Fusion

Integrated Reading and Writing **Book 1**

Enhanced Edition

KEMPER / MEYER / VAN RYS / SEBRANEK

Dave Kemper

Verne Meyer
Dordt College

John Van Rys
Redeemer University College

Pat Sebranek

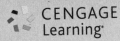
CENGAGE
Learning·

Australia • Brazil • Mexico • Singapore • United Kingdom • United States

CENGAGE
Learning·

Fusion: Integrated Reading and Writing,
Enhanced Edition, Book 1
Dave Kemper, Verne Meyer, John Van
Rys, and Pat Sebranek

Product Director: Annie Todd

Senior Content Developer:
Marita Sermolins

Associate Content Developer: Beth Rice

Product Assistant: Luria Rittenberg

Senior Media Developer: Amy Gibbons

Senior Marketing Manager: Lydia LeStar

Content Project Manager:
Rosemary Winfield

Art Director: Faith Brosnan

Manufacturing Planner: Betsy Donaghey

Rights Acquisition Specialist:
Ann Hoffman

Text and Cover Designer: Sebranek, Inc.

Cover Image: Sebranek, Inc.

Production Service and Compositor:
Sebranek, Inc.

For product information and technology assistance, contact us at
Cengage Learning Customer & Sales Support, 1-800-354-9706.
For permission to use material from this text or product, submit all requests online at **www.cengage.com/permissions.**
Further permissions questions can be emailed to
permissionrequest@cengage.com.

Library of Congress Control Number: 2011942007

ISBN-13: 978-1-285-46499-2

ISBN-10: 1-285-46499-0

Cengage Learning
200 First Stamford Place, 4th floor
Stamford, CT 06902
USA

Cengage Learning is a leading provider of customized learning solutions with office locations around the globe, including Singapore, the United Kingdom, Australia, Mexico, Brazil, and Japan. Locate your local office at **international.cengage.com/region.**

Cengage Learning products are represented in Canada by Nelson Education, Ltd.

For your course and learning solutions, visit **www.cengage.com.**

Purchase any of our products at your local college store or at our preferred online store **www.cengagebrain.com.**

Instructors: Please visit **login.cengage.com** and log in to access instructor-specific resources.

Printed in the U.S.A.
1 2 3 4 5 6 7 17 16 15 14 13

Fusion 1 Brief Contents

Preface   xx

Part I: Reading and Writing for Success   1

Jaimie Duplass, 2011 / Used under license from Shutterstock.com

R. Gino Santa Maria, 2013 / Used under license from Shutterstock.com

eurobanks, 2013 / Used under license from Shutterstock.com

Preface

Fusion: Integrated Reading and Writing, Book 1, is the first text to connect the reading and writing processes in every chapter. *Fusion* uses parallel strategies to teach students how to analyze readings and generate writing. Throughout, grammar instruction is integrated with writing instruction using high-interest readings.

We wanted to find out how instructors expect to teach the combined course, and what they need in order to teach it more effectively. *Fusion* is the direct result of extensive research conducted across the country, which indicated that a textbook addressing instructors' needs would

- provide instructor support, with particular attention paid to teaching reading;
- cover essential reading skills and two levels of writing (paragraph and essay development);
- present lessons following a pattern of reading, writing, analyzing, and grammar;
- provide support for those new to teaching in an integrated reading and writing environment;
- integrate a variety of interesting readings;
- incorporate online technology (**Aplia**™) to promote skill development and allow for tracking of learning outcomes; and
- promote better outcomes, persistence, and retention by giving students a chance to move through the developmental sequence and into credit-bearing courses more quickly.

NEW in the Enhanced Edition

More Reading Strategies to Better Prepare Students. Expanded reading coverage helps students learn and practice the key concepts associated with reading skills.
- *Chapter 2 "Academic Reading and Learning" coverage now includes*
  - asking questions as part of prereading;
  - understanding the structure of textbooks and textbook chapters;
  - drawing inferences with practice opportunities;
  - using additional note-taking systems, such as topic outlines, sentence outlines, and clusters; and
  - additional vocabulary coverage providing examples of vocabulary notebook entries across disciplines, and additional examples of and practice with context clues and word parts.
- *Chapter 3 "The Traits of Academic Reading" coverage now includes*
  - identifying the topic with additional practice, and
  - identifying implied main ideas with additional practice.

Additional Readings for Practice. Additional readings that challenge students' critical thinking skills, enrich their college-ready vocabulary, and reflect the types of reading and writing expected of them in their college courses provide opportunities for practice and interaction.

- **In Part 1, new "Review and Enrichment"** sections allow students to immediately practice reading and writing skills as they are introduced.

- **Part 2 chapters now include a paragraph-length reading and two essay-length readings.** New apparatus helps students implement the reading process through background information, guiding prereading questions, prompts to annotate and take notes as they read, and vocabulary questions.

- **In Part 2, all "Reading and Reacting"** reading samples now provide **more background information, prereading questions, vocabulary questions, and drawing inference prompts.**

Chapter Features

Fusion reflects the best research on reading, writing, and learning, so students can be confident that following the explanations and guidelines in each chapter will promote success. Here are the key features in the text:

- **Integrated reading and writing guidance in every chapter.** *Fusion's* integrated approach is reciprocal and reinforcing. Parallel reading and writing strategies are introduced in Chapter 1, "The Reading-Writing Connection."

- **Brief, approachable learning units.** Every chapter has several assignments with a clear learning objective and a clear stopping point. This purposeful design allows students to stay focused. Insight boxes sprinkled throughout each chapter explain or reinforce concepts.

- **Grammar instruction in every modes chapter.** *Fusion* integrates relevant grammar coverage in the context of students' reading and writing assignments. Additional practice and instruction appears in the book's "Workshop" sections.

- **Pedagogy that emphasizes critical thinking and vocabulary.** Purposeful use of learning aids, like *Consider the Traits* boxes, thought-provoking quotes, followed by a *"What do you think?"* question, and integrated *Drawing Inference* activities, reinforces key concepts, promotes skill development, and encourages students to think analytically. Challenging words are defined on-page, and integrated vocabulary exercises provide students practice in defining words.

Additional Support for *Fusion*

Aplia™ for *Fusion*. Through diagnostic tests, succinct instruction, and engaging assignments, **Aplia™** for *Fusion: Integrated Reading and Writing* reinforces key concepts and provides students with the practice they need to build fundamental reading, writing, and grammar skills:

- Diagnostic tests provide an overall picture of a class's performance, allowing instructors to instantly see where students are succeeding and where they need additional help.

- Assignments include immediate and constructive feedback, reinforcing key concepts and motivating students to improve their reading and writing skills.

- Grades are automatically recorded in the Aplia grade book, keeping students accountable while minimizing time spent grading.

- **The Individualized Study Path (ISP).** An ISP course generates a personalized list of assignments for each student that is tailored to his or her specific strengths and weaknesses. ISP assignments are randomized, auto-graded problems that correspond to skills and concepts for a specific topic. Students get as much help and practice as they require on topics where they are weak. Conversely, if there are topics they understand well, no remediation is necessary and no additional assignments will be present.

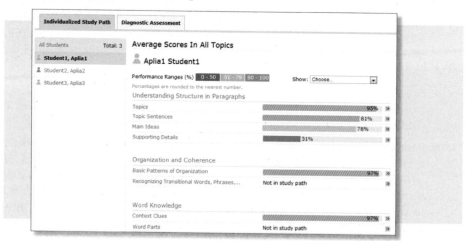

Contact your Cengage Learning representative for assistance with packaging access to Aplia. For more information and a demonstration, go to www.aplia.com /developmentalenglish.

Instructor Manual and Test Bank. The Instructor Manual and Test Bank is located on the Instructor Companion Site in a convenient printable format. This supplement features a wealth of resources for course enrichment, including

- test bank material: chapter quizzes, a midterm exam, and a final exam;
- detailed sample syllabi, including syllabi mapped to North Carolina, Texas, and Virginia state objectives;
- a variety of writing prompts to be used in class or as homework assignments;
- a success story about how Aplia and *Fusion* can be used together in the classroom; and
- a guide to teaching ESL learners using *Fusion*.

Cognero®. Cengage Learning testing powered by Cognero® is a flexible, online system that allows you to author, edit, and manage test-bank content from multiple Cengage Learning solutions, including the quizzes and exams available on Fusion's Instructor Companion Site. Multiple test versions can be created in an instant, and tests can be delivered from your LMS or your classroom.

Instructor Companion Site. Access the Instructor's Manual and Test Bank, and PowerPoint slides organized around topics covered in the book with a high level chapter overview, as well as an opening and closing activity.

Write Experience 2.0. Students need to learn how to write well in order to communicate effectively and think critically. Cengage Learning's Write Experience provides students with additional writing practice without adding to your workload. Utilizing artificial intelligence to score student writing instantly and accurately, it also provides students with detailed revision goals and feedback on their writing to help them improve. Write Experience is powered by e-Write IntelliMetric Within— the gold standard for automated scoring of writing—used to score the Graduate Management Admissions Test (GMAT) analytical writing assessment. Visit www.cengage.com/writeexperience to learn more.

Course Redesign for Developmental Education. Course Redesign is one of the latest trends impacting the landscape of higher education and developmental studies. Cengage Learning's trained consultants, instructional designers, subject matter experts, and educational researchers offer a variety of services to guide you through the process of redesigning your curriculum. Combining that with a wealth of powerful digital and print offerings allows us to personalize solutions to your state or institution's needs. Contact your Learning Consultant to learn more about these services or visit www.cengage.com/services.

Acknowledgements

Many thanks to the many reviewers who have helped to shape *Fusion* into the text you have before you:

Wes Anthony, *Cleveland Community College;* Joe Antinarella, *Tidewater Community College;* Stacey Ariel, *Santa Rosa Junior College;* Margaret Bartelt, *Owens Community College; Jon Bell, Pima College;* Christina Blount, *Lewis and Clark Community College;* Mary Boudreaux, *San Jacinto College;* Kimberly Bovee, *Tidewater Community College;* Janice Brantley, *University of Arkansas at Pine Bluff;* Robyn Browder, *Davenport University;* Doris Bryant, *Thomas Nelson Community College; Jennifer Call, Cape Fear Community College;* Jana Carter, *Montana State University Great Falls;* Roberta Cohen, *Union County Colleg*e; Annette Dammer, *Fayetteville Technical Community College;* Melissa DuBrowa, *Berkeley College;* Arlene Edmundson, *United Tribes Technical College;* Mary Etter, *Davenport University;* Shannon Fernandes, *Yakima Valley Community College;* JoAnn Foriest, *Prairie State College;* Marty Frailey, *Pima Community College;* Johnanna Grimes, *Tennessee State University;* David Harper, *Chesapeake College;* Gina Henderson, *Tallahassee Community College;* Eric Hibbison, *J. Sargeant Reynolds Community College;* Donna Hill, *College of the Ouachitas;* Brent Kendrick, *Lord Fairfax Community College;* Shayna Kessel, *Los Angeles City College;* Sara Kuhn, *Chattanooga State Community College;* Glenda Lowery, *Rappahannock Community College;* Deborah Maness, *Wake Technical Community College;* Katherine McEwen, *Cape Fear Community College;* Carolyn Miller, *Chattanooga State Community College;* Miriam Moore, *Lord Fairfax Community College;* Ann Moser, *Virginia Western Community College;* Ray Orkwis, *Northern Virginia Community College;* Jay Peterson, *Atlantic Cape Community College;* Laura Powell, *Danville Community College;* Pam Price, *Greenville Technical College;* Carole Quine, *Baltimore City Community College;* Janet Rico Everett, *Southern Arkansas University Tech;* David Robinson, *College of Southern Maryland;* Mary S. Leonard, *Wytheville Community College;* Brenda Sickles, *Tidewater Community College;* Virginia Smith, *Carteret Community College;* Suba Subbarao, *Oakland Community College;* Claudia Swicegood, *Rowan-Cabarrus Community College;* Jennifer Taylor Feller, *Northern Virginia Community College-Woodbridge;* Nicole Tong, *Northern Virginia Community College;* Patricia Tymon, *Virginia Highlands Community College;* Kathy Tyndall, *Wake Technical Community College;* Julie Voss, *Front Range Community College;* Michelle Zollars, *Patrick Henry Community College*

Enhanced Edition

Brenda Ashcraft, *Virginia Western Community College;* Teena Boone, *Rowan-Cabarrus Community College;* Mike Coulehan, *El Paso Commuity College;* Kris DeAngelis, *Central Piedmont Community College;* Meribeth Fields, *Central Florida Community College;* Cynthia Gomez, *Hodges University;* Eric Hibbison, *J. Sargeant Reynolds Community College;* Marcia Hines, *Saint Mary's University of Minnesota;* Alice Kimara, *Baltimore City Community College;* Kimberly Koledoye, *Houston Community College;* Kina Lara, San Jacinto College South; Alice Leonhardt, *Blue Ridge Community College;* Glenda Lowery, *Rappahannock Community* College; Breanna Lutterbie, *Germanna Community College;* Gail Malone, *South Plains College;* Deborah Maness, *Wake Technical Community College;* Abigail Montgomery, *Blue Ridge Community College;* Miriam Moore, *Lord Fairfax Community College;* Lana Myers, *Lone Star College-Montgomery;* Elizabeth Powell, *Forsyth Technical Community College;* Tony Procell, *El Paso Community College;* Robert Sandhaas, *San Jacinto College South Campus;* Melissa Shafner, *Mitchell College;* Deborah Spradlin, *Tyler Jr. College;* Claudia Swicegood, *Rowan-Cabarrus Community College;* Gene Voss, *Houston Community College;* Shari Waldrop, *Navarro College;* Dawn White, *Davidson County Community College;* Lori Witkowich, *College of Central*

Part I:

Reading and Writing for Success

Part I: Reading and Writing for Success

1

> "Whoever cares to learn will always find a teacher."
> —German Proverb

The Reading-Writing Connection

Reading and writing are really two sides of the same coin, meaning they are "different but closely related." You read to learn, and you write to learn. You use reading to help you with your writing. You use writing to help you understand your reading. Reading is thinking; writing is thinking. The connections go on and on.

This chapter introduces the reading-writing connection and offers three strategies that will help you with your college-level reading and writing assignments: (1) using questions to identify the key parts of assignments, (2) using the traits of writing to help you analyze your reading and develop your writing, and (3) using graphic organizers to arrange ideas in your reading and writing.

The next four chapters in this section take a closer look at academic reading and writing.

Learning Outcomes

LO1 Understand reading and writing assignments.

LO2 Use the traits for reading and writing.

LO3 Use graphic organizers for reading and writing.

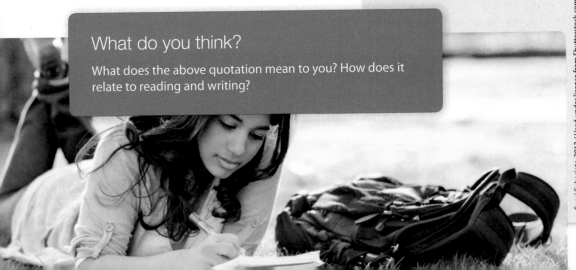

What do you think?

What does the above quotation mean to you? How does it relate to reading and writing?

Supri Suharjoto, 2013 / Used under license from Shutterstock.com

LO1 Understanding Reading and Writing Assignments

At the start of a reading or writing assignment, you should identify exactly what is expected of you. The main features of an assignment are similar to the key features in a recipe. If you forget any one of them, the final product will suffer.

The STRAP Strategy

You can use the STRAP strategy to analyze your writing and reading assignments. The strategy consists of answering questions about these five features: *subject, type, role, audience,* and *purpose*. Once you answer the questions, you'll be ready to get to work. This chart shows how the strategy works:

For Reading Assignments		For Writing Assignments
What specific topic does the reading address?	**Subject**	What specific topic should I write about?
What form (*essay, text chapter, article*) does the reading take?	**Type**	What form of writing (*essay, article*) will I use?
What position (*student, responder, concerned individual*) does the writer assume?	**Role**	What position (*student, citizen, employee*) should I assume?
Who is the intended reader?	**Audience**	Who is the intended reader?
What is the goal of the material?	**Purpose**	What is the goal (*to inform, to persuade*) of the writing?

The STRAP Strategy in Action

Suppose you were given the following reading assignment.

Assignment: Read the paragraph on page 178. Then identify the 5 W's (*who? what? when? where?* and *why?*) of the experience that the writer shares. Below are the answers to the STRAP questions for this assignment.

Subject:	Preparing to skydive for the first time
Type:	Narrative paragraph
Role:	Adult looking back at a memorable experience
Audience:	Readers in general
Purpose:	To share a personal experience

Respond for Reading   Analyze the following reading assignment by answering the STRAP questions that follow it.

Assignment: Read "Crime-Scene Investigation of Blood" on page 258. Then list the steps involved in the process.

Subject: What specific topic does the reading address?

_____

Type: What form (*paragraph, article, textbook chapter*) does the reading take?

_____

Role: What position (*observer, participant, expert, student*) does the writer assume?

_____

Audience: Who is the intended audience (*students, general readers, experts*)?

_____

Purpose: What is the goal of the text (*to inform, to persuade, to entertain, to describe*)?

_____

Additional Practice: Use the questions above to analyze this assignment:

- Read the descriptive essay on pages 167–169. Then identify the specific topic of the description and at least five or six sensory details that stand out to you.

Respond for Writing   Analyze the following writing assignment by answering the STRAP questions that follow it.

Assignment: Write a paragraph explaining how to use a social networking Web site such as Facebook. Your writing is intended for older adults who have little experience with social media.

Subject: What specific topic does the writing assignment address?

_____

Type: What form (*paragraph, essay, blog posting*) should my writing take?

_____

Role: What position (*teacher, student, observer, participant*) should I assume?

_____

Audience: Who is the intended audience (*classmates, older adults, general audience*)?

_____

Purpose: What is the goal of my writing (*to persuade, to explain, to classify*)?

_____

Additional Practice: Use the STRAP questions above to analyze this assignment.

- Think of one of your favorite interests (*working out, fashion, cars, reality television, and so on*). Then write an essay classifying different categories or types for a specific topic related to this interest. For example, if you enjoy working out, perhaps you could classify different types of leg exercises.

LO2 Using the Traits for Reading and Writing

You can use the traits of writing to help you gain a full understanding of reading assignments and develop your own paragraphs and essays. The traits identify the key elements of written language, including ideas, organization, voice, word choice, sentence fluency, and conventions. Pages 45–90 discuss how to use the traits when reading, and pages 119–146 discuss how to use them when writing.

INSIGHT

Using the traits answers these two questions: "What elements should I look for in each of my reading assignments?" and "What elements should I consider when developing my writing assignments?"

The Traits in Action

This chart shows the connection between using the traits for reading and writing assignments.

Read to identify . . .	The Traits	Write to shape . . .
■ the topic. ■ the thesis (main point). ■ the key supporting details.	**Ideas**	■ a thesis or focus. ■ your thoughts on the topic. ■ effective supporting details.
■ the quality of the beginning, middle, and ending parts. ■ the organization of the supporting details.	**Organization**	■ an effective beginning, middle, and ending. ■ a logical, clear presentation of your supporting details.
■ the level of the writer's interest in and knowledge about the topic.	**Voice**	■ a voice that sounds interesting, honest, and knowledgeable.
■ the quality of the words. (Are they interesting and clear?)	**Word Choice**	■ words that are specific, clear, and fitting for the assignment.
■ the effectiveness of the sentences. (Do they flow smoothly, and are they clear?)	**Sentence Fluency**	■ smooth-reading, clear, and accurate sentences.
■ to what degree the writing follows conventions (and why or why not).	**Conventions**	■ paragraphs or essays that follow the conventions, or rules.

Note Design, or the appearance of a text, is sometimes included in a list of the traits. The key consideration of design is readability: Does the design add to or take away from the reading of a text?

Respond for Reading To get a feel for using the traits, answer the questions below for the paragraph "Cross-Cultural Miscues" on page 344.

NOTE: The questions on this page cover the first three traits of effective reading and writing.

Questions to Answer for Reading

Ideas: What is the topic of this paragraph or essay?

What specific details stand out? Name two.

Organization: How does it start?

What is included in the middle part?

How does it end?

Voice: Does the writer seem interested in and knowledgeable about the topic? Why or why not?

Extra Practice: Answer the questions above for "A Penny for Your World-Saving Thoughts" on pages 206–208.

Respond for Writing To get a feel for using the traits for writing, answer the questions below for this assignment:

■ Write a paragraph explaining how to use a social networking Web site such as Facebook. Your writing is intended for older adults who have little experience with the Internet.

Questions to Answer for Writing

Ideas: What topic will you write about?

What main point about the topic could you focus on?

What types of details could you include (*explanations, examples, descriptions, personal thoughts,* etc.)? Name two.

Organization: How could you begin your writing?

How will you organize your details (*by time order, by order of importance, by logic*)?

Voice: How will you sound in your writing (*formal and factual, informal and friendly, or somewhere in between*)? Explain.

Extra Practice: Answer the questions above for this writing assignment:

■ Think of one of your favorite interests (*working out, fashion, cars, reality television, and so on*). Then write a paragraph classifying different categories or types for a specific topic related to this interest. For example, if you enjoy working out, perhaps you could classify different types of leg exercises.

LO3 Using Graphic Organizers for Reading and Writing

Graphic organizers help you map out ideas or concepts and are commonly used to organize the ideas that you collect for writing assignments. You can use the same organizers to "chart" the key information in reading assignments.

Charting a Reading Assignment

Provided below is a line diagram that charts the key points in the classification paragraph "Effective Discipline" on page 286.

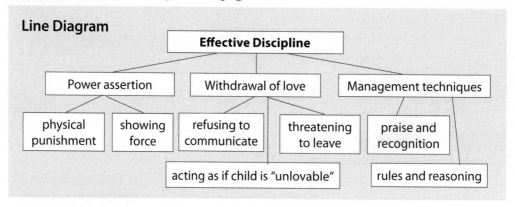

Respond for Reading   Use a line diagram to chart the key points in the classification paragraph "My Condiments to the Chef" on page 295.

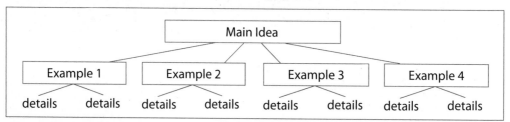

Respond for Writing   Use a line diagram to chart the main categories or examples for a specific topic related to one of your favorite interests. (You've already done some planning for this assignment on the previous page.)

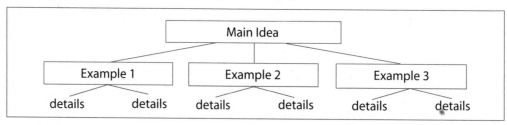

Sample Graphic Organizers

Time Line Use for personal narratives to list actions or events in the order they occurred.

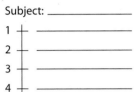

Subject: _____

1
2
3
4

Line Diagram Use to collect and organize details for informational essays.

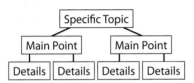

Cause-Effect Organizer Use to collect and organize details for cause-effect essays.

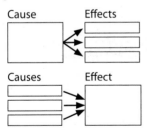

Evaluation Chart Use to collect supporting details for essays of evaluation.

Subject: _____

Points to Evaluate	Supporting Details
1	
2	
3	
4	

Process Diagram Use to collect details for science-related writing, such as the steps in a process.

Topic: _____

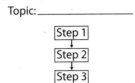

Venn Diagram Use to collect details to compare and contrast two topics.

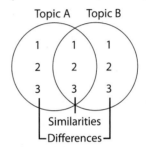

Problem-Solution Web Use to map out problem-solution essays.

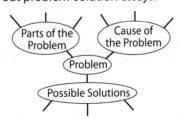

Cluster Use to collect details for informational essays.

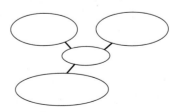

Reviewing the Reading-Writing Connection

Complete these activities as needed to help you better understand the reading-writing connection.

Understand the Assignment Answer these questions about the STRAP strategy. (See pages 4–5.)

- What is the STRAP strategy? _____
- What does each letter in STRAP stand for? _____

Assignment: Use the STRAP strategy to analyze "Support Wind Farm Energy" (page 372).

Subject: _____

Type: _____

Role: _____

Audience: _____

Purpose: _____

Use the Traits Answer these questions about the traits of reading and writing. (See pages 6–7.)

- Which is the first and most important trait?

  _____

- Which trait deals with the arrangement of details in writing?

  _____

- Which trait deals with the rules for using the language correctly?

  _____

Assignment: Write a paragraph in which you describe a favorite place. Be sure to include specific details arranged so they are easy to follow.

Ideas: _____

_____

Organization: _____

_____

Voice: _____

_____

2

Academic Reading and Learning

We all do it sometimes. We listen without really hearing, letting someone's words breeze past us like mere puffs of air. Honest listening means paying attention, hearing what is being said, considering it, and providing some sort of response.

The same is true with reading. It isn't enough to just let our eyes roam casually across the page and forget the words there as quickly as we read them. Instead, we must actively engage the text, paying attention, considering what it means. Active reading means thinking about the words as we read them, connecting them to what we have read before, predicting what the text will say next, and evaluating the ideas as they present themselves.

In this chapter, you will learn strategies for learning the most from your academic reading.

Learning Outcomes

LO1 Read to learn.
LO2 Understand the reading process.
LO3 Understand the structure of textbooks.
LO4 Use basic reading strategies (annotating, note taking, outlining, summarizing).
LO5 Read critically.
LO6 Draw inferences.
LO7 Improve vocabulary.
LO8 Read graphics.

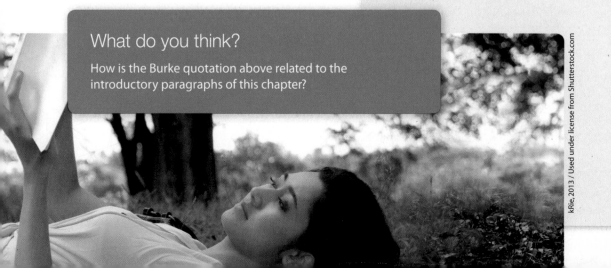

What do you think?

How is the Burke quotation above related to the introductory paragraphs of this chapter?

"Today a reader, tomorrow a leader."
—Margaret Fuller

LO1 Reading to Learn

To be the best musicians, athletes, or public speakers, people study the techniques of that skill and put those techniques into practice. You'll find that academic reading has its own techniques that can help you best understand and remember what you read.

Traits

In effective text, the reader will find strong ideas, logical organization, a clear voice, precise words, and smooth sentences. These traits are the working parts of a text.

Effective Academic Reading

Follow the guidelines listed below for all of your reading assignments.

1. **Divide the assignment into doable parts.** Don't try to read long texts all at once. Instead, try to read for 15–30 minutes at a time.

2. **Find a quiet place.** You'll need space to read and write without distractions. (Quiet background music is okay, if it helps you stay on task.)

3. **Gather your materials.** Have on hand a notebook, related handouts, Web access, and so on.

4. **Approach your reading as a process.** Academic reading requires that you do a number of things, usually in a certain order. (See pages 13–16.)

5. **Use proven reading strategies.** For example, taking notes and annotating a text gets you actively involved in your reading. (See pages 20–26.)

6. **Know what to look for when you read.** There are key ideas or elements that you need to identify in order to understand a text. (See pages 27–28.)

7. **Summarize what you have learned.** Also note any concepts or explanations that you don't understand. (See page 25.)

8. **Review your reading from time to time.** Doing this will help you internalize the information so you can apply it in your writing and class work.

Practice Choose the star below that best describes your academic reading skills. Then, in a brief paragraph, explain your choice. In your paragraph, consider which of the guidelines above you do or do not follow.

Weak ★ ★ ★ ★ ★ Strong

LO2 Understanding the Reading Process

If you cook, you know how important it is to follow the steps in a recipe. The more difficult the recipe, the more important it is to follow the steps. Otherwise you risk leaving out an essential ingredient.

You can apply a step-by-step process to your academic reading, as well. Following the steps will help you learn the most from your reading.

> **Think about it.**
> Reading allows you to discover what other people are thinking about important subjects.

The Steps in the Process

The process described below helps you pace yourself and read thoughtfully. See pages 14–15 for a closer look.

Process	Activities
Prereading	First become familiar with the text and establish a starting point for reading.
Reading	Read the assignment once to get a basic understanding of the text. Use reading strategies such as the ones on pages 20–26.
Rereading	Complete additional readings and analysis as needed, until you have a clear understanding of the text's key elements or traits.
Reflecting	Evaluate your reading experience: *What have you learned? What questions do you have about the material? How has this reading changed or expanded what you know about the topic?*

The Process in Action

This graphic shows the reading process in action. The arrows show how you may move back and forth between the steps. For example, after beginning your reading, you may refer back to something in your prereading.

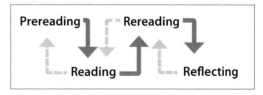

Practice What observations can you make about the reading process after reviewing the information above? One observation is provided below; list three or four more on your own paper.

Academic reading can't be done quickly.

A CLOSER LOOK at the Process

Each step in the reading process requires a special type of thinking and planning. Following these steps will help you become a more confident reader and learner.

Prereading addresses what you should do *before* your actual reading. A coach reviews scouting reports in order to prepare for an opponent; prereading helps you to prepare for a reading assignment. Here are the basic prereading tasks.

- **Review the title.** Many readers give the title very little thought. Bad move. The title often identifies the topic of the reading and helps you understand the author's attitude or feeling about it.

- **Learn about the author.** Read the brief biography that may be provided with the text, or check online for information about the writer. This information may help you appreciate the author's approach or point of view taken in the text.

- **Preview the text.** Read the first paragraph or two to get a general idea about the topic, the level of language used, the writer's tone, and so on. Next, skim the text for headings, bold words, and graphics. Then read the final paragraph or two to see how the text ends. Finally, consider the author's purpose and audience.

- **Establish a starting point for reading.** Once you have done all of these things, write down your first thoughts about the text. Consider what you already know about the topic, what questions you have, and what you expect to learn.

- **Ask questions.** Forming a set of prereading questions will help you stay on task as you read. A common practice is to base your questions on information that you've gleaned while previewing the text's title, objectives, headings, subheadings, first sentences in paragraphs, bold-faced terms, and visuals. Here are three prereading questions from a chapter in a criminal justice textbook:
  - The learning objective **"Explain when searches can be made without a warrant"** can be turned into this question: **When can searches be made without a warrant?**
  - The heading **"The Fourth Amendment"** can be turned into this question: **How does the Fourth Amendment protect the rights of the people?**
  - The bold-faced term **"probable cause"** can be turned into this question: **What is meant by probable cause?**

Reading a text requires your undivided attention. These are your goals during the first reading.

- **Confirm the author's purpose and audience.** Is the material intended to explain, describe, or persuade? And does it address general readers, college students, professionals, or someone else?
- **Identify the focus or main idea** of the text. (See pages 50–60.)
- **Locate the evidence**—the facts and details that support the main idea. (See pages 61–70.)
- **Consider the conclusion**—the closing thoughts of the writer.
- **Answer the questions** you posed during prereading.

Rereading a text helps you to better understand its main points. These are your goals during your rereading.

- **Confirm your basic understanding of the text.** Are you still sure about the main idea and details? If not, adjust your thinking.
- **Analyze the development of the ideas.** Is the topic timely or important? Does the main idea seem reasonable? What types of support are provided—facts, statistics, or examples? Does the conclusion seem logical?
- **Consider the organization of the material.** How does the writer organize his or her support? (See pages 71–77.)
- **Check the voice and style of the writing.** Does the writer seem knowledgeable about the topic and interested in it? Are the ideas easy to follow?

Reflecting helps you fine-tune your thinking about the material. Writing about your reading is the best way to reflect on it. These are your goals during this step.

- **Explain what you have learned.** What new information have you gained? How will you use it? Does this new information change your thinking?
- **Explore your feelings about the reading.** Did the reading surprise you? Did it disappoint you? Did it answer your questions?
- **Identify what questions you still have.** Then try to answer them.

Apply You will use this process to read and react to the reading selections in this book, starting with the one on page 152. Also use it for all of your college reading assignments.

Other Reading Processes

Two other reading processes—KWL and SQ3R—are variations on the reading process described on the previous pages.

KWL

KWL stands for what I _know_, what I _want_ to know, and what I _learned_. Identifying what you know (K) and want to know (W) occurs during prereading. Identifying what you learned (L) occurs after your reading, rereading, and reflecting.

Using a KWL Chart

1. Write the topic of your reading at the top of your paper. Then divide the paper into three columns labeled **K, W,** and **L.**
2. In the **K** column, identify what you already know.
3. In the **W** column, identify the questions you want answered.
4. In the **L** column, note what you have learned.

Topic:		
K	**W**	**L**
Identify what you **KNOW.**	Identify what you **WANT** to know.	List what you **LEARNED.**

SQ3R

SQ3R is a thorough reading process, very similar to prereading, reading, rereading, and reflecting. The letters SQ3R stand for _survey, question, read, recite,_ and _review._

Using SQ3R

Survey: When you survey, skim the title, headings, graphics, and first and last paragraphs to get a general idea about the text.

Question: During this step, ask questions about the topic that you hope the text will answer.

Read: While you do the reading, take careful notes, reread challenging parts, look up unfamiliar words, and so on.

Recite: At the end of each page, section, or chapter, state out loud what you have learned. (This could involve answering the 5 W's and H—_who? what? when? where? why?_ and _how?_) Reread as necessary.

Review: After reading, you study your notes, answer questions about the reading, summarize the text, and so on.

LO3 Understanding the Structure of Textbooks

In many of your college courses, you will be assigned a textbook, and your instructor will regularly ask you to read particular chapters as background for class lectures and discussions.

Since reading textbooks plays such an important role in your coursework, it is important that you first recognize and understand the main parts they usually include.

Parts of a Textbook

- The **title page** is usually the first printed page in a book. It provides the full title of the book, the authors' names, the publisher's name, and the place of publication.
- The **copyright page** comes right after the title page. This page gives the year in which a copyright was issued, which is usually the same year the book was published. The copyright gives an author or publisher the legal right to the production, publication, and use of the text.
- The **table of contents** shows the major divisions (units, parts, chapters, and topics) in the textbook. It contains page numbers to locate the different divisions. (Many textbooks precede the full table of contents with a table of contents in brief used as a quick guide to the text.)
- A **preface, foreword,** and/or **introduction** often follows the table of contents and introduces the reader to the book.
- The **body** is the main part of the book, containing the actual text.
- Following the body an **appendix** is sometimes included. This section gives extra information, often in the form of charts, tables, letters, or copies of official documents.
- If included, the **glossary** follows the appendix and serves as the dictionary portion of the book. It is an alphabetical listing of key terms, with an explanation or definition for each one.
- Some textbooks then provide a **reference** section identifying the books or articles the authors used during the development of the text.
- The **index** at the end of a textbook lists alphabetically the important topics, terms, and names appearing in the book and the page location for each one.

Practice Locate the different parts of each of your textbooks, including this one. Do any of your textbooks not contain all of these parts, and do any of them contain other parts?

Parts of a Textbook Chapter

As you approach each textbook reading assignment, be aware that most chapters share common features. These features are designed to help you carry out your reading, so it's important that you know what they are and that you use them.

Key features in a chapter from *American Government and Politics Today* are identified and explained. Each one is an important part of the text.

- The **chapter title** identifies the topic of the chapter.
- **Learning outcomes** identify the different things that you can expect to learn from that chapter.
- Many chapters provide **special opening text** to prompt you to think about the chapter.
- **Key terms** are often highlighted and defined.
- **Main headings** are the largest headings and announce each main part of the topic to be discussed.
- **Subheadings** are similar headings and help direct the reading of each main part. (There can be different levels of subheadings. As they get more detailed, they are reduced in size.)
- **Graphics** provide visual representations of important facts and figures.
- **Photographs** and **captions** enhance the discussion in the main text.
- **Side notes** can have a variety of uses, depending on the textbook. They can define key terms, identify learning outcomes, or provide interesting facts or ideas, among other things.
- **Summaries** at the end of chapters review the main ideas and details covered in the reading.
- **Resources** to additional reading or viewing may also be provided at the end of a chapter.

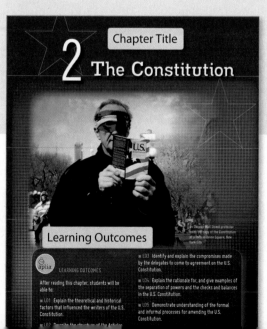

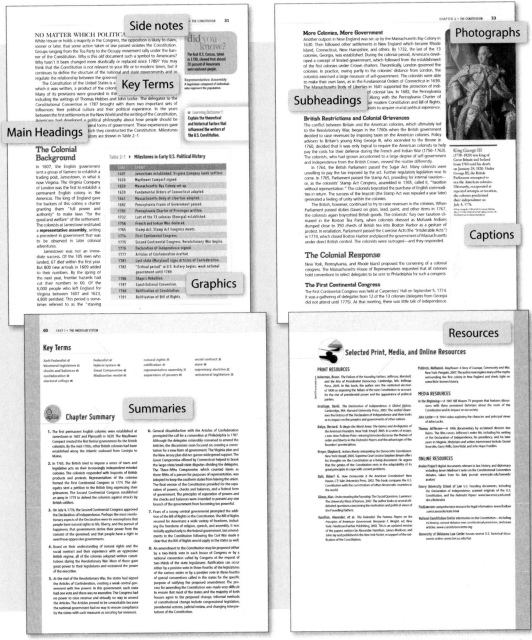

From Schmidt/Shelley/Bardes/Ford, American Government and Politics Today, 2013-2014 Edition, 16E. © 2014 Cengage Learning

Practice Review the parts of one chapter from one of your textbooks as well as this one. How are they similar or different from the parts you just learned about? Be prepared to discuss the makeup of one textbook chapter with your classmates.

LO4 Using Basic Reading Strategies

To make sure that you gain the most from each reading assignment, carry out the reading strategies on the next few pages.

Annotating a Text

To annotate means "to add comments or make notes in a text while you are reading." Annotating a text allows you to interact with the ideas in a reading selection. Here are some suggestions:

- Write questions in the margins during your previewing, and answer them during your reading.
- Underline or highlight the main idea and key details.
- Define new terms.
- Make connections to other parts.

> **NOTE:**
> Annotate reading material only if you own the text or if you are reading a photocopy.

Annotating in Action

Here is an example of one student's annotations of a paragraph.

Margin notes	Text
Good question.	*Don't feelings of hunger originate in the stomach?* To find out, Walter Cannon and A.L. Washburn (1912) decided to see if stomach contractions cause hunger. In an early study, Washburn
A century ago!	
Contraction = the act of reducing in size	trained himself to swallow a balloon, which could be inflated through an attached tube. (You, too, will do anything for science, right?) This allowed Cannon to record the movements
This detail answers the question.	of Washburn's stomach. When Washburn's stomach contracted, he reported that he felt "hunger pangs." In view of this, the two scientists concluded that hunger is nothing more than the contractions of an empty stomach. (This, however, proved to be
A bad pun.	an inflated conclusion.)

From COON/MITTERER. *Psychology: A Journey*, 4E. © 2001 Cengage Learning

INSIGHT

Highlighting or underlining alone are not good ways to annotate, because you may forget later why you marked that text. It is important to also write notes in the margin as reminders of what you were thinking while reading.

Annotate Carefully read the paragraph below. Then, if you own this book, annotate the text according to the following directions:

- Circle the main idea of the paragraph.
- Underline or highlight two ideas that you either agree with, question, or are confused by. Then make a comment about each idea in the margin.
- Circle one or two words that you are unsure of. Research those words, and then define or explain them.

The Reading Process

Prereading   Rereading

Reading   Reflecting

With knowledge obtained from the Greeks, the Romans realized that   *1*

some diseases were connected to filth, contaminated water, and poor   *2*

The Romans

sanitation. They began the development of sanitary systems by building   *3*

sewers to carry away waste and aqueducts (waterways) to deliver clean   *4*

water. They drained swamps and marshes to reduce the incidence   *5*

of malaria. They created laws to keep streets clean and eliminate *I agree*   *6*

because

garbage. The first hospitals were also established in ancient Rome when   *7*

physicians began caring for injured soldiers or ill people in their homes.   *8*

From SIMMERS. *Diversified Health Occupations*, 7E. © 2009 Cengage Learning

Taking Effective Notes

Taking notes helps you to focus on reading material and understand it more fully. Notes change information you have read about to information that you are working with. Of course, taking effective notes makes studying for an exam much easier.

Note-Taking Tips

- Use your own words as much as possible.
- Record only important ideas and details rather than complicated sentences.
- Consider **boldfaced** or *italicized* words, graphics, and captions as well as the main text.
- Employ abbreviations and symbols to save time (vs., #, &, etc.).
- Decide on a system to organize or arrange your notes so they are easy to follow.

Using Two-Column Notes

To make your note taking more active, use a two-column system called the Cornell Method. One column (two-thirds of the page) is for your main notes, and the other column (one-third of the page) is for questions and key terms. Fill in this column after you're done with your main notes.

INSIGHT

To review your notes, cover the main notes, and answer the questions in the left column.

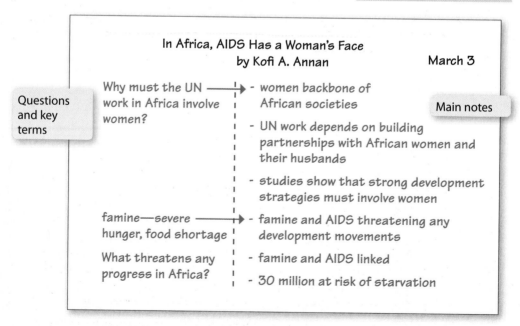

In Africa, AIDS Has a Woman's Face
by Kofi A. Annan   March 3

Questions and key terms

Why must the UN work in Africa involve women?

famine—severe hunger, food shortage

What threatens any progress in Africa?

Main notes

- women backbone of African societies
- UN work depends on building partnerships with African women and their husbands
- studies show that strong development strategies must involve women
- famine and AIDS threatening any development movements
- famine and AIDS linked
- 30 million at risk of starvation

Note: Save space at the bottom of the page to summarize the notes after class.

Using an Outline

An outline shows how ideas fit together in a reading. The ideas in a *topic outline* are expressed in words and phrases. The ideas in a *sentence outline* are expressed in sentences. In a traditional outline, each new division represents another level of detail. As shown below, if you have a "I," you should have at least a "II." If you have an "A," you should at least have a "B," and so on.

Topic Outline

Suppose you have read a chapter about North American trees. Here's the start of a topic outline for this chapter.

Chapter subject: Common North American trees
- I. Trees used in landscaping
  - A. Cold climate trees
    - 1. Hardy evergreens
      - a. Norway pine
      - b. Scotch pine
    - 2. Colorful maple trees
      - a. Red maple
      - b. Silver maple
  - B. Warm climate trees . . .
- II. Trees used in agriculture . . .

Important: Unless your instructor says otherwise, adapt your outline to meet your needs rather than worrying if you've followed all the rules.

Sentence Outline

Here is a sentence outline for the paragraph "Cross-Cultural Miscues" on page 344.

- I. Differences between American and British English can cause misunderstandings.
  - A. Each uses different words to refer to the same thing.
    - 1. The Brits refer to dustbins, lifts, and flats.
    - 2. Americans call them garbage cans, elevators, and apartments.
  - B. Sometimes the same word is used, but for different meaning.
    - 1. "Homely" means "warm and friendly" for Brits and plain for Americans.
    - 2. "To table a motion" means "giving an important place on an agenda" for Brits and "postponing action on an issue" for Americans.
    - 3. "Rubber" means "eraser" for Brits and "condom" for Americans.

Practice Outline the paragraph "Effective Discipline" on page 286. For a special challenge, also outline the essay "Movies at Work" on pages 289–290.

Using Clusters or Webs

Clustering or webbing is a more graphic way to collect and organize the key points in a reading assignment. Begin a cluster with a nucleus word or idea—most often, the main idea in the reading. Then you cluster key points and supporting details around the nucleus concept. Circle each point or detail and connect it to the closest related word. The end result should be a structure that graphically shows you at a glance all the important information in a reading selection.

Clustering in Action

"A Penny for Your World-Saving Thoughts" is an illustrative essay on pages 206–208. This essay illustrates four inexpensive ideas that aid the world's poor. Study the cluster that follows to see how it shows how the important information fits together.

Tip Suppose you want to explore your thoughts and feelings about a text. You can do so in a cluster or, as it is sometime called, a mind map. Simply start with an appropriate nucleus word (perhaps the title of the selection) and record and connect your ideas. Clustering in this way may help you gain a firmer understanding of the text.

Practice Read the illustrative paragraph "Heading in the Right Direction" on page 213 in your book. (Or use another selection recommended by your instructor.) Then use a cluster to gather and connect the important information in the text. Afterward, share clusters and discuss the value of this reading strategy.

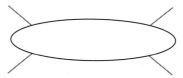

Summarizing a Text

Summarizing a reading assignment will tell you how well you understand the information. Summarizing means "to present the main points in a clear, concise form using your own words." Generally speaking, a summary should be about one-third as long as the original.

Summarizing Tips

- Start by clearly stating the main idea of the text.
- Share only the essential supporting facts and details (names, dates, times, and places) in the next sentences.
- Present your ideas in a logical order.
- Tie all of your points together in a closing sentence.

Example Summary

The example below summarizes a two-page essay by Kofi A. Annan concerning the suffering caused by AIDS and famine in southern Africa.

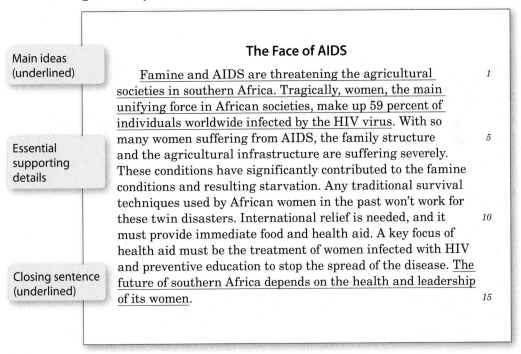

Main ideas (underlined)

Essential supporting details

Closing sentence (underlined)

The Face of AIDS

Famine and AIDS are threatening the agricultural   *1*
societies in southern Africa. Tragically, women, the main
unifying force in African societies, make up 59 percent of
individuals worldwide infected by the HIV virus. With so
many women suffering from AIDS, the family structure   *5*
and the agricultural infrastructure are suffering severely.
These conditions have significantly contributed to the famine
conditions and resulting starvation. Any traditional survival
techniques used by African women in the past won't work for
these twin disasters. International relief is needed, and it   *10*
must provide immediate food and health aid. A key focus of
health aid must be the treatment of women infected with HIV
and preventive education to stop the spread of the disease. The
future of southern Africa depends on the health and leadership
of its women.   *15*

Practice   On your own paper, summarize one of the paragraphs on pages 147–438 or a paragraph provided by your instructor. Use the tips above as a guide.

Forming Personal Responses

To thoughtfully interact with a text, you need to write about it. Reserve part of your class notebook for these personal responses. Personal responses to a text help you think about it—to agree with it, to question it, to make connections with it. The following guidelines will help you do this:

- **Write several times,** perhaps once before you read, two or three times during the reading, and one time afterward.
- **Write freely and honestly** to make genuine connections with the text.
- **Respond to points of view** that you like or agree with, information that confuses you, connections that you can make with other material, and ideas that seem significant.
- **Label and date your responses.** You can use these entries to prepare for exams or complete other assignments.
- **Share your discoveries.** Your entries can provide conversation starters in discussions with classmates.

> ### INSIGHT
> If you are a visual person, you may understand a text best by clustering or mapping its important points. (See page 24 for a sample cluster.)

Types of Personal Responses

Here are some specific ways to respond to a text:

Discuss	Carry on a conversation with the author or a character to get to know her or him and yourself a little better.
Illustrate	Create graphics or draw pictures to help you figure out parts of the text.
Imitate	Continue the article or story line, trying to write like the author.
Express	Share your feelings about the text, perhaps in a poem.

Practice Follow the guidelines on this page to explore your thoughts about one of your next reading assignments. Afterward, assess the value of forming personal responses to a text.

LO5 Reading Critically

Critical reading involves a lot of analyzing and evaluating. Analyzing refers to, among other things, classifying and comparing ideas as well as looking for cause-effect relationships. Evaluating refers to weighing the value of a text and considering its strengths and weaknesses.

An educational psychologist named Benjamin Bloom created a list of thinking skills, moving from simpler, surface thinking to deeper levels of thinking. In this taxonomy, analyzing and evaluating are clearly deeper levels of thinking.

Bloom's New Taxonomy

Whenever you are asked to . . .	Be prepared to . . .
Remember	collect basic information, identify key terms, and remember main points.
Understand	explain what you have learned, give examples, and restate information.
Apply	identify crucial details, organize key points, and model or show understanding.
Analyze	carefully examine the topic, classify the main points, show cause-effect relationships, and make comparisons.
Evaluate	judge the value of information, identify strengths and weaknesses, and argue for or against the ideas.
Create	develop something new from what you have learned.

Apply Study the chart above. Then explain in a brief paragraph how many of these thinking skills you apply to your own academic reading or perhaps in your test taking.

_____

_____

_____

A CLOSER LOOK at Critical Reading

When reading critically, you are, in effect, asking and answering thoughtful questions about a text. Here are some thoughtful questions that a critical reader may ask about a nonfiction text:

Asking Critical Questions

- What is the purpose of the reading (to inform, to entertain, to persuade)?
- Who is the intended audience (general readers, students, professionals)?
- What parts does the text include (title, headings, graphics, introduction, and so on)?
- What logical pattern of reasoning does it follow? (See below.)
- What is the focus or main idea in the reading?
- How is the focus supported or developed (facts, examples, definitions, and so on)?
- What parts of the text seem especially important, and why?
- What questions do you still have about the topic?
- How will you use this information?

Deductive and Inductive Thinking

Almost all texts that you read will follow either deductive or inductive patterns of reasoning. **Deductive thinking** moves from a general focus (topic sentence) to specific supporting details. Most texts follow this form of thinking. **Inductive thinking** moves from specific facts and details to a general conclusion.

Use these questions to check for deductive thinking.

- Does the text start with a thesis (main point or major premise)?
- Do the details logically support or follow from the focus?
- Does the conclusion logically follow the ideas that come before it?

Use these questions to check for inductive thinking.

- Does the text start with a series of facts, examples, and explanations?
- Do they logically lead up to the general conclusion?
- Does the general conclusion make sense in terms of the preceding evidence (facts, examples, and so on)?

Apply Use the "critical questions" on this page as a general guide for your next information reading assignment. Afterward, share your reading experience with your classmates.

LO6 Drawing Inferences

An *inference* is a logical conclusion that you make about something that is not actually said or stated in a text. A thoughtful inference results from a careful reading of a text. Suppose a newspaper article shows a famous athlete's illegal use of performance enhancement drugs for the years 2009-2011. This same athlete has claimed earlier that the only time he used such drugs was from 2003 to 2005. With the new finding, you could reasonably infer that the athlete was cheating in the years between the two reports as well.

Steps to Follow

To make thoughtful inferences, follow these steps:

- Carefully read and reread the text, using the reading process.
- Identify the main idea and supporting details.
- Then ask yourself: *What other conclusions can I draw from the reading?*

Inferring in Action

The following passage comes from the Bureau of Alcohol, Tobacco, Firearms, and Explosives (ATF) Web site. Note the inferences that were arrived at after a careful reading of the passage.

> The [ATF] director is appointed by the secretary of the Treasury and   *1*
> reports to the under secretary (enforcement). ATF headquarters are in
> Washington, D.C., although most personnel and many ATF operations
> are decentralized throughout the country, with a few stations overseas.
> ATF agents, inspectors, and support staff are involved in investigating   *5*
> some of the most violent crimes in society, in regulating some of the most
> important and sensitive industries in America, and in collecting over $13
> billion in annual revenue. ATF is a young federal agency, yet it is heir
> [someone who inherits] to the whole experience and proud tradition of
> "these United States."   *10*
>
> From Bureau of Alcohol, Tobacco, Firearms and Explosives Web site
> http://www.atf.gov/kids/about/history/

1. What is the main idea in the passage?

   "ATF is a young federal agency, yet is heir to the whole experience and proud tradition of 'these United States.'"

2. What detail supports the main idea?

   (1) The agency has operations throughout the country. (2) It investigates violent crimes and regulates sensitive industries.

3. What inferences can you draw from the passage? Here is one.

   ATF was probably involved in the investigation of the shooting in Newtown, CT, because this tragedy was certainly a violent crime.

Practice   To practice drawing inferences, carefully read each passage below. Then answer the questions following each passage.

1.   On a global basis, we have plenty of freshwater, but it is not   *1*
distributed evenly. Differences in average annual precipitation and
economic resources divide the world's continents, countries, and people
into water haves and have-nots. For example, Canada, with only 0.5
percent of the world's population, has 20 percent of the world's liquid   *5*
freshwater, while China, with 19 percent of the world's people, has only
7 percent of the supply. Asia has 60 percent of the population but only 30
percent of the water supply.   From Miller, *Living in the Environment*, 17E. © 2012 Cengage Learning

a. What is the main idea in the passage? (Hint: Look for the topic sentence.)

_____

b. What key type of detail supports the main idea? Circle one: definitions, statistics, quotations.

c. What inferences (conclusions) can you draw from the passage?

_____

2.   The diet debates over low-fat versus low-carbohydrate versus high-   *1*
protein have raged for years. Which is best? Several studies over recent years
found little difference in the ultimate results. The largest-ever controlled
study of dietary methods reached a clear conclusion: It doesn't matter
whether you count carbohydrates, protein, or fat—as long as you eat less.   *5*
    In the study, more than 800 overweight men and women were assigned
to one of four diets, each loosely based on popular weight loss programs, such
as the Atkins high-protein diet and Dean Ornish's low-fat approach. . . .
    Each participant consumed about 750 calories less than normal, but all
ate at least 1,200 calories a day. After six months every diet group had lost   *10*
about the same amount of weight, regardless of the weight loss plan, for an
average of 13 pounds per person. About 15 percent lost more than 10 percent
of their body weight by the end of the two-year study. Those who lost the most
attended more counseling sessions and followed the diets more closely than
the others.   From Hales, *An Invitation to Health*, 7E. © 2012 Cengage Learning   *15*

a. What is the main idea in this passage? (Hint: Focus on the first paragraph.)

_____

b. What main detail from the controlled study supports this idea?

_____

c. What inferences (conclusions) can you draw from this passage?

_____

3.

Disinformation

In October 1986, the press learned that two months earlier the Reagan *1* administration had launched a disinformation campaign to scare Libyan leader Muammar Qaddafi. Selected U.S. government sources had planted stories with reporters that U.S. forces were preparing to strike Libya.

The first report about the bogus preparations appeared in the *5* August 25, 1986, issue of *The Wall Street Journal,* which first used the word **disinformation** to describe the practice of government officials intentionally planting false information with reporters.

On the basis of a statement by White House spokesman Larry Speakes that the *Journal's* article about an impending strike on Libya was *10* "authoritative," other newspapers, including *The Washington Post,* carried the story. This example brings up the ethical question of the government's responsibility to tell the truth and not to use the news media for its own ends. State Department spokesman and former television reporter Bernard Kalb resigned when he learned about the disinformation campaign, saying, "Faith *15* in the word of America is the pulse beat of our democracy."

Disinformation also was at the center of the 2007 trial of presidential advisor I. Lewis Libby, in which Libby was found guilty of perjury and obstruction of justice for leaking the name of CIA operative Valerie Plame to journalists and then denying before a Washington, D.C., grand jury that he *20* had done so. . . .   From Biagi, *Media/Impact: An Introduction to Mass Media,* 10E. © 2011 Cengage Learning

a. What is the main idea in this passage?

_____

_____

b. What details from the passage support this main idea?

_____

_____

_____

c. What inferences (conclusions) can you draw from the passage? Name two.

_____

_____

_____

LO7 Improving Vocabulary

To understand and truly benefit from your academic reading, you need to build a fairly strong reading vocabulary, which you will do if you become a regular reader. You also need strategies right now to unlock the meaning of new words, which you are sure to find in college-level texts. Referring to a dictionary is one such strategy, but that can disrupt your reading if you use it too much. Here are other strategies that are more reader friendly for understanding new words.

Keeping a Vocabulary Notebook

Proactive means "acting in advance" or "acting before." Reserving part of your classroom notebook for new words is proactive because you are taking control of your vocabulary building. This strategy will prove especially helpful in challenging courses, when you are introduced to many new words. The examples show the kinds of information to include for words you list in your notebook.

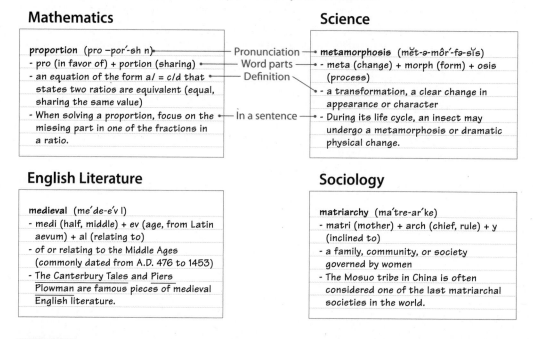

Mathematics

proportion (pro –por´-sh n) — Pronunciation
- pro (in favor of) + portion (sharing) — Word parts
- an equation of the form a/ = c/d that — Definition
  states two ratios are equivalent (equal,
  sharing the same value)
- When solving a proportion, focus on the — In a sentence
  missing part in one of the fractions in
  a ratio.

Science

metamorphosis (mĕt-ə-môr´-fə-sĭs)
- meta (change) + morph (form) + osis
  (process)
- a transformation, a clear change in
  appearance or character
- During its life cycle, an insect may
  undergo a metamorphosis or dramatic
  physical change.

English Literature

medieval (me´de-e´v l)
- medi (half, middle) + ev (age, from Latin
  aevum) + al (relating to)
- of or relating to the Middle Ages
  (commonly dated from A.D. 476 to 1453)
- The Canterbury Tales and Piers
  Plowman are famous pieces of medieval
  English literature.

Sociology

matriarchy (ma´tre-ar´ke)
- matri (mother) + arch (chief, rule) + y
  (inclined to)
- a family, community, or society
  governed by women
- The Mosuo tribe in China is often
  considered one of the last matriarchal
  societies in the world.

Identify   For each of the following words, create a vocabulary entry like the ones above. Identify the pronunciation, helpful word parts, a primary definition, and the word used in a sentence. (For assistance, refer to a dictionary and the glossary of word parts on pages 623–631 in your book.)

- intercede
- anthropology
- supernova
- numerical

Using Context

Instead of skipping new words in your reading, try to figure out what they mean in context—or by looking for clues in the other words and ideas around them. Here is how using context can work:

In some cases, the context clues can be very easy to identify. In the following passage from a science text, the word "pasture" is defined right in the same sentence (underlined).

> Cattle, sheep, and goats graze on about 42 percent of the world's   *1*
> grassland. The 2005 Millennium Ecosystem Assessment estimated that
> this could increase to 70 percent by 2050. Livestock also graze in *pastures,*
> <u>which are managed grasslands or fenced meadows usually planted with</u>
> <u>domesticated grasses.</u> . . .   *5*

In other cases, you must study a text more carefully for context clues. In this passage from a sociology text, an antonym in one sentence (underlined) helps you understand the word "monopolize" in a previous sentence.

> Most people don't consistently try to *monopolize* conversations. If they   *1*
> did, there wouldn't be much talk in the world. In fact, <u>turn-taking</u> is one
> of the basic norms that govern conversations; people literally take turns
> talking to make conversation possible. . . .

Types of Context Clues

There are many types of context clues, as you will see in the list that follows.

- **Cause-effect relationships:** Suggesting the use of seat belts didn't work, so the state officials made seat-belt use *mandatory.*
- **Definitions built into the text:** Dr. Williams is an *anthropologist,* a person who scientifically studies the physical, social, and cultural development of humans.
- **Comparisons and contrasts:** Lynn Dery lives in New York, so she is used to a fast-paced life; Mandy Williams lives in the country, so she is used to a more *serene* lifestyle.
- **Words in a series:** Spaghetti, lasagna, and *ziti* all have their own special shape.
- **Synonyms (words with the same meaning):** Hector's essay contains too many *banal,* overused phrases.
- **Antonyms (words with the opposite meaning):** Mrs. Wolfe still seemed strong and energetic after the storm, but Mr. Wolfe looked *haggard.*
- **The tone of the text:** The street was filled with *bellicose* protesters who pushed and shoved their way through the crowd. The scene was no longer peaceful and calm, as the marchers promised it would be.

Define Define or explain the italicized word or term in each passage that follows. Also indicate the type of context clue that helped you understand the word.

1.   How do you navigate around the town you live in? Have you simply   *1*
learned to make a series of right and left turns to get from one point to
another? More likely, you have an overall mental picture of how the town
is laid out. This *cognitive map* acts as a guide even when you must detour
or take a new route. A cognitive map is an internal representation of an   *5*
area, such as a maze, city, or campus.   From Coon/Mitterer. *Psychology*, 12E. © 2012 Cengage Learning,

Definition/explanation: _____

Type of context clue: _____

2.   [When taking lecture notes] put the lecture in your own words for
the most part, but write down formulas, definitions, charts, diagrams,   *1*
and specific facts *verbatim*. Also, write down good points made by
classmates. . . .   From Staley/Staley, *FOCUS on College and Career Success*, 1E. © 2012 Cengage Learning.

                                                                                4
Definition/explanation: _____

Type of context clue: _____

3.   In 2008, a number of *hydrologists* warned that the current rate of
withdrawal of water from the Colorado River is not sustainable. Water   *1*
experts also project that if the climate continues to warm as projected,
mountain snows that feed the river will melt faster and earlier, and
the melted water will evaporate in greater amounts, making less water
available in the river system. . . .   From Miller, *Living in the Environment*, 17E. © 2012 Cengage Learning   *5*

Definition/explanation: _____

Type of context clue: _____

4.   Because partners can pool their funds, a partnership usually has
more capital available than a *sole proprietorship* does. This additional   *1*
capital, coupled with the general partner's unlimited liability, can form
the basis for a better credit rating. Banks and suppliers may be more
willing to extend credit or approve larger loans to such a partnership than
a sole proprietorship. This does not mean that partnerships can borrow all   *5*
the money they need.   From Pride/Hughes/Kapoor, *Foundations of Business*, 3E. © 2013 Cengage Learning

Definition/explanation: _____

Type of context clue: _____

Understanding Word Parts

You may have heard of the following terms: *roots* (base words), *prefixes*, and *suffixes*. Many words in our language are made up of combinations of these word parts. (See pages 623–631 for a listing of common word parts.)

- **Roots** like *liber* (as in <u>liber</u>ate) or *rupt* (as in inter<u>rupt</u>) are the starting points for most words.
- **Prefixes** like *anti* (as in <u>anti</u>biotic) or *un* (as in <u>un</u>real) are word parts that come before roots to form new words.
- **Suffixes** like *dom* (as in bore<u>dom</u>) or *ly* (as in hour<u>ly</u>) are word parts that come after roots to form new words.

Sample Words

The following examples show how multiple word parts can be combined to form words.

Transportation **combines . . .**
- the prefix *trans* meaning "across" or "beyond,"
- the root *port* meaning "carry,"
- and the suffix *tion* meaning "act of."

So, *transportation* **means "the act of carrying across or beyond."**

Biographic **combines . . .**
- the root *bio* meaning "life,"
- the root *graph* meaning "write,"
- and the suffix *ic* meaning "nature of" or "relating to."

So, *biographic* **means "relating to writing about life."**

Micrometer **combines . . .**
- the root *micro* meaning "small"
- and the root *meter* meaning "measure."

So, a *micrometer* **is "a device for measuring small distances."**

STILLFX, 2013 / Used under license from Shutterstock.com

Identify Using the examples above as a guide, analyze and define these words.

- nominate (nomin + ate)
- hemisphere (hemi + sphere)
- senile (sen + ile)
- translucent (trans + luc + ent)

Within a Text

Note the word *multiculturalism* in the following passage from a sociology textbook. You may already know the meaning of this word. If not, studying its parts can help you unlock its meaning.

> In contrast, for the past several decades, advocates of   *1*
> *multiculturalism* have argued that school and college curricula should
> present a more balanced picture of American history, culture, and
> society—one that better reflects the country's ethnic and racial diversity
> today (Nash, Crabtree, and Dunn, 12977).   *5*
>
> From BRYM/LIE, *Sociology*, 2E. © 2007 Cengage Learning

Analysis of the word *multiculturalism*:

Word parts: *Multi* is a prefix meaning "many" (see page 624). *Culture* is a root or base word meaning "the way a group conducts life." The suffixes *al* and *ism* basically mean "of or relating to" (see page 625).

Definition/explanation of the word: *Multiculturalism* logically means "of or relating to many cultures" or "of or relating to the many ways that groups conduct their lives."

Practice   Study the italicized word in each of the following passages. Break it into recognizable word parts, explain what each part means, and then define the word. Use the example above as a guide. (Also see pages 623–631.)

1.   The United States should limit carbon emissions and lessen its   *1*
           dependence on fossil fuels. To *counteract* its dependence on fossil fuels,
           the U.S. must invest in wind farms for its energy needs. A wind farm
           is made up of a group of large wind turbines, which convert wind into   *5*
           electric energy. . . .

Analysis of the word *counteract*:

Word parts: _____

Definition/explanation of the word: _____

2.   Not all Greeks were able to find the truth they needed in philosophy.   *1*
           Probably the large majority of people were not exposed to the complex
           reasoning of the philosophers, so they turned instead to religion. Like
           most of the other peoples we have discussed, the Greeks were *polytheistic*.   *5*
           . . .   From Adler/Pouwels, *World Civilizations*, 6E. © 2012 Cengage Learning

Analysis of the word *polytheistic*:

Word parts: _____

Definition/explanation of the word: _____

LO8 Reading Graphics

In many of your college texts, a significant portion of the information will be given in charts, graphs, diagrams, and drawings. Knowing how to read these types of graphics, then, is important to your success as a college student. Follow these reading guidelines.

- **Scan the graphic.** Consider it as a whole to get an overall idea about its message. Note its type (bar graph, pie graph, diagram, table, and so forth), its topic, its level of complexity, and so on.
- **Study the specific parts.** Start with the main heading or title. Next, note any additional labels or guides (such as the horizontal and vertical guides on a bar graph). Then focus on the actual information displayed in the graphic.
- **Question the graphic.** Does it address an important topic? What is its purpose (to make a comparison, to show a change, and so on)? What is the source of the information? Is the graphic out of date or biased in any way?
- **Reflect on its effectiveness.** Explain in your own words the main message of the graphic. Then consider its effectiveness, how it relates to the surrounding text, and how it matches up to your previous knowledge of the topic.

Analysis of a Graphic

Review the bar graph below. Then read the discussion to learn how all of the parts work together.

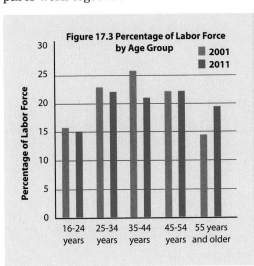

Discussion: This bar graph compares the labor force in 2001 to the labor force in 2011 for five specific age groups. The heading identifies the subject or topic of the graphic. The horizontal line identifies the different age groups, and the vertical line identifies the percentage of the labor force for each group. The key in the upper right-hand corner of the graphic explains the color-coded bars. With all of that information, the graphic reads quite clearly—and many interesting comparisons can be made.

React   Read and analyze the following graphics, answering the questions about each one on your own paper. Use the information on the previous page as a guide.

Graphic 1

1. This graphic is called a pictograph rather than a bar graph. What makes it a "pictograph"?

   _____

   _____

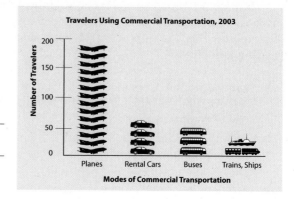

2. What is the topic of this graphic?

   _____

3. What information is provided on the horizontal line? On the vertical line?

   _____

4. What comparisons can a reader make from this graphic?

   _____

Graphic 2

1. This graphic is called a line diagram, and it maps a structure. What structure does this diagram map?

   _____

   _____

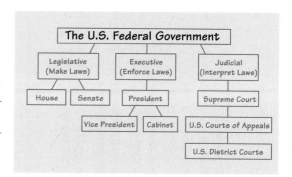

2. From the following items, choose the two working parts in this diagram: *words, lines, symbols.*

   _____

3. What are the three main branches in this graphic?

   _____

Review and Enrichment

On the next six pages you will review and enrich your understanding of the concepts in this chapter.

Reviewing the Chapter

Reading to Learn Explain in a few sentences how you should approach your academic reading to get the most out of each assignment. (See page 12.)

_____

_____

Understanding the Reading Process List the four steps in the reading process. Identify two things that you should do during each step. (See pages 13–15.)

1. _____   3. _____

2. _____   4. _____

Using Reading Strategies Answer the following questions about reading strategies. (See pages 20–22.)

■ What does it mean to annotate a text?

_____

■ What are two-column notes?

_____

Reading Critically What does it mean to analyze a text? (See page 27.)

_____

_____

Drawing Inferences What are inferences? (See pages 29–31.)

_____

Improving Vocabulary Explain what it means to use context clues to figure out the meaning of new words. (See page 33.)

_____

_____

Reading

The reading selection "Television: Changing Channels," which starts on page 41, comes from a textbook called *Media/Impact: An Introduction to Mass Media*. It is the type of reading you will typically find in an introductory college textbook. As you read this text, be sure to follow the steps in the reading process. Also be sure to apply one or more of the reading strategies introduced in this chapter, including annotating and note taking, to help you gain a full understanding of the text.

> "All television is educational television. The question is: what is it teaching?"
> —Nicholas Johnson

About the Author

Shirley Biagi is a professor in the Department of Communication Studies at California State University, Sacramento. *Media/Impact* is in its tenth edition and is also published in Canadian, Greek, Spanish, and Korean editions.

Prereading

Television impacts us all to one degree or another. It can serve as a learning tool, a source of entertainment, an annoying distraction, and on and on. Like all aspects of life, it is probably best used or consumed in moderation. Write freely for 3–5 minutes about your own viewing habits.

_____

_____

Identify   Before you read, answer these three questions:

1. What do the title, beginning paragraph, headings, and graphic tell you about the text?

_____

2. What are your first thoughts about the author's purpose?

_____

3. What do you expect to learn?

_____

What do you think?

Consider the quotation above. What does television "teach"? Think of many possibilities.

Reading and Rereading

As you read, make it your goal to (1) find or state the main idea of the selection, (2) identify the key supporting details, and (3) study the closing paragraph. Be especially aware of the different types of support the author includes: the thoughts of experts, references to reports and studies, and statistics.

Tip Annotate the text (page 20) and/or take notes (page 22) as needed to help you with your reading.

Television: Changing Channels

"Television is the pervasive American pastime," writes media observer Jeff Greenfield. "Cutting through geographic, ethnic, class, and cultural diversity, it is the single binding thread of this country, the one experience that touches young and old, rich and poor, learned and illiterate. A country too big for homogeneity, filled by people from all over the globe, without any set of core values, America never had a central unifying bond. Now we do. Now it is possible to answer the question, 'What does America do?' We watch television."
1

5

Television is turned on in today's American household, on average, more than eight hours a day, according to the A.C. Nielsen Company, which monitors television usage for advertisers. (See Illustration 8.1.) Even though people in your household may not watch TV this much, the percentage of households in the United States that use television a lot counterbalances the smaller amount of time people at your house spend with their television sets.
10

15

How Much Time Each Day Do People Watch Television?

The time people spend watching TV has increased every year since 1950. These statistics reflect total viewing per household, which means the total combined time that all people in the average household have the TV turned on each day.
16

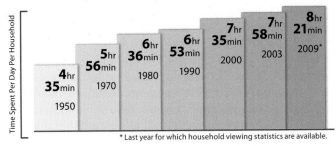

Time Spent Per Day Per Household

| 1950 | 1970 | 1980 | 1990 | 2000 | 2003 | 2009* |
| 4hr 35min | 5hr 56min | 6hr 36min | 6hr 53min | 7hr 35min | 7hr 58min | 8hr 21min |

* Last year for which household viewing statistics are available.

Source: nielsenwire, "Average TV Viewing for 2008-09 TV Season at All-Time High," http://blog.nielsen.com/nielsenwire/media_entertainment;average-tv-viewing-for-2008-09-tv-season-at-all-time-high/.

Television Transforms Daily Life

It's not surprising that the effects of such a pervasive medium   *20*
have attracted so much attention from parents, educators, social
scientists, religious leaders, public officials, and anyone else who wants
to understand society's habits and values. TV has been blamed for
everything from declines in literacy to rises in violent crime to the
trivialization of national politics. Every once in a while it is praised, too,   *25*
for giving viewers instant access to world events and uniting audiences
in times of national crisis.

An industry with this much presence in American life is bound to
affect the way we live. Someone who is watching television is not doing
other things: playing basketball, visiting a museum, or looking through a   *30*
telescope at the planets, for instance. Television can, however, bring you
to a museum you might never visit or to a basketball game you cannot
attend or to the surface of a planet you can only see through a telescope.

Television technology, by adding pictures to the sounds of radio,
truly transformed Americans' living and learning patterns. The word   *35*
television, which once meant programs delivered by antennas through
over-the-air signals, now means a television screen, where several
different types of delivery systems bring viewers a diversity of programs.

The programs Americans watch today are delivered by antennas,
cables, and satellites, but they all appear on the same television screen,   *40*
and as a viewer, you can't tell how the program arrived at your television
set and probably don't care. What you do know is that television gives
you access to all types of programs—drama, comedy, sports, news, game
shows, and talk shows. You can see all types of people—murderers,
public officials, foreign leaders, reporters, soldiers, entertainers, athletes,   *45*
detectives, and doctors. The television screen is truly, as scholar Erik
Barnouw observed, a "tube of plenty."

About 1,600 television stations operate in the United States.
Three out of four of these are commercial stations, and the others
are noncommercial stations. About half the commercial stations are   *50*
affiliated with a network.

According to TV commentator Jeff Greenfield, "The most common
misconception most people have about television concerns its product. To
the viewer, the product is the programming. To the television executive,
the product is the audience. Strictly speaking, television networks and   *55*
stations do not make money by producing a program that audiences
want to watch. The money comes from selling advertisers the right to
broadcast a message to that audience. The program exists to capture the
biggest possible audience."   *59*

From Biagi, *Media/Impact: An Introduction to Mass Media,* 10E. © 2011 Cengage Learning

Reflecting

After your reading, answer the following questions. Afterward, share your responses with your classmates.

1. What main idea is developed in the text? (Or is there more than one main idea?)

_____

_____

_____

2. What supporting evidence is provided? (Give two key examples.)

_____

_____

_____

3. What information is presented in the graphic?

_____

_____

_____

4. What is the main method of organization employed in this selection—chronological, spatial, logical? (See page 71.)

5. One scholar has called television a "tube of plenty." What is meant by that term?

_____

_____

6. Has this text changed or expanded your understanding of the topic? If so, how?

_____

_____

7. How would you rate this reading, and why?

   Weak ★ ★ ★ ★ ★ Strong

_____

_____

Vocabulary Practice

Pages 33–34 explain one strategy—using context clues—that will help you understand new words in your reading. Context clues are clues provided by familiar words and ideas around unfamiliar ones.

Identify Use context clues to define or explain the following words in "Television: Changing Channels."

1. homogeneity (line 5)

clues: _____

definition: _____

2. counterbalances (line 14)

clues: _____

definition: _____

3. access (line 22)

clues: _____

definition: _____

Drawing Inferences

Pages 29–31 explain that an inference is a logical conclusion that you make about something that is not actually said or stated in a text. A thoughtful inference results from a careful reading, after you have identified the main point that is developed.

Explain Draw inferences from "Television: Changing Channels" by answering the following questions.

1. What message may be suggested to the individual TV viewer?

_____

_____

_____

2. What will television's impact be in the future, and why?

_____

_____

3

> "Reading is a basic tool of the living of a good life."
> —Joseph Addison

The Traits of Academic Reading

Here's one thing you know for sure: As a college student, you will do a lot of reading. Because reading is so important, you need to know the best way to understand and learn from each assignment. The last chapter, "Academic Reading and Learning," provided a starting point by discussing important skills such as note taking and vocabulary building. This chapter takes a closer look at reading.

You will learn about the traits or building blocks of a reading assignment. The basic traits include ideas (topics, main ideas and details), organization, voice, word choice, and sentences. Knowing how to identify and analyze these traits will make you a better reader. And becoming a better reader will help you succeed in all of your classes.

Remember: Reading may be your most important learning tool in college, so you need to know how to learn from your reading assignment.

Learning Outcomes

LO1 Topics, main ideas, and supporting details
LO2 Organization
LO3 Voice (Tone)
LO4 Word choice and sentences

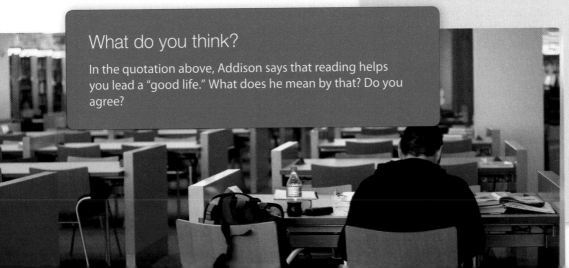

What do you think?

In the quotation above, Addison says that reading helps you lead a "good life." What does he mean by that? Do you agree?

LO1   Topics, Main Ideas, and Supporting Details

Ideas are the key trait in everything that you read. Every other trait—*organization, voice, word choice*—depends on the ideas. In this section you will learn about identifying the topic, main idea, and supporting details in a text.

Identifying the Topic

Any paragraph, essay, article, or textbook chapter has to be about something, and that something is called the **topic**. A topic may be a specific person (*Pope Francis*), a place (*the Great Barrier Reef*), an object (*the rotary phone*), or an idea (*transparency*). Identifying the topic is naturally an important first step when carrying out a reading assignment. In essence, you need to know what the reading is about. A topic is usually not a complete sentence, but rather a word or phrase.

Luckily, this task is seldom complicated, because the topic is often stated in the title, in the first sentence in a paragraph, or in one of the first few paragraphs in a longer piece of writing.

Steps to Follow

1.   For paragraphs, read the title and first sentence. If you're still not sure, check the closing sentence, too.

2.   For essays, read the title, any headings, and the first paragraph. If you're still not sure, simply keep reading. As you go along, you're sure to identify the topic.

Topics in Context

Topic Stated in a Heading and First Sentence: Here is the first part of a multi-paragraph passage in a chapter from *World Civilizations,* a college history textbook. The topic, the Black Death, is stated in the heading and bold-faced in the first sentence. It is also referred to regularly as the text progresses.

The Black Death

The **Black Death** of the mid- and late fourteenth century is the most massive epidemic on record and by far the most lethal in the history of Europe, Asia, and parts of Africa. What was it, and why did it deal such a blow to Old World populations . . . ?   From Adler/Pouwels, *World Civilizations,* 6E. © 2012 Cengage Learning

---

Topic Stated at the End of First Paragraph: In the following paragraph from a multi-paragraph article, the topic—brown paper bags—is identified at the end of the first paragraph in the article's thesis statement.

> That much reviled bottleneck known at the American supermarket   *1*
> checkout lane would be an even greater exercise in frustration were it not for
> several technological advances. The Universal Product Code and the decoding
> laser scanner, introduced in 1974, tally a shopper's groceries far more quickly
> and accurately than the old method of inputting each purchase manually into
> a cash register. But beeping a large order past the scanner would have led only   *5*
> to a faster pileup of cans and boxes down the line, where the bagger works, had
> it not been for the introduction, more than a century earlier, of an even greater
> technological masterpiece: the square-bottomed paper bag.
>
> From *American Scholar* 72.4 (Autumn 2003)

Delayed Identification of a Topic: In this personal essay, the writer doesn't state his topic—the tidal wave of new technologies—until the middle of his essay.

> ### No Technology? No Problem
>
> As MIT graduates go, I realize I am unusual. I run a rickshaw service in   *1*
> downtown St. Louis, where I live. I make soap at home, and my wife sells it at
> the local farmer's market on Saturdays. We travel on foot or by bicycle to get
> the day's errands done and tote our groceries in **capacious**, foldable rear bike-
> baskets, carting our children behind using "Trail-Bikes," attachments that
> convert an adult bicycle into a tandem for a child.   *5*
>   Either one of my sons or myself mows our yard with a hand-powered
> cutting cylinder. My wife, assisted by our children, does the laundry using
> an old-fashioned, swing handled washing tub. We don't have a computer,
> television, or VCR, although we do listen to the radio and drive a car when
> the need arises (a 1983 Honda). I will go to the library by bicycle, and use the   *10*
> Internet at times. . . .
>   Compared to the world's silent majority, I am markedly better off, even
> pampered, and I don't consider myself radical or extreme in my practices. It
> is the Americans around me. I am merely wading in technology. They are
> drowning in it, dog-paddling to keep their heads above water. If a certain   *15*
> amount of something is good, it does not follow that lots of it is. King Midas
> tried to do a famous **alchemical** experiment, and we know what happened: he
> learned that too much of a good thing is not a good thing. . . .
>
> From "No Technology? No Problem" from "What Matters?" *MIT Alumni Journal*, October 2004

capacious
able to hold a lot

alchemical
unscientific, enchanting

Practice   Identify the topic in each of the following texts by circling the correct choice. Also state where the topic is first stated.

1.

The Growth of Franchising

Franchising, which began in the United States around the time of the   *1*
Civil War, was used originally by large firms, such as the Singer Sewing
Company, to distribute their products. Franchising has been increasing
steadily in popularity since the early 1900s, primarily for filling stations and
car dealerships; however, this retailing strategy has experienced enormous   *5*
growth since the mid-1970s. The franchise proliferation [great growth]
generally has paralleled the expansion of the fast-food industry. Three of
Entrepreneur magazine's top-rated franchises for 2010 were in this category.

a. the first franchise

b. the history of franchising

c. the growth of franchising

2.

The Pregnancy Trap

In my short time as a teacher in Connecticut, I have muddled through   *1*
President Bush's No Child Let Behind Act, which tied federal funding of
schools to various reforms, and through President Obama's Race to the Top
initiative, which does much the same thing, though with different benchmarks.
Thanks to the Feds, urban schools like mine are swimming in money. Our   *5*
facility is state-of-the-art, thanks to a recent $40 million face-lift, with
gleaming new hallways and bathrooms and a fully computerized library.

Here's my prediction: The money, the reforms, the gleaming porcelain,
the hopeful rhetoric about saving our children—all of it will have a limited
impact, at best, on most city schoolchildren. Urban teachers face an intractable   *10*
[difficult] problem, one that we cannot spend or even teach our way out of:
teen pregnancy. This year, all of my favorite girls are pregnant, four in all,
future unwed mothers every one. There will be no innovation in this quarter,
no race to the top. Personal moral accountability is the electrified rail that no
politician wants to touch.   *15*

My first encounter with teen pregnancy was a girl named Nicole, a pretty
15-year-old who had rings on every finger and great looped earrings and a red
pen with fluffy pink feathers and a heart that lit up when she wrote with it. . . .

From *Readings for Writers*, 14E © 2013 Cengage Learning

a. school reform

b. teen pregnancy

c. problems with pregnancy

3.   The **sheriff** is a very important figure in American law enforcement. *1*
Almost every one of the more than 3,000 counties in the United States (except
those in Alaska) has a sheriff. In every state except Rhode Island and Hawaii,
sheriffs are elected by members of the community for two- or four-year terms
and are paid a salary set by the state legislature or county board. As elected *5*
officials who do not necessarily need a background in law enforcement, modern
sheriffs resemble their counterparts from the political era of policing in many
ways. Simply stated, the sheriff is also a politician.

From GAINES/MILLER, Cengage Advantage Books: *Criminal Justice in Action*, 6E. © 2011 Cengage Learning

   a. American law enforcement
   b. sheriffs in American law enforcement
   c. politicians and law

---

4.   ### From "The Race to Codlandia"

   A medieval fisherman is said to have hauled up a three-foot-long cod, which *1*
was common enough at the time. And the fact that the cod could talk was not
especially surprising. But what was astonishing was that it spoke an unknown
language. It spoke Basque.

   The Basque folktale shows not only the Basque attachment to their orphan *5*
language, indecipherable to the rest of the world, but also their tie to the
Atlantic cod, *Gadus morhua,* a fish that has never been found in Basque or even
Spanish waters.

   The Basque are enigmatic [mysterious]. They have lived in what is now the
northwest corner of Spain and a nick of the French southwest for longer than *10*
history records, and not only is the origin of their language unknown, but the
origin of the people themselves remains a mystery also. According to one theory,
these rosy-cheeked, dark-haired, long-nosed people were the original Iberians,
driven by invaders to the mountainous corner between the Pyrenees, the
Cantabrian Sierra, and the Bay of Biscay. Or they may be indigenous [native] to *15*
this area.

   They graze sheep on impossibly steep, green slopes of mountains that are
thrilling in their rare, rugged beauty. They sing their own songs and write their
own literature in their own language, Euskera. . . . They also have their own
sports, most notably jai alai, and even their own hat, the Basque beret, which is *20*
bigger than any other beret.

From *Cod: A Biography of the Fish That Changed the World*. New York: Walker, 1997

   a. the Basque people
   b. the Atlantic cod
   c. the history of the Euskera langauge

Identifying the Main Idea

Almost everything that you read—be it an essay, an article, or a textbook chapter—develops a **main idea**. This idea is usually stated in the topic sentence in paragraphs and in the thesis statement in essays or other longer texts. The main idea consists of the topic and usually a particular feeling or idea about it.

There are times, however, when the main idea comes later in the text, perhaps as a concluding or closing statement. You may also read some essays or articles where the main idea is only implied rather than stated directly. (See page 59.) You may even read some longer texts that have more than one main idea or a main idea and one or two secondary (lesser) ideas.

What the Main Idea Tells You

In a *narrative* text, the main idea will tell you what experience the writer is going to share:

- "My final moments on stage during the musical *Grease* are ones I'll never forget."

In an *informational* text, the main idea will tell you what the author is going to explain or discuss:

- "One word in medical reports strikes fear into people everywhere, and that word is pandemic."

In a *persuasive* text, the main idea will tell you what claim or opinion the writer is going to argue for:

- "Text messaging should be banned in all states because it is making U.S. roads dangerous."

INSIGHT

Every piece of writing needs a spark to ignite, or, start a piece of writing. A main idea serves this purpose.

SPECIAL NOTE: The way that a sentence is worded might tell you that it states the main idea: "It has been more than two years since my telephone rang with the news . . . ," "There are several steps . . . ," or "All the flavors a person can taste are made up of . . . ."

Steps to Identifying the Main Idea

Follow the steps below to help you identify the main idea in a text. In paragraphs, you usually need to look no further than the first sentence—the topic sentence, because this sentence will name the topic and a particular idea or feeling about it. In an essay, you most often will find the main idea in one of the opening paragraphs.

Steps to Follow

1. Study the title and the first and last sentences of paragraphs. For essays, study the title and first and last paragraphs (just as you would to identify the topic).

2. Then read the paragraph from start to finish. For an essay read the opening few paragraphs to gain a general understanding of the topic.

3. Next, in a paragraph, look for a sentence (usually the first one) that directs the writing. In an essay, look for this sentence at the end of one of the opening paragraphs.

4. Write this statement down, or underline it if you own the text or are reading a copy. (If you can't find such a statement, try to state it in your own words.)

5. Read the paragraph again (or the essay completely) to make sure that this statement makes sense as the main idea. In a paragraph, each new sentence should support or develop this idea. In an essay, each new paragraph should support or develop it.

6. If your thinking changes, identify or write down what you now believe to be the main idea.

INSIGHT

A paragraph is really an essay in miniature. That is, it should contain the same traits or working parts. Essays, of course, provide more information because the support comes in the form of paragraphs rather than sentences. (See the graphic on page 76 to see how the two forms compare.)

Topic Sentences and Thesis Statements

A topic sentence or thesis statement usually consists of two parts: (1) a specific topic plus (2) a particular feature or feeling about it. Together, these two parts express the main idea. Here are three examples:

- "The United States must invest in wind power *(topic)* to resist our dependence on fossil fuel *(feeling/opinion)*."
- "Captain Chesley 'Sully' Sullenberger *(topic)* performed an emergency landing in the Hudson River *(feature)*."
- "The Don Quixote statuette my dad gave me *(topic)* isn't worth much to other people *(feeling)*."

In Context

Example 1

Study the following paragraph in which the writer explains Braille.

Communicating by Braille

Braille is a system of communication used by the blind. It was 1
developed by Louis Braille, a blind French student, in 1824. The code
consists of an alphabet using combinations of small, raised dots. The
dots are imprinted on paper and can be felt, and thus read, by running
the fingers across the page. The basic unit of the code is called a "cell," 5
which is two dots wide and three dots high. Each letter is formed by
different combinations of these dots. Numbers, punctuation marks, and
even a system for writing music are also expressed by using different
arrangements. These small dots, which may seem insignificant to the
sighted, have opened up the entire world of books and reading for the blind. 10

Discussion: A paragraph, by definition, is a group of sentences sharing ideas about a main point, which is usually stated in the topic sentence. The topic sentence in the above paragraph is underlined. It identifies the topic *(Braille)* and an important feature of it *(is a system of communication used by the blind)*. The sentences in the body of the paragraph give facts about the topic.

leungchopan, 2011 / Used under license from Shutterstock.com

Example 2

Read the following paragraph, in which the writer recalls a memorable gym teacher.

Duck-Walking

<u>Mr. Brown, my middle school gym teacher, did not allow any fooling around in his classes</u>. Unfortunately, two of my friends learned this the hard way. At the end of the first day of flag football, Mr. Brown blew his whistle. Most of us knew enough to stop and fall in line. He had made it very clear on the first day of class that when he blew his whistle, we had to stop our activity. Immediately. Kerry Schmidt and Jesse Johnson ignored the whistle and continued throwing a football. With fire in his eyes, Mr. Brown quickly sent the rest of us in. We all watched from the locker room doorway while Mr. Brown made Kerry and Jesse duck-walk on the football field. By the time they went 20 yards, they were really struggling. He sent them in after another 10 yards when their duck-walk had turned into more of a crawl. We couldn't help giving a few duck calls when they limped into the locker room, but we didn't quack too loudly because we didn't want Mr. Brown to make us walk like a duck or any other type of animal.

1
5
10

Piotr Tomicki, 2011 / Used under license from Shutterstock.com

Discussion: The topic sentence, which is underlined above, identifies the topic (*Mr. Brown*) and a feeling about him (*did not allow any fooling around in his classes*). The sentences in the body describe one experience that supports the topic sentence.

Example 3

Read the title, opening paragraph, and numbered main points from a book entitled *Focus on College and Career Success*.

Be Advised! Advising Mistakes Students Make

One of the most important relationships you'll have as a college 1
student is the one you build with your academic advisor. In your college
this person may be an advisor, a counselor, or a faculty member who can
steer you toward courses you can handle and instructors you can learn
best from. An advisor can keep you from taking classes that bog you down 5
academically or unnecessary ones that take you extra time to earn your
degree. <u>Here's a list of advising mistakes students make from real advisors
who work with college students every day.</u>

1. Not using the campus advising office or your faculty advisor. . . . 10

2. Not planning ahead. . . .

3. **Procrastinating**. . . .

4. Skipping **prerequisites**. . . .

From STALEY/STALEY. *FOCUS on College and Career Success*, 1E. © 2012 Wadsworth, a part of Cengage Learning, Inc.

Discussion: The title and general comments in the opening paragraph about the topic lead up to the thesis statement (underlined). Each of the numbered points that follow identifies an advising mistake. So clearly, the underlined statement is the thesis of the essay.

procrastinating putting off doing something	**prerequisites** courses that are needed

Example 4

Read the title and opening part of a section from *Sociology: Your Compass for a New World* in which the authors discuss clothing as a symbol of status.

Status and Style

Often rich people engage in **conspicuous** displays of **consumption**,   *1*
waste, and leisure not because they are necessary, useful, or pleasurable
but simply to impress their peers and inferiors (Veblen, 1899). This is
evident if we consider how clothing acts as a sort of language that signals
one's status to others (Lurie, 1981).   *5*

For thousands of years, certain clothing styles have indicated rank. In
ancient Egypt, only people in high positions were allowed to wear sandals.
. . .

European laws governing the dress styles of different groups fell into
disuse after about 1700. That is because a new method of control emerged   *10*
as Europe became wealthier. . . .

Today we have different ways of using clothes to signal status.
Designer labels loudly proclaim the dollar value of garments. . . .

From BRYM/LIE. *Sociology: Your Compass for a New World, 2E.* © 2006 Thompson, a part of Cengage Learning, Inc.

Discussion: The underlined statement in the opening paragraph essentially restates the claim made in the title—which suggests that it is the main idea or thesis of the text. The start of the next three paragraphs show that the underlined idea will be explored in the main part of the text.

conspicuous
easy to notice

consumption
the act or process of buying

Practice　Identify the topic sentence in the two paragraphs that follow. For the essay on page 58, identify the thesis statement. Then explain each of your choices (how the statement relates to the other sentences in the text).

Tip

Use the guidelines on page 52 to help you find the topic sentence or thesis statement for each sample text.

Practice 1

Defying Gravity

Unlike race cars or trains, roller coasters do not rely on powerful engines for speed. Instead, roller coasters let gravity do much of the work. (Gravity is the force that constantly pulls objects of mass toward the ground.) When a roller-coaster track slopes down, the passenger cars accelerate forward because gravity pulls the front car downward. When the track tilts up, the cars decelerate because gravity pulls the back car downward. But gravity is not the only factor in maintaining speed. Another factor is momentum. On most roller coasters, the first drop is the tallest and steepest. Coasters are designed this way to create enough momentum to carry them forward through the rest of the track. Momentum is especially needed to make it up hills and through loops, as gravity pulls the cars in the opposite direction. This tug-of-war between gravity and momentum makes for exciting rides.

1

5

10

Topic sentence: _____

_____

_____

Explain your choice: _____

_____

_____

_____

Practice 2

The Value of Serving

Community service requirements give students life-changing   *1*
experiences not available in the classroom. First, they learn the
importance of basic job skills such as being on time, teamwork, and
completing tasks. Volunteer Anna Hernandez said, "I had to be at the
senior center right at 3:00 p.m. when the board games started. The   *5*
residents expected me to be there." Community service work also helps
students appreciate the problems and challenges facing Burlington. Scott
Thompson, part of a clean-up crew, never realized how thoughtless people
can be until he started cleaning up after them. As he stated, "Some people
really trash the parks." Most importantly, students learn about giving   *10*
back. For many students, community service is the first time they have
helped people in the community. According to Ms. Sandra Williams, the
community service advisor, "Working in the community shows students
that a lot of people need help." Critics feel that this requirement seems
almost like a punishment. However, participants quickly discover the   *15*
value of their efforts. Essentially, community service gives students a taste
of real life at just the right time.

Topic sentence: _____

_____

_____

Explain your choice: _____

_____

_____

_____

Practice 3

Dietary Diversity

Whatever your cultural heritage, you have probably sampled Chinese, *1*
Mexican, Indian, Italian, and Japanese foods. If you belong to any of these
ethnic groups, you may eat these **cuisines** regularly. Each type of ethnic
cooking has its own nutritional benefits and potential drawbacks.

Mediterranean Diet Several years ago **epidemiologists** noticed *5*
something unexpected in the residents of regions along the Mediterranean
Sea: a lower incidence of deaths from heart disease. . . .

Ethnic Cuisines The cuisine served in Mexico features rice, corn, and
beans, which are low in fat and high in nutrition. However, the dishes
Americans think of as Mexican are far less healthful. . . . *10*

African American cuisine traces some of its roots to food preferences
from west Africa (for example, peanuts, okra, and black-eyed peas). . . .

The mainland Chinese diet, which is plant-based, high in
carbohydrates, and low in fats and animal protein, is considered one of the
most healthful in the world. . . . *15*

Many Indian dishes highlight healthful ingredients such as vegetables
and legumes (beans and peas). However, many also use ghee (a form of
butter) or coconut oil; both are rich in saturated fats. . . .

From HALES. *An Invitation to Health*, 7E. © 2012 Brooks/Cole, a part of Cengage Learning, Inc.

Thesis statement: _____

_____

_____

Explain your choice: _____

_____

_____

_____

cuisines
manners or styles of preparing food

epidemiologists
medical professionals who study the
causes and control of diseases

Implied Main Ideas

As is mentioned on page 50, there are times when the main idea is implied or suggested rather than directly stated. You will know that this is the case in a paragraph if no one sentence seems to direct the writing. When this is the case, follow these steps:

Steps to Follow

1. Identify the topic in the first reading.

2. Pay close attention to each set of details in additional readings.

3. Write down the important idea that can "cover" all of the details.

4. Read the paragraph again to make sure that this idea accurately covers the details. (Revise your statement as needed.)

Implied Main Idea in Context

Here is a paragraph about the homeless. While the topic is easy to identify, the main idea of the paragraph is not because it isn't stated. Read the paragraph and then see below how the implied main idea is identified.

> It was estimated in October of this year that almost all of the food supplied *1* by the Temporary Emergency Assistance Program had gone to those who were not homeless. Anna Kondratas of the Department of Agriculture explains, " When you're homeless, you don't carry around a five-pound block of cheese" (qtd. in Whitman 34). Food programs such as this are of value only to those who already *5* have places to store and prepare food they are given. A federal program called the voucher system allows low-income families to live wherever they can find housing, regardless of cost, but they must pay at least 30 percent of their income in rent. So while this program has provided shelter and a place to prepare food for the truly needy, it has also, in a way, promoted additional homelessness. How so? With the *10* voucher system, a low-income family can raise its income by becoming "homeless" (Coulson 16). In addition, for the voucher system to be truly successful, there needs to be a lot of available housing. And this is not the case.

- **Topic:** Programs to help the homeless
- **Key details:** One set talks about food supplied by the Temporary Emergency Assistance Program. The program didn't work.

  Another set deals with a federal program (voucher system) that offers housing, but there are problems with it, too.
- **Implied idea that "covers" the details:** Two specific programs haven't worked.

Practice   Carefully read the following paragraphs. Then identify the implied main idea by filling in the chart that follows. (See the example on the previous page for help.)

1.   Some parts of the brain respond to the body, and some respond to other   *1*
parts of the brain. Some parts produce thoughts, some parts help process
thoughts, and some parts store thoughts. Some parts produce the thinking
we are best known for: reflecting. Other parts produce and coordinate animal
reflexes as well as automatic functions of the body. The parts most essential   *5*
for survival, the brain stem and medulla, are huddled deep inside masses of
brain tissue. Injury to one part of the brain can remove a single function, such
as speaking, while leaving other functions unharmed. At any given time, the
brain may be working on several levels: conscious thinking, memory, physical
motion, imagination, and so on. Sometimes the parts work in concert, and   *10*
sometimes they are in conflict.

Topic: _____

Key details: _____

Implied idea that "covers" the details: _____

_____

_____

2.   In the United States, Mara Salvatrucha (MS-13) has about 10,000   *1*
members and a presence in 42 states. The FBI has set up a task force to
deal exclusively with this gang. U. S. immigration officials routinely deport
members back to their home countries in Central America. One of these
countries, El Salvador, has responded to the influx of violent gang members   *5*
with strict anti-gang legislation. These laws make it easier for police to detain
suspects who exhibit certain characteristics, such as having gang tattoos or
loitering in known gang areas. Still, several years ago, MS-13 members fired
on two crowded buses in San Salvador, killing 17 people and intensifying
outrage over gang violence. Under a new law, merely belonging to a gang is   *10*
punishable by four to six years in prison, even if no other criminal activity is
proved.

From GAINES/MILLER, Cengage Advantage Books: *Criminal Justice in Action*, 6E. © 2011 Cengage Learning

Topic: _____

Key details: _____

Implied idea that "covers" the details: _____

_____

_____

Recognizing and Analyzing Supporting Details

The main idea serves as the starting point for writing. The supporting details explain or develop the main idea. To gain a complete understanding of a reading assignment, you must be able to identify and understand the supporting information.

Recognizing the Types of Support

The next two pages demonstrate different types of supporting details that you will find in informational texts. The examples come from an article about the Crazy Horse Memorial in South Dakota.

> "The great gift we can bestow on others is a good example."
> —Thomas Morrell

- **Facts and statistics** give specific details about a main point or topic.

  > The head of Crazy Horse will be 87 feet high, which is 20 feet higher than any of the heads of the presidents at Mount Rushmore.

- **Explanations** move the discussion along.

  > There is no verifiable photograph of Crazy Horse. What will be captured in the carving is the spirit of this man.

- **Examples** show or demonstrate something.

  > Crazy Horse was that last leader to surrender to the U.S. military, and he did so because the people who followed him were suffering so much. *(This example shows that Crazy Horse tried to stay true to the Lakota ways of life as long as he could.)*

- **Descriptions** or observations show how something or someone appears.

  > Crazy Horse will be seen leaning over his horse's head, pointing his left hand toward his sacred lands.

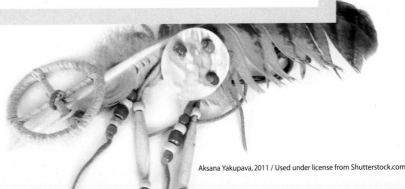

- **Reasons** answer the question "Why?" about something.

  > Crazy Horse is being memorialized because he was known as a courageous fighter, a humble man, a giver and provider, and someone true to the Lakota way of life.

- **Quotations** share the specific thoughts of people knowledgeable about the main point.

  > "The development of this memorial is not without controversy. For example, descendants of Crazy Horse feel that the family wasn't properly consulted at the outset of the project," stated local historian Marcie Smith.

- **Reflections** offer the writer's personal thoughts and feelings.

  > Because of Crazy Horse's private nature, one can only assume that he would have had little interest in such a memorial.

- **Analysis** shows the writer's critical thinking about the topic.

  > The memorial seems like a good idea, a way to honor a great man. Unfortunately, it is also a reminder of the difficult history of Native Americans.

Additional Support

Listed below are other types of support that you may find in your reading assignments.

- **Analogies** often compare something unfamiliar with something familiar.
- **Definitions** explain complex terms.
- **Experiences** share events in the writer's life, sometimes in the form of flashbacks.
- **Anecdotes** provide a slice of life (a brief story) to illustrate something.
- **References** to experts or studies add authority to an essay.

INSIGHT

A text may contain any combination of supporting details in any number. Knowing this will help you follow its development.

Supporting Details in Context

Here is a paragraph from a student essay in which the writer identifies an unusual plant, the banyan tree. The writer uses *facts, explanations,* and *examples* in his explanation.

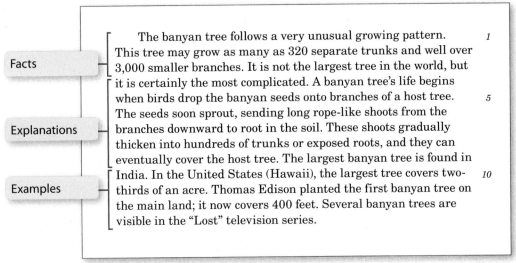

Facts

Explanations

Examples

> The banyan tree follows a very unusual growing pattern.   1
> This tree may grow as many as 320 separate trunks and well over
> 3,000 smaller branches. It is not the largest tree in the world, but
> it is certainly the most complicated. A banyan tree's life begins
> when birds drop the banyan seeds onto branches of a host tree.   5
> The seeds soon sprout, sending long rope-like shoots from the
> branches downward to root in the soil. These shoots gradually
> thicken into hundreds of trunks or exposed roots, and they can
> eventually cover the host tree. The largest banyan tree is found in
> India. In the United States (Hawaii), the largest tree covers two-   10
> thirds of an acre. Thomas Edison planted the first banyan tree on
> the main land; it now covers 400 feet. Several banyan trees are
> visible in the "Lost" television series.

Here is another paragraph from a textbook, *Sociology: Your Compass for a New World.* The writer discusses religious sects using *explanations, examples,* and *analysis.*

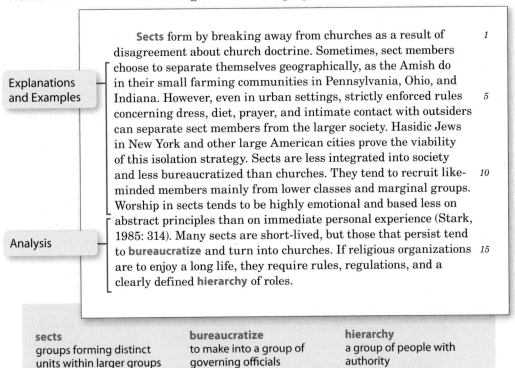

Explanations and Examples

Analysis

> **Sects** form by breaking away from churches as a result of   1
> disagreement about church doctrine. Sometimes, sect members
> choose to separate themselves geographically, as the Amish do
> in their small farming communities in Pennsylvania, Ohio, and
> Indiana. However, even in urban settings, strictly enforced rules   5
> concerning dress, diet, prayer, and intimate contact with outsiders
> can separate sect members from the larger society. Hasidic Jews
> in New York and other large American cities prove the viability
> of this isolation strategy. Sects are less integrated into society
> and less bureaucratized than churches. They tend to recruit like-   10
> minded members mainly from lower classes and marginal groups.
> Worship in sects tends to be highly emotional and based less on
> abstract principles than on immediate personal experience (Stark,
> 1985: 314). Many sects are short-lived, but those that persist tend
> to **bureaucratize** and turn into churches. If religious organizations   15
> are to enjoy a long life, they require rules, regulations, and a
> clearly defined **hierarchy** of roles.

sects	**bureaucratize**	**hierarchy**
groups forming distinct units within larger groups	to make into a group of governing officials	a group of people with authority

Lastly, here is a personal essay in which student writer Eric Dawson explains his fascination with car racing. He uses *reflections, explanations, descriptions,* and *analysis* to share his story.

The Thrill of Victory

My fascination started the first time I saw my dad race. That was back in 1982. Ever since then, racing has been my main interest. I will never forget the afternoon when my dad told me I could drive and that he would build a race car for me. That was probably the most exciting day of my life. That was the day my dad passed down the legacy of racing to me.   *1*   *5*

Reflections

You wouldn't believe the feeling that I had the first day I hit the track with my brand-new Buick stock car. I was a 13-year-old kid with absolutely no driving experience, being strapped into a 400-horsepower stock car. It was a very scary but exciting experience. All it took was one afternoon at the track, and I was hooked. I became the youngest driver ever to race at the Lake Geneva Raceway.   *10*

Explanation and Description

I guess you could say that my first year racing was a big learning experience. Driving race cars was not as easy as it appeared. I finished 18th overall out of 70 cars. It was a rough year. Because of my age and inexperience, many people had little or no faith in me, and I was sponsorless all season. Racing is a very expensive sport. Without some type of sponsorship or financial backing, it is almost impossible to maintain a race team. After that year, my future looked grim. I had no money and no sponsorship offers, but I did have some respectable finishes.   *15*   *20*

I managed to get enough funds together to build a new and more competitive car for the following season. The racing year started off great. I pulled off two second-place finishes in the first two races. Then disaster struck. I was leading the final race of the night, when my brand-new Monte Carlo hit an oil slick and slid headfirst into the wall, at just over 100 miles per hour. My car was destroyed. I was sent to the hospital with a broken wrist and a separated shoulder. I thought my racing career was over. I had spent every nickel I had on this car, and I was still sponsorless.   *25*   *30*

Analysis

Just when I thought I was through with racing, a miracle happened. When I returned from the hospital, there were two men waiting to speak to me. The men were from B. F. Goodrich. They not only wanted to sponsor me, but also wanted to give me a new race car. My future did a 180-degree turnaround.   *35*

This year will be my third year with B. F. Goodrich, and everything looks great. This year I have switched from Dodge to Jeep, and I am getting backing from Mopar Performance. Jeep Motorsports is another of my sponsors. It looks like all my hard work and dedication is starting to pay off.   *40*

Practice Identify the type of support used in the underlined information. Use pages 61–64 as a guide. (The first one is done for you.)

1. <u>By the 1800s, there were believed to be between 3,000 and 5,000 wolves living in the state</u> (Wydeven). Around the same time, many European settlers arrived in the area.

   fact/statistic

2. When I was in first grade, our circus field trip was one huge disappointment. <u>First of all, I couldn't see much of anything because we were sitting in one of the last rows.</u> I could barely make out tiny figures scurrying around the three rings.

3. Rent control is a main factor in determining the number of homeless a city will have. <u>For example, the number of homeless in Santa Monica, California, is so great that the city has been called "The Homeless Capital of the West Coast."</u>

4. The emotional outburst known as road rage is a factor in as many as two-thirds of nonfatal accidents. . . . <u>Psychologist Arnold Nerenberg of Whittier, California, a specialist in motorway mayhem, estimates 1.78 billion episodes of road rage occur each year.</u> . . . From Hales, *An Invitation to Health*, 7E. © 2012 Cengage Learning

   Quotation

5. <u>Webster's defines "eclectic" (i-klek´-tik) as selecting elements from different sources or systems.</u> Eclectic suggests variety. But what a great way to say variety. Variety sounds so plain, so Brand X. But eclectic is rich with imagination.

   Definition

6. <u>My grandmother's rose garden was a symphony of color, and she was the conductor.</u> Shears in hand, she would step confidently toward the rose trellis and spread her hands. With a quick downbeat, her sheers sliced through the sharp thorns.

   Experience

Practice   Here is part of an essay by Lois Krenske in which she discusses an unusual happening in nature, whale **strandings**. Try to identify different types of support used in each paragraph. Work on this activity with one or more of your classmates if your instructor allows it.

Suicide by Strandings

Mass whale suicides, or "strandings," as they are called, occur with   *1*
disturbing consistency. Many men have tried to understand these bizarre
suicides. Even Aristotle, the ancient Greek philosopher, considered
them. Although he decided the suicides may indeed happen "without any
apparent reason," modern biologists are not so easily convinced.   *5*

_____

_____

One researcher has pointed out that the whales are descended
from land-dwelling animals. He decided the whales may simply be
"remembering" their ancient roots and beach themselves to go home. This
habit, however, would have put the whales close to extinction years ago.
The idea had to be dismissed.   *10*

_____

_____

A newer theory suggests that the whales blindly follow the earth's
magnetic forces. The whales travel wherever these forces lead, almost as
if they were following a road map. Unfortunately, the magnetic flow will
sometimes **intersect** the shore and guide the whales along a collision course
with the beach.   *15*

_____

_____

Biologists realize, of course, that none of these findings are complete
explanations. They feel that the strandings must have a number of causes.
To make this point, they compare beached whales to crashed planes. One
theory will never explain them all.

_____

_____

strandings
occurrences of swimming onto a beach

intersect
cut across, form a cross

Analyzing the Support

Identifying the different details in a reading assignment is the first step. You should also decide how effective the details are. Reading without analyzing the details is like attempting to play soccer without defining the boundaries of the field: One of the key elements is missing.

A Guide to Careful Analysis

Use the following questions as a guide when you analyze the support in a paragraph or an essay that you read. Your answers will help you better understand the text and judge its value.

Questions to Ask

1. What supporting evidence seems especially strong? Why?

   _____

2. Does this information seem reliable and well researched? Explain.

   _____

3. What evidence, if any, does not seem that effective? Explain.

   _____

4. How would you rate the overall quality of the supporting information, and why?

   Weak ★ ★ ★ ★ ★ Strong

   _____

5. What have you learned from this text?

   _____

6. What questions do you still have about it?

   _____

INSIGHT

Answering questions like these helps you connect with your reading assignment and remember the key points in it.

> "The book to read is not the one [that] thinks for you, but the one [that] makes you think."
> —Harper Lee

Analysis in Action

Here is a paragraph that shares a story about coming to America. The topic sentence is underlined. The supporting information includes explanations and descriptions. The analysis follows the paragraph.

<u>I saw the pain in Frances Opeka's eyes as she talked about fleeing Yugoslavia when the Russian and communist troops were moving in.</u> Sometime in May of 1945, at 4:00 a.m., my grandfather's brother knocked on the window of Frances' home and said, "If you're coming with us, we're leaving in a half an hour." So my grandma, who was seven months pregnant, and my great-aunt (Frances) woke up my grandma's three children and left. They didn't have time to say good-bye to their parents, relatives, or friends. They just left. Their first stop was a camp in Austria, and then they went to Italy where they lived for five difficult years in a refugee camp. Living conditions were primitive, to say the least. At times, they slept on the cold ground, or if they were lucky, they slept on a thin covering of hay. At night, Frances would often go without her coat because she wanted to cover her pregnant sister to keep her warm. For food, they usually received bread and soup. They would cup their hands around the bread so they would not lose even a crumb. To get a potato was a treat. Germs and colds spread easily in the camp, so they all went through their sick times. My great-uncle Greg had the measles, and being so young, he thought he was going to die. My grandma and great-aunt had high fevers multiple times. Well, my grandmother had her child, my mother, and her family was the first one that was allowed to come to America.

Sample Analysis

Main point as stated in the topic sentence (underlined): Fleeing her homeland was a painful experience for the writer's great-aunt.

1. What supporting information is especially strong? Why?

The information held my interest because it showed what the family had to do to remain free. One detail that stands out is this one: The family left early in the morning without saying goodbye to anyone. Also, not wasting even a crumb of bread showed how hungry they were.

2. Does this information seem reliable and well-researched?

    This information comes from one of the refugees, so it should
    be reliable. But Frances Opeka is recalling something that
    happened a long time ago, so some of the details might be
    fuzzy. The experience of people fleeing communist rule could be
    checked on the Internet to learn more about this time.

3. What evidence, if any, does not seem that effective? Why?

    For the most part, the story seems realistic and believable.
    There were no really questionable ideas shared. Anyway, why
    would anyone try to make this up?

4. How would you rate the overall quality of the supporting information, and why?

    Weak ★ ★ ★ (★) ★ Strong

    The supporting information got my attention because the story
    is so dramatic. But at times, more details would have made it
    better. For example, how did the family actually get to Austria
    and Italy?

5. What have you learned from this text?

    The end of World War II did not bring an end to the suffering of
    people in Europe. For this family, the suffering continued for at
    least five more years.

6. What questions do you still have about it?

    Two questions were identified in question 4. Also, I would like to
    know how many people attempted to flee Yugoslavia and how
    many actually succeeded.

Practice   Analyze the following paragraph. To get started, carefully read the paragraph; then underline the topic sentence and consider the different types of support that it includes. Next, answer the analysis questions that follow the paragraph.

Drug Deal

    I was an eyewitness to a drug deal, and the smoothness and quickness   *1*
of the transaction will be in my mind forever. I was busy at work when
I happened to observe the deal. My work place, a restaurant, opens onto
an alley. About 25 feet from the rear of the restaurant is a dumpster. I
was taking a break and glanced out the back door. I saw a well-dressed   *5*
man come from the left and a raggedy-looking man come from the right.
They both met by the dumpster in clear view of me. The both looked
around, watching for anyone who might be in the alley. Then they quickly
exchanged packages and checked what they received. The slick man
flipped through the roll of bills he received and nodded. The raggedy   *10*
man checked his package and gave a quick nod. Both men slipped their
packages in their pockets and after a few quick glances, each went the way
he had come. The whole incident took about 45 seconds.

Analysis

  1. What main point is stated in the topic sentence or thesis statement?

    _____

  2. What supporting evidence seems especially strong? Why?

    _____

  3. Does this information seem reliable and well-researched? Explain.

    _____

  4. What evidence, if any, does not seem that effective? Why?

    _____

  5. How would you rate the overall quality of the supporting information, and why?
     Weak ★　★　★　★　★ Strong

    _____

  6. What have you learned from this text? What questions do you have about it?

    _____

Special Challenge   Answer the questions above for the essay on page 64.

LO2 Organization

When you read, remember that the ideas and organization work together to create meaning. Unless the ideas are organized, it is almost impossible to follow them.

Common Patterns of Organization

Factual texts may follow one of these basic patterns. Knowing how these patterns work will help you follow the ideas in a text.

- **Chronological** – Paragraphs that recall experiences or explain how something works or how to do something usually follow chronological, or time, order.

- **Spatial** – Paragraphs that describe something or someone are often organized spatially, or by location—working from top to bottom, right to left, and so on.

- **Logical** – Paragraphs that simply present supporting ideas in a sensible or reasonable order are organized logically.

- **Cause-effect** – Paragraphs that explain the relationship between causes and effects usually explore the causes first, then the effects.

- **Comparison-contrast** – Paragraphs that compare show the similarities and differences between two ideas. Comparative essays may discuss one subject first, then the next subject; they may discuss all of the similarities between the two and then their differences; or they make a point-by-point comparison.

- **Problem-solution** – Paragraphs that explore a particular problem often begin with a summary of the problem, follow with possible solutions, and then focus on the best solution.

- **Order of importance (argumentative)** – Paragraphs that support a claim or an opinion may be organized from the most important argument to the least important or the other way around. Objections to the claim or arguments often come first or last.

INSIGHT ───

While a text usually follows one main pattern, other patterns may be used in a few specific parts.

The Patterns in Action

Each paragraph that follows shows how a writer uses a common pattern of organization to arrange his or her ideas.

Chronological Order

This paragraph narrates an interesting historical story about growing up in the American frontier. (The words and phrases in italics show that time order is used.)

Frances Anne Slocum

Frances Anne Slocum was born in Rhode Island in March of 1773. The *1*
next year her family moved to Pennsylvania. There, *until she was five,* she
lived a happy childhood. But *on November 2, 1778,* Delaware Indians raided
her home during the absence of the father. No one was hurt, but Frances was
taken from the family and lost for 57 years. Then *in January of 1835,* a fur *5*
trader named Colonel Ewing stopped at the house of a widow of the Chief of
the Miami Indians. Colonel Ewing became interested in the mistress of the
house because her features and coloring seemed different to him. Ewing *later*
learned she was born of white parents and that her father's name was Slocum.
He announced this discovery in a Lancaster, Pennsylvania, newspaper. *10*
Eventually, one of Frances's brothers read the article and was *soon* reunited
with his long-lost sister.

Comparison-Contrast

This paragraph compares and contrasts two main types of lightbulbs by first identifying their similarities and then discussing their differences.

See the Light

To select a lightbulb, you need to understand the differences between the *1*
traditional incandescent bulb and the compact fluorescent ones. Both bulbs
are similar in that they come in many shapes, sizes, and brightnesses. But
they are different in many important ways. For example, the compacts have
some limitations in their usability. Because of their odd shape, they may not *5*
fit in the bulb sockets on some lamps. Compacts also may not work well in
very cold temperatures, and they can't be used with a dimmer switch. On the
other hand, compact bulbs are four times more efficient than incandescent
ones. A 15-watt compact bulb produces as many lumens of light as a 60-watt
incandescent bulb. Cost is another factor to consider. A compact may cost *10*
about $15.00, while an incandescent can be purchased for a dollar. However,
the compact burns less electricity and lasts seven to ten times longer. So in
the long run, it should be less expensive. This information may help you decide
what bulbs to choose in your own room or apartment.

Cause-Effect

This paragraph identifies the causes and effects of job opportunities in journalism. (The words in italics identify the cause-effect order used.)

Wanted: Newspaper Jobs

Students interested in journalism may want to consider other professions. *1*
The *cause* is simple: Fewer and fewer people are buying newspapers. Many
individuals, especially young people, are getting their news on the Internet.
Fewer buyers of newspapers and magazines mean less income from sales.
Fewer readers also mean fewer ad dollars, which is a major source of revenue. *5*
As a result, newspapers are going out of business or cutting back, and
magazines are folding. This situation has forced publishers to re-form their
companies. Newspapers are now offering electronic alternatives to their print
products, but readers get this news for free or pay a small fee that in no way
offsets the huge losses the companies are facing. The *effect* of this situation *10*
on journalists is predictable: There are not enough jobs for experienced
journalists, let alone college graduates. However, not all is lost. The Internet
may offer exciting new career choices in the Information Age, especially for
people who understand and appreciate the power of electronic communications.

Problem-Solution

This problem-solution paragraph discusses a serious issue in older urban dwellings, lead poisoning. (The words in italics show the pattern of organization used.)

Dangers of Lead Poisoning

Young children unprotected from almost any amount of lead may *1*
suffer serious health problems. Lead poisoning can lead to everything from
headaches to periods of confusion to learning problems. Inner-city dwellings
built before 1960 may contain lead-based paints, the major source of the
problem. If the lead paint is peeling, very young children will eat the paint *5*
chips. Even the dust from this paint can be harmful. Unfortunately, once
someone suffers from lead poisoning, there are no complete cures. The
best *solutions* for families are **preventive**, such as daily house cleaning and
regularly washing hands. Long-term solutions include painting over the old
lead paint, but without sanding beforehand. The Mayo Clinic Web site on lead *10*
poisoning reminds renters that they have rights protecting their health and
safety. Landlords are required by law to find and address sources of lead.

preventive
a remedy that prevents something

Practice   Label the main pattern of organization used in the following paragraphs. Use pages 71–73 as a guide for your work.

1.   **Those Were the Days**

    The old man grumbled a bit as he wiped his eyes with the back of his   *1*
gnarled hand. From his perch above the crowd, he watched the proceeding.
He then glanced at his wife standing a short distance away. She, too, was old,
but he still saw her as a much younger woman. His thoughts went back. He
recalled the black and white dishes on which she had so proudly served him   *5*
home-cooked meals. The chairs, the tables, the curtains, things that had made
their home—all raced before his eyes. Then the auctioneer's voice brought
his thoughts back to the present. He shifted in the seat of his old John Deere
tractor. It was now being auctioned off and would soon be plowing someone
else's field. Then the other machinery was to be sold, piece by piece. Within the   *10*
next hour or so, the things he had worked for all his life would be gone. A half
century of thoughts and feelings went with everything on display.

Pattern of organization:

_____

_____

2.   **Religion and School**

    Americans have the right to practice the religion of their choice, but   *1*
practicing religion in public schools touches on sensitive ground. Religion
in public schools goes against the Constitution of the United States. Most
specifically and importantly, the First Amendment clearly states its desire
to leave religion out of public schooling. The establishment clause in this   *5*
amendment says there can be no official religion. The free-exercise clause
states how people can practice whatever religion they choose. If religious
education were **mandated** in public schools, both of these rights would be
violated. In addition, the Fourteenth Amendment contains an equal protection
clause that makes clear the separation of church and state. The Supreme   *10*
Court has also voiced its opinion that having religion affiliated with public
schooling is unconstitutional. So it is clear that the writers of the Constitution
wanted to keep religion separate from public institutions such as the education
system.

Pattern of organization:

_____

_____

3.

TV and Your Health

Regardless of where they live, Americans spend most of their leisure   *1*
time watching television: on average, more than 30 hours a week. Yet the
more time spent in front of the TV, the greater the risk of obesity and related
chronic diseases. Compared with other **sedentary** activities, such as reading,
writing, or driving, watching TV lowers **metabolic** rate, so people burn fewer   *5*
calories. Every hour spent watching television may increase your risk of dying
prematurely from any cause by 11 percent, from **cardiorespiratory** disease by 18
percent, and from cancer by 9 percent, according to recent research. Compared
with those who watched less than two hours per day, individuals who watched
more than four hours had an 80 percent greater risk of premature death from   *10*
heart-related causes.

From HALES. *An Invitation to Health*, 7E. © 2012 Brooks/Cole, a part of Cengage Learning, Inc.

Pattern of organization:

_____

_____

4.

About Race

Race is often the first thing people think of when they hear the word diversity.   *1*
But some experts say race is a relatively modern idea. Centuries ago people tended
to classify other people by status, religion, or language, for example, not by race.
Actually, most of us are a blend of **ethnicities**, and how we perceive ourselves may
be different from the way others see us. People may assume that a Pacific Islander
with light-brown skin, dark hair, and dark eyes, for example, is Hispanic. And a   *5*
classmate you may assume is white may think of himself as black. Or consider
this: If you have a Chinese mother and a white father, you may not know which
"race box" to check on standard forms. Should you choose Mom or Dad? Biologists
tell us that there's more variation within a race than there is between races. Race
isn't biological, they say, but *racism* is real.   *10*

From STALEY/STALEY. *FOCUS on College and Career Success*, 1E. © 2012 Wadsworth, a part of Cengage Learning, Inc.

Pattern of organization:

_____

_____

mandated required or commanded by **sedentary** requiring much sitting	**metabolic** dealing with the chemical processes occurring within an organism to sustain life	**cardiorespiratory** of or relating to the heart and the respiratory system **ethnicities** ethnic character and background

LO3 Voice (Tone)

Another main trait of a text is voice—the special way in which the writer speaks to the reader. Voice is sometimes referred to as tone. In this discussion they are one and the same thing. It may help to think of voice as the personality in a piece of writing. Most informational texts will speak to you in one of three ways:

> "Voice is the aspect of writing closest to the writer."
> —Dan Kirby

- **Academic voice:** Writers of professional materials use a serious academic voice.
- **Personal voice:** Writers of essays, articles, and blog postings often use a casual personal voice.
- **Satiric voice:** Occasionally, writers use a satiric voice when they want to criticize or make fun of someone or something.

Types of Voice

Academic Voice

An academic voice is used in most textbooks, professional journals, and in thoughtful, serious research. An academic uses **formal English** and sounds serious and objective (sticking to the facts). The following informational text uses an academic voice.

> According to the Sierra Club, pollutants from farm run-off are 1
> steadily seeping into streams, lakes, reservoirs, and wells. Because much
> of the drinking water comes from these sources, warnings are posted in
> a number of U.S. and Canadian communities, and many more postings
> might be needed in the future (Sierra Club, 2005). As the Sierra Club 5
> argues, the pollution and related warnings are serious, and failure to heed
> them could be deadly. . . .

SPECIAL NOTE: Serious texts may contain brief personal introductions or brief passages containing the writer's personal thoughts and feelings and still be academic in voice.

formal English
a serious, straightforward style used in most academic writing including textbooks; characterized by objectivity (sticking to the facts)

Arkorn, 2011 / Used under license from Shutterstock.com

Personal Voice

A personal voice used in personal essays, articles in popular magazines, and personal blog postings uses **informal English** and sounds somewhat relaxed and subjective (including the writer's personal thoughts and feelings). The following description uses a personal voice.

> One Capewell photograph is proudly displayed in our house. It's a black-   *1*
> and-white photograph of two people neatly attired in their best military
> uniforms, and it was taken during World War II in a small studio in Leicester,
> England. . . . What makes this photograph so special to our family is the
> occasion that prompted it. It's my great-grandparents' wedding picture. They   *5*
> were both on leave to get married. Their honeymoon had to wait until after the
> war. This photograph is one of the few keepsakes that we have left from their
> military experience and wedding day, and we take very special care of it.

Satiric Voice

A satiric voice is used in essays and commentaries in which the writer speaks humorously or **sarcastically** about someone or something. A satire may be objective or subjective. The following passage from a personal blog posting uses a satiric voice. (King Arne refers to Arne Duncan, the Department of Education Secretary.)

All Hail to the King

> King Arne made a visit to Milwaukee, and at one point during his visit, he   *1*
> toured a downtown public high school. A photograph in the newspaper shows
> the king marching down a hall with his attendants following close behind.
> The king was impatient with his subjects here because in his estimation,
> they weren't making enough school improvements. And of course, when the   *5*
> king speaks, everyone listens because the king controls the coffers (stimulus
> money). He has $10 billion to invest in education, and this is only part of the
> money for education that he controls. (Talk about a power high.)

| **informal English** a relaxed style used in most personal essays; characterized by subjectivity (the writer's personal thoughts and feelings) | **satiric** the use of humor, fake praise, or sarcasm to make fun of someone or something | **sarcastically** related to the act of making critical comments |

Practice Carefully read the following passages. Then identify the voice used in each one—academic, personal, or satiric.

1. I recently sat in on a meeting that made my eyes droop and my toes curl. The purpose of the meeting was clear, but it dragged on and on without anything getting accomplished. And here's why: One person wouldn't stop talking. . . .

   Voice: _____

2. Several factors contributed to the tragedy in Walkerton, Ontario, including human error. First, according to *The Edmonton Journal,* a flaw in the water treatment system allowed the infested water to enter Walkerton's well (Blackwell, 2001). Even after the manure washed into Walkerton's well, the chlorine should have killed the bacteria. . . .

   Voice: _____

3. Then there comes an odor in the cafeteria. No, more than an odor. It is a heavy choking presence that overpowers the senses and settles on the skin, leaving a thin greasy film. The food line lurches forward once more, and doomed students mover closer to their noon meal. . . .

   Voice: _____

4. On a cold August morning, the stars blanketed the night sky over the outskirts of Quito, Ecuador. I stood on the street corner, shaking underneath my wool sweater, waiting for a guide to show me around this massive market. . . .

   Voice: _____

5. The major danger associated with texting is the distraction it causes to the driver. When a driver's eyes are concentrating on a phone instead of the road, he or she is more likely to get in an accident. Some critics say teenage drivers are the problem, but 20 percent of adults in a recent AAA study admitted regularly texting while driving. . . .

   Voice: _____

LO4 Word Choice and Sentences

Two other important traits are word choice and sentences.

Word Choice

Word choice is closely connected to voice, in that the words used help create the writer's voice. For example, textbook writers will naturally use many specific words associated with the topic. These content-specific words help create the academic voice in the text. Personal essayists, on the other hand, usually rely on more familiar words, which helps create a more personal or conversational voice.

Academic passage with content-specific words (underlined)

Wind farms are a clean energy source. Unlike power plants, which   *1*
emit dangerous pollutants, wind farms release no pollution into the air,
meaning less smog, less acid rain, and fewer greenhouse emissions. The
American Wind Energy Association reports that running a single wind
turbine has the potential to displace 2,000 tons of carbon dioxide, or the   *5*
equivalent of one square mile of forest trees.

Passage from a personal essay with mostly familiar words:

There was this old guy I used to know. His name was Jimmy, but I   *1*
called him "Admiral" because he had been in some war. He was about five
feet tall and smelled of cigar smoke mixed with coffee and other scents I
didn't recognize. He had smoke-stained teeth that were crooked. His white
hair always looked like it needed to be washed, and he wore the same   *5*
wrinkled clothes. But he had beautiful blue eyes, the deepest blue I've
ever seen.

Practice   Team up with a classmate to find one passage (two or three sentences) in a paragraph in this book that uses many content-specific words. Write the passage down and underline these words. Then write down a passage from a paragraph that seems more personal and uses very familiar terms. Be prepared to discuss your findings.

Sentences

Sentences come in all shapes and sizes. Some of them are very brief and direct. Others flow along very smoothly like a lazy country stream. Then, of course, there are sentences that are very complex and require multiple readings to understand.

Academic Sentences

The sentences in most textbooks are often long and complex, sometimes containing many ideas. These sentences suggest that the writer has been very careful in her or his thinking. This makes sense because textbooks must share information thoroughly and accurately. Here are some longer sentences from academic texts. In each one, the core sentence is underlined. Notice all of the additional information added to each one.

Public housing was built in Chicago because of the Great Migration, the name given to the movement of African Americans from the South to the North.

Over time, the first musical instruments, which were stone and clay sound-producing objects, evolved into wind instruments including flutes and windpipes.

While North American wealth grew out of the Industrial Revolution, today's capitalism is a system largely based on consumerism—an attitude that values the purchase of goods in the belief that it is necessary.

In the past couple of decades, the status of the flight attendant (i.e., the position of the flight attendant in relation to others) has changed. In the era of shoe searches, deep-discount no-frill service, and packaged peanut snacks, little of the glamour remains.

Sentences in Personal Essays

The sentences in personal essays are usually simpler than the ones that you will find in academic texts. As such, they are easier to follow and move along rather quickly. As a general rule, you will find more variety in the sentence length and structure. Notice how easy it is to read the following passages from personal essays.

The smell of burnt oil was the first thing I would notice in my grandfather's garage. On the right wall, he had pictures of the Smith Family. Some days, I would study all of the smiling faces on the pictures.

I had locked myself in the walk-in freezer. I knew I would get out. Someone *had* to open the door. But when? All around me, I saw frozen shrimp, crab legs, and lobsters. I couldn't even eat any of it.

My Indian culture is important to me, but that doesn't mean that I don't value my independence. During this semester, I have had a chance to think about my life. And I realize that I am an Indian and an American.

Have questions about your love life? Wonder what fashions to wear this fall? Want to know about the latest in hip food? Trendy magazines geared for young women address "deep" issues like these. Am I the only female that is both embarrassed and offended by these magazines?

Practice   Carefully read the following sets of sentences. Then identify each set as either academic or personal in structure. (Word choice, of course, plays a role in the level of difficulty or complexity in these sentences.)

1. The fourth type of Latin American music known as urban popular music combines a dynamic sound with calls for social change and appeals to many young listeners.

   Sentence style: _____

   _____

2. It's laundry night for me, and the Laundromat is buzzing, thumping, whirring. All the seats by the window are taken, as usual. The vending machines are doing overtime. A very pregnant young woman is folding clothes. Her toddler son is trying to climb into a dryer.

   Sentence style: _____

   _____

3. Waking up is hard. I'd rather dream I've won the tournament than get up and face the scale. But I'm hopeful. I've been strict and focused, in the gym and at the table. This tournament is the toughest one for the year, by far.

   Sentence style: _____

   _____

4. The Dutch fear of Islamic extremism has also increased, brought on in part by international attacks such as September 11 (2001) and later attacks in Madrid and London. This fear was further intensified when two well-known Dutch politicians were assassinated.

   Sentence style: _____

   _____

5. Sethe lives in house number 124, a house generally believed to be haunted and "full of baby venom" (Morrison 3). The child's ghost living in the house throws things around, shakes the floor, and stomps up the stairs.

   Sentence style: _____

   _____

Special Challenge   Find two sentences in the models in *Fusion 1* that are clearly academic because of their length and complexity. Then find two sentences that are personal in structure. Share your work with your classmates.

Review and Enrichment

On the next six pages you will review and enrich your understanding of the concepts in this chapter.

Reviewing the Chapter

Ideas   Answer the following questions about the ideas in writing. (See pages 46–70.)

1. What is the first step to follow to find the main idea in a paragraph? The last step?

2. What is the name of the sentence that contains the main idea in a paragraph? In an essay?

3. What two parts does this sentence usually contain?

4. What is the purpose of the supporting details in a paragraph?

5. What are four types of supporting details?

6. What type of support includes the writer's personal thoughts and feelings?

Organization   Explain the following patterns of organization. (See pages 71–75.)

Chronological

Spatial

Comparison-contrast

Order of importance

Organization Explain the three-part structure in a paragraph and an essay. Create a graphic that will help you remember these three parts. (See page 76.)

_____

_____

Voice Answer the following questions about voice. (See pages 78–80.)

1. What is voice in a text?

_____

_____

2. What is meant by academic voice? Find an example in one model.

_____

_____

3. What is meant by personal voice? Find an example in one model.

_____

_____

4. What is meant by satiric voice? Find an example in one model.

_____

_____

Word Choice and Sentences Answer the following questions about word choice and sentences. (See pages 81–84.)

1. What are the main features of academic word choice and sentences?

_____

_____

2. What are the main features of personal word choice and sentences?

_____

_____

"We all worry about the population explosion, but we don't worry about it at the right time."

—Art Hoppe

Reading

The reading selection "The Population of Earth," which starts on page 88, comes from *World Civilizations*, a history textbook. It appears in the chapter entitled "Decolonization of the Nonwestern World," and it discusses the status of an important worldwide issues. Be sure to use the reading process as a guide when you read.

CONSIDER THE TRAITS

As you read, pay careful attention first to the **ideas**—the main idea and the supporting details in the text. (You may have to read this text many times to follow all of the details.) Also consider the **organization** or the logical order in which the details are presented. Upon completion of the reading, ask yourself what effect the reading has on you.

About the Authors

Philip J. Adler taught courses in world history for nearly 30 years. He has published widely in the historical journals of this country and German-speaking Europe. **Randall L. Pouwels** has published widely. His book *Horn and Crescent: Cultural Change and Traditional Islam on the East African Coast, 800-1900* has become a standard work on African history. He taught for many years at LaTrobe University in Melbourne, Australia, and at UCLA.

Prereading

Almost certainly, you have discussed population on different occasions during your high school career. It happens to be one of those topics, like global warming, that we talk a lot about, especially in terms of the disturbing consequences if its increase goes unchecked.

Identify Before you read, answer these three questions.

1. What do the title and beginning paragraph tell you about the text?
2. What do you already know about the topic?
3. What questions do you have about it?

What do you think?

Consider the quotation above. Hoppe says "we don't worry about it (the population explosion) at the right time." What does he mean by that?

Reading and Rereading

As you read, make it your goal to (1) find or state the main idea of the selection, (2) pay careful attention to the supporting details, and (3) decide if your questions were answered.

Tip Annotate the text (page 20) and/or take notes (page 22) as needed to help you with your reading.

The Population of the Earth

A book appeared in the 1970s with the arresting title *The Population Bomb.* Written by a respected biologist, Paul Ehrlich, at an American university, it warned that a time was rapidly approaching when the earth would face massive, prolonged famine. The rate of population growth in the less-developed countries, it said, threatened to overwhelm the earth's capacity to grow food.   *5*

Professor Ehrlich's prognosis of early famine proved erroneous. The Green Revolution, plus a series of good crop years around the globe, actually increased the ratio of available food to mouths, but many believe that Ehrlich's basic argument is still valid: Inevitably, starvation will   *10* come. They point to the examples of the African Sahel (a semi-arid area of western and north-central Africa), Bangladesh since independence, and many of the Andean populations in South America to assert that the number of consumers is exceeding the available resources. It is just a matter of time, they argue, until the well fed will be using lethal weapons   *15* to hold off the starving hordes.

Other observers, however, argue that Ehrlich and similar doomsayers are not taking the so-called demographic transition into account. This transition occurs when parents stop viewing many children as a familial and economic necessity and instead produce a smaller number of better-   *20* cared-for children. Historically, this has occurred when a society becomes industrialized and urbanized. Children then become less economically necessary to the family, and a lower mortality rate means that most will live to maturity. Hence, parents no longer need to have many children to ensure that some will survive to care for them in their old age. Because   *25* the three continents where the large majority of nonindustrial peoples live (Africa, Asia, and South America) are rapidly developing urban and industrialized societies, it was hoped that birthrates would drop substantially within a generation, but this has not happened.

In Latin America, parts of Asia, and much of Africa, birthrates have   *30* remained at levels that are double or triple Western rates. The "gap" between the present-day medical and technological capacities to preserve and prolong life and the cultural demands to have children early and

frequently so that some will survive into adulthood has not closed as
swiftly as was hoped. Efforts to lower the birthrate by artificial means   *35*
have worked in some places (China, for instance) but failed in most others.

Yet, some means of controlling the hugely increasing demands of the
world's population on every type of natural resource (including privacy,
quietude, and undisturbed contemplation) must be found soon, presumably.

The human inhabitants of Spaceship Earth are increasing in   *40*
geometric fashion. The earth's first half-billion inhabitants took perhaps
50,000 years to appear, and the second half-billion appeared over 500
years (1300-1800), but nearly 2 billion people out of the 2009 total of 6.64
billion came aboard in a period of eighteen years! Most of this proportion
lives in the less-developed countries, where the rate of natural increase—   *45*
births over deaths without counting migration—is two to four times the
industrial world.

From Adler/Pouwels, *World Civilizations*, 6E. © 2012 Cengage Learning

Reflecting

After your reading, answer the following questions.

1. What main idea is developed in the text? (Or is there more than one main idea?)

   _____

2. What supporting details are provided? (Give two examples.)

   _____

3. How would you describe the main pattern of organization of this text— chronological, spatial, or logical? Choose one and explain your choice.

   _____

4. Is this text academic or personal in terms of voice, word choice, and sentence structure? Explain.

   _____

5. How has this text changed or expanded your understanding of the topic? Identify one or two key ways.

   _____

6. How would you rate this reading, and why?

   Weak ★ ★ ★ ★ ★ Strong

   _____

Vocabulary Practice

Identify Create a notebook entry for each of the following words. Identify the pronunciation, helpful word parts, a primary definition, and the word used in a sentence. (For assistance, refer to a dictionary and the glossary of word parts on pages 623–631 in your book.)

1. **erroneous** (line 7)

2. **doomsayers** (line 17)

3. **contemplation** (line 39)

Drawing Inferences

Pages 29–31 explain that an inference is a logical conclusion that you make about something that is not actually said or stated in a text. A thoughtful inference results from a careful reading, after you have identified the main idea.

Explain Draw inferences from "The Population of the Earth" by answering the following questions.

1. What conclusion can you make about family planning?

2. To what degree will population be important in future political decisions?

Special Challenge: Summarizing the Text

Write a summary of "The Population of the Earth" using page 25 as a guide. Remember that summarizing means "to present the main points of a text in a clear, concise form using your own words."

4

> "The pen is the tongue of the mind."
> —Miguel de Cervantes

Academic Writing and Learning

You may not consider yourself a writer, but chances are you write more than you realize. Think about how many text messages, social media posts, or emails you have responded to in the last week alone. All of these examples involve using written words to communicate. Indeed, writing is an essential communication tool, especially with today's technology at your fingertips.

For a lot of you, this social aspect of writing comes naturally, while writing in the classroom is more difficult. Do not feel alone. Academic writing challenges even the most experienced writers. This chapter will outline guidelines and strategies to help make the demands of academic writing more manageable. Along the way, you will learn that writing is more than a way to share ideas—it is also a tool for *learning* new ideas.

Learning Outcomes

LO1 Write to learn.
LO2 Write to share learning.
LO3 Understand the writing process.
LO4 Use writing strategies.
LO5 Understand strong writing.
LO6 Use Standard English.
LO7 Think critically and logically.

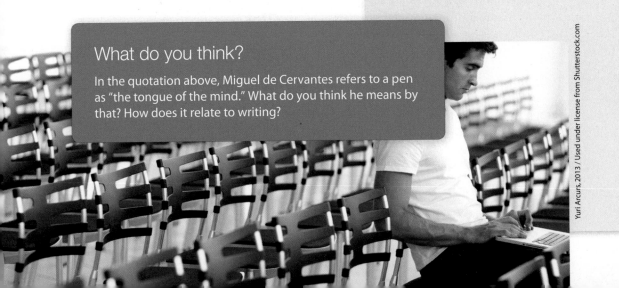

What do you think?

In the quotation above, Miguel de Cervantes refers to a pen as "the tongue of the mind." What do you think he means by that? How does it relate to writing?

Yuri Arcurs, 2013 / Used under license from Shutterstock.com

> "Don't think and then write it down. Think on paper."
> —Harry Kemelman

LO1 Writing to Learn

When athletes and other entertainers perform at exceedingly high levels, you often hear them talk about entering "the zone," a special place where the mind slows down and achieving something extraordinary feels ordinary.

Experienced writers will tell you that writing allows you to enter a similar state of mind. The act of filling up a page triggers their thinking and leads to meaningful learning. The key is to rid your mind of distractions and let your thoughts flow onto the paper.

Changing Your Attitude

If you think of writing in just one way—as an assignment to be completed—you will never discover its true value. Writing works best when you think of it as a learning tool. A series of questions, a list, or a quick note can be a meaningful form of writing if it helps you think and understand. If you make writing an important part of your learning routine, you'll change your attitude about writing (for the better), and you'll become a better thinker and learner.

Keeping a Class Notebook

Keeping a class notebook or journal is essential if you are going to make writing an important part of your learning routine. Certainly, you can take notes in this notebook, but it is also helpful to reflect on what is going on in the class. These writing activities will help you think about your course work.

- Write freely about anything from class discussions to challenging assignments.
- Explore new ideas and concepts.
- Argue for and against any points of view that came up in class.
- Question what you are learning.
- Record your thoughts and feelings about an extended project.
- Evaluate your progress in the class.

Reflect Write freely for 5 to 10 minutes about your writing experiences. Consider how you feel about writing, your strengths and weaknesses as a writer, whether you have ever used writing to learn, and so on. Then share your thoughts with your classmates.

LO2 Writing to Share Learning

The second important function of writing is to *share* what you have learned. When you write to learn, you write to gather your thoughts and make conclusions about subjects. But when you write to share, you present what you have learned to an audience, including your instructors and classmates. Writing to share involves making your writing clear, complete, and ready to be read by others.

Understanding the Learning Connection

As this graphic shows, improved thinking is the link between the two functions of writing. Writing to learn involves exploring and forming your thoughts, and writing to share learning involves clarifying and fine-tuning those thoughts.

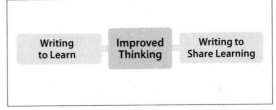

INSIGHT

Following the steps in the writing process is the best way to develop writing to share. This process helps you pace yourself so you don't try to do everything all at once. (See pages 94–99.)

Reviewing the Range of Writing

The forms of writing to share cover a lot of territory, as you can see in the chart to the right. As a college student, your writing will likely cover the entire spectrum, with a focus on the more formal forms, such as essays and reports.

React Answer these questions about the chart: What forms of writing do you most often engage in? How does your writing approach change at different points along the spectrum?

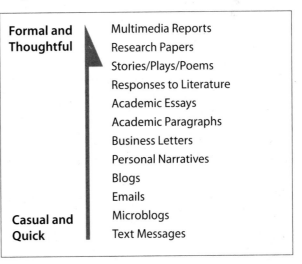

LO3 Understanding the Writing Process

Attempting to start and finish a writing project all at once can cause you undue stress. A writing project is much more manageable when you approach it as a process. This section will introduce you to the steps in the writing process.

The Steps in the Process

You cannot change a flat tire with one simple action. It takes a number of steps to get the job done right. The same goes for writing. If you expect to complete a paper in one general attempt, you (and your instructor) will be disappointed in the results. On the other hand, if you follow the writing process, you'll complete the job in the right way—one step at a time.

Process	Activities
Prewriting	Start the process by (1) selecting a topic to write about, (2) collecting details about it, and (3) finding a focus to direct your writing.
Writing	Then write your first draft, using your prewriting plan as a general guide. Writing a first draft allows you to connect your thoughts about a topic.
Revising	Carefully review your first draft, and have a classmate read it as well. Change any parts that need to be clearer, and add missing information.
Editing	Edit your revised writing by checking for style, grammar, punctuation, and spelling errors.
Publishing	During the final step, prepare your writing to share with your instructor, your peers, or another audience.

Reasons to Write

Always use the writing process when you are writing to share learning and when you are writing certain personal forms. You don't need to use it when you are simply writing to learn.

Reason	Forms	Purpose
Writing to share learning	Informational paragraphs, summaries	To show your understanding of subjects you are studying
Personal writing	Personal paragraphs, blog postings, short stories, plays	To share your personal thoughts, feelings, and creativity with others

Reflect Explain how the writing process explained above compares with your own way of completing assignments. Consider what you normally do first, second, third, and so on.

"If you start in the right place and follow all the
steps, you will get to the right end."
—Elizabeth Moon

The Process in Action

As the chart to the right indicates, there can be forward and backward movement between the steps in the writing process. For example, after writing a first draft, you may decide to collect more details about your topic, which is actually a prewriting activity.

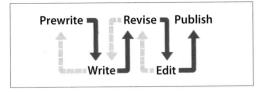

Points to Remember

When using the writing process, you need to understand the following points.

1. All the steps require some type of writing. Prewriting (planning), revising, and editing are writing activities as much as composing the first draft is.

2. It is unlikely that the process will work the same for any two writing assignments. For one assignment, you may struggle with gathering details. For another, you may have trouble starting the first draft.

3. No two writers develop their writing in the same way. Some writers need to talk about their writing early on, while others would rather keep their ideas to themselves. Some writers need to step away from their writing. Other writers can't stop until they produce a first draft. Your own writing personality will develop as you gain more writing experience.

4. All the information about the writing process won't make you a better writer unless you make a sincere effort to use it. You wouldn't expect to play the piano just by reading about it—you must follow the instructions and practice. The same holds true for writing.

INSIGHT

When you respond to a writing prompt on a test, use an abbreviated form of the writing process. Spend a few minutes gathering and organizing your ideas; then write your response. Afterward, read what you have produced and quickly revise and edit it.

Create Make a chart that shows your own process—the one you described on page 94. Share your chart with your classmates.

A CLOSER LOOK at the Process

Each step in the writing process requires a special type of thinking. Following these steps will help you become a more confident writer and learner.

Prewriting is the first step in the writing process. In many ways, it is the most important step because it involves all of the decisions and planning that come before writing a first draft. If you plan well, you will be well prepared to work through the rest of the process. These are the basic prewriting tasks.

- **Identify a meaningful writing idea.** Choose a topic that meets the requirements of the assignment and that truly interests you. Begin your topic search by writing freely about the assignment or by simply listing your ideas.

- **Collect plenty of details.** Explore your own thoughts and feelings about the topic. Then gather additional information, either through firsthand experience (observations, interviews, and so on) or by reading about the topic in books, magazines, and on the Internet.

- **Establish a focus.** Just as a skilled photographer focuses or centers the subject before taking a photograph, you must identify a special part or feeling about the topic before writing your first draft. This focus, or emphasis, is usually expressed in a topic sentence. (See pages 52–55.)

- **Choose a pattern of arrangement.** Once you have established a focus, decide what details to include in your writing and how to organize them. You can arrange your details chronologically (by time), logically, by order of importance, and so on. (See pages 71–73.)

- **Organize your information.** With a pattern of arrangement in mind, you can organize your details in one of three basic ways:

  - Make a quick list of main points and support.

  - Create an outline—a more formal arrangement of main points and subpoints.

  - Fill in a graphic organizer—arranging main points and details in a chart or diagram. (See page 9.)

Supri Suharjoto, 2011 /
Used under license from Shutterstock.com

Drafting is the next step in the writing process. You have one important task during this step—to connect your thoughts and ideas about your topic. Just put these thoughts on paper so you have something to work with. They do not have to be perfectly worded. Here is a basic guide to drafting.

- **Strike while you're hot.** Write your first draft while your planning is still fresh in your mind.

- **Refer to your prewriting.** Use all of your planning and organizing as a basic writing guide. But also be open to new ideas as they come to mind.

- **Write as much as you can.** Keep writing until you get all of your ideas on paper, or until you come to a natural stopping point. Concentrate on forming your ideas rather than on making everything correct.

- **Form a meaningful whole.** A meaningful whole for a paragraph means a topic sentence, body sentences, and a closing sentence.

- **Pay special attention to each part.** All three parts—the opening, the middle, and the closing—play important roles in your writing. Give each part special attention. (See pages 100–105.)

   Opening Sentence
   The opening gets the reader's interest and states your thesis.

- **Look back to move forward.** Stop and reread what you have written to help you add new ideas.

   Middle
   The middle supports your thesis.

- **Write naturally and honestly.** "Talk" to your readers, as if a group of classmates were gathered around you.

- **Remember, it's a draft.** A first draft is your first look at a developing writing idea. You will have plenty of opportunities to improve upon it later in the process.

   Closing
   The closing offers important final thoughts about the topic.

A CLOSER LOOK at the Process (continued)

Revising is the third step in the process. During this step, you shape and improve the ideas in your first draft. Here is a basic guide to revising.

- **Step away from your draft.** Your time away will help you see your first draft more clearly and with a fresh outlook.

- **Revisit your purpose.** Are you writing to explain, to persuade, to describe, or to share?

- **Read your draft many times.** Read it silently and out loud to get an overall impression of your work.

- **Have peers read it.** Their comments and questions will help you decide what changes to make.

- **Check your overall focus.** Decide if your focus still works and if you have provided enough support for it.

- **Review each part.** Be sure that the opening sets the proper tone for your writing, the middle part supports your focus, and the closing provides worthy final thoughts about the topic.

- **Know your basic moves.** There are four basic ways to make changes—adding, cutting, rewriting, or reordering information. Each change or improvement that you make will bring you closer to a strong finished paper.

Add information to . . .
- make a main point more convincing.
- complete an explanation.
- improve the flow of your writing.

Cut information if it . . .
- doesn't support the thesis.
- seems repetitious.

Rewrite information if it . . .
- seems confusing or unclear.
- appears too complicated.
- lacks the proper voice.

Reorder information if it . . .
- seems out of order.
- would make more sense in another spot.

- **Plan a revising strategy.** Decide what you need to do first, second, and third, and then make the necessary changes.

Editing is the fourth step, when you check your revised writing for style and correctness. Editing becomes important *after* you have revised the content of your writing. Here is a basic guide to editing.

- **Start with clean copy.** Do your editing on a clean copy of your revised writing; otherwise, things get too confusing.

- **Check first for style.** Make sure that you have used the best words, such as specific nouns and verbs and smooth-reading sentences.

- **Then check for correctness.** Start by checking your spelling, then move on to end punctuation, and so on.

- **For spelling, read from the last word to the first.** This strategy will force you to look at each word. (A spell checker will not catch every error.)

- **Circle punctuation.** This strategy will force you to look at each mark.

- **Refer to an editing checklist.** You'll find an example on page 165. Also refer to pages 439–617 for sentence, grammar, punctuation, and mechanics rules.

- **Use editing symbols.** These symbols provide an efficient way to mark errors.

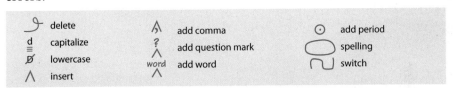

- **Get help.** Ask a trusted classmate to check for errors as well. You are too close to your writing to notice everything.

Publishing is the final step in the writing process. During this step, you prepare your writing before submitting or sharing it.

- **Prepare a final copy.** Incorporate all of your editing changes.

- **Follow design requirements.** Format your final copy according to the requirements established by your instructor.

- **Proofread the text.** Check your writing one last time for errors.

LO4 Using Writing Strategies

The writing strategies and instruction on the next ten pages will help you write strong paragraphs.

Creating an Effective Topic Sentence

The topic sentence is the most important sentence in a paragraph, because it introduces the topic and establishes a focus for the rest of the writing. In most cases, the topic sentence is also the first sentence of the paragraph. Use this formula to create effective topic sentences for your paragraphs.

A specific topic		a specific feeling, feature, or part		An effective topic sentence
arrival of Hernán Cortéz in Mexico	**+**	marked the beginning of the end for the Aztec empire	**=**	The arrival of Hernán Cortéz in Mexico marked the beginning of the end of the Aztec empire.

Patryk Kosmider, 2013 / Used under license from Shutterstock.com

INSIGHT

A topic sentence is sometimes called a controlling sentence, because it establishes boundaries for your writing and helps you decide what information to include about your topic. A paragraph without a topic sentence lacks direction and can steer readers off course.

Analyzing the Topic Sentence

Analyze   Carefully read the following paragraph, paying special attention to how the topic sentence controls the direction of the paragraph. Then answer the questions below.

There are three main types of solar eclipses, each of which occurs when the moon passes between the sun and the earth. The first type is called a total solar eclipse. During a total solar eclipse, the moon blocks out the entire central portion of the sun, resulting in the sky darkening as if it were night. The second type is called a partial solar eclipse. With this type, only part of the sun's surface is blocked out, and the sky may dim slightly. Finally, an annular solar eclipse occurs when the sun and moon are exactly in line, but the moon appears smaller than the sun. As a result, the sun looks as if it has a bright ring around a dark center. Despite their differences, all three types of solar eclipses do share one thing in common: They are rare to see since the moon passes between the sun and earth only twice a year on average.

1. What specific topic is introduced in the topic sentence?

   _____

2. What special part or feature about the topic is stated in the topic sentence?

   _____

3. How does the topic sentence control the direction of the other details in this paragraph?

   _____

4. How would you rate this topic sentence, and why?

   Weak ★ ★ ★ ★ ★ Strong

   _____

Developing the Middle Part

In the middle sentences, you develop all of the main points that support your topic statement. Use your planning (quick list, outline, graphic organizer) as a general guide when you develop this part of a paragraph. Here are a few tips for getting started.

- **Keep your topic sentence in mind as you write.** All of your details should support or explain this statement.
- **Use plenty of details** to fully explain your ideas.
- **Use your own words,** except on those few occasions when you employ a quotation to add authority to your writing.
- **Be open to new ideas that occur to you,** especially if they will improve your paragraph.
- **Try any of the basic writing moves** that are appropriate to your topic.

Basic Writing Moves

The sentences in the middle part of a paragraph should, among other things, *explain, describe, define, classify,* and so on. What follows is a list and definitions of these basic writing moves.

Narrating	sharing an experience or a story
Describing	telling how someone or something appears, acts, or operates
Explaining	providing important facts, details, and examples
Illustrating	providing examples to support a main point
Analyzing	carefully examining a subject or breaking it down
Comparing	showing how two subjects are similar and different
Defining	identifying or clarifying the meaning of a term
Reflecting	connecting with or wondering about
Evaluating	rating the value of something
Arguing	using logic and evidence to prove something is true
Classifying	breaking down a subject into categories, or types

Special Challenge   Read two different paragraphs in this book. On your own paper, list the different moves that the writer uses in the middle sentences of the paragraph. For example, the writer may *explain* in one or more sentences, *reflect* in another, and so on.

Analyzing the Middle Sentences

Analyze   Carefully read the following paragraph, paying special attention to the middle sentences. Then answer the questions below.

> There are three main types of solar eclipses, each of which occurs *1*
> when the moon passes between the sun and the earth. The first type is
> called a total solar eclipse. During a total solar eclipse, the moon blocks
> out the entire central portion of the sun, resulting in the sky darkening as
> if it were night. The second type is called a partial solar eclipse. With this *5*
> type, only part of the sun's surface is blocked out, and the sky may dim
> slightly. Finally, an annular solar eclipse occurs when the sun and moon
> are exactly in line, but the moon appears smaller than the sun. As a result,
> the sun looks as if it has a bright ring around a dark center. Despite their
> differences, all three types of solar eclipses do share one thing in common: *10*
> They are rare to see since the moon passes between the sun and earth only
> twice a year on average.

1. How do the middle sentences relate to the topic sentence?

   _____

2. Do the middle sentences do enough to support the topic sentence? Explain.

   _____

3. What basic writing move (or moves) does the writer use in this paragraph? (See previous page.)

   _____

4. How would you rate the middle sentences, and why?

   Weak ★ ★ ★ ★ Strong

   _____

Writing a Strong Closing

While the opening part of your writing offers important *first* impressions, the closing part offers important *final* impressions. More specifically, the closing helps the reader better understand and appreciate the importance of your topic sentence.

The Basic Parts

Consider the strategies below when writing your closing. Note that it may take more than one sentence to appropriately close a paragraph.

- Remind the reader of the focus of the topic sentence.

  > Exploring the basics of sleeplessness makes it clear why we have sleep disorder clinics: There are a lot of people who aren't getting a good night's sleep.

- Summarize the main point.

  > As you can see, sometimes young adults seem to be everywhere and nowhere at the same time.

- Reflect on the explanation or argument you've presented in the middle part.

  > Let's make all of our roads a safer place; the time has come to make text messaging while driving illegal in every state.

- Offer a final thought to keep the reader thinking about the topic.

  > With all the senses to appeal to, chefs can make every dish a unique work of art.

INSIGHT ————

You may need to write two or three versions of your closing before it says exactly what you want it to say.

Example Closing Sentence

Analyze Carefully read the same paragraph, paying special attention to the closing sentence. Then answer the questions below.

There are three main types of solar eclipses, each of which occurs   *1*
when the moon passes between the sun and the earth. The first type is
called a total solar eclipse. During a total solar eclipse, the moon blocks
out the entire central portion of the sun, resulting in the sky darkening as
if it were night. The second type is called a partial solar eclipse. With this   *5*
type, only part of the sun's surface is blocked out, and the sky may dim
slightly. Finally, an annular solar eclipse occurs when the sun and moon
are exactly in line, but the moon appears smaller than the sun. As a result,
the sun looks as if it has a bright ring around a dark center. Despite their
differences, all three types of solar eclipses do share one thing in common: *10*
They are rare to see since the moon passes between the sun and earth only
twice a year on average.

1. In what way does the closing sentence remind the reader of the topic sentence?

   _____

   _____

2. What basic closing strategy (or strategies) does the writer use in this paragraph? (See the previous page.)

   _____

   _____

3. How would you rate the end of this paragraph, and why?

   Weak ★ ★ ★ ★ ★ Strong

   _____

   _____

LO5 Understanding Strong Writing

The traits (ideas, organization, voice, and so on) are the key ingredients in writing. Each one contributes to a successful essay or report. (See pages 119–146.)

The traits-based checklist below serves as a guide to strong writing. Your writing will be clear and effective when it can "pass" each point. This checklist is especially helpful during revising, when you are deciding how to improve your writing.

> "The first draft is the down draft—you just get it down. The second draft is the up draft—you fix it up."
> —Anne Lamont

INSIGHT

Word choice and sentence fluency are not as important early in the revising process, when you are focused on content. But they do become important later on, during editing.

A Guide to Strong Writing

Ideas

- Does an interesting and relevant topic serve as a starting point for the writing?
- Is the writing focused, addressing a specific feeling about or a specific part of the topic? (Check the topic sentence.)
- Are there enough specific ideas, details, and examples to support the thesis?
- Overall, is the writing engaging and informative?

Organization

- Does the writing form a meaningful whole—with opening, middle, and closing parts?
- Does the writing follow a logical pattern of organization?
- Do transitions connect ideas and help the writing flow?

Voice

- Does the writer sound informed about and interested in the topic?
- Does the writer sound sincere and genuine?

Word Choice

- Does the word choice clearly fit the purpose and the audience?
- Does the writing include specific nouns and verbs?

Sentence Fluency

- Are the sentences clear, and do they flow smoothly?
- Are the sentences varied in their beginnings and length?

React   Carefully read the following paragraph. Then answer the questions below.

Cutting Down the Atmosphere

Trees make up an essential part of the earth's ecosystem, but rapid   1
deforestation is having harmful effects on the planet. Deforestation refers
to the clearance of forests through logging and burning. The main cause
of deforestation is the use of trees for lumber and fuel. Forests are also
cut down to make room for farming. But while deforestation can provide   5
a short-term boost to struggling economies, it is also causing harm to
the environment. Adverse effects of deforestation include erosion of soil,
disruption of the water cycle, loss of biodiversity, and flooding and drought.
The most harmful effect, though, may be on the climate. Deforestation
leads to a greater accumulation of carbon dioxide in the atmosphere, which   10
in turn may warm the planet. Those who practice deforestation must
determine if the economic benefits outweigh the negative impact on the
earth.

Ideas
- Is the topic relevant and interesting?
- Is the topic sentence clear?
- Does the paragraph contain a variety of specific details?

Organization
- Does the topic sentence include the key elements of an effective opening?
- Do the middle sentences follow a logical pattern of organization?

Voice
- Does the writer sound informed and interested in the topic?
- Does the writer sound sincere and honest?

LO6 Using Standard English

Standard English (SE) is English that is considered appropriate for school, business, and government. You have been learning SE throughout your years in school. The chart that follows shows the basic differences between non-Standard English (NS) and SE.

Differences in . . .	NS	SE
1. Expressing plurals after numbers	10 mile	10 miles
2. Expressing habitual action	He always be early.	He always is early.
3. Expressing ownership	My friend car . . .	My friend's car . . .
4. Expressing the third-person singular verb	The customer ask . . .	The customer asks . . .
5. Expressing negatives	She doesn't never . . .	She doesn't ever . . .
6. Using reflexive pronouns	He sees hisself . . .	He sees himself . . .
7. Using demonstrative adjectives	Them reports are . . .	Those reports are . . .
8. Using forms of *do*	He done it.	He did it.
9. Avoiding double subjects	My manager he . . .	My manager . . .
10. Using *a* or *an*	I need new laptop. She had angry caller.	I need a new laptop. She had an angry caller.
11. Using the past tense of verbs	Carl finish his . . .	Carl finished his . . .
12. Using *isn't* or *aren't* versus *ain't*	The company ain't . . .	The company isn't . . .

"Standard English is not a language— but a variety of English among many."
—Peter Trudgill

Read   Carefully read the following narrative paragraph. As you will see, it contains underlined examples of non-standard variations of American English (NS).

As I rode up the mountain trail, my thighs ached and my lungs   *1*
burned, but I couldn't be happier. Fifty feet in front of me pedaled my
brother, Keith, fresh off his tour with the Marines. This mountain biking
adventure was his idea. The green, forest-lined trail <u>be bumpy</u>, with sharp
turns and steep descents. It <u>ain't for beginners</u>. At one point <u>we hit patch</u>   *5*
<u>of fog</u> and I lost sight of Keith. It felt as if we were riding through clouds.
Keith couldn't even <u>see hisself</u>. The ghostly air <u>be damp</u> and smelled like
rain. I slowed down and called for my brother. "Are you still up there?"
"Would I be anywhere else?" he yelled back. When the fog disappeared,
we stopped for a breather on a ridge that overlooked a vast valley. A   *10*
sea of pointy evergreens stretched for miles, ending near the peak of a
distant mountain. While <u>I snack on my</u> peanut butter granola bar, <u>Keith</u>
<u>he</u> glanced over at me. "This is fun, isn't it?" he commented. "It's good
having you back, man," I responded. With that we hopped on our bikes and
continued our adventure.   *15*

Discuss   In small groups or as a class, identify the number that describes each underlined NS form, using the chart on page 108 as a guide. Then explain how to express each one using Standard English (SE).

LO7 Thinking Critically and Logically

Critical thinking is careful, logical thinking—the kind of thinking that you should use for your academic reading and writing. (See pages 11–44 and 91–118.) The questions below will help you to think critically and logically about your writing projects.

Asking Critical Questions

- What is the purpose of my writing (to inform, to entertain, to persuade)?
- Who is my intended audience (general readers, my instructor, my peers)?
- Can my topic be separated into parts? If so, what are they?
- How well do I know my topic?
- What will the reader gain from reading about this topic?
- What logical pattern of thinking should I follow? (See below.)
- What will be the focus, or topic sentence, of my paragraph? (See pages 100–101.)
- How will I support my topic sentence?

Deductive and Inductive Thinking

Most of your academic writing will follow either a deductive or an inductive pattern of thinking. **Deductive thinking** moves from a general focus to specific supporting details. This is the most common pattern of thinking that you will use. **Inductive thinking** moves from specific facts and details to a general conclusion.

Use these questions to check for deductive thinking.

- Do I include a topic and a focus in my topic sentence?
- Do the details logically support or follow from my topic sentence?
- Does the conclusion logically follow the ideas that come before it?

Use these questions to check for inductive thinking.

- Do I start with a series of facts, examples, and explanations?
- Do the details logically lead up to a general conclusion?
- Is the general conclusion reasonable?

Apply For your next writing assignment, use the questions on this page as a general guide to critical and logical thinking.

A CLOSER LOOK at Logic

Logic is the science of reasonable and accurate thinking. Your writing will be logical if it contains relevant and provable evidence.

Reliable and Logical Evidence

Observation: I happily waited in line with scores of others at the Columbia Public Market.

Quotation: Christie George of Willis Bakery said, "Our booth has generated goodwill for our business."

Statistic: The number of markets in the United States increased by 18.3 percent from 2004 to 2006.

Explanation: According to the United States Department of Agriculture . . .

Faulty Logic

Exaggerating the Facts: Eating fast food causes obesity, even if you eat it only once or twice a month.

Distracting the Reader: Processed food is not only bad for your health, but it looks gross and the wrappers add to the problem of littering.

Offering Extremes: If you don't start buying locally grown food, all farmers will lose their jobs.

Telling Only Part of the Truth: Eating fresh, locally grown food is the only way to eat healthy.

Appealing to a Popular Position: You should eat locally grown food because a lot of celebrities are saying it's a good idea.

Practice Write two or three of your own examples of faulty logic (without naming the type). Then exchange your work with a partner and discuss each other's examples.

_____

_____

Review and Enrichment

On the next seven pages you will be asked to review and enrich your understanding of the concepts in this chapter.

Reviewing the Chapter

Writing to Learn   Answer these questions about writing to learn. (See page 92.)

1. How is writing to learn different from traditional writing assignments?

   _____

   _____

2. How can you write to learn in your classes? Name two ways.

   _____

Understanding the Writing Process   Answer the following questions about the writing process. (See pages 94–99.)

1. What are the steps in the writing process?

   _____

2. Explain the forward and backward movement of this process.

   _____

3. Which steps deal with planning to write? With improving the first draft?

   _____

Using Writing Strategies   Answer the following questions about the writing strategies and instruction covered in this chapter. (See pages 100–105.)

1. What are the three main parts of an academic paragraph?

   _____

2. What is Standard English?

   _____

Thinking Critically and Logically   Answer the following questions about critical and logical thinking. (See pages 110–111.)

1. What is critical thinking?

   _____

2. What is meant by faulty logic? Give one example.

   _____

Reading

In the first part of this section, you will read and react to "The Legal System Based on *Sharia*," a special essay appearing in a chapter on the American court system in *American Government and Politics Today*. In the second part you will develop a piece of writing in response to your reading.

> "Depend not on fortune, but on conduct."
> —Publilius Syrus

About the Authors

Steffen W. Schmidt is professor of political science at Iowa State University. He has published 12 books and more than 122 journal articles. He also has a political talk show on WOI Public Radio. Mack C. Shelley II is professor of political science at Iowa State University. He has served as co-editor of *Policy Studies Journal* and has written numerous publications on public policy. **Barbara A. Bardes** is professor *emerita* (retired but retaining her professional title) of political science. She has written extensively on public opinion, foreign policy, and women and politics. **Lynne E. Ford** is professor of political science and associate provost (administrator) for curriculum and academic administration at the College of Charleston. She has authored many articles and books on women and politics.

Prereading

Laws are designed to set limits on behavior in society. As a general population, we have secular (not related to religion) laws to obey. For many in the Muslim faith, there is a system of law called *sharia* as well. Do you know of other faiths that have a system of law? Explain.

CONSIDER THE TRAITS

As you read, pay careful attention to the **ideas**—the main idea and supporting details in the text. Also consider the authors' **voice** and **word choice:** To what degree do they use a tone and words that are understandable to you?

_____

_____

_____

_____

_____

What do you think?

Consider the quotation above: How would you explain this idea in your own words?

Identify Before you read "The Legal System Based on *Sharia*," answer these three questions.

1. What do the title, first paragraph, and headings tell you about the text?

   _____

2. What do you already know about the topic?

   _____

3. What do you expect to learn?

   _____

Reading and Rereading

As you read, make it your goal to (1) identify the main idea, (2) pay careful attention to the supporting details, and (3) come to a clear understanding of the text.

Tip: Turn the headings into questions; then answer the questions as you read.

"The Legal System Based on *Sharia*"

Hundreds of millions of Muslims throughout the world are governed by   *1*
a system of law called *sharia*. In this system, religious laws and precepts
are combined with practical laws relating to common actions, such as
entering into contracts and borrowing funds.

The Authority of *Sharia*

It is said that *sharia*, or Islamic law, is drawn from two major sources   *5*
and one lesser source. The first major source is the **Qur'an** (Koran) and the
specific guidelines laid down in it. The second major source, called *sunnah*,
is based on the way the **Prophet Muhammad** lived his life. The lesser source
is called *ijma*; it represents the consensus of opinion in the community
of Muslims. *Sharia* law is comprehensive in nature. All possible actions   *10*
of Muslims are divided into five categories: obligatory, meritorious,
permissible, reprehensible, and forbidden.

The Scope of *Sharia* Law

Sharia law covers many aspects of daily life, including the following:

- Dietary rules
- Relations between married men and women
- The role of women
- Holidays
- Dress codes, particularly for women
- Speech with respect to the Prophet Muhammad
- Crimes, including adultery, murder, and theft
- Business dealings, including the borrowing and lending of funds

Where *Sharia* Law Is Applied

The degree to which *sharia* is used varies throughout Muslim societies today. Several of the countries with the largest Muslim populations (e.g., Bangladesh, India, and Indonesia) do not have Islamic law. Other Muslim countries have dual systems of *sharia* courts and secular courts.

In 2008, many British citizens were surprised by the remarks of the Archbishop of Canterbury, the religious leader of all Episcopalians, that there was a need for accommodation of *sharia* law in Great Britain.* He was referring to a system of *sharia* courts that has been functioning in Muslim neighborhoods for the last 20 years. The comments followed news that a *sharia* court had released some Somali youths who had stabbed another young man after ordering the assailants to compensate the victim and apologize. This incident led to national debate over whether the *sharia* court was performing functions that should be reserved for criminal and civil courts. In other parts of England, *sharia* courts deal mainly with Islamic laws regarding divorce and the rights of women, much in the same way the Catholic Church decides the status of its own members.**

Canada, which has a *sharia* arbitration court in Ontario, is the first North American country to establish a *sharia* court. Some countries, including Iran and Saudi Arabia, maintain religious courts for all aspects of **jurisprudence**, including civil and criminal law. Recently, Nigeria has reintroduced *sharia* courts.

*"Sharia Law Courts Are Already Dealing with Crime on the Streets of London, It Has Emerged," *Evening Standard*, London, February 8, 2008.

**"The View from Inside a Sharia Court," BBC News, February 11, 2008.

From Schmidt/Shelley/Bardes/Ford, *American Government and Politics Today*, 2013-2014 Edition, 16E. © 2014 Cengage Learning

15

20

25

30

35

40

Qur'an (Koran)
the sacred text of Islam

Prophet Muhammad
the prophet of the Islam religion

jurisprudence
the science of law

Reflecting

After your reading, answer the following questions:

1. What main idea is developed in the text? (Or is there more than one main idea?)

   _____

   _____

   _____

2. What supporting details do you find the most interesting and important? Name two.

   _____

   _____

3. What information is provided in the bulleted list?

   _____

   _____

   _____

4. Has this text introduced you to a new topic, confirmed what you already new about the topic, or changed or expanded you understanding of it? Explain your choice.

   _____

   _____

   _____

5. How would you rate this reading, and why? (Use "A Guide to Strong Writing" on page 106 to help you form your rating.)

   Weak ★ ★ ★ ★ ★ Strong

   _____

   _____

   _____

Vocabulary Practice

Pages 35–36 explain one strategy—understanding word parts—that will help you understand new words in your reading. Use this strategy to look for recognizable parts (prefixes, suffixes, and roots) in new words to help you unlock their meaning.

Identify Analyze the words below from the text: First, identify word parts that you recognized. Then check the glossary of word parts on pages 623–631 to see if other parts are explained there. Then define each word. Afterward, check with a dictionary to see how you did.

1. **meritorious** (line 11)

_____

_____

2. **dietary** (line 14)

_____

_____

3. **reintroduced** (line 41)

_____

_____

Drawing Inferences

Pages 29–31 explain that an inference is a logical conclusion that you make about something that is not actually said or stated in a text. A thoughtful inference results from a careful reading, after you have identified the main idea that is developed.

Explain Draw inferences from "The Legal System Based on *Sharia*" by answering the following questions.

1. What would be the value of two or more court systems? Drawbacks?

_____

_____

2. How is religion a factor in law?

_____

_____

LO1 Ideas

Ideas are the first and most important trait to consider when you are writing. Without ideas you have nothing to work with. Just as a cook needs ingredients to make something, a writer needs ideas to develop a piece of writing. When choosing ideas, you need to consider a topic first and then details to support it.

> "As soon as you connect with your true subject, you will write."
> —Joyce Carol Oates

Selecting a Topic

Always try to select a topic that attracts you; otherwise, you will have a hard time working with it through the steps in the writing process. Granted, your choices may be limited for many of your writing assignments. Even so, do your best to select a topic that truly has some meaning to you.

Limiting Your Choices

In most cases, a writing assignment will identify a general subject area, and your first job is to find a specific writing idea related to this subject. This graphic shows how the selecting process should work from the general subject area to a specific topic.

Assignment: Write a paragraph explaining a stress-related condition.

INSIGHT

A topic for a research report must be broad enough to offer plenty of information. For a more limited assignment (a one- or two-page essay), the topic should be more specific.

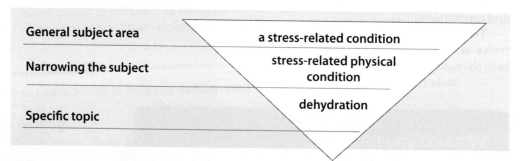

General subject area	a stress-related condition
Narrowing the subject	stress-related physical condition
Specific topic	dehydration

Select Identify a specific topic for the following assignment.

Assignment: Write a paragraph explaining an important environmental problem.

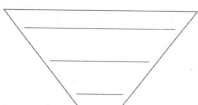

1. General subject area
2. Narrow this subject
3. Specific topic

Selecting Strategies

Always review your class notes, textbook, and Web sites for possible topics. You may also want to try one of the selecting strategies that follow.

- **Clustering** Begin a cluster (or web) with a nucleus word or phrase related to the assignment. (The general subject area or narrowed subject would work.) Circle it and then cluster related words around it. As you continue, you will identify possible writing ideas.

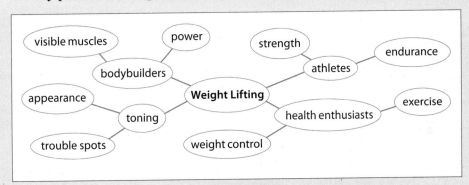

- **Listing** Freely list ideas as you think about your writing assignment. Keep going as long as you can. Then review your list for possible topics.
- **Freewriting** Write nonstop for 5–10 minutes about your assignment to discover possible topics. Begin by writing down a particular thought about the assignment.

Practice Use one of the strategies explained above to identify possible topics related to one of the following general subject areas:

exercise	popular music	careers	freedom/rights	technology

_____

_____

_____

_____

_____

_____

Gathering Details

To write about a topic, you need plenty of supporting details. Some of these details may come from your own thoughts about the topic. Other details will come from reading and learning about the topic.

Identifying What You Already Know

To learn what you already know about a topic, try one of these strategies.

- **Clustering** Create a cluster with your topic as the nucleus word. (See page 121.)
- **Listing** List your thoughts and ideas about your topic as well as questions that come to mind. Keep your list going as long as you can.
- **Freewriting** Write nonstop for 5-8 minutes to see what ideas you can discover about your topic. Go where your thoughts take you, one after another.
- **Developing a Dialogue** Create a dialogue (written conversation) about your topic. In this dialogue, talk about your topic. Keep the dialogue going as long as you can. Here's one way to get started:

   (Your name): Luis, do you know anything about (your topic)?

   Luis: I know a little bit. How about you?

Collect Use one of the strategies above to gather your thoughts about a topic you identified on the last page. (Select an activity different from the one you used on page 121.)

_____

_____

_____

_____

CONSIDER THE TRAITS

Remember that at this stage, the most important trait is ideas. Gather them, discover them, hunt them down. More is better.

> "Knowledge is of two kinds. We know subjects ourselves, or we know where we can find information about it."
> —Samuel Johnson

Learning More About a Topic

Your own thoughts will not be enough for many writing assignments. You will need to collect additional information through research. You can read about a topic or learn about it some other way. You can also try one of these strategies.

Answering Key Questions   Create a list of questions about the topic that you would like to answer during your research. Let's say that you are writing about an event. You could list questions based on the 5 W's and H to answer.

- **When** did the event take place?

  _____

- **What** exactly happened?

  _____

- **Who** was involved?

  _____

- **Why** did it occur?

  _____

- **Where** did it take place?

  _____

- **How** did everything go? (Were there any problems?)

  _____

Analyzing   You can explore your topic from different angles by answering these questions.

- What parts does my topic have? _(Break it down.)_

  _____

- What do I see, hear, or feel when I think about my topic? _(Describe it.)_

  _____

- What is it similar to and different from? _(Compare it.)_

  _____

- What value does it have? _(Evaluate it.)_

  _____

- How useful is it? _(Apply it.)_

  _____

Collect   Use either of the above strategies to discover more about the topic you worked with on the last page. (Answer at least three of the questions after doing some quick research.)

_____

_____

Understanding Supporting Details

When you collect information, you need to know that there are different types of details that you can use in your writing. These details will help you explain or support your topic.

Types of Details

The following list identifies the common types of details.

- **Facts and statistics** give specific information that can be checked.

  > Peregrine falcons have the same mate for life and produce three or four eggs each season.

- **Examples** demonstrate or show something.

  > **Main point:** Americans responded in many ways during the latest oil crisis.
  >
  > **Example:** Many homeowners in the Northeast voluntarily turned down their home thermostats.

- **Definitions** explain new terms.

  > A pandemic is an "infectious disease covering a wide geographic area and affecting a large part of the population."

- **Quotations** provide the thoughts of people knowledgeable about the topic.

  > Chris Woolston of the Consumer Health Interactive says, " Fatty, unbalanced, and oversized. That, in a nutshell, is the American diet."

- **Reasons** answer the question "Why?" about an idea.

  > Huck and Jim both escaped from civilization. They were both fleeing from an unbearable situation.

Identify List two or three different types of details that you could use to support the topic you have been working with in this chapter.

_____

_____

_____

Levels of Details

List two or three different types of details that you could use to support the topic you have been working with in this chapter.

- **Level 1:** A **controlling sentence** names a topic and makes a point about it.
- **Level 2:** A **clarifying sentence** explains a level 1 sentence.
- **Level 3:** A **completing sentence** adds details to complete the point.

Details in Action

In the passage that follows, the level 1 sentence (a topic sentence) is supported by two level 2 sentences. Each level 2 sentence is supported by two level 3 sentences.

> (**Level 1**) Cartoons helped to shape the way I think. (**Level 2**) Most   *1*
> of them taught me never to take life too seriously. (**Level 3**) Many of the
> characters made their way through life with smirks on their faces. (**Level
> 3**) And all but a few of them seized the day, living for the moment. (**Level
> 2**) In an offhanded way, cartoons also provided me with a guide on how   *5*
> to act. (**Level 3**) Good versus evil was usually clearly defined. (**Level 3**)
> Other cartoons stressed the importance of loyalty.

Identify   After reading the following passage, label its levels of detail. Work on this activity with a partner if your instructor allows it.

> (_____) Jim Thorpe was one of the star athletes   *1*
> representing the United States in the 1912 Summer Olympics in Sweden.
> (_____) Thorpe, a Native American, was an extremely versatile
> athlete, but he was especially skilled in track and field. (_____)
> He won a gold medal in the pentathlon, a track-and-field event of five   *5*
> parts. (_____) He also won a gold medal in the decathlon, a ten-
> part track-and-field event.

Special Challenge   Write a brief paragraph describing a favorite television show. Label your sentences with a 1, 2, or 3, depending on the level of detail they include. (Your paragraph may or may not have level 3 details.)

LO2 Focus or Thesis

Focus is not one of the basic traits of writing, but it is included here because it helps you plan how to use the ideas that you collect.

Choosing a Focus

A focus is a particular feeling or part of the topic that you want to emphasize in your writing.

Let's say you are writing about the food in your school's union. More specifically, you want to complain about the huge amount of food that goes to waste. Your feelings about the waste could serve as the focus for your writing.

Topic: food in your school union

Focus: amount of food that is wasted

Your writing will be hard to follow if it lacks focus. So it's important to identify a clear and reasonable focus. To try to describe everything about the food in the union would be unreasonable because there would be too much to say.

Evaluating a Focus

Your writing will be hard to follow if it lacks focus. As a result, it's important to identify a clear and reasonable focus. To try to describe every activity related to an annual community event would be too general, whereas focusing on one or two unique activities would seem reasonable.

Review   Rate the effectiveness of each focus below by circling the appropriate star. Consider whether the focus is clear, reasonable, and worth developing. Explain each of your choices.

1. **Topic:** sports drinks **Focus:** the best choice during long workouts
weak ★ ★ ★ ★ ★ strong _____

_____

2. **Topic:** society's view of beauty **Focus:** seems good
weak ★ ★ ★ ★ ★ strong _____

_____

3. **Topic:** cultural comparisons between Korea and the United States **Focus:** contrasting views on cleanliness
weak ★ ★ ★ ★ ★ strong _____

_____

Forming a Topic Sentence or Thesis Statement

State your focus in a **topic sentence** for a paragraph and in a **thesis statement** in an essay. The following formula can be used to write a topic sentence or thesis statement. The following example is for an informational paragraph.

A specific topic	**+** a particular feeling, feature, or part	**=** an effective topic sentence or thesis statement (main idea).
arrival of Hernán Cortés in Mexico	marked the beginning of the end of the Aztec empire	The arrival of Hernán Cortés in Mexico marked the beginning of the end of the Aztec empire.

Create Identify a focus and then write a topic sentence or thesis statement for each of the following assignments. The first one is done for you.

1. **Writing assignment:** Paragraph describing a specific style of clothing

   Specific topic: Zoot suit

   Focus: Popular during the swing era

   Topic sentence: The zoot suit (specific topic) became a popular fashion symbol in the swing era (a particular feature).

2. **Writing assignment:** Paragraph explaining how to do something

   Specific topic: Using chopsticks

   Focus: _____

   Topic sentence: _____

   _____

3. **Writing assignment:** Paragraph analyzing a popular type of cooking

   Specific topic: Cajun cooking

   Focus: _____

   Thesis statement: _____

   _____

4. **Writing assignment:** Paragraph exploring technology and education

   Specific topic: Electronic textbooks

   Focus: _____

   Thesis statement: _____

   _____

---

topic sentence
the controlling idea in paragraph

thesis statement
the controlling idea in an essay

LO3 Organization

You should next think about the pattern of organization that you plan to use to develop your topic sentence (or thesis statement). Here's one way to do this:

1. **Study your topic sentence or thesis.** It will usually indicate how to organize your details. Consider the following topic sentence:

   > Eating locally grown produce will improve the local economy.

   This topic sentence suggests arranging the information by order of importance (see below) because the writer is trying to prove a point.

2. **Then review the details you have gathered.** Decide which details support your topic sentence; also decide on the best pattern of organization to arrange them. For the example topic sentence, the writer would arrange his or her details (reasons) from most important to least important or the other way around.

Patterns of Organization

Listed below are some of the common patterns that you will use in your writing.

- Use **chronological order** (time) when you are sharing a personal experience, telling how something happened, or explaining how to do something.
- Use **spatial order** (location) for descriptions, arranging information from left to right, from top to bottom, from the edge to the center, and so on.
- Use **order of importance** when you are taking a stand or arguing for or against something. Arrange your reasons either from most important to least important or the other way around.
- Use **logical order** if you want to follow your topic sentence or thesis statement with supporting details (reasons, examples, and so on) that naturally and logically follow one another.
- Use **compare-contrast organization** when you want to show how one topic is different from and similar to another one.

CONSIDER THE TRAITS

Think about your purpose as you choose a pattern of organization. Often, your working thesis statement will suggest how you should organize details.

Choose Study each of the following topic sentences and thesis statements. Then choose the best method of organization to develop it. The first one is done for you. (Work on this activity with a classmate if your instructor allows it.)

1. **Topic sentence:** The bottom of the hill in my childhood neighborhood offered everything young boys wanted.

   Appropriate method of organization: _spatial order_

   Explain: _The topic sentence suggests that the writer will describe the area_

   at the bottom of the hill, so using spatial order seems appropriate.

   _____

2. **Topic sentence:** In most cases, people involved in recreational fishing should use barbless hooks.

   Appropriate method of organization: _____

   Explain: _____

   _____

   _____

3. **Topic sentence:** To become an effective leader, a person must develop three main traits.

   Appropriate method of organization: _____

   Explain: _____

   _____

   _____

4. **Thesis statement:** Meeting my grandmother for the first time rates as one of my most important personal encounters.

   Appropriate method of organization: _____

   Explain: _____

   _____

   _____

5. **Thesis statement:** (Choose one that you wrote on page 127.)

   Appropriate method of organization: _____

   Explain: _____

   _____

   _____

Arranging Details

Here are three basic strategies for arranging the supporting details after selecting a pattern of organization.

- **Make a quick list** of main points.
- **Create an outline**—an organized arrangement of main points and subpoints.
- **Fill in a graphic organizer,** arranging main points and details in a chart or diagram. (See pages 8–9.)

Using a Quick List

A quick list works well when you are writing a short piece or when your planning time is limited. Here is a quick list for a descriptive paragraph about zoot suits. (The list organizes details in spatial order, from top to bottom.)

Sample Quick List

Topic sentence: The zoot suit became a popular fashion symbol in the swing era.
- begins with a stylish wide-brimmed hat turned down
- follows with an oversized, tapered long jacket
- under jacket, a dress shirt with a tie
- pleated pants taper to narrow bottoms
- ends with two-tone, thin-soled shoes

Create   Write a topic sentence and a quick list for a narrative paragraph about a funny, scary, or otherwise significant personal experience. Include four to six details in your list, organized chronologically.

Topic sentence:

_____

_____

Quick list:

_____

_____

_____

_____

Using an Outline

An outline shows how ideas fit together for your writing. Topic and sentence outlines follow specific guidelines: If you have a "I," you must at least have a "II." If you have an "A," you must at least have a "B," and so on. You can also change or simplify an outline to meet your needs. Outlines are often used to arrange the ideas in essays and other longer pieces of writing.

Simplified Outline

Here is the first part of a simplified outline that includes main points stated in complete sentences and supporting details stated as phrases.

Thesis statement: Humpback whales are by far the most playful and amazing whale species.

1. Most observers note that humpbacks appear to enjoy attention.
   - lift bodies almost completely out of water (breaching)
   - slap huge flippers against the water
   - thrust their flukes (tail portion) straight out of water

2. Humpback whales "sing" better than other whales.
   - song lasts up to 30 minutes
   - head pointed toward ocean floor when singing
   - seem to engage in group singing

Develop   Create a simplified outline for an essay about becoming a leader. A thesis statement and three main points are provided. Put the main points in the most logical order, and make up two or three details to support each one. (Work on this activity with a classmate if your instructor allows it.)

Thesis statement: To become an effective leader, a person must develop three main traits.

Main points: Leaders must earn the respect of others. Leaders must display good work habits. Leaders must be confident.

1. _____

_____

_____

_____

2. _____

_____

_____

_____

LO5 Word Choice and Sentences

The words and sentences that you use carry the meaning in your writing. So it is important that they are clear, interesting, and honest. Also be sure that they fit the type of writing that you are doing. As you learned on the last two pages, the language you use for an informational paragraph will be different from the language you use in a narrative recalling a personal experience.

Using Specific Nouns and Verbs

Generally speaking, specific words (*LeBron soars*) are better to use than general ones (*the basketball player jumps*). And fresh words (a *drop-dead* beauty) are usually better to use than overused ones (a *real* beauty).

It's especially important to use specific nouns and verbs because they carry the most meaning in your sentences. The charts below show different examples of general versus specific nouns and verbs.

General nouns:	personal computer	adventure	performer
Specific nouns:	iMac	bungee jumping	Jennifer Lopez

General verbs:	laugh	run	look	build
Specific verbs:	giggle	sprint	inspect	erect

Study List examples of specific nouns and verbs that come to mind when you inspect the photograph to the right. Afterward, compare lists with your classmates.

Samot, 2013 / Used under license from Shutterstock.com

Specific Nouns	Specific Verbs

Avoiding Weak Words

If the words you use help to create clear and interesting paragraphs, essays, and reports, then you have probably used the right ones. The following information discusses word-related issues to consider:

Watch for . . .

- **Vague adjectives** (modifiers of nouns) such as *neat, big, pretty, small, cute, fun, bad, nice, good, great,* and *funny.* Use more specific adjectives instead.

    > **Vague adjective:** Josie makes a good pizza crust.
    >
    > **Specific adjective:** Josie makes a thin and crisp pizza crust.

- **Too many adjectives in general.** Being "adjective happy" detracts from rather than adds to writing.

    > **Too many adjectives:** Part-time help can complete high-profile, high-impact workplace tasks without adding full-time employees.
    >
    > **Fewer adjectives:** Part-time help can complete important tasks without adding full-time employees. (simpler and clearer)

- **Too many "be" verbs** (*is, are, was, were,* and so on). Instead, use specific action verbs.

    > **"Be" verb:** Laura is a powerful diver.
    >
    > **Specific action verb:** Laura dives powerfully.

- **The same word used over and over.** Such repetition calls undo attention to the word.

    > **Overuse of a word:** I noticed a woman dressed in a crisp, navy blue suit. The woman appeared to be in charge. I soon realized that the woman was the owner.
    >
    > **Variety added:** I noticed a woman dressed in a crisp, navy blue suit who appeared to be in charge. I soon realized that she was the owner.

- **Words used incorrectly.** Words such as *their, they're,* and *there* and *its* and *it's* are commonly misused.

    > Most engineers get their (not they're or there) training on the job.
    >
    > Jogging has its (not it's) most impact if it's (not its) done regularly.

Create Write your own example for at least three of the problems discussed above. For each one, provide a new sentence with improved word choice. Afterward, share your work with your classmates.

Writing Clear Sentences

To write strong, clear sentences, you must first understand the basics. By definition, a simple sentence expresses a complete thought and contains a subject and a verb. But not all sentences are "simple." There are compound sentences and complex sentences, as well as other types.

The most common sentence errors include fragments *(incomplete sentences)*, comma splices *(two sentences connected only with a comma),* and run-on sentences *(two sentences joined without punctuation).* The examples that follow show what is and what isn't a sentence. (See pages 487–506 for more explanations and practice activities.)

A Basic Guide to Sentences

Correct sentences

Simple sentence:	Jackson chews his fingernails. *(one complete idea)*
Compound sentence:	Max watches the presentation, but his mind is really somewhere else. *(two complete ideas)*
Complex sentence:	Sonja takes quick notes, while Connie sketches tiny flowers. *(one main idea and one subordinate or lesser idea)*

Sentence errors

Fragment:	Popcorn all over the floor. *(no verb)*
	Popcorn *spilled* over the floor. *(verb added)*
Fragment:	Couldn't help laughing. *(no subject)*
	We couldn't help laughing. *(subject added)*
Comma Splice:	Josie and I ordered coffee, we decided to split a cookie. *(missing a connecting word or end punctuation)*
	Josie and I ordered coffee, *and* we decided to split a cookie. *(connecting word added)*
Run-on:	Taking my dog for a walk frustrates me he has to sniff every tree and shrub in front of him. *(no punctuation)*
	Taking my dog for a walk frustrates me. He has to sniff every tree and shrub in front of him. *(punctuation added)*

Develop   Write for 5 minutes about your favorite late night snack (or snacks). Then use the information above to check your sentences for correctness. Ask a classmate to check them as well. Correct any sentence errors that you find.

Checking Sentences for Style

There are other issues to consider when it comes to writing effective sentences. The information that follows identifies four of them.

Watch for . . .

■ **Short, choppy sentences.** Too many short sentences in a row will sound choppy. To correct this problem, combine some of the ideas.

> **Choppy sentences:** A Harley roared past us. The cycle was jet black. It stopped in front of a food stand. The food stand sells fresh fish tacos.
>
> **Combined sentences:** A jet-black Harley roared past us and stopped in front of a food stand that sells fresh fish tacos.

■ **Sentences with the same beginning.** (This problem often creates choppy sentences.) To correct this problem, vary some of your sentence beginnings and lengths.

> **Sentences with no variety:** Keeping a daily planner is important. It keeps track of your schedule. It lists your assignments. It helps you plan your time during the day.
>
> **Varied sentences:** Keeping a daily planner is important. In addition to keeping track of your schedule, it lists your assignments and helps you plan your time.

■ **Sentences with passive verbs.** With a passive verb, the subject is acted on rather than doing the action. (See pages 540–541 for more information and activities.) To fix this problem, change the passive verbs into active ones.

> **Passive verb:** The 16-ounce porterhouse steak was *attacked* by the Chihuahua.
>
> **Active verb:** The Chihuahua *attacked* the 16-ounce porterhouse steak.

Check Use the following strategy to evaluate the sentences that you used in the activity on page 136.

1. List the opening words in your sentences. Decide if some sentence beginnings need to be varied.

   _____

2. List the number of words in each sentence. Decide if some sentence lengths need to be varied.

   _____

3. List the main verbs used. Decide if you need to replace any overused "be" verbs (*is, are, was, were*) with action verbs.

   _____

LO6 Conventions

The conventions are the rules for grammar, usage, and mechanics that you need to follow in your writing. But be sure to focus on the correctness of your writing at the best time, when you have completed the revising of your writing. Once all of your ideas are in place, then checking for the conventions becomes important.

If you're working on a computer, do your correcting on a printout of your work. Then enter the changes on the computer. Be sure to save the edited printout so you have a record of the changes you've made.

If you're working with pen and paper, do your editing on a neat copy of your revised writing. Then make a new copy of your writing and save the edited copy. Once you develop a final copy, be sure to proofread it for correctness before you submit it.

Strategies for Editing

When checking for errors, examine your writing word for word and sentence by sentence. The following strategies will help you edit thoroughly and effectively.

- Work with a clean copy of your writing, one that includes your revising changes.
- Check one element at a time—spelling, punctuation, and so on.
- For spelling, start at the bottom of the page to force yourself to look at each word. (Remember that your spell-checker will not catch all errors.)
- For punctuation, circle all the marks to force yourself to look at each one.
- Read your work aloud at least once, noting any errors as you go along.
- Refer to a list of common errors.
- Have an editing guide (see pages 439–617 in this text) and a dictionary handy.
- Ask a trusted classmate to check your work as well.

Preview When you have questions about punctuation, grammar, or any other convention, turn to pages 439–617. This part of the book is divided into three major workshops. Answer the following questions about this section.

1. What are the names of the three workshops in this section?

2. How will these workshops prove helpful when you are editing your writing?

3. Which one or two of these workshops will you probably turn to more than the others? Why?

Using Editing Symbols

You can use editing symbols to mark errors in your writing. Listed below are some of the most common symbols.

<u>c</u> chicago	Capitalize a letter.	first my⋀speech	Insert here.
F̶all	Make lowercase.	⋀ ⋀ ⋀	Insert a comma, a colon, or a semicolon.
Mr⨀Ford	Insert (add) a period.	˅ ˅ ˅	Insert an apostrophe or quotation marks.
Sp. or ⟨recieve⟩	Correct spelling.	? ! ⋀ ⋀	Insert a question mark or an exclamation point.
Mr. Lott ̶h̶e̶	Delete (take out) or replace.	⌐possible⟍worst⌐	Switch words or letters.

Edit   Use the editing symbols above to mark the errors in the following piece and show how they should be corrected.

> When we lived on Maple street, we had a neighbor who seemed to   *1*
> have two personalities his name was Mr. Bunde. I worked for him one
> Summer while I was in grade school, cutting his lawn and doing other yard
> work. After a few months of working for him I'd had more than enough. In
> general, he was a nice enough guy, and he likes to joke around some of the   *5*
> time. Unfortunately, it was hard to tell if he was really kidding or if his
> mood was suddenly changing. When he was in one of his moods I couldn't
> do anything rite. Sometimes he would complain about other neighbors and
> he would expect me to agree with him, even though he new they were my
> friends. I not only have to concentrate on my work but I also had to be on   *10*
> my guard, trying to predict Mr. Bunde's mood. Why did I have to work for
> him

Review and Enrichment

On the next seven pages you will review and enrich your understanding of the concepts in this chapter.

Reviewing the Chapter

Ideas Answer the following questions about this section. (See pages 120–125.)

- What does it mean to narrow a subject?

_____

- What are four different types of supporting details?

_____

Identifying a Focus Explain the importance of a topic sentence or thesis statement. (See pages 126-127.)

_____

_____

Organization Explain three patterns listed in this section. (See pages 128–131.)

1. _____

2. _____

3. _____

Voice Explain the following: (See pages 132–133.)

- Academic Voice: _____

_____

- Personal Voice: _____

_____

Word Choice and Sentences Answer the following: (See pages 134–137.)

- Why is it important to use specific nouns and verbs? _____

_____

- Why should you vary your sentence beginnings and lengths? _____

_____

Conventions Explain when in the writing process you should check for conventions and why the "timing" is important. (See pages 138–139.)

_____

_____

Reading

In the first part of this section, you will read and react to a personal essay entitled "A Very Lucky Daughter." This essay is the type of writing that is commonly found in magazines and memoirs or autobiographies. In the second part you will develop a piece of writing in response to your reading.

> "When I was a boy of 14, my father was so ignorant I could hardly stand to have the old man around. But when I got to be 21, I was astonished at how much the old man had learned in seven years."
> —Mark Twain

About the Author

Sharon Liao is a freelance writer and editor specializing in health, nutrition, and fitness. He writing has appeared in many magazines. This essay appeared in *Reader's Digest* and the *Washingtonian* (a magazine) in 2001.

Prereading

Traveling can put people in difficult or embarrassing situations, especially when there are language barriers. That is what happens to the author in this essay. You may have had a similar experience yourself. Write for 3–5 minutes about one of your own difficult or challenging traveling experiences.

CONSIDER THE TRAITS

As you read, pay careful attention to the **ideas**—especially the details that you learn about the author's parents. Also consider the author's **voice**—the way in which she speaks to you in the writing. Upon completion of your reading, ask yourself to what degree the text informed you and engaged your interest.

What do you think?

Consider the quotation above: Through the use of humor, what point is Mark Twain really trying to make?

Identify   Before you read "A Very Lucky Daughter," answer these three questions.

1. What do the title and first 10 lines tell you about the text?

2. Who might be the author's intended audience?

3. What do you expect to learn in this essay?

Reading and Rereading

As you read, make it your goal to (1) follow all of the details in the author's story, (2) notice her use of dialogue and description, and (3) carefully consider the ending part.

Tip: Consider annotating the text (page 20) and /or taking notes (page 22) as you read.

A Very Lucky Daughter

I should have been just another face in the hotel lobby in Zhangjiajie, a   *1*
city in central China. But my words singled me out.

"*Yun dou*," I repeated to the clerk. Maybe he understood English: "Do
you have a gym here?"

The clerk blinked, and then reached behind the counter and pulled out   *5*
an iron.

I smiled blankly. My brain rooted through my limited Chinese
vocabulary. Just then my dad strolled up, his eyebrows arched in amused
triangles.

"She wants to know where the gym is," he supplied in rapid Mandarin   *10*
Chinese, his native language. He turned to me and explained gently, "*Yun
dong* is exercise, Sharon. *Yun dou* means iron."

I mumbled a sheepish apology to the laughing clerk and glanced at my
dad. A look of recognition flashed through his eyes. We'd gone through this
before. Only this time, the tables were turned.   *15*

When I was younger, I would try to imagine my parents growing up
in China and Taiwan. But I could only envision them in the grainy black-
and-white of their faded childhood pictures. Their childhood stories didn't
match the people I knew. I couldn't picture my domestic mom, unsure of
her halting English, studying international economics at a Taiwanese   *20*
university. I laughed at the image of my stern father, an electrical
engineer, chasing after chickens in his Chinese village.

I related to my parents' pre-American lives as only a series of events,
like facts from some history exam. My dad fled to Taiwan in 1949 as a
14-year-old, after the Communists won the civil war. His father fought   *25*
for the losing side, the Nationalists. My mom's father, a Nationalist navy
captain, also retreated to Taiwan. My mom, who was born in Taiwan, grew
up thinking that her family would eventually return to China, after the
Nationalists reclaimed their homeland.

But that didn't happen. As young adults, my parents moved to the 30
United States to lead better lives. They did not step onto Chinese soil for
more than 50 years. Then their friends arranged a trip to China. And they
asked me to join them on the six-city tour.

My list of why-nots was jam packed. And yet something inside–I could
not explain what—urged me to go. 35

When the plane jerked to a stop in Shanghai, our first destination, all
of those reasons I decide to go materialized in the expression on my parents'
faces. My mom folded and unfolded her hands impatiently in her lap. I was
surprised and slightly scared to see my stoic dad's eyes glimmering with
emotion. He slipped his hand, soft and spotted with age, in mine. 40

"Last time I was here," he said, " my parents going from north to south,
away from the Communists. So much bombing. A lot of people starving."
He leaned close. "You very lucky, Sharon."

That was my dad's line. When I would whine as a child, my dad's
response was inevitable: "Some people not as lucky as you." 45

But I never cared about being lucky. I just wanted to be like the other
American kids.

My parents, however, intended for me to become a model Chinese
American. Starting when I was six, they would drag me away from Saturday
cartoons to Chinese church. I would squirm like a worm in my seat while a 50
teacher recited Chinese vocabulary. I dutifully recited my *bo po mo fos*—the
ABCs of speaking Mandarin. But in my head, I rearranged the chalk marks
that made up the characters into pictures of houses and trees.

When I turned nine, I declared I wasn't going to Chinese school
anymore. "This stinks," I yelled. "None of my friends have to go to extra 55
school. Why do I have to go?"

"Because you Chinese," my mom replied coolly.

"Then I don't want to be Chinese," I shouted back. "It's not fair. I
just want to be normal. Why can't you and Dad be like everybody else's
parents? I wish I were somebody else's kid." 60

I waited for my mom to shout, but she just stared at me with tired
eyes. "If you don't want to go, don't have to," she said. . . .

My mom speaks English like I speak Chinese, slowly and punctuated
by ums and ahs. When someone speaks English too rapidly, my mom's eyes
cloud with confusion. I instantly recognize her I-don't-get-it look, and I 65
know it's time to explain something.

About a month before we left for China, I helped my mom return a
purchase to Wal-Mart.

The clerk rudely ignored my mom's slow English, speaking to me
instead. 70

Later my mom thanked me for my help. "*Xie xie*, Sharon," she said,
patting my shoulder. "I have a good American daughter."

"It's nothing, Mom," I said.

In the airport before we departed for China, my parents' friends herded around me. "Your parents so proud of you," said one man. "Always talking about you." 75

His words surprised me. I felt like I barely spoke with my parents. Did they really know who I was? Then another question, the one I always managed to skirt, surfaced in my conscience: Did I even come close to understanding them . . . ? 80

Often during the tour, my own face resembled my mom's I-don't-get-it look. At meals, my parents answered my constant questions about each colorful bowl that would rotate on a lazy Susan.

My parents chuckled at the response when a waiter put a bowl of soup on our table. While the other diners shouted with excitement, I was 85 horrified to see the remnants of a turtle floating in the clear yellow broth.

My table cried in dismay when I let the soup circle past me. "Strange," said one man, shaking his head. "Such good soup."

A few days after "the iron incident," as my run-in with the hotel clerk became known in our tour group, my parents and I sat on a bench 90 overlooking monoliths [giant rocks or stones]. "Too bad I don't speak fluent Chinese," I said. "I should have listened when you tried to teach me."

My dad looked at me with understanding. "It's okay," he said. "You learning it now."

My mom smiled supportively. "Never too late," she said. 95

From Sharon Liao, "A Daughter's Journey" in *The Washingtonian*, January 2001

Reflecting

After your reading, answer the following questions:

1. Why did the author share this particular experience?

   _____

2. What specific detail (action or explanation) stands out to you, and why?

   _____

3. What type of voice does the author employ—academic or personal? Explain.

   _____

4. How would you rate this reading, and why? (Use "A Guide to Strong Writing" on page 106 to help you form your rating.)

Weak ★ ★ ★ ★ ★ Strong

Vocabulary Practice

Pages 33–34 explain one strategy—using context clues—that will help you understand new words in your reading. Context clues are clues provided by the words and ideas around unfamiliar words.

Identify   Use context clues to define the following words in "A Very Lucky Daughter."

1. sheepish (line 13)

    clues: _____

    definition: _____

2. stoic (line 39)

    clues: _____

    definition: _____

3. remnants (line 86)

    clues: _____

    definition: _____

Drawing Inferences

Explain   Draw two inferences from "A Very Lucky Daughter" by answering the following questions. (See pages 29–31 for help.)

1. What can be learned in the narrative about the relationship between parents and their children?

    _____

    _____

2. How does language define us?

    _____

    _____

Writing

What follows are possible writing activities to complete in response to the reading. Use the writing process (pages 94–99) and the traits of writing (pages 120–139) to help you develop your paragraphs and essays.

Prewriting

Choose one of the following writing ideas, or create your own idea.

Writing Ideas

1. **Blog (Journal) Writing:** For one day, pay careful attention to the conversations that you hear and participate in. Then write a blog or journal entry exploring your thoughts about these conversations.
2. **Paragraph Writing:** Describe an experience in which language led to misunderstanding, embarrassment, or worse.
3. Share interesting facts and details about someone in your family's past.
4. **Essay Writing:** In an expository or argumentative essay, explore the value of learning a second (or even a third) language.
5. Reveal something important about your relationship with your parents or grandparents through one or more personal experiences.

When planning . . .

Refer to page 96 and the tips below to help with your prewriting and planning.
- Select a topic (experience) that means a lot to you.
- Gather your thoughts and ideas about the topic.
- Decide on an interesting or revealing way to develop it.

Writing and Revising

Refer to pages 97–98 and the tips below to help you write and revise your first draft.

When writing . . .
- Get all of your thoughts and ideas on paper.
- Don't worry about correctness at this point.
- Form a meaningful whole, with a beginning, middle, and ending.

When revising . . .
- Let your first draft sit unread for a bit. Then reread it carefully.
- Check for clarity and completeness. (Have you left anything out?)
- Ask a classmate to react to your first draft.
- Make the necessary improvements in the content of your writing.

Editing

Refer to the checklist on page 165 when you are ready to edit your writing.

II:

Reading and Writing Paragraphs

Part II: Reading and Writing Paragraphs

6

"As we read we discover the importance of physical details. . . ."
—John Gardner

Description

Have you ever thought about what makes dogs and cats different? It's more than just size: Some cats are very large, and some dogs are quite tiny. Both are mammals. Both are pets. Both have four legs and a tail. Both are primarily carnivorous. Unlike dogs, however, cats possess retractable claws, and they purr. Dogs have shoulder blades, which cats do not, and, of course, dogs bark.

Details help us to tell the two creatures apart. The more descriptive details that are presented, the more we learn about the subjects, and the more confidently we can talk about them.

In this chapter, you will read and react to two professional descriptions. Then you will write a descriptive paragraph of your own. In the process, you should come to value the importance of descriptive details in all forms of communication.

Learning Outcomes

LO1 Understand description.

LO2 Learn reading strategies (identify details and consider organization).

LO3 Read and react to a professional paragraph.

LO4 Read and react to a professional description.

LO5 Practice reading skills (identify tone and mood).

LO6 Plan a description.

LO7 Write the first draft.

LO8 Revise the writing.

LO9 Edit the writing.

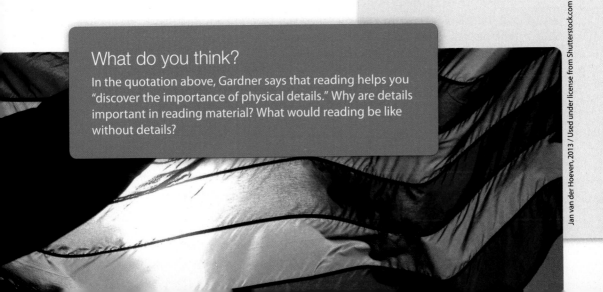

What do you think?

In the quotation above, Gardner says that reading helps you "discover the importance of physical details." Why are details important in reading material? What would reading be like without details?

LO1 Understanding Description

In the film *Enter the Dragon,* Bruce Lee describes thinking as a finger pointing at the moon. "Don't concentrate on the finger," he says, "or you will miss all that heavenly glory." Notice how Lee's description uses a few well-chosen details—the finger, the moon, the heavenly glory—to convey its message.

Descriptive writing relies upon these sorts of details. The purpose of such writing is not merely to list, however. Instead, it is to choose the best details and present them in the best manner to describe the subject. Descriptive writing helps readers to feel they have experienced the subject for themselves.

> "A good description is a magician that can turn an ear into an eye."
> —Unknown

Many Purposes

For this reason, other types of writing often include some description. A narrative (story) may describe a scene and a character. An explanation may use description in its examples. Process writing may describe each step. Classifications and comparisons may use description to make their subjects easier to understand.

Description in Academic Texts

Your reading assignments in academic texts will seldom be pure descriptions. But even within a typical explanation or analysis, there's a good chance some description will occur. For example, in an analysis of the traditional family, a sociologist might provide a description of a day in the life of the family members. In an explanation of gender differences, a health expert might provide a detailed description of each gender.

INSIGHT

Descriptions don't have to include every detail. Rather, authors usually choose the key details to picture the subject they are writing about.

Practice Think of a favorite magazine or Web site. Then name two or three topics that might be described in it. For example, *People* magazine might describe the favorite fashions of an up-and-coming actress.

_____

_____

_____

Reading

Reading descriptions can be entertaining and enlightening. They can create powerful images in your head and help you visualize topics.

LO2 Learning Reading Strategies

To best understand descriptive writing, pay attention to the details included and the order they are presented.

Identifying Details

Descriptive texts typically include sensory details—the sights, sounds, smells, tastes, and textures of a subject. Use a chart like the one below to note the sensory details in the descriptive texts you read. You can also use this chart to gather sensory details for your own descriptive writing.

Sensory Chart

Sights	Sounds	Smells	Tastes	Textures

Considering Organization

The order in which details are revealed also plays an important role in the effectiveness of descriptive writing. Common descriptive organizations include the following.

> **INSIGHT**
> Not every description will appeal to every sense. A description of a meal might focus on tastes, smells, sights, and textures, but not at all on sound.

- **Spatial Organization:** Details are arranged by location—top to bottom, right to left, foreground to background, or so on. Settings are often described this way.
- **Chronological Organization:** Details are presented according to the passage of time. Events are typically described this way.
- **Logical Order:** The details simply follow one another predictably or naturally. Academic texts often use this order to explain or define.

LO3 Reading and Reacting to a Professional Paragraph

In this paragraph, the author describes a statue he received from his father. The statue holds a special place in the author's life. Use the reading process (see below) to help you with your reading.

Prereading   Before you read, answer these three questions:

1. What do the title and first sentence tell you about the text?

_____

2. What might be the author's purpose?

_____

3. What questions would you like answered? (Name two.)

_____

_____

Reading and Rereading   As you read, make it your goal to (1) identify the topic and main idea, (2) locate the key supporting details, and (3) study the ending sentence. Consider annotating the text (page 20) during your reading.

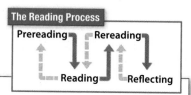

The Reading Process

A Battered Statue

    The **Don Quixote** statuette my dad gave me isn't worth much. It is a statue of a gaunt, old man in battered armor sitting astride a swayback horse. The helmet on Quixote's head is dented, its visor bent above bushy eyebrows, squinting eyes, a wide wedge of a nose, and an unruly mustache and beard. His breastplate and shield are so worn that whatever emblems they once held have been lost. The statue looks like roughcast pewter, but when I accidentally knocked it over, it smashed on the floor, revealing itself to be painted plaster. I scooped up the jaggy chunks and did my best to stick them back together. Now a few seams of seeping glue and off-color paint crisscross the figure, and electrician's tape clings to the bent lance. Despite these flaws, despite dust and cobwebs, Quixote still manages to stare out with a look of hope. The statuette wasn't worth much when Dad gave it to me, and it's worth even less now. But somehow, after all this time and all this glue and tape, the statue means even more to me.

1

5

10

Don Quixote (ke-ho′-te)
the hero in a Spanish novel of the same name; impractical knight battling life's injuries but failing miserably

Reflecting After you read, answer these questions. Then share your reflections with your classmates.

1. What is the main idea?

   _____

2. What supporting details are provided? Name two.

   _____

3. What have you learned in this reading?

   _____

4. What questions, if any do you still have about the topic?

   _____

5. How would you rate the paragraph, and why?

   Weak ★ ★ ★ ★ ★ Strong

   _____

Vocabulary Practice

Identify Define the word parts as indicated. Then try to explain the meaning of the complete word. (See pages 35–36 and 623–631 for help.)

1. **unruly** (line 4) un + rul + ly

   _____

   _____

2. **roughcast** (line 6) rough + cast

   _____

   _____

Drawing Inferences

Explain Answer the following question to help you draw an inference about the text. (See pages 29–31 for help.)

- Why does the statuette mean more to the author after the "glue and tape"?

   _____

   _____

LO4 Reading and Reacting to a Professional Description

In this excerpt, the author describes a topic all of us have seen in history or geography books. As you will see, he gives his description an artistic twist. Use the reading process to help you with your reading.

About the Author

Philip M. Isaacson worked full-time as a lawyer as well as writing regularly about art and architecture. He was also an accomplished photographer of architecture.

Prereading   Before you read, answer these questions:

1. What do the title and first sentence tell you about the text?

2. What is the author's purpose?

3. What main question do you expect to be answered about the topic?

Reading and Rereading   As you read, make it your goal to (1) identify the topic and main idea, (2) find the key supporting details, and (3) study the final sentence. Consider annotating the text (page 20) during your reading.

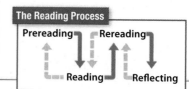

From *A Short Walk Around the Pyramids*

At Giza, a few miles north of Saqqara, sit three great pyramids, each   1
named for the king—or Pharaoh—during whose reign it was built. No
other buildings are so well known, yet the first sight of them sitting in
their field is breathtaking. When you walk among them, you walk in a
place made for giants. They seem too large to have been made by human   5
beings, too perfect to have been formed by nature, and when the sun is
overhead, not solid enough to be attached to the sand. In the minutes
before sunrise, they are the color of faded roses, and when the last rays
of the desert sun touch them, they turn to amber. But whatever the light,
their broad proportions, the beauty of the limestone, and the care with   10
which it is fitted into place create three unforgettable works of art.
What do we learn about art when we look at the pyramids?
First, when all of the things that go into a work—its components—
complement one another, they create an object that has a certain spirit,
and we can call that spirit harmony. The pyramids are harmonious   15
because limestone, a warm, quiet material, is a cordial companion for a
simple, logical, pleasing shape. In fact, the stone and the shape are so
comfortable with each other that the pyramids seem inevitable—as though
they were bound to have the form, color, and texture that they do have.

From *A Short Walk Around the Pyramids* by Philip M. Isaacson, copyright © 1993 Knopf Doubleday
Publishing Group

Reflecting   Answer the following questions about the excerpt. Then discuss your answers with your classmates.

1. What is the main idea of this selection?

   _____

2. What are two details that seem especially artistic?

   _____

3. How has this selection changed or expanded your understanding of the topic?

   _____

4. How would you rate this selection, and why?

   Weak ★ ★ ★ ★ ★ Strong

   _____

Vocabulary Practice

Identify   Use context clues to explain or define the following words. (See pages 33–34 for help.)

1. **complement** (line 14)

   clues: _____

   definition: _____

2. **cordial** (line 16)

   clues: _____

   definition: _____

Drawing Inferences

Explain   Answer this question to help you draw an inference about the text. (See pages 29–31 for help.)

■ Why does the author seem to overstate or exaggerate the appearance of the pyramids?

   _____

   _____

LO5 Practicing Reading Skills

As noted in the chapter introduction, most descriptive writing tries to do more than merely describe. Descriptive writing often communicates an attitude or a feeling. The strategies here will help you identify it.

Identifying Tone

To recognize an author's tone or voice in descriptive writing, it may help to make a chart like the one below. List descriptive words in the first column and your thoughts about their effect in the second. (An example is included.)

Word	Effect
battered	Adds to a sense of worthlessness or uselessness

Identify Use a chart like the one above to analyze the tone of the description paragraph on page 152. List at least three or four descriptive words.

Understanding Mood

Mood is the feeling generated in the reader. A writer's tone or voice can help to create a particular mood. In "A Battered Statue," for example, the author uses words with a tone of wear and defeat. And the paragraph moves from a description of Quixote as a character to the broken plaster of the statuette to the rebuilding of it.

One way to understand the mood of a descriptive piece is to freewrite about it to see how it makes you feel.

Freewrite Write nonstop for about 5 minutes about the excerpt you have just read on page 154. Consider how pyramids are described and how the details make you feel about them. This writing will help you identify the mood of the piece.

_____

_____

_____

_____

_____

Writing

It is time now to begin planning and writing your own description paragraph about a person, place, or thing that is important to you. Remember to use the writing process to help you do your best work.

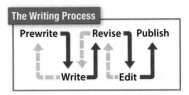

The Writing Process

Prewrite → Write → Revise → Edit → Publish

LO6 Planning a Description

According to one old tale, a boy was asked to bring a wizard something no one had ever seen before. The boy brought an egg. When the chick inside hatched out, the wizard was the first to see it.

The point is that your descriptive paragraph doesn't have to be about something unusual. What makes a description effective instead is how you see the topic and present it to your readers.

Selecting a Topic

To select a topic, you can start by listing items in the general categories of person, place, or thing. Then jot down one or more specific examples of each. Circle the one you would like to write about. See one student's example below.

Select List two or three possible topics for each of the categories below. A sample topic for each category is provided.

Person	Place	Thing
Teachers	**Shops**	**Pets**
Ms. Rucki	Starbucks	parakeet
Neighbors	Apple Store	**Cars**
Mr. Vogt	**Restaurants**	my first one
Wilson Kendall	Staniford's Pizza	**Clothes**
Celebrities	**Parks**	leather jacket
Matt Damon	North Beecham	
	Hoversten State Park	

List Create your own chart of people, places, and things. Circle the item you feel most excited about as the topic for your description paragraph.

Sergii Figurnyi, 2013 / Used under license from Shutterstock.com

Gathering Details

Sensory details help readers to "picture" your subject in their own minds. In the example below, a student used a sensory chart to list details about her first car. Part of her sensory chart is shown below. Notice the tone of her words.

Sensory Details

Sights	Sounds	Smells	Tastes	Textures
– faded paint, tomato soup color – huge dent in driver's door	– roaring motor – rattle in door – buzzing speakers	– dirty oil – pine cleaner – stale cheese	– none	– "dusty" paint – cracked upholstery

Gather On a sensory chart, write down key sensory details about the subject you have chosen.

Organizing Details

It's important to present your details in an order that makes your description easy to follow. The student from the above example decided to use chronological order in describing her first car, starting when she first saw it.

1. Dent in driver's door

2. Pale "tomato soup" paint

3. Cracked upholstery inside

4. Inside smelled like 1. oil, 2. pine, and 3. stale cheese

5. The engine roared

Organize List the details you plan to include in an appropriate order. (See page 128 for help.)

_____

_____

_____

_____

LO7 Writing the First Draft

A first draft is a chance to get your thoughts down on paper without worrying about perfect grammar or spelling. Even your organization and details can be changed later, during revision.

Student Model

Read   Read and enjoy the following descriptive paragraph.

Tomato Can

Topic Sentence

It was a Saturday morning when my uncle Elijah took me   *1*
to buy my first car. He had discovered it on Craigslist. Outside, the car was depressing. Its red paint had faded to a dusty tomato soup color that came off on your fingers. The driver's side door was one big dent, and it rattled when I opened it.   *5*
Inside, the fake leather seats were cracked, and crumbly orange foam padding showed through. The interior stank of dirty motor oil and what smelled like old cheese, even through the stench of a new pine freshener the seller had hung on the rearview mirror. When my uncle said, "Start it up," I turned   *10*
the key to the roar of a broken exhaust. I shut it off and next

Body Sentences

tried the radio. The speakers buzzed like angry hornets. When Elijah said, "We'll take it," I almost felt like crying. I drove his car home, while he drove the junk heap to his house to work on. Later that night, he brought the "Tomato Can" back to my   *15*
house to switch vehicles. I couldn't believe it was the same car. He had used a restoring wax, and the paint was now a deep, shiny red. A new exhaust pipe made the engine purr. Polka dot seat covers hid the old upholstery, and new speakers were playing one of my favorite songs. The driver's door was still   *20*
one big dent, but it didn't rattle when I opened it. "I found a coat hanger inside," he said. I could still smell cheese, but that would fade with time. I had my first set of wheels.

Closing Sentence

Consider the Craft

1. What do you like best about this paragraph?

2. What are two of your favorite details?

3. How much time does the event cover?

4. Does the writer say just enough about the experience, too much, or too little?

Drafting Tips

When writing a descriptive paragraph, you are trying to capture the sights, sounds, and other details related to your topic. To do this, consider the following strategies.

In the opening sentence . . .

- Identify the topic to be described.
- Get your reader's interest.

In the middle sentences . . .

- Include specific sensory details.
- Use chronological order, order of location, or logical order to organize your details.

In the closing sentence . . .

- Sum up your own feelings about the subject (either directly or by suggestion).
- Or leave the reader with something to think about.

> **CONSIDER THE TRAITS** ——
>
> Voice is very important in descriptive writing. Choose words that show your own interest in the topic and are appropriate for the assignment.

The Working Parts of a Paragraph

As shown on the previous page, a paragraph has three main parts, each with its own purpose.

Topic Sentence: A topic sentence introduces your topic and gets your reader's interest.

Body Sentences: The sentences in the middle part describe the topic with sensory details.

Closing Sentence: A closing sentence (or two) often summarizes the topic. Or it may leave the reader with something to think about.

Write Prepare your first draft using the information above and your planning on pages 157–158 as a guide.

Daniel Ochoa IFOTOCHOA, 2013 / Used under license from Shutterstock.com

LO8 Revising the Writing

Start the revising process by reading your first draft two or three times to get a feel for your work so far. Then have one of your classmates react to your work.

Using Transitions

Transitions are words and phrases that link ideas in writing so that the reader can clearly follow your ideas. Transitional words and phrases that show time include *first, next, then, when, after that,* and so on. Transitions that indicate location include *above, below, at the bottom,* and so on. When describing, you may need to use both types of transitions.

Revising in Action

Read aloud the unrevised and then the revised version of the following passage. The revised version includes the transitions.

It was Saturday morning when my uncle Elijah took me to buy my first car. He had discovered it on Craigslist. *Outside,* The car was depressing. Its red paint had faded to a dusty tomato soup color that came off on your fingers. The driver's side door was one big dent, and it rattled when I opened it. *Inside,* The fake leather seats were cracked, and crumbly orange foam padding showed through. The interior stank of dirty motor oil. . . . *When* My uncle said, "Start it up," I turned the key to the roar of a broken exhaust. I shut it off and *next* tried the radio.

Revise Improve your writing, using the checklist below and your classmate's comments on the response sheet.

Using a Revising Checklist

Ideas

- ☐ 1. Do I focus on a specific topic to describe?
- ☐ 2. Do I include enough sensory details?

Organization

- ☐ 3. Have I included a topic sentence, body sentences, and a closing sentence?
- ☐ 4. Have I organized my details in the best way?
- ☐ 5. Do I use transitions to connect my ideas?

Voice

- ☐ 6. Do I sound interested and knowledgeable?

LO9 Editing the Writing

When you edit, you check your revised writing for the proper use of capitalization, punctuation, grammar, usage, and spelling. This should be one of the last things that you do during the writing process.

Basic Capitalization

Correct capitalization will be one of the most basic things to check for. In your description, there are essentially two basic capitalization rules that you will need to check for: (1) first words of sentences, and (2) proper nouns and adjectives. Proper nouns and adjectives are the specific names of people, places, things, and so on.

First Word in a Sentence

- The driver's door was one big dent, and it rattled when I opened it.
- Inside, the fake leather seats were cracked, . . .

First Word of a Direct Quotation *(what someone says)*

- When my uncle said, "**S**tart it up," I turned the key to the roar of a broken exhaust.

Proper Nouns and Adjectives

- It was a **S**aturday morning when my uncle **E**lijah took me to buy my first car.
- He had discovered it on **C**raigslist. *(the specific name of a Web site)*

Capitalization Practice   Read the sentences below. Correct any capitalization errors that you find. Use the information above as a guide. The first one is done for you.

1. I stood in the parking lot near the stadium where the New York mets play their spring training games.
2. all of a sudden david wright pulled up in his car.
3. I walked over to him with his card and said, "could you please sign this?"
4. without hesitation, he said, "no problem" and signed it for me.
5. A few minutes later, another player pulled up in a black corvette.
6. he was one of the coaches, and I wasn't interested in him.
7. Then I walked toward digital domain park, the team's spring stadium.
8. just to my right, I saw r. a. dickey, one of the mets' main pitchers.

Additional Practice: For additional practice, see pages 582–583.

Apply   Check your revised paragraph for capitalization using the information above as a guide.

Basic Punctuation

Be sure that you use proper end punctuation—periods, question marks, or exclamation points—at the end of your sentences. Also be sure that you use a comma in compound sentences. A compound sentence is two or more simple sentences connected by *and, but, or,* and so on.

End Punctuation

- Rock climbing is popular at Devils Lake State Park. *(statement)*
- Does rock climbing interest you? *(question)*
- Signs in the park say: Watch for snakes! *(exclamation mark)*

Practice Read the following passage, and add the correct end punctuation.

What does the future hold for our energy needs Will we rely mostly on wind power and solar power Some people feel biodegradable sources of energy like corn and seaweed have potential In the near future, we might discover even more exciting sources of energy In other words, the best may be yet to come

Commas in Compound Sentences

- Todd works out and runs all of the time, **but** I am woefully out of shape.
- He likes to keep active all of the time, **and** I enjoy sedentary, restful activities.

Punctuation Practice Read the sentences below. Insert commas as needed in any compound sentences.

1. The initial explosion from the bomb injured people and many cars and buildings were destroyed.
2. The explosion also created tremendous amounts of smoke, dust, and heat.
3. The smoke and dust immediately turned day into night but the darkness eventually gave way to light as many fires started.
4. Buildings near the center of the city went up in flames first and the surrounding structures caught fire from exposed wires and damaged gas lines.
5. People did what they could to escape the heat yet their efforts were futile.

Additional Practice: For additional practice, see pages 592–593.

Apply Check your revised writing for end punctuation and commas in compound sentences.

Marking a Paragraph

The model that follows has a number of errors.

Editing Practice   Correct the following paragraph, using the correction marks below. One correction has been done for you.

Easter Island Mystery

Unknown sculptors carved huge stone statues in an old volcano on
easter island. The statues were carved in a quarry within the crater of
an old volcano and they were somehow moved to their present locations
around the island. The sculptors worked with stone tools. It is not believed
that they had wood for lifting, ropes for pulling or wheels for moving. More
than 250 of these statues stand guard on the volcano's slopes, and 300
additional statues lie scattered around the island The statues is different
heights—the average being between 17 and 26 feet. The tallest towers
are 72 feet, and the shortest measures 10 feet. The statues are known for
there large, broad noses and jutting chins. they are thought to be modeled
after the faces of primitive Polynesians, emigrant peoples from peru, or
early Caucasian visitors. These works of art are on of the world's wonderful
mysteries

1

5

10

Correction Marks

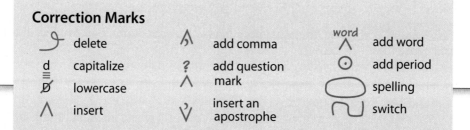

⌿ delete	⋏ add comma
d̲̲ capitalize	? add question mark
D̸ lowercase	⋏
⋀ insert	⋁ insert an apostrophe

word
⋀ add word
⊙ add period
⎌ spelling
↻ switch

Using an Editing Checklist

With your paragraph revised, it is now time to edit it for correctness.

Edit   Prepare a clean copy of your paragraph and use the following checklist to look for errors. Continue working until you can check off each item in the list.

Words

☐ **1.** Have I used the right word *(their, they're, there)*?

☐ **2.** Have I used more action verbs than "be" verbs? (See page 536.)

Sentences

☐ **3.** Have I varied the beginnings and lengths of sentences? (See pages 136–137.)

☐ **4.** Have I avoided fragments and run-ons? (See pages 488–491, 494–495.)

Conventions

☐ **5.** Do I use correct verb forms *(he saw,* not *he seen)*? (See pages 542, 544.)

☐ **6.** Do my subjects and verbs agree *(she speaks,* not *she speak)*? (See pages 472–481.)

☐ **7.** Have I capitalized first words and proper nouns and adjectives? (See page 582.)

☐ **8.** Have I checked for end punctuation? (See page 163.)

☐ **9.** Have I used commas in compound sentences? (See page 592.)

☐ **10.** Have I carefully checked my spelling?

Adding a Title

A title should grab a reader's attention and generate curiosity about the paragraph. To make an attention-grabbing title, you can use one of these strategies.

- Use an interesting phrase or idea from the paragraph.

  Easter Island Mystery

- Use repetition of similar vowel sounds.

  Island Art

- Capture the main idea of the paragraph.

  Primitive Stone Art

Create   Invent an attention-grabbing title for your own descriptive paragraph.

Enrichment: Reading

On the following three pages, you will find the descriptive essay "Hispanic USA: The Conveyor-Belt Ladies" to read and respond to. As you read this essay, use the steps in the reading process as your guide. Your reading activities are followed by a number of writing ideas to choose from to write a descriptive paragraph or essay of your own.

> "Description is what makes the reader a sensory participant in the story."
> —Stephen King

About the Author

Rose Del Castillo Guilbault is a columnist on Hispanic issues, an associate editor at Pacific News Service, and the editorial director of the ABC-afflliate station KGO-TV in San Francisco.

Prereading

The way an author describes something can reveal as much about him- or herself as it does about the topic itself. The details included, and the order they are presented, are decisions that say something about the author. No two people will describe the same topic in quite the same way.

This is part of the fun of reading and writing descriptions. In reading, you get a chance to learn about a topic but also to meet the author. In writing, you are able to describe topics on your own terms and share a little bit of yourself in the process. Name an experience that you could describe that would reveal something about you and the topic.

CONSIDER THE TRAITS

As you read this selection, consider first the **ideas**—the explanations, descriptions, and dialogue that move the essay along. Also consider the author's **voice,** or tone. Does Guilbault speak personally to the reader, or does she sound more formal and distant?

_____

_____

_____

What do you think?

Consider the quotation above. Why do details increase the impact or value of a piece of writing?

Identify   Before you begin your reading, answer the following questions.

1. What do the title and the first few paragraphs tell you about the text?

   _____

2. What might be the author's purpose for this essay?

   _____

3. What do you expect to learn?

   _____

Reading and Rereading

Read the following essay by Rose Del Castillo Guilbault. As you will see, the author addresses a theme that may be familiar to you, working at an unappealing job to pay for college. She also shares revealing details about her special coworkers, primarily migrant mothers.

As you read, make it your goal to (1) identify the main idea, (2) pay careful attention to the descriptive details and dialogue, and (3) think about the different levels of meaning in the text. Consider annotating the text (page 20) during your reading.

Hispanic USA: The Conveyor-Belt Ladies

The conveyor-belt ladies were the migrant women, mostly from Texas, I worked with during the summers of my teenage years. I call them conveyor-belt ladies because our entire relationship took place while sorting tomatoes on a conveyor belt.   *1*

We were like a cast in a play where all the action occurs on one set. We'd return day after day to perform the same roles, only this stage was a vegetable-packing shed, and at the end of the season there was no applause. The players could look forward only to the same uninspiring parts on a string of grim real-life stages.   *5*

The women and their families arrived in May for the carrot season, spent the summer in the tomato sheds, and stayed through October for the bean harvest. After that, they emptied the town, some returning to their homes in Texas (cities like McAllen, Douglas, Brownsville), while others continued on the migrant trail, picking cotton in the San Joaquin Valley or grapefruits and oranges in the Imperial Valley.   *10*   *15*

Most of these women had started in the fields. The vegetable-packing sheds were a step up, easier than the back-breaking, grueling work the field demanded. The work was more tedious than strenuous, paid better, and provided fairly steady hours and clean bathrooms. Best of all, you weren't subjected to the elements.   *20*

The summer I was 16, my mother got jobs for both of us as tomato sorters. That's how I came to be included in the seasonal sorority of the conveyor belt.

The work consisted of standing and picking flawed tomatoes off the conveyor belt before they rolled off into the shipping boxes at the end of the line. These boxes were immediately loaded onto waiting delivery trucks, so it was crucial not to let imperfect tomatoes through.   25

The work could be slow or intense, depending on the quality of the tomatoes and how many there were. Work increased when the company's deliveries got backlogged or after rainy weather had delayed picking.   30

During those times, it was not unusual to work from 7 A.M. to midnight, playing catch-up. I never heard anyone complain about the overtime. Overtime meant desperately needed extra money.

I was not happy to be part of the agricultural work force. I would have preferred working in a dress shop or baby-sitting, like my friends. But I   35 had a dream that would cost a lot of money—college. And the fact was, this was the highest-paying work I could do.

But it wasn't so much the work that bothered me. I was embarrassed because only Mexicans worked at packing sheds. I had heard my schoolmates joke about the "ugly, fat Mexican women" at the sheds. They   40 ridiculed the way they dressed and laughed at the "funny way" they talked. I feared working with them would **irrevocably stigmatize** me, setting me further apart from my Anglo classmates.

At 16 I was more American than Mexican and, with adolescent arrogance, felt superior to these "uneducated" women. I might be one of   45 them, I reasoned, but I was not like them.

But it was difficult not to like the women. They were a gregarious, entertaining group, easing the long, monotonous hours with bawdy humor, spicy gossip, and inventive laments. They poked fun at all the male workers and did hysterical impersonations of a **dyspeptic** Anglo supervisor.   50 Although he didn't speak Spanish (other than "Mujeres, trabajo, trabajo!" Women, work, work!), he seemed to sense he was being laughed at. That would account for the sudden rages when he would stamp his foot and forbid us to talk until break time.

"I bet he understands Spanish and just pretends so he can hear what   55 we say," I whispered to Rosa. . . .

We were often shifted around, another strategy to keep us quiet. This gave me ample opportunity to get to know everyone, listen to their life stories, and absorb the gossip.

Pretty Rosa described her romances and her impending wedding to   60 a handsome field worker. Bertha, a heavy-set, dark-skinned woman, told me that Rosa's marriage would cause nothing but headaches because the man was younger and too handsome. Maria, large, moon-faced, and placid, described the births of each of her nine children, warning me about the horrors of childbirth. Pragmatic Minnie, a tiny woman who always wore   65 printed cotton dresses, scoffed at Maria's stupidity, telling me she wouldn't have so many kids if she had ignored that good-for-nothing priest and gotten her tubes tied . . . !

My mother, no stranger to suffering, suggested I was too impressionable when I emotionally told her the women's stories. "That's nothing," she'd say lightly. "If they were in Mexico, life would be even harder. At least there's opportunities here, you can work."

My icy arrogance quickly thawed, that first summer, as my respect for the conveyor-belt ladies grew.

I worked in the packing sheds for several summers. The last season also turned out to be the last time I lived at home. It was the end of a chapter in my life, but I didn't know it then. I had just finished junior college and was transferring to the university. I was already over-educated for seasonal work, but if you counted the overtime, no other jobs came close to paying so well, so I went back one last time.

The ladies treated me with warmth and respect. I was a college student, deserving of special treatment.

Aguedita, the crew chief, moved me to softer and better-paying jobs within the plant. I went from the conveyor belt to shoving boxes down a chute and finally to weighing boxes of tomatoes on a scale—the highest-paying position for a woman.

When the union's dues collector showed up, the women hid me in the bathroom. They had decided it was unfair for me to have to join the union and pay dues, since I worked only during the summer.

"Where's the student?" the union rep would ask, opening the door to a barrage of complaints about the union's unfairness.

Maria (of the nine children) tried to feed me all summer, bringing extra tortillas, which were delicious. I accepted them guiltily, always wondering if I was taking food away from her children. Others would bring rental contracts or other documents for me to explain and translate.

The last day of work was splendidly beautiful, warm and sunny. If this had been a movie, these last scenes would have been shot in soft focus, with a crescendo of music in the background,

But real life is anti-climatic. As it was, nothing unusual happened. The conveyor belt's loud humming was turned off, silenced for the season. The women sighed as they removed their aprons. Some of them just walked off, called "Hasta la proxima!" Until next time!

But most of the conveyor-belt lades shook my hand, gave me a blessing or a big hug.

"Make us proud!" they said.

I hope I have.

Rose Del Castillo Guilbault, *San Francisco Chronicle*, April 15, 1990

irrevocably
being impossible to take back or retract

stigmatize
to identify or describe in negative terms

dyspeptic
bad-tempered

Reflecting

After your reading, answer the following questions. Then share your responses with your classmates.

1. What main idea is developed in the essay? (Or is there more than one main idea?)

   _____

   _____

   _____

2. What descriptions seem the most important? Identify two.

   _____

   _____

   _____

3. What is one exchange or dialogue that seemed important to you?

   _____

   _____

   _____

4. What is the main method of organization employed in this essay— chronological, spatial, or logical?

   _____

5. Has the text changed or expanded your understanding of the topic? If so, how?

   _____

   _____

   _____

6. How would you rate this reading, and why?
   Weak ★ ★ ★ ★ ★ Strong

   _____

   _____

Vocabulary Practice

Identify Use context clues to explain or define the following words. (See pages 33–34 for help.)

1. **grueling** (line 17)

   clues: _____

   definition: _____

2. **flawed** (line 24)

   clues: _____

   definition: _____

3. **arrogance** (line 45)

   clues: _____

   definition: _____

4. **gregarious** (line 47)

   clues: _____

   definition: _____

5. **impressionable** (line 70)

   clues: _____

   definition: _____

Drawing Inferences

Explain Answer the following questions to help you draw inferences from the reading. (See pages 29–31 for help.)

1. Why do you think the writer shared this experience?

   _____

   _____

2. How was the writer alike and/or different from the other women?

   _____

   _____

Writing

What follows are possible writing activities to complete in response to the reading. Use the writing process (pages 94-99) to help you develop your writing.

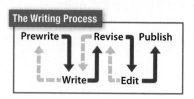

Prewriting

Choose one of the following writing ideas. Or decide upon another idea related to the reading.

Writing Ideas

1. **Writing to Learn:** Develop a letter or email message to someone whom you once worked with. Share your thoughts about the person, discuss pleasant and not-so pleasant memories, reflect on the value of the experience, and so on. (Whether you send the message is up to you.)

2. **Paragraph Writing:** Write a descriptive paragraph about one of the topics you identified on page 157.

3. Or describe in detail your best work experience or your worst work experience.

4. **Essay Writing:** In a descriptive essay, share an important experience or time in your life.

5. In an expository essay, share information about one important aspect of migrant work.

When planning . . .

Refer to pages 157–158 to help with your prewriting and planning. Also use the tips below.

- Choose a topic you care deeply about. Writing about something you find interesting is always easiest.
- Gather as many sensory details as possible.
- From those details, select the ones that will most effectively capture the subject.
- Choose a pattern of organization that immediately draws your readers in and carries them along to the end.
- When revising, make sure your tone is appropriate for the topic. For example, your tone should sound exciting if the topic is exciting and sound serious if the topic is serious.

Writing and Revising

Refer to pages 159–161 to help you write and revise your first draft. Also use the tips below to help with your drafting and revising.

When writing . . .

- Include an effective beginning, middle, and ending in your descriptive piece. Each part has its own role to play. (See page 160.)
- Write your first draft freely, allowing yourself to be immersed in the experience again.
- Add new ideas as they come to mind during your writing, but only if they seem important to include.

When revising . . .

- Let your first draft sit unread for a while. Then read it carefully, with fresh eyes. Reading a printed copy can help you see it differently.
- Consider where sensory details seem missing, and fill them in.
- Also consider where sensory details seem unnecessary or slow the reading, and cut them.
- Make sure your chosen organization works well and helps your reader follow your ideas.
- Ask a classmate or another writer to review and critique your writing. Use a Peer Review Sheet to guide the critique. (See page 622.)

Editing

Refer to the checklist on page 162 when you are ready to edit your descriptive writing for style and correctness.

Reflecting on Description Writing

Answer the following questions about your descriptive reading and writing experience in this chapter.

1. Why is description so common in essays and articles?

   _____

2. What is your favorite descriptive writing in this chapter? Why?

   _____

3. What reading strategy in this chapter do you find most helpful? Explain.

   _____

4. What is the most important thing you learned about reading a descriptive paragraph or essay?

   _____

5. What do you like most about the descriptive piece you wrote for this chapter? Why?

   _____

6. What is one thing you would like to change in your writing?

   _____

7. What is the most important thing you have learned about writing descriptive paragraphs and essays?

   _____

- **Sensory details**—the sights, sounds, smells, tastes, and touch sensations of a descriptive subject.
- **Chronological order**—details arranged by time of occurrence.
- **Spatial order**—details arranged by their location in a setting.
- **Logical order**—details arranged from most important to least, or from least important to most.

7

Narration

"We write to taste life twice, in the moment, and in retrospection."
—Anaïs Nin

Early on, you may have been lucky enough to have had someone read you bedtime stories. If so, then you know "in your bones" the elements of a good story. Storytellers hold a young child's interest by building drama and suspense. At least, this is the opinion of William Zinsser, who has skillfully written about the craft of writing in his famous book *On Writing Well*.

This chapter deals with narrative writing, the sharing of personal stories. To narrate is "to give an account of an event." First you will learn about the importance and popularity of the narrative form. Then you will read and react to two professional narratives before developing one of your own. And along the way, you will experience the power of storytelling.

Learning Outcomes

LO1 Understand narration.

LO2 Learn reading strategies (use a time line and the 5 W's and H).

LO3 Read and react to a professional paragraph.

LO4 Read and react to a professional narration.

LO5 Practice reading skills (find and analyze showing details).

LO6 Plan a narrative.

LO7 Write the first draft.

LO8 Revise the writing.

LO9 Edit the writing.

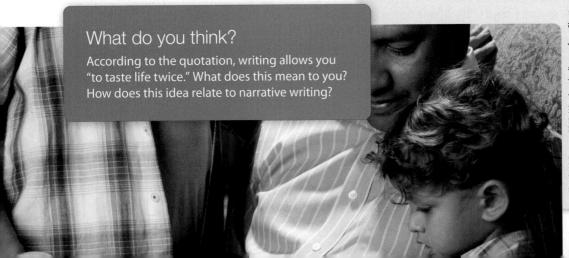

Glenda M. Powers, 2013 / Used under license from Shutterstock.com

What do you think?

According to the quotation, writing allows you "to taste life twice." What does this mean to you? How does this idea relate to narrative writing?

LO1 Understanding Narration

American author William Faulkner said, "The past is never dead; it's not even past." If you think about your own life, you can understand this idea. You hold many memories about growing up and reaching adulthood, so your past is in no way dead. Neither is it over, because your experiences continue to help shape who you are and what you will become.

Importance of the Past

If you were to review the autobiography section in a local bookstore, you would see how important the past is to writers. Their past experiences are in their bones, and they need to write about them. And the popularity of these books shows that readers are definitely interested in the lives of others, from the rich and famous to ordinary people much like you and your classmates.

> "Story is everything. All writing of whatever kind begins with narrative."
> —John Rouse

Writing about their past experiences helps writers make sense of life, the world, and their place in it. Their personal writing says, "For better or worse, here's what I've experienced and how I feel about it. I'd like to share my story with you." Autobiographies share interesting details about the writer's life and reveal important truths about life in general.

Autobiography Versus Personal Narrative

An autobiography shares the story of a writer's life; a personal narrative focuses on one specific event or experience. In a sense, an autobiography is a collection of personal narratives, because it covers key events in the writer's life. A single narrative highlights a memorable moment or a life-changing event.

Insight

What motivates an autobiographical writer? Just about anything, including successes, setbacks, self-discovery, pride, and recovery.

Identify Suppose you were assigned to read or watch an autobiography about one of the following individuals. Circle the one you would pick; then explain your choice. (A quick check online will identify any of these people.)

Michelle Obama   Spike Lee

Mark Zuckerberg   Oprah Winfrey

Beyoncé   Michael Moore

Mariano Rivera

_____

_____

_____

_____

Reading

Reading narratives can be an extremely enjoyable experience. After all, who doesn't enjoy a good story? You can also learn a lot about life from narratives.

LO2 Learning Reading Strategies

These two strategies—using a time line and answering the 5 W's and H—will help you read narrative texts.

Using a Time Line

When reading a narrative, it's important that you follow the key actions in the order they occur. A graphic organizer called a time line works well for this purpose. With this type of organizer, you list the main actions of a story chronologically, or by time.

Time Line	
1.	(Key actions in order)
2.	
3.	
4.	
5.	

Answering the 5 W's and H

In one way, you can simply enjoy a narrative that holds your interest from beginning to end as a good story. But to understand a narrative, you need to identify the key actions. To do this, you can answer the 5 W's and H about the story. (This is a strategy used by reporters when they gather details for a news story.)

5W's and H

Who was involved in the experience?

What happened?

When did it happen?

Where did it happen?

Why did it happen?

How did it happen?

Tip
Sometimes you will not find answers to all of these questions, but stories usually reveal most of the 5 W's and H details.

Evangelos, 2013 / Used under license from Shutterstock.com

LO3 Reading and Reacting to a Professional Paragraph

In the following narrative the author shares a once-in-a-lifetime moment. Most of the before and all of the after details are left to the reader's imagination.

Prereading   Before you read, answer these three questions:

1. What do the title and first sentence or two tell you about the text?

_____

2. What might be the author's purpose?

_____

3. What questions would you like answered? (Name one or two.)

_____

Reading and Rereading   As you read, make it your goal to (1) identify the topic and main idea, (2) locate the supporting details, and (3) study the ending. Consider answering the 5 W's and H about the story during this step. (See the previous page.)

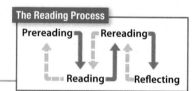

The Reading Process

Prereading   Rereading

Reading   Reflecting

The Earth Below Us

Some 9,000 feet off the ground, I peered down at the clouds below me   *1*
and realized I had reached a point of no return. I was about to jump out of
an airplane. Earlier that day, when I asked my brother about his first time
skydiving, he singled out this moment as his most frightening. "Dude, I'm
telling you—I almost blacked out," he offered, only half-jokingly. Those   *5*
words were embedded in my mind as my tandem partner, Dale, tightened
the harness that held us together and guided us to the open exit door. With
half of my body dangling outside of the plane, I reached out and gripped
a support bar under the right wing. I had to tighten my grip to fight the
wind, which pushed with the force of a charging linebacker. Below me   *10*
I could see perfectly square plots of farmland in between breaks in the
clouds, and I almost missed Dale's final instructions over the buzz of the
Cessna's twin engines. "When you are ready, cross your arms over your
chest, and we'll jump," he yelled. Surprisingly, I didn't black out. I was
ready. So I crossed my arms, and we jumped.   *15*

Reflecting   After you read, answer these questions. Share your responses with your classmates.

   1. What is the main idea?

   _____

   2. What two supporting details stand out to you?

   _____

   3. What have you learned in this reading?

   _____

   4. How would you rate this paragraph, and why?

   Weak ★ ★ ★ ★ ★ **Strong**

   _____

Vocabulary Practice

Identify   Use context clues to explain or define the following words. (See pages 33–34 for help.)

   1. peered (line 1)

   clues: _____

   definition_____

   2. embedded (line 6)

   clues: _____

   definition_____

Drawing Inferences

Identify   Answer the following questions to help you draw inferences from the reading. (See pages 29–31 for help.)

   1. Why did the writer remember so many details about this particular moment?

   _____

   2. Why did he choose to end the narration as he did?

   _____

LO4 Reading and Reacting to a Professional Narration

This narrative focuses on a tragic experience—the murder of the writer's brother. The writer most assuredly relives the experience over and over again in his mind.

About the Author

After receiving a PhD from the University of Chicago, Brent Staples worked as an adjunct professor of psychology at colleges in Pennsylvania and Chicago, then as a reporter for the *Chicago Sun-Times,* and most recently as an editorial writer for the *New York Times.*

Prereading Before you read, answer these three questions:

1. What do the title and first sentence of the paragraphs tell you about the text?

_____

2. What might be the author's purpose?

_____

3. What main question do you expect to be answered about the topic?

_____

Reading and Rereading As you read, make it your goal to (1) identify the topic and main idea, (2) find the key supporting details, and (3) study the final sentences. Consider annotating the text (page 20) during your reading.

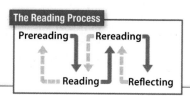

A Brother's Murder

   It has been more than two years since my telephone rang with the   *1*
news that my younger brother Blake—just 22 years old—had been
murdered. The young man who killed him was only 24. Wearing a ski
mask, he emerged from a car, fired six times at close range with a massive
.44 Magnum, then fled. The two had once been inseparable friends. A   *5*
senseless **rivalry**—beginning, I think, with an argument over a girlfriend—
escalated from posturing, to threats, to violence, to murder. . . .
   As I wept for Blake, I felt wrenched backward into events and
circumstances that had seemed **light-years** gone. Though a decade apart,
we both were raised in Chester, Pennsylvania, an angry, heavily black,   *10*
heavily poor, industrial city southwest of Philadelphia. There, in the 1960s,

I was introduced to mortality, not by the old and failing, but by beautiful young men who lay wrecked after sudden explosions of violence. . . .

As I fled the past, so Blake embraced it. On Christmas of 1983, I traveled from Chicago to a black section of Roanoke, Virginia, where he then lived. . . . One evening . . . standing in some Roanoke dive among drug dealers and grim, hair-trigger losers, I told him I feared for his life. He had **affected** the image of the tough he wanted to be. But behind the dark glasses and the swagger, I glimpsed the baby-faced toddler I'd once watched over. I nearly wept. I wanted desperately for him to live. The young think themselves immortal, and a dangerous light shone in his eyes as he spoke laughingly of making fools of the policemen who had raided his apartment looking for drugs. He cried out as I took his right hand. A line of stitches lay between the thumb and index finger. Kickback from a shotgun, he explained, nothing serious. Gunplay had become part of his life.

I lacked the language simply to say: Thousands have lived this for you and died. I fought the urge to lift him bodily and shake him. This place and the way you are living smells of death to me, I said. Take some time away, I said. Let's go downtown tomorrow and buy a plane ticket anywhere, take a bus trip, anything to get away and cool things off.

He took my alarm casually. We arranged to meet the following night—an appointment he would not keep. . . .

As I stood in my apartment in Chicago holding the receiver . . . I felt as though part of my soul had been cut away. I questioned myself then, and I still do.

Did I not reach back soon or **earnestly** enough for him? For weeks I awoke crying from a recurrent dream in which I chased him, urgently trying to get him to read a document I had, as though reading it would protect him from what had happened in his waking life.

His eyes shining like black diamonds, he smiled and danced just beyond my grasp. When I reached for him, I caught only the space where he had been.

rivalry
the condition of competing

light-years
an extremely large measure of time

affected
adopted or pretended

earnestly
seriously or with deep feeling

Reflecting   Answer the following questions about the selection. Then discuss your answers with your classmates.

1. What is the topic of this selection?

   _____

2. Circle the types of details the author uses—sensory details, dialogue, personal thoughts and feelings?

3. How does the author open the narrative? How does he close it?

   _____

4. How would you rate this narrative, and why?

   Weak ★ ★ ★ ★ ★ Strong

   _____

Vocabulary Practice

Identify   Define the word parts as indicated. Then try to explain the meaning of the complete word. (See pages 35–36 and 623–631 for help.)

1. **mortality** (line 12) mort + al + ity

   _____

   _____

2. **recurrent** (line 37) re + cur(r) + ent

   _____

   _____

Drawing Inferences

Explain   Answer these questions to help you draw inferences about the text. (See pages 29–31 for help.)

1. What is meant in lines 26–27: "Thousands have lived this for you and died"?

   _____

2. What conclusions about the narrator can you draw from this narrative?

   _____

LO5 Practicing Reading Skills

Most often, a writer will mix telling and showing details in a narrative. Telling involves reporting what happened; showing involves re-creating the experience. Showing details in narratives are far more interesting to read. Writers use the following techniques to show what happens in their narratives.

Showing Details

- **Sensory details** share sights, sounds, smells, tastes, and textures.
  The smell of old cigarettes and expired perfume turns my stomach.
  The weight of my backpack thrusts me forward in the rush-hour crowd.
- **Dialogue shares** the conversation between people.
  "So where are you from?" I asked.
  "Sudbury. My boyfriend is in jail, and they're letting him go today."
- **Personal thoughts and feelings** reveal the writer's state of mind.
  I have no idea how to talk to this woman, but she seems to like me.

Select Identify two or three showing details from the paragraph on page 178 that you especially like.

1. _____

2. _____

3. _____

Analyzing the Details

Explain Carefully review the narrative on pages 180–181 for the types of details used: sensory details, dialogue, and personal thoughts. As you will see, the writer's personal thoughts dominate the text. Identify two or three of these thoughts and explain what they tell you about the writer.

_____

_____

_____

_____

_____

Writing

Starting on this page, you will plan and write a narrative paragraph about a special moment in your life. Be sure to use the writing process to help you do your best work. (See pages 94–99.)

The Writing Process

Prewrite — Revise — Publish
Write — Edit

LO6 Planning a Narrative

Remember that special moments are different for different people. Not everyone has bumped into a famous person, won the lottery, or survived a tsunami.

Selecting a Topic

Below, a writer listed four experiences that he clearly remembers. He decided to write about his backpacking trip with his brother.

> the first day on my first job
>
> my grandfather's funeral
>
> my high school track championship
>
> ✓ my backpacking trip

"I've never tried to block out the memories of the past, even though some are painful. . . . Everything you live through helps to make you the person you are now."
—Sophia Loren

Select List four important memories from your life. Then put a check next to one memory you would like to write about in a personal narrative paragraph.

Using Chronological Order

Once you have selected a topic, think carefully about the order of events as you remember them. In most cases, narrative paragraphs are arranged chronologically (by time).

Identify Use a time line like the one to the right to list the main events of your experience in time order.

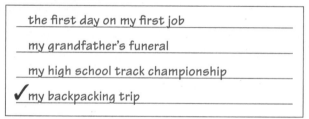

Time Line

1.	pedaling with brother on a mountain trail
2.	lose track of brother because of fog
3.	fog lifts and stop to rest on a ridge
4.	I and my brother share feelings

Gathering Sensory Details

The most vivid narrative paragraphs use plenty of sensory details. Such details allow the reader to picture, hear, and touch what you describe. You can use a sensory chart to list specific sensory details about an experience.

Sensory Chart

Sights	Sounds	Smells	Tastes	Feelings/Textures
-forests of evergreens -dirt path -mountain ranges -thick fog	-talk with brother -birds chirping -crunching leaves	-fresh air -smell of rain	-peanut butter granola bar	-achy thighs -burning lungs

INSIGHT

To gather the best details, try talking about the experience with someone or writing freely and rapidly about it.

Kayros Studio "Be Happy!", 2013 / Used under license from Shutterstock.com

Collect Complete a sensory chart like the one below. Collect any sights, sounds, smells, tastes, feelings, or textures that you may want to include in your narrative. (Not all senses will necessarily pertain to your experience.)

Sights	Sounds	Smells	Tastes	Feelings/Textures

LO7 Writing the First Draft

Writing a first draft is your first attempt to connect the thoughts you have gathered about your topic. Don't try to make everything perfect. Instead, simply get all of your ideas on paper.

Read Carefully read and enjoy this writer's paragraph about a special time in his life.

A Rugged Ride

Topic Sentence

   As I rode up the mountain trail, my thighs ached and my   1
lungs burned, but I couldn't be happier. Fifty feet in front of me
pedaled my brother, Keith, fresh off his tour with the Marines.
This mountain biking adventure was his idea. The green,
forest-lined trail was rugged, with sharp turns and steep   5
descents. At one point we hit a patch of fog, and I lost sight of
Keith. It felt as if we were riding through clouds. The ghostly

Body Sentences

air was damp and smelled like rain. I slowed down and called
for my brother, "Are you still up there?" "Would I be anywhere
else?" he yelled back. When the fog disappeared, we stopped   10
for a breather on a ridge that overlooked a vast valley. A sea
of pointy evergreens stretched for miles, ending near the peak
of a distant mountain. While I snacked on a peanut butter
granola bar, Keith glanced over at me and said, "This is fun,

Closing Sentence

isn't it?" "It's good having you back, man," I responded. With   15
that, we hopped on our bikes and continued our adventure.

Consider the Craft

1. What do you like best about this paragraph?

2. What are two of your favorite details?

3. How much time does the event cover?

4. Does the writer say just enough about the experience, too much, or too little?

Drafting Tips

When you write a narrative paragraph, you are essentially sharing a story. Consider these storytelling techniques to interest your readers.

READING-WRITING CONNECTION

Review the model narratives in this chapter for approaches or techniques that may help you with your writing.

- **To make your beginning special,** start right in the middle of the action (rather than starting with a more traditional topic sentence).
- **To keep your reader in suspense,** leave out certain details that give the ending away. Instead, offer clues about what might happen, or give false clues so that the real outcome is truly a surprise. Make a mystery out of your personal story.
- **To give your story impact,** include dialogue, but be selective. Make sure the conversation enhances or adds to the story.
- **To bring your writing to an effective end,** look around you. Cars screech to a halt. A jet trail eventually drifts away. Bathtubs swirl for a while, then gurgle. What will your ending do?

INSIGHT

How you develop your story depends on what you want it to do—inform, entertain, amuse, surprise, or shock.

The Working Parts of a Paragraph

A paragraph consists of three main parts, and each has a special function. The information that follows explains each part.

Topic Sentence:	A topic sentence sets the stage for the paragraph. It identifies your topic and puts it in perspective in an interesting way.
Body Sentences:	The body sentences support the topic sentence. Specific details are included to make each main point clear to the reader.
Closing Sentence:	A closing sentence (or two) captures the importance of the experience.

Write Develop your first draft using the information on this page and your planning on pages 184–185 as a guide.

Punctuation Used with Quotation Marks

As you edit your narrative paragraph, pay special attention to the punctuation marks used with quotation marks. Here are three rules to follow:

- When periods or commas follow the quotation, place them before the closing quotation mark.

  "Never be afraid to ask for help," advised Mr. Lee.

  "With the evidence we now have," Professor Howard said, "many scientists believe there could be life on Mars."

- When question marks or exclamation points follow the quotation, place them before the closing quotation mark if they belong with the quoted words. Otherwise, place them after the quotation mark.

  "Bill, do you want to go to the gym with me?" I asked.

  Were you telling the truth when you said, "Let's go home"?

- When semicolons or colons follow the quotation, place them after the quotation mark.

  He said, "Absolutely not"; however, he relented and left work early.

Punctuation Practice   In each sentence, correct the misplaced punctuation marks. (Use the transpose sign ∩∪ .) Refer to the rules above for help.

1. "Please hand your papers in by the end of the week", advised Professor Hopkins.

2. Mark said, "See you soon;" however, he missed his flight.

3. "With everything that happened", my boss said, "it might be best to take Friday off."

4. "Don't be late"! exclaimed Lisa.

5. "Should we meet tomorrow"? asked Renee.

6. Did you really mean it when you said, "We are just looking?"

7. "Remember, you have a doctor's appointment on Thursday", my mom reminded me.

8. "Can you pass me the ketchup"? I asked.

Additional Practice: For more practice see pages 602–603.

Apply   Read your narrative paragraph. Check the punctuation of dialogue closely.

Marking a Paragraph

The model that follows has a number of errors.

Editing Practice Correct the following paragraph, using the correction marks below.

Creature of Habit?

People say I'm a creature of habit but that's not entirely true. For   *1*
instance I like try new foods. When I was in New hampshire, I ate raw
oysters. People say they taste like the ocean Indeed they are very salty.
I do enjoy the thrill of a new food, oysters will not become a staple of my
diet. Besides eating bizarre foods, I also enjoy going on weeknd adventures.   *5*
Last saturday, my friends and I went camping outside the city. We
didn't even set up tents, deciding to sleep under the stars. Unfortunately
the rising sun woke us up at about 6:00 a.m. I got only about for hours of
sleep, so I tired and crabby for the rest of the day. I guess that's won way I
am a creature of habit. I like my sleep. Another unusual activity I enjoy is   *10*
Pilates. For some reason my friends think this makes me a wimp but I bet
they couldn't make it threw one class. I would love to see them try

---

Correction Marks

⊱ delete	⩓ add comma	*word* ∧ add word
d̲ capitalize	? add question	⊙ add period
∅̲ lowercase	∧ mark	⬭ spelling
∧ insert	⌄ insert an apostrophe	⎍ switch

INSIGHT

You have seen how quotation marks are used before and after direct quotations. Quotation marks are also used around special words: (1) to show that a word is being discussed as a word, (2) to indicate that a word is slang, or (3) to point out that a word is being used in a humorous or ironic way.

(1) In our society, the word **"honesty"** is often preceded by the modifier **"old-fashioned."**

(2) You are wearing an **"old-school"** style of jeans.

(3) In an attempt to be popular, he works very hard at being **"cute."**

Additional Practice: For more practice see pages 602–603.

Using an Editing Checklist

Now it's time to correct your own paragraph.

Edit Create a clean copy of your revised writing, and use the following list to check for errors. Continue working until you can check off each item in the list.

Words

☐ **1.** Have I used specific nouns and verbs? (See page 134.)

☐ **2.** Have I used more action verbs than "be" verbs? (See page 536.)

Sentences

☐ **3.** Have I varied the beginnings and lengths of my sentences? (See pages 136–137.)

☐ **4.** Have I combined short, choppy sentences? (See page 137.)

☐ **5.** Have I avoided shifts in sentences? (See page 500.)

☐ **6.** Have I avoided fragments and run-ons? (See pages 136, 488–491, 494–495.)

Conventions

☐ **7.** Do I use correct verb forms (*he saw,* not *he seen*)? (See pages 542, 544.)

☐ **8.** Do my subjects and verbs agree (*she speaks,* not *she speak*)? (See pages 472–481.)

☐ **9.** Have I used the right words (*their, there, they're*)?

☐ **10.** Have I capitalized first words and proper nouns and adjectives? (See page 582.)

☐ **11.** Have I punctuated dialogue correctly? (See pages 189–190.)

☐ **12.** Have I carefully checked my spelling?

Adding a Title

Make sure to add an attention-getting title. Here are three simple strategies for creating one.

- Use a phrase from the paragraph:

  Creature of Habit?

- Use a main idea from the paragraph:

  Taking a Bow

- Use strong, colorful words from the paragraph:

  A Rugged Ride

Create Prepare a clean final copy of your paragraph, and proofread it before you share it.

Enrichment: Reading

On the following two pages, you will find the extended narrative "The Key to Language" to read and respond to. As you read this narrative, use the steps in the reading process as your guide. Your reading activities are followed by a number of writing ideas to choose from to write a narrative of your own.

> "The universe is made of stories, not of atoms."
> —Muriel Rukeyser

About the Author

Helen Keller lost her sight and hearing at the age of 18 months. With the help of Anne Sullivan, she gained the ability to communicate and eventually earned a college degree in 1904. Keller became a leading social activist and humanitarian. Her autobiography, *The Story of My Life,* was turned into the 1977 television drama *The Miracle Worker.* (The Internet has a wealth of information about Helen Keller, including video of her early life.)

Prereading

Many of your most memorable experiences involve home life and family. You may have had a life-changing experience as a kid, or you may have become reacquainted with a family member after many years. Think of experiences involving your home life and family that have influenced you in a significant way. List a few of them below.

CONSIDER THE TRAITS

As you read the narrative that follows, focus on the **ideas**—the main idea and supporting details and dialogue in the story. Also pay attention to the **organization**, especially the way that the narrative begins (right in the middle of the action).

_____

_____

_____

_____

What do you think?

Consider the quotation above: What does it say about the importance of stories in the life of the author of the quotation? Why do you think she feels this way?

Identify   Before you begin your reading, answer these questions:

1. What do the title and first sentences in the opening paragraphs tell you about the text?

_____

2. Who is Keller's intended audience?

_____

3. What do you expect to learn?

_____

Reading and Rereading

Read the following narrative, which is included in *The Story of My Life* by Helen Keller. As you will see, the author shares an incredible, life-changing experience that reveals the power of something that most of us take for granted: language.

As you read, make it your goal to (1) carefully follow the story line, (2) appreciate the descriptions and dialogue, and (3) consider any questions that the story brings to mind. Consider annotating the text (page 20) during your reading.

The Key to Language

We walked down the path to the well-house, attracted by the fragrance of   *1*
the honeysuckle with which it was covered. Someone was drawing water, and
my teacher placed my hand under the spout. As the cool stream gushed over one
hand, she spelled into the other the word "water," first slowly, then rapidly. I stood
still, my whole attention fixed upon the motions of her fingers. Suddenly I felt a   *5*
misty consciousness, as of something forgotten—a thrill of returning thought;
and somehow the mystery of language was revealed to me. I knew then that
"w-a-t-e-r" meant the wonderful cool something that was flowing over my hand.
That living word awakened my soul, gave it light, hope, joy, set it free. There were
barriers still, it is true, but barriers that could, in time, be swept away.   *10*

I left the well-hose eager to learn. Everything had a name, and each name
gave birth to a new thought. As we returned to the house, every object [that] I
touched seemed to quiver with life. That was because I saw everything with the
strange, new sight that had come to me. On entering the door I remembered the
doll I had broken. I felt my way to the hearth and picked up the pieces. I vainly   *15*
tried to put them together. Then my eyes filled with tears; for I realized what I
had done, and for the first time I felt repentance and sorrow.

I learned a great many new words that day. I do not remember what they all
were; but I do know that mother, father, sister, teacher were among them—words
that were to make the world blossom to me. It would have been difficult to find a   *20*
happier child than I was as I lay in my crib at the close of that eventful day and

lived over the joys it had brought me and, for the first time, longed for a new day to come. . . .

I had now the key to all language, and I was eager to learn to use it. Children who hear acquire language without any particular effort; the words that fall from others' lips they catch on the wing, as it were, delightedly, while the little deaf child must trap them by a slow and often painful process. But whatever the process, the result is wonderful. Gradually, from naming an object we advance step by step until we have traversed the vast distance between our first stammered syllable and the sweep of thought in a line of Shakespeare. 30

At first, when my teacher told me about a new thing, I asked very few questions. My ideas were vague, and my vocabulary was inadequate, but as my knowledge of things grew, and I learned more and more words, my field of inquiry broadened, and I would return again and again to the same subject, eager for further information. Sometimes a new word revived an image that 40 some earlier experiences had engraved on my brain.

I remember the morning that I first asked the meaning of the word "love." This was before I knew many words. I had found a few early violets in the garden and brought them to my teacher. She tried to kiss me; but at that time I did not like to have anyone kiss me except my mother. Miss Sullivan put her arm 45 gently around me and spelled into my hand "I love Helen."

"What is love?" I asked.

She drew me closer to her and said, "It is here," pointing to my heart, whose beats I was conscious of for the first time. Her words puzzled me very much because I did not then understand anything unless I touched it. 50

I smelt the violets in her hand and asked, half in words, half in signs, a question [that] means, "Is love the sweetness of flowers?"

"No," said my teacher.

Again I thought. The warm sun was shining on us.

"Is this not love?" I asked, pointing in the direction from which the heat 55 came, "Is this not love?"

It seemed to me that there could be nothing more beautiful than the sun, whose warmth makes all things grow. But Miss Sullivan shook her head, and I was greatly puzzled and disappointed. I thought it strange that my teacher could not show me "love." 60

A day or two afterward I was stringing beads of different sizes in symmetrical groups—two large beads, three small ones, and so on. I had made many mistakes, and Miss Sullivan had pointed them out again and again with gentle patience. Finally I noticed a very obvious error in the sequence and, for an instant, I concentrated my attention on the lesson and tried to think how 65 I should have arranged the beads. Miss Sullivan touched my forehead and spelled with decided emphasis, "Think."

In a flash, I knew that the word was the name of the process that was going on in my head. This was my first conscious perception of an abstract idea.

Reflecting

After your reading, answer the following questions. Then share your responses with your classmates.

1. What main idea is developed in the narrative? (Or is there more than one main idea?)

_____

_____

_____

2. Circle the type of detail that seems to be used the most—sensory details, dialogue, or personal thoughts and feelings.

3. What is the main pattern of organization used in the narrative? (See page 128.)

_____

_____

4. How has the text changed or expanded your understanding of the topic?

_____

_____

5. Are there any questions that you still have? If so, what are they?

_____

_____

6. How would you rate this narrative, and why?
   Weak ★ ★ ★ ★ ★ Strong

_____

_____

_____

Vocabulary Practice

Identify   For each of the following words, create a vocabulary entry. Identify the pronunciation, helpful word parts, a primary definition, and the word used in a sentence. (Refer to a dictionary and pages 32–36 in this book for help.)

1. **consciousness** (line 6)

   _____

   _____

2. **repentance** (line 17)

   _____

   _____

3. **traversed** (line 29)

   _____

   _____

4. **symmetrical** (line 62)

   _____

   _____

Drawing Inferences

Explain   Answer one or both of the following questions to help you draw inferences about the reading. (See pages 29–31 for help.)

1. Why was a word such as "water" easier for Keller to realize than a word such as "think"?

   _____

   _____

2. How were Keller's special needs being met?

   _____

   _____

Writing

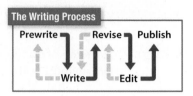

What follows are possible writing activities to complete in response to the reading. Use the writing process (pages 94–99) to help you develop your writing.

Prewriting

Choose one of the following writing ideas. Or decide upon another idea related to the reading.

Writing Ideas

1. **Writing to Learn:** Respond to a photograph from your childhood in a personal blog. Be sure that your writing answers the 5 W's (who? what? when? where? and why?) about the experience.

2. **Paragraph Writing:** Write a narrative paragraph for another one of the topics that you identified on page 184.

3. Or in a paragraph, share an experience related to one of your own special needs.

4. **Essay Writing:** Using Keller's essay as a guide, share an experience that changed you in some important way.

5. In an expository essay, share information about the ways in which the blind and/or hearing impaired develop their communication skills in today's world.

When planning . . .

Use the tips that follow and the information on pages 184–185 to help you with your prewriting and planning.

- Choose a specific personal experience to write about.
- Consider your purpose (*to inform, to entertain,* and so on), your audience (*peers, family members,* and so on), and the main point you would like to share.
- Collect plenty of details (*sensory details, dialogue, personal thoughts*).
- Review the narratives in this chapter to see how they are developed.

Writing and Revising

Use the tips that follow and the information on pages 186–187 to help you with your drafting and revising.

When writing . . .

- Include an opening, a middle, and a closing in your narrative. Each part has a specific role. (See page 187.)
- Follow your planning notes, but feel free to include new ideas that pop into your mind as you write. Some of these new ideas may be your best ones.
- Remember that sensory details include more than what you see. Also consider sounds, smells, tastes, and feelings/textures.
- Include dialogue and personal thoughts to re-create the experience for your reader.

When revising . . .

- Determine if you've done too much telling and not enough showing.
- Also ask yourself if your story will interest and engage your reader. If it doesn't, determine what changes need to be made.
- Have at least one trusted peer react to your narrative. Ask for his or her honest reaction.

Editing

Refer to the checklist on page 192 when you are ready to edit your narrative for style and correctness.

Reflecting on Narrative Writing

Answer the following questions about your narrative reading and writing experiences in this chapter.

1. What makes a personal narrative enjoyable to read?

   _____

2. What is your favorite narrative in this chapter? Explain.

   _____

3. What reading strategy highlighted in this chapter seems most helpful? Explain.

   _____

4. What do you like the most about the narrative that you wrote in this chapter? Explain.

   _____

5. What is one thing that you would like to change in this writing?

   _____

6. What is the most important thing that you have learned about writing a narrative?

   _____

Key Terms to Remember

When you read and write narratives, it's important to understand the following terms.

- **Autobiography**—the story of a person written by that person
- **Personal narrative**—an account of one specific experience in the writer's life
- **Sensory details**—specific sights, sounds, smells, tastes, and feelings/textures
- **Dialogue**—conversation between characters
- **Chronological order**—organized according to time
- **5 W's and H strategy**—answering *who? what? when? where? why?* and *how?* about an experience

8

Illustration

"Good writing is clear thinking made visible."
—Bill Wheeler

The backbone of any good piece of writing is the details that support the main idea. Without them, the writing simply won't hold up. This fact holds true for newspaper stories, magazine articles, text chapters, and blog posts. A newspaper columnist stating that violence in a city has reached unacceptable proportions will provide examples to make the statement credible. A fashion writer's positive review of a new clothing line will include reasons for her approval.

An illustration paragraph supports a general idea with specific examples. Recognizing key examples in reading will help you analyze texts and remember important information. Meanwhile, offering key examples in your writing will help you communicate your ideas more convincingly.

In the first part of this chapter, you will read and react to two professional examples of illustrative writing. In the second part, you will write one of your own.

Learning Outcomes

LO1 Understand illustration.

LO2 Learn reading strategies (identify the main idea and support; use a line diagram).

LO3 Read and react to a professional paragraph.

LO4 Read and react to a professional illustration.

LO5 Practice reading skills (recognize signal words and create the organization).

LO6 Plan an illustration.

LO7 Write the first draft.

LO8 Revise the writing.

LO9 Edit the writing.

What do you think?

According to the quotation, good writing demonstrates clear thinking. What do you think is the connection between the two?

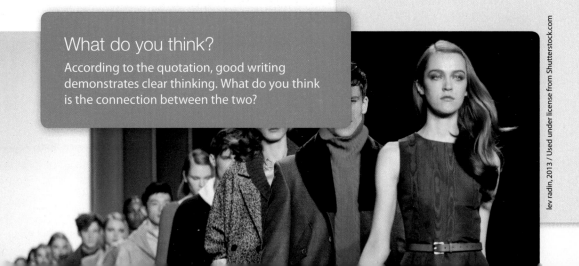

lev radin, 2013 / Used under license from Shutterstock.com

LO1 Understanding Illustration

What comes to mind when you think about the word *illustration?* If it is something art-related, you are not wrong. After all, drawings, sketches, and paintings are all considered illustrations. How then does illustration relate to writing? To answer this question, consider that *illustration* is defined in one sense as "the act of clarifying or explaining." Artists provide clarity by offering a visual representation of things. Writers clarify ideas by offering written explanations. Illustration paragraphs, in particular, clarify and explain ideas by offering examples.

> "No man with a conscience can just bat out illustrations. He's got to put all his talent and feeling into them!"
> —Norman Rockwell

A Familiar Structure

In most cases, illustration paragraphs generally follow a similar organizational pattern. They begin with a main idea, followed by examples and other types of details that support the idea. The following passage demonstrates this pattern.

> *(Main idea)* Climate change is already having a serious impact on the world around us. *(First example)* According to NASA, average temperatures have climbed 1.4 degrees Fahrenheit around the world since 1880, with most of the warm-up occurring in the last few decades. *(Second example)* Arctic ice is rapidly disappearing, and the loss of habitat is endangering polar bears. *(Third example)* Glaciers and mountain snows are rapidly melting. . . .

This pattern—main point, followed with examples—is a main feature in almost all forms of informational writing.

INSIGHT

Examples help a writer illustrate or support a main point. Other common types of supporting details in informational writing include facts, statistics, reasons, quotations, and definitions. (See pages 61–62.)

Identify Find a passage (similar to the one above) in one of your textbooks or on a Web site in which the writer illustrates a main idea. Identify the main idea and supporting examples in the text. Share the passage with your classmates.

Reading

Illustrating a main idea is the most common arrangement of ideas in academic writing. The strategies that follow will help you read texts that follow this arrangement.

LO2 Learning Reading Strategies

Identifying the Main Idea and Support

The main idea in an illustration paragraph is generally located in the first sentence—the topic sentence. It expresses a point about the topic that the writer illustrates throughout the rest of the paragraph. Once you determine the main idea, look for examples that support it. The examples and other details should be provided in the sentences that follow.

The number of supporting examples and details in a paragraph depends on the main idea. One writer may share a single example or story in great detail to support the main idea. Another writer may use three, four, or five brief examples. It all depends on what the writer feels is the best way to develop her or his main idea.

Using a Line Diagram

To keep track of the key components, consider using a line diagram. Identify the main idea along the top of the diagram and the supporting examples on the legs. If the paragraph includes additional details about any of the examples, add support legs to the example.

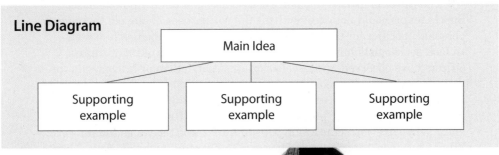

Line Diagram

Main Idea		
Supporting example	Supporting example	Supporting example

funflow, 2013 / Used under license from Shutterstock.com

Practice Use these strategies for your next illustration reading assignment. Afterward, discuss your work with a classmate.

LO3 Reading and Reacting to a Professional Paragraph

The illustrative paragraph below comes from *Sociology: Your Compass for a New World*. It discusses a trait important to the success of groups.

Prereading Before you read, answer these three questions:

1. What do the title and the first few sentences tell you about the paragraph?

   _____

2. What might be the authors' purpose?

   _____

3. What do you expect to learn?

   _____

Reading and Rereading As you read, make it your goal to (1) identify the topic, (2) locate the supporting evidence, and (3) judge the importance of the ending sentences. Consider annotating the text (page 20) during your reading.

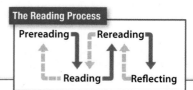

The Reading Process

Groupthink

The power of groups to ensure conformity is often a valuable asset.   *1*
Sports teams could not excel without the willingness of players to undergo
personal sacrifice for the good of the group, nor could armies function.
In fact, sociologists have demonstrated, and as high-ranking military
officers have observed, group cohesion—not patriotism or bravery—is the   *5*
main factor motivating soldiers to engage in combat (Stouffer et al., 1949;
Marshall, 1947: 160-1). As one soldier says in the 2001 movie *Black Hawk
Down*: "When I go home people will ask me: 'Hey, Hoot, why do you do it,
man? Why? Are you some kinda war junkie?' I won't say a goddamn word.
Why? They won't understand. They won't understand why we do it. They   *10*
won't understand it's about the men next to you. And that's it. That's all
it is."

Works Cited

Stouffer, Samuel A., et al. 1949. *The American Soldier*, 4 vols. Princeton, NJ: Princeton
   University Press.
Marshall, S.L.A. 1947 *Men Against Fire: The Problem of Battle Command in Future
   War*. New York: Morrow.

Reflecting After you read, answer these questions. Then share your reflections with your classmates.

1. What is the main idea of the paragraph?

   _____

   _____

2. What examples are used to illustrate the main idea?

   _____

   _____

3. How would you rate the paragraph, and why?
   Weak ★ ★ ★ ★ ★ Strong

   _____

Vocabulary Practice

Identify Define the word parts as indicated. Then try to explain the meaning of the complete word. (See pages 35–36 and 623–631 for help.)

1. **conformity** (line 1) con + form + ity

   _____

   _____

2. **cohesion** (line 5) co + hes + ion

   _____

   _____

Drawing Inferences

Explain Answer the following question to help you draw an inference about the text. (See pages 29–31 for help.)

- How can you apply the main idea in this paragraph to more than sports or the military?

   _____

   _____

LO4 Reading and Reacting to a Professional Illustration

The essay below illustrates how inventors are addressing serious problems with simple solutions. The work of these inventors may inspire you to come up with some creative solutions of your own. To gain a full understanding of the text follow the reading process.

About the Author

Robert King is coauthor of *Inquire: A Guide to 21st Century Learning* as well as two dozen novels.

Prereading Before you read, answer these three questions:

1. What do the title and first paragraph tell you about the text?

_____

2. What is the author's purpose?

_____

3. What questions do you hope to have answered in the essay?

_____

Reading and Rereading As you read, make it your goal to (1) identify the topic and main idea, (2) note the key supporting details, and (3) pay special attention to the closing paragraph. Consider annotating the text (page 20) and/or taking notes (page 22) during your reading.

The Reading Process

Prereading → Rereading → Reading → Reflecting

A Penny for Your World-Saving Thoughts

Most people in the developed world think of technology as the newest $300 cell phone or the best $50,000 hybrid vehicle or one of our many $40,000,000 predator drones. In the developing world, however, a whole different breed of entrepreneurs is working on technologies that cost very little and use materials as simple as corncobs and discarded 2-liter bottles. These inventors don't care so much about the future as about the present, in which over a billion people live without access to safe drinking water (World). With a rare combination of ingenuity and compassion, a generation of inventors is fixing the world's worst problems with the simplest solutions.

1

5

10

For example, Amy Smith, an instructor at MIT, works in the Peruvian Andes to turn corncobs into charcoal. Like 800 million others in the world, the locals of El Valle Sagrado de los Incas currently heat their homes with agricultural waste products such as dung, straw, and corncobs. These fuels produce a great deal of smoke, which causes respiratory infections, *15* the leading cause of death for those under five in such homes. By turning corncobs into charcoal, Smith converts a high-smoke fuel to a low-smoke one, not only heating homes but saving lives. Her process involves corncobs, matches, a 55-gallon drum with a lid, and patience. She jokingly calls her creations "carbon macro-tubes" (Ward). *20*

While Smith works in Peru to bring clean heat to family homes, a man called "Solar Demi" is working to bring light to the slums of Manila, Philippines. In these tight-packed quarters, electricity is scarce, and most people live in total darkness. Demi takes discarded two-liter bottles, strips off their labels, cleans them, and fills them with a mixture of distilled *25* water and bleach. He then cuts a hole in the roof of a home and fits the bottle in place with a watertight flange. This simple arrangement costs $1 per installation and produces 55 watts of free solar lighting. The Liter of Light Project aims to bring solar bottle lighting into one million homes in the Philippines (Ambani). *30*

In South Africa, the problem is not lack of light but lack of water. Traditionally in many tribes, women and girls carry water in containers on their heads, a technique that requires numerous trips (keeping girls out of school) and causes stress injuries to necks. To solve this problem, architect Hans Hendrikse and his brother Piet have developed a wheel- *35* shaped plastic drum that can hold up to 50 liters and is durable enough to roll across the ground behind a person. Four trips for water turn into one, and backbreaking loads turn into an easy stroll with a sloshing drum behind. By working with global partners, the Hendrikses are providing the Q-drum cheaply to those who need it most (Hendrikse). *40*

Throughout the developing world, unsafe drinking water is a huge problem. It causes diarrhea, which kills 1.5 million children every year— more than AIDS and malaria combined. The company Vestergaard Frandsen wants to put a stop to it, so it has developed the LifeStraw—a compact filtering device that is about the size of a fat ballpoint pen. *45* Children can carry this straw with them and drink surface water without fear of getting waterborne diseases. The straw costs about $20 in the developed world, but Vestergaard Frandsen is working with international partners to provide the straw affordably to those elsewhere who do not have safe supplies of water ("LifeStraw"). *50*

It's become fashionable to talk about how the future belongs to the innovators, and people who say such things are often thinking about space elevators and the like. But the present also belongs to the innovators—those who make corncob coal and soda-bottle lights and drums and straws that deliver water. All of these inventions are simple, elegant solutions to   *55* the world's oldest problems. With thinking like this, not only is our future bright, but our present can be as well.

Works Cited

Ambani, Priti. "An Innovative and Cheap 'Solar Bottle Bulb' Solution Lights Homes in Manilla." *Ecoprenurist.* N.p. Web. 14 Sept. 2011. 21 October 2011.

Hendrikse, Piet. "The rolling water container for developing countries." *WHCC Health Innovations.* WHCC. Web. N.d. 21 October 2011.

"LifeStraw Introduction." *Vestergaard Frandsen.* VF. N.d. Web. October 2011.

Ward, Logan. "MIT's Guru of Low-Tech Engineering Fixes the World on $2 a Day." *Popular Mechanics* 1 Aug. 2008: 68-72. Print.

World Health Organization. "Access to safe drinking water improving; sanitation needs greater efforts." *World Health Organization.* 15 March 2010. Web. 21 October 2011.

Reflecting   Answer the following questions about the selection. Then discuss your answers with your classmates.

1. What is the main idea of the essay?

   _____

2. How many supporting examples are included? Which one do you find most valuable?

   _____

   _____

3. How has this selection changed or expanded your understanding of entrepreneurs and inventors?

   _____

   _____

4. What information does the writer provide in the final paragraph?

   _____

   _____

5. How would you rate the essay, and why?

   Weak ★ ★ ★ ★ ★ Strong

   _____

Vocabulary Practice

Identify   Create a vocabulary entry for each of the following words. Identify the pronunciation, helpful word parts, a primary definition, and the word used in a sentence. (See a dictionary and pages 32–36 in this book for help.)

1. **entrepreneurs** (line 4)

2. **waterborne** (line 47)

3. **innovators** (line 53)

Drawing Inferences

Explain   Answer these questions to help you draw one inference about the essay. Then try to write another inference of your own. (See pages 29–31 for help.)

1. What does this essay have to say about human nature in general?

2. Why were each of these solutions necessary? (Consider the "state" of many parts of the world.)

3. What other inferences can you make from the essay?

LO5 Practicing Reading Skills

Understanding the use of signal words and the structure of illustrations will help you read them more effectively.

Recognizing Signal Words

In illustration paragraphs, look for signal words or transitions to indicate that an example is being identified. Common ones include "for example" and "in addition." As you read illustration selections, look for words like the ones in the chart below. Whenever you see one of these words or phrases, expect an example to follow it.

Words that can be used to add examples:

for example	another	for instance
also	moreover	additionally
next	in addition	along with

THE READING-WRITING CONNECTION

Use the signal words listed above to help you identify or introduce examples in your own illustrative paragraphs.

Creating the Organization

Knowing how the details are organized can help you recognize the type of paragraph you are reading. Unlike paragraphs that describe a process or share a story, the details of an illustration paragraph often have equal value, meaning they can be reordered and the paragraph will still seem clean and coherent.

Since the 1970s, the culinary world has experienced an explosion of fusion food, which blends elements of different cuisines. For example, Chinese pot stickers may be filled with European ingredients. Japanese sushi rolls may include California staples like smoked salmon and avocado. A Mexican-South Korean eatery may combine traditional Mexican offerings (chicken, cilantro, and cheese) with South Korean offerings (fried egg, tofu, and soy sauce) to make a single burrito. As global cultures continue to blend together, so too will the cuisines.

Evaluate Study the supporting details in the two selections you have read. Would they still make sense with the examples in a different order?

Writing

In your own paragraph, you will illustrate something about modern culture or life. Be sure to use the writing process to help you do your best work. (See pages 94–99.)

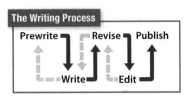

The Writing Process

Prewrite — Revise — Publish

Write — Edit

LO6 Planning an Illustration

Selecting a Topic

The topic for your paragraph should be related to modern culture—a type of television show, a type of technology, a brand of clothing, and so on. You should be able to think of any number of interesting topics to illustrate your main idea.

Select List possible topics under at least three of the categories below. (One example is provided for you.) Then circle the one that you want to write about in an illustration paragraph.

Favorite type of . . .				
books	movie/ television	music	sports	other
			football	

Deciding on a Focus

Once you choose a topic, decide on a feature of this topic that you could illustrate in your paragraph. For example, in the paragraph on page 204, the writer focuses on situations when teamwork is essential for success. To write about a feature of football, a writer might illustrate changes that are being made because of head injuries.

Explain In the space below, explain the feature or part of this topic that you will illustrate in your paragraph.

_____

_____

_____

INSIGHT _____

Finding a focus for your writing is a crucial part of prewriting. It gives you direction to move forward with your planning and writing. Make sure the topic is not so broad that it will not fit in a paragraph.

Identifying Your Examples

Once you have established a focus, you need to identify the examples that will help illustrate this feature.

Identify List three or four examples that you could use to illustrate your focus. The writer of a paragraph that illustrates the measures taken to prevent head injuries in football listed these three examples.

> Better in-game concussion testing
>
> Limits on full-contact and off-season practice time
>
> Stricter fines and penalties for illegal "head" hits

Gathering Details

After you think of examples, you may have to come up with additional details to clarify each example. For example, the writer of the paragraph about football safety would need to explain how players are tested during games for concussions.

Collect Identify details that are necessary to clarify any of your examples. You may have to do some research to complete this part.

Forming Your Topic Sentence

Your topic sentence should state your topic and identify your focus. The following formula can help you write your sentence.

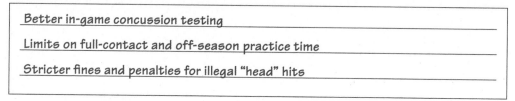

The topic	a feature or part of the topic	topic sentence.
Head injuries in the NFL	**+** additional safety measures	**=** Numerous head injuries in the NFL have led to additional safety measures.

Create Write your topic sentence using the formula above as a guide. If necessary, write two or three versions and then choose the best one.

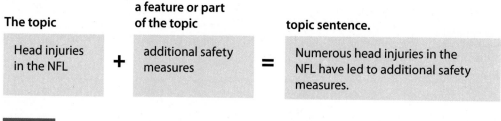

LO7 Writing the First Draft

After you have completed your prewriting and planning, you are ready to write your paragraph. Provided below is another sample illustration paragraph to consider before you write.

Read Read the paragraph, noting the distinct beginning, middle, and ending parts.

Heading in the Right Direction

Topic Sentence

Numerous head injuries in the NFL have led to additional   *1*
safety measures. New studies conclude that concussions can
lead to long-term, crippling brain damage. As a result, the
league has beefed up its baseline testing for players who suffer

Example 1

head injuries during a game. Before gaining permission to   *5*
reenter the game, a player in question must now pass a six-
to eight-minute test that measures things such as memory,
balance, and concentration. The NFL is also cutting back on

Example 2

practice time and off-season programs, as well as limiting full-
contact practices in the pre-season and regular season. With   *10*
less time to bang heads, fewer concussions should happen. In
addition, the league is enforcing stricter fines and penalties
for illegal helmet-to-helmet hits—those hits where a player
launches himself headfirst to strike an opposing player's

Example 3

helmet. The measures listed above are just a few of the steps   *15*
the NFL is taking to make the game safer. Still, the media,
lawmakers, and former players say the league is failing to do
enough to protect players. It will be interesting to see what

Closing Sentence

additional safety measures will come in the future. The game
may soon look much different than it does today.   *20*

Consider the Craft

1. What do you like best about the paragraph?
2. What are your two favorite details?
3. Do the examples help clarify the main idea?
4. Does the writer sound knowledgeable?

Drafting Tips

When you write an illustration paragraph, you are clarifying an idea by providing examples. Consider the following techniques to give your reader a clear understanding of your main idea.

- Use at least three strong examples or other types of support to illustrate your main idea.

- Arrange the examples in an order that makes the best sense. (Remember that examples in illustration paragraphs may work in more than one order.)

- Clearly explain each example so it is clear to the reader.

- Review the models you have read in this chapter for ideas for your own paragraph.

The Working Parts of a Paragraph

A paragraph consists of three main parts, each of which has a special function. The information that follows explains each part.

Topic Sentence:	The topic sentence states the topic and the focus of the paragraph.
Body Sentences:	The body sentences provide examples and other details that illustrate the main idea, which was established in the topic sentence.
Closing Sentence:	The closing sentence sums up the main point or recasts it in a new or interesting way.

Tip

Remember the transitional words used to add information: *additionally, along with, also, another, as well, finally, for example, for instance, in addition, next, other,* and so on.

Write Develop your first draft using the information on this page and your planning on pages 211–212 as a guide.

LO8 Revising the Writing

Start the revising process by reading your first draft two or three times to get a feel for your work so far. Then have one of your classmates read and react to your work using a response sheet as a guide. (See page 428.)

Cutting Unnecessary Ideas

Unnecessary ideas repeat what was already said or include unrelated or inaccurate information. They should be deleted.

> **Repeated Idea:** The power of groups to ensure conformity is often a valuable asset. ~~It can be very useful.~~
>
> **Unrelated Idea:** With their immersion in social media, millennials are being called the "Elsewhere Generation." ~~Young people don't understand the value of hard work.~~
>
> **Inaccurate Information:** The NFL is enforcing stricter fines and penalties for illegal helmet-to-helmet hits. ~~If a referee judges a tackle as a helmet-to-helmet, he can penalize the guilty player five yards.~~ *(The penalty is 15 yards.)*

Revising in Action

Read aloud the unrevised and then the revised version of the following passage. Notice that an unrelated idea and a repeated idea have been cut.

> Hurricane Katrina led to the largest displacement of Americans since the Civil War. More than a half-million people sought shelter outside their homes ~~elsewhere.~~ The New Orleans area was hit hardest, with more than 90 percent of its residents evacuated. ~~New Orleans is known as "The Big Easy" because of its easy-going, laid-back attitude.~~

Revise Improve your writing, using the following checklist and your classmate's comments on the response sheet. Continue working until you can check off each item.

Using a Revising Checklist

Ideas

☐ 1. Have I created a strong topic sentence for my paragraph?
☐ 2. Do I include at least three examples to illustrate my main idea?

Organization

☐ 3. Does my paragraph have effective opening, middle, and closing parts?
☐ 4. Do I use transitions, if necessary, between examples? (See page 210.)

Voice

☐ 5. Do I sound knowledgeable and interested?

LO9 Editing the Writing

The main work of editing is to check the effectiveness of individual words and sentences and correct any errors in your revised writing.

Capitalizing Proper Nouns and Adjectives

You know most of the basic rules related to capitalization, but it is useful to review them before you edit your writing. In addition to capitalizing the first word in a sentence, here are three other rules to remember.

- **Sections of the country** are capitalized, but words that indicate direction are not: Paul moved to the **Northwest** last year. He lives **south** of Seattle.

- **Titles used with the name of a person** are capitalized, but titles used by themselves are not: **Mayor Henderson** solved the city's sewage problem, a problem that the former **mayor** failed to address.

- **The first word in a direct quotation** is capitalized, but only if it begins a full sentence: Shawna asked, **"Does** anyone want to meet at the coffee shop?" I would have said **"yes,"** but I was busy.

Capitalization Practice   Rewrite the following sentences, adding capitalization where needed and lowercasing any letters that should not be capitalized.

1. The midwest in the United States is made up of 12 states.
2. The Southern half the midwest is composed of kansas, Missouri, Illinois, Indiana, and Ohio.
3. Before becoming President, Barack Obama worked as a Senator in Illinois.
4. The Midwest is East of president Obama's birthplace—Honolulu, Hawaii.
5. Bill Bryson said, "you can always tell a midwestern couple in Europe because they will be standing in the middle of a busy intersection looking at a wind-blown map and arguing over which way is west."
6. Many people from other regions, especially the northeast, are used to busy intersections.

Additional Practice: For additional practice, see pages 582–585.

Apply   Check your illustration paragraph for the capitalization rules above. (For more information, see pages 582–585.)

Additional Capitalization

Here are three additional rules about capitalization that are important to understand when you edit your writing.

- **Specific names of special events** (historic events, holidays, sporting events, and so on) are capitalized, but general terms for the events are not: Americans celebrate **Veterans Day** every November 11. The **day** honors living and dead **veterans** of war.
- **Specific names of places** (mountains, rivers, buildings, bridges, and so on) are capitalized, but general references to them are not: Chicago's **Sears Tower** was officially renamed the **Willis Tower** in 2009. With 108 stories and standing 1,451 feet high, the **tower** was the tallest in the world from 1973 to 1998.
- **Specific names of organizations** (military groups, sports teams, political parties, and so on) are capitalized, but general references to them are not: The **New York Rangers** played the **New Jersey Devils** in hockey. The proximity of both **teams** makes them natural rivals.

NOTE: Capitalize the first and last word and other important words for a specific name of something. Do not capitalize words such as *of, on, for, the,* or *a* if they are within the name.

United States of America   Susan G. Komen for the Cure

Practice   Rewrite the following sentences, adding capitalization where needed and lowercasing any letters that should not be capitalized.

1. My favorite holiday is thanksgiving because our family dines at leroy's cafe.

2. Each labor day, my family drives along the Mississippi river to my aunt's house in st. louis.

3. My uncle belongs to the Republican party, and my mom belongs to the democratic party, but I am independent of any party affiliation.

4. Many tourists visit the empire State Building in New York; the Plaza hotel is a favorite tourist stop as well.

5. A restaurant called tavern on the green has closed, but it was once a popular eating place in Central park.

6. Rescue missions are common in most large cities; the unity rescue mission in Quincy helps many people.

Additional Practice: For additional practice, see pages 582–587.

Apply   Check your illustration paragraph to make sure that you have followed the capitalization rules above.

Marking a Paragraph

The model that follows has a number of errors.

Editing Practice Correct the following paragraph, using the correction marks below. One correction has been done for you.

Forged by Pain

Frida Kahlos path toward political and artistic fame was paved by   1
pain. As a child, Kahlo were bedridden for nine months with polio. Then,
at age 18, she was critically injured in an autobus acident. During the
collision Kahlo was impaled by a handrail and suffer fractures in her spine
and pelvis. it took months of painful rehab to walk again, and the pain   5
and injuries lingered throughout her lifetime. But during the months of
agonizing rehab, kahlo took up painting. It was during this period when
Kahlo started working on her first of many famous self-portraits. The
physical pain she epxerienced as a youth and the emotional pain from her
unsteady marriage is reflected in her self-portraits many people belief that   10
is what makes the paintings so powerful.

Correction Marks

⊃ delete	⋏ add comma	word ∧ add word
d capitalize	? add question	⊙ add period
⊘ lowercase	∧ mark	spelling
∧ insert	⋎ insert an apostrophe	switch

Using an Editing Checklist

Now it's time to correct your own paragraph.

Apply   Create a clean copy of your revised paragraph and use the following checklist to check for errors. Continue working until you can check off each item in the list.

Words

☐ 1. Have I used specific nouns and verbs? (See page 134.)

☐ 2. Have I used more action verbs than "be" verbs? "Be" verbs include words like *is, are, was, were.* (See page 536.)

Sentences

☐ 3. Have I avoided sentence errors such as fragments and run-ons? (See pages 488–491, 494–495.)

Conventions

☐ 4. Do I use correct verb forms (*he saw,* not *he seen*)? (See pages 542, 544.)

☐ 5. Do my subjects and verbs agree (*she speaks,* not *she speak*)? (See pages 472–481.)

☐ 6. Have I used the right words (*their, there, they're*)?

☐ 7. Have I capitalized first words and proper nouns and adjectives? (See page 582.)

☐ 8. Have I used the proper punctuation marks at the end of my sentences?

☐ 9. Have I used commas after long introductory word groups? (See pages 592–595.)

☐ 10. Have I used apostrophes correctly in contractions and to show possession? (See pages 608–609.)

Adding a Title

Make sure to add an appropriate title for your essay. Here are three strategies to try.

■ Highlight the main idea:

Groupthink

■ Think creatively:

The Elsewhere Generation

■ Make a bold statement:

Forged by Pain

composting, beekeeping, and other skills. L. Pearson King, a junior *20*
environmental studies major, taught his peers how to carve spoons in a
woodworking guild last year.

At Dickinson College, students like Claire Fox, who just graduated
with a double major in international studies and environmental studies,
can get a practical education on the college's 180-acre working farm. "It *25*
truly enhanced my education," says Fox, who had never had contact with
agriculture before leaving suburban New Jersey to go to Dickinson.

At Unity College in Maine, students have had a hand in constructing
some of the college's buildings, tending its garden, and working on
renewable-energy projects out in the field with Michael "Mick" Womersley, *30*
an associate professor of human ecology. A former maintenance engineer
in the British Royal Air Force, Womersley tells his students that a lot of
relatively simple projects, like installing a $42 programmable thermostat in
a home, can make a big difference in energy use, yet few people bother. Why?

"A lot of us are bred out of actually doing things," he said when I met *35*
him at a Maine sheep farm, where he was setting up wind-measurement
equipment with the help of two students. "I find that is a big failing of the
sustainability movement—we are so busy talking about things, but there is
a ton of stuff to do."

Or consider Green Mountain College, a once-troubled institution in rural *40*
Vermont. Green Mountain, which now lands at the top of national rankings
of sustainable colleges, has torn up a portion of its athletics fields to start
a small farm that trains students in both cutting-edge and old-fashioned
techniques of growing food without the help of petroleum. That means using
and maintaining human- and animal-powered machines, using solar energy *45*
in innovative ways, learning the importance of crop rotations and animal
manures, and, of course, getting the basics of growing carrots and tomatoes.

The professors there routinely tie the skills on the farm to the
sustainability lessons in the classroom. "Many educational institutions
pride themselves on preparing students to lead a life of inquiry," writes *50*
Philip Ackerman-Leist, an associate professor of environmental studies who
founded the college farm, in *Up Tunket Road: The Education of a Modern
Homesteader*, a book about building his home and farm in Vermont. But "few
actually challenge and support students to embrace the ecological questions
and immediately begin living the possible solutions—not later but in the *55*
midst of the educational experience itself. . . ."

Derek Larson, an associate professor of environmental studies and
history at the College of Saint Benedict and Saint John University,
gets his students to imagine the future by reading **techno-utopian** and
postapocalyptic fiction. James Howard Kunstler's *World Made by Hand*, *60*
which describes America after an influenza pandemic and an oil shortage,
left them shaken.

"I asked each of them, 'What skills would you have that would be applicable in that world?'" Larson says. "And they all said, 'Nothing.' They were actually kind of despairing at this. They said, 'I'd die. What would I be able to do? I would have no valuable skills.'" When the environmental-studies curriculum went through a revision recently, he says, students made one request: Include more practical and hands-on learning. 65

Work colleges have long met that anxiety (the feeling of not being able to fix anything) by teaching the rewards of self-reliance. "When people ask me, 'What do you get out of the work program?' I say, 'Skills, maybe. Confidence, absolutely,'" says Ian Robertson, dean of work at Warren Wilson College, where students are required to put in hours as woodworkers, farm hands, janitors, carpenters, cooks, landscapers, and anything else the college needs to operate in exchange for room and board. 70 75

"The Future of American Colleges May Lie, Literally, in Students' Hands" by Scott Carlson in *The Chronicle of Higher Education* ("The Chronicle Review" section), February 5, 2012

niches
special areas

aesthetic
beautiful or pleasing

techno-utopian
the use of digital technology to create a greater good

postapocalyptic
after widespread devastation

Reflecting

After your reading, answer the following questions. Then share your responses with your classmates.

1. What main idea is developed in the text? (Or is there more than one main idea?)

   _____

   _____

2. What types of supporting examples are provided?

   _____

   _____

3. What example (school) interests you the most, and why?

   _____

   _____

4. How is the text organized—chronologically, spatially, or logically? Circle one. (See page 128.)

5. How has the essay confirmed, changed, or expanded your understanding of a college education?

   _____

   _____

6. What questions do you still have about the topic?

   _____

   _____

7. How would you rate this reading, and why?
   Weak ★ ★ ★ ★ ★ Strong

   _____

   _____

Vocabulary Practice

Identify Use context clues to explain or define the following words. (See pages 33–34 for help.)

1. **stagnant** (line 2)

   clues: _____

   definition: _____

2. **cutting-edge** (line 43)

   clues: _____

   definition: _____

3. **despairing** (line 65)

   clues: _____

   definition: _____

Drawing Inferences

Explain Answer the following questions to help you draw inferences about the reading. (See pages 29–31 for help.)

1. What is meant by this idea from the essay: "A lot of us are bred out of actually doing things"?

   _____

   _____

   _____

2. What does it mean to become educated?

   _____

   _____

   _____

Writing

What follows are possible writing activities to complete in response to the reading. Use the writing process (pages 94–99) to help you develop your writing.

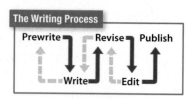

Prewriting

Choose one of the following writing ideas. Or decide upon another idea related to the reading.

Writing Ideas

1. **Writing to Learn:** For a week, write blog or journal entries in which you examine how you have supported and/or ignored sustainability in all of its versions. At the end of the week, pull your thoughts together in a final entry.

2. **Paragraph Writing:** Write an illustrative paragraph about one of the topics you identified on page 211.

3. Write a paragraph that in some way illustrates your resourcefulness.

4. **Essay Writing:** Reflect on your job, your neighborhood, your group of friends, your favorite music, or so on. Then write an essay in which you illustrate some important feature of your topic.

5. In an expository essay, share information about one specific aspect of sustainability.

When planning . . .

Refer to pages 211–212 to help you with your prewriting and planning. Also use the tips below.

- Choose a topic that you care about. Writing about something you like helps you put more effort into your work.
- Decide on an interesting focus or feature of the topic to illustrate.
- Be able to identify at least three examples to illustrate your topic. Make sure the examples clearly illustrate the main idea for your readers.
- Review the written illustrations in this chapter to see how they are developed. Some of the techniques those writers used may help you shape your own thoughts and ideas.

Writing and Revising

Refer to pages 213–214 to help you write and review your first draft. Also use the tips below to help you with your drafting and revising.

When writing . . .

- Write your first draft freely, generally following your planning. But also be open to new ideas.
- Don't worry about getting anything just right in this writing.
- Include an effective beginning, middle, and ending in your illustration piece. Each part plays its own role. (See page 214.)
- Clearly explain each one of the examples.
- When necessary, use transitional words to connect the examples in the paragraph.

When revising . . .

- Let your first draft sit unread for a bit. Then reread it carefully, with fresh eyes.
- Determine if your writing answered key questions readers might have about your topic.
- Decide if all of your ideas are necessary—or directly related to your topic and focus.
- Be prepared to do further research if you need more examples or details.
- Ask a classmate to review your writing, using a peer review sheet. (See page 622.)

Editing

Refer to the checklist on page 219 when you are ready to edit your illustration piece for style and correctness.

Reflecting on Illustration Writing

Answer the following questions about your illustration reading and writing experiences in this chapter.

1. What are the two key parts of illustration writing?

   _____

2. Why are examples so important in this type of writing?

   _____

3. Which reading strategy in this chapter seems the most helpful?

   _____

4. What is your favorite model in this chapter? Explain.

   _____

5. How will your understanding of illustrating a topic help you with your academic reading?

   _____

6. What is the easiest thing about writing an illustration essay? The hardest?

   _____

7. What do you like best about your writing?

   _____

8. What is one thing you would like to change in it?

   _____

Key Terms to Remember

When you read and write illustration essays, it's important to understand the following terms.

- **Illustration**—the act of clarifying or explaining in writing
- **Example**—something that represents the whole group
- **Line diagram**—a graphic organizer used to identify the main idea and examples in writing

9

Definition

> "Words mean more than what is set down on paper. . . ."
> —Maya Angelou

Read any word in a dictionary, and you'll find other words to define it. Each one of these words has its own definition. This web of words creates the enormous network that is our language.

A paragraph or essay of definition may start with a dictionary definition, but then it includes other types of information such as synonyms for the word, examples of the word in use, and its history. In other words, a dictionary definition is only a launching point for a fuller explanation.

In this chapter, you will learn about this form of writing. First you will read and react to two professional examples of definition writing. Finally, you will write a definition paragraph of your own. During your work, you will begin to appreciate what it means to define a term.

Learning Outcomes

LO1 Understand definition.

LO2 Learn reading strategies (consider the term and support).

LO3 Read and react to a professional paragraph.

LO4 Read and react to an extended definition.

LO5 Practice reading skills (consider specific terminology and general use).

LO6 Plan a definition.

LO7 Write the first draft.

LO8 Revise the writing.

LO9 Edit the writing.

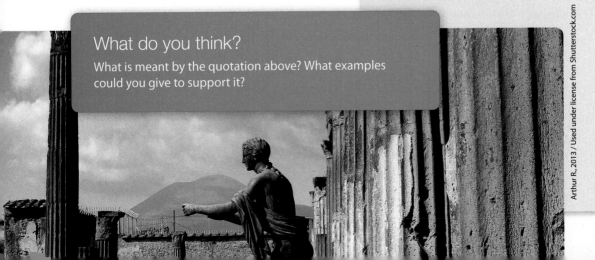

What do you think?

What is meant by the quotation above? What examples could you give to support it?

Arthur R., 2013 / Used under license from Shutterstock.com

LO1 Understanding Definition

On the surface, a definition paragraph looks like a basic form of informational writing—sharing the meaning of a word. Many times, however, definition paragraphs go into much greater detail about a word, requiring research from a number of primary and secondary sources. In such cases, writing a definition paragraph becomes a practice in research writing.

The paragraphs that you will read in this chapter involved quite a bit of research. So too will the definition paragraphs you encounter in your college reading and writing.

> "We do not see first, then define. We define first and then see."
> —Walter Lippman

Professional Versus Student Paragraphs

Professional paragraphs of definition are generally written for one of two reasons. First, they are directed at the reader, to present information (as is usually the case in your textbooks). Second, they are directed more to the writer, to explore a term in order to better understand it. Often you may see this second sort of writing in personal essays and opinion pieces.

For your own writing in this chapter, you will focus on the second approach: writing to explore a word. Your task will be to consider a term that interests you, and then write about it in a way that increases your understanding of the word. At the same time, you will be sharing what you've learned with your readers.

INSIGHT ————————————————————————————

When writing a definition paragraph, you must make sure that you understand the term and its background. You must also gather your own thoughts about the term.

Identify   Identify two possible topics for definition in each of the following categories. (One idea is provided.) Then discuss your responses with your classmates.

History: _democracy_____

Technology: _____

Health: _____

The arts: _____

Environment: _____

Reading

Reading a definition paragraph involves connecting new information to what you already know about the topic.

LO2 Learning Reading Strategies

The following reading strategies can help you get the most from definition paragraphs.

Considering the Term

Before reading the definition, consider the following questions.

- **What do I already know about the term?** Have you encountered it before? If not, do you recognize the root word and any prefixes or suffixes?
- **What is the context of this definition?** Is it presented within a particular course of study? What do you know about the author that might affect the definition? Is the definition intended to inform or to explore? (See "Professional Versus Student Paragraphs" on page 230.)
- **What do I expect to learn from the definition?** With the previous questions in mind, what might you predict about the definition? What do you hope to learn, and what do you expect the author may have to say?

Understanding the Support

Support for a definition paragraph may include dictionary definitions, personal definitions, word histories, encyclopedia information, synonyms and antonyms, comparisons, quotations, examples, and so on. It may help to chart the different types of support when you read a definition paragraph. Here is the start of a support chart:

Support Chart

Term defined: _____

- Dictionary definition: _____

- Personal definitions: _____

- Word history: _____

LO3 Reading and Reacting to a Professional Paragraph

This paragraph, which first appeared in a textbook entitled *An Invitation to Health*, defines a word that is common to us all. To gain a full understanding of the paragraph, follow the reading process.

Prereading Before you read, answer these three questions:

1. What do the title and first sentence tell you about the paragraph?

2. Why might the author have written this paragraph?

3. What do you expect to learn from it?

Reading and Rereading As you read, make it your goal to (1) identify the topic and main idea, (2) consider the supporting details, and (3) judge the value of the closing part.

Tip: Annotating the text (page 20) will help you react to the information as you read.

The Reading Process

Prereading → Rereading

Reading → Reflecting

The Three Most Difficult Words

While "I forgive you" may be three of the most difficult words to say, they are also three of the most powerful—and the most beneficial for the body as well as the soul. Being angry, harboring resentments, or reliving hurts over and over again is bad for your health in general and your heart in particular. The word *forgive* comes from the Greek for letting go, and that's what happens when you forgive: You let go of all the anger and pain that have been demanding your time and wasting your energy. To some people, forgiveness seems a sign of weakness or submission. People may feel more in control, more powerful, when they're filled with anger, but forgiving instills a much greater sense of power. Forgiving a friend or family member may be more difficult than forgiving a stranger because the hurt occurs in a context in which people deliberately make themselves vulnerable. When you forgive, you reclaim the power to choose. It doesn't matter whether someone deserves to be forgiven; you deserve to be free. However, forgiveness isn't easy. It's not a one-time thing but a process that takes a lot of time and work involving both the conscious and unconscious mind. . . .

1

5

10

15

From HALES. *An Invitation to Health,* 7E. © 2012 Brooks/Cole, a part of Cengage Learning, Inc. Reproduced by permission. www.cengage.com/permissions

Reflecting After you complete your reading, answer these questions. Share your responses with your classmates.

1. What is defined in this paragraph?

   _____

2. What supporting details are provided? Name two.

   _____

3. Do you agree or disagree with the author's main idea?

   _____

4. How would you rate this paragraph, and why?

   Weak ★ ★ ★ ★ ★ Strong

   _____

Vocabulary Practice

Identify Define the word parts as indicated. Then try to explain the meaning of the complete word. (See pages 35–36 and 623–631 for help.)

1. **resentments** (line 3) re + sent + ments

   _____

   _____

2. **unconscious** (line 16) un + con + sci + ous

   _____

   _____

Drawing Inferences

Explain Answer the following questions to help you draw inferences from the text.

1. What is meant by the following statement: "When you forgive, you reclaim the power to choose"?

   _____

   _____

2. What synonyms and antonyms for "forgive" come to mind? Explain each one.

   _____

   _____

LO4 Reading and Reacting to an Extended Definition

The model below is the text of a graduation speech in which the speaker examines the concept of the American dream. Follow the steps in the reading process to help you gain a full understanding of the text.

About the Author

Martin C. Jischke, PhD, was president of Purdue University from 2000–2007. He has served on many prominent boards in education and industry and has received many awards for his accomplishments in science and education.

Prereading   Before you read, answer these three questions:

1. What is your understanding of the American dream?

   _____

2. Why do you think that the speaker picked this topic?

   _____

3. What do you expect to learn in your reading?

   _____

Reading and Rereading   As you read, make it your goal to (1) consider the importance of the topic, (2) carefully note of the supporting details, and (3) judge the impact of the final few paragraphs.

Tip: Consider annotating the text (page 20) and/or taking notes (page 22) during your reading.

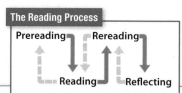

The American Dream

What is the American dream? What does it mean to you? Is it your *1*
own prosperity? Is it becoming more successful than your parents?

I can tell you what it meant to James Truslow Adams. He wrote
that the American dream is the "dream of a land in which life should
be better and richer and fuller for everyone, with opportunity for each *5*
according to ability or achievement. It is not a dream of motor cars and
high wages merely, but a dream of a social order in which each man
and each woman shall be able to attain to the fullest stature of which
they are innately capable and be recognized by others for what they are,
regardless of birth or position." *10*

Standing here before you—the grandson of a German immigrant with little education, the son of a grocer—I have experienced the incredible opportunity of serving as a president of Purdue. I am surely living the American dream.

I believe the American dream was the concept Thomas Jefferson was 15 crafting when he wrote: "We hold these truths to be self-evident: That all men are created equal, that they are endowed by their creator with certain unalienable rights, that among these are life, liberty, and the pursuit of happiness."

I believe the American dream is much more than the dreams of 20 individuals. I believe the American dream is the dream of this nation.

I believe the American dream is the opportunity to live in a nation in which diversity is celebrated as the source of strength and beauty.

I believe the American dream is the opportunity not only to acquire, but to give and to serve other people in need.   25

I believe the American dream is the opportunity to pursue knowledge freely, through a lifetime of learning, growing, changing, and evolving.

I believe the American dream is the opportunity to share these great possibilities with people throughout the world, no matter where they live, no matter what their circumstances.   30

All of this is the American dream to me.

Martin Luther King Jr. said: "America is essentially a dream, a dream as yet unfulfilled. It is a dream of a land where [people] of all races, of all nationalities, and of all creeds can live together as brothers and [sisters]."   35

Dr. King was right. Even today we struggle to fulfill the incredible full promise of the American dream. But I believe it can be fulfilled. I believe it must be fulfilled. And I believe you are the ones who will do it.

There are those today who will tell you the American dream is finished and gone. There are those who will tell you that all dreams are 40 foolish, beyond the harsh realities of life and a waste of our time. Don't believe them. Brooks Atkinson was a 20th-century American drama critic who said: "Our nation was built by pioneers who were not afraid of failure, scientists who were not afraid of the truth, thinkers who were not afraid of progress, and dreamers who were not afraid of action."   45

What is the American dream?

Ultimately, you are the American dream. . . .

From Martin C. Jischke, "The American Dream," *Vital Speeches of the Day 73*, No. 7 (July 2007): 314-315.

Writing

It is time now to begin planning and writing your own definition paragraph about a term you wish to better understand. Remember to use the writing process to help you do your best work. (See pages 94–99.)

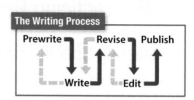

LO6 Planning a Definition

As you've seen, a word can mean different things to different people. Part of the enjoyment of writing a definition paragraph is in discovering just what a particular term means to you and other people.

> "Nothing in life is to be feared. It is only to be understood."
> —Marie Curie

Selecting a Topic

To decide upon a topic, think of a term that either . . .

- means something important to you, or
- you would like to better understand.

Here are the terms that a student might list for consideration.

Terms that are important to me	Terms that I'd like to better understand
– loyalty	– faith
– independence	– pandemic ✔
– hipness	– willingness

The student chose to write about "pandemic" after hearing the word on a news report.

List Make a list of at least three terms that are important to you and three that you would like to better understand. Check the term that you would like to define in a paragraph.

Terms that are important to me	Terms that I'd like to better understand

Gathering Details: Terminology and Context

Once you have selected a term, gather details about it to use in your definition paragraph. In the example below, a student used a support chart to keep track of his details.

Support Chart

Term defined: *pandemic*

Dictionary definition	an "infectious disease covering a wide geographic area and affecting a large proportion of the population"
Comparison	Pandemic and epidemic
History	Pandemic comes from the Greek *pandemos*. The greek root *pan* means "every" or "all" and *demos* means "common people."
Examples	Black Death during the Dark Ages; flu pandemic in 1918 (killed 40 to 50 million); H1N1; and HIV

Collect Gather details for your paragraph, and use a support chart to keep track of your supporting ideas. Try to collect at least three types of support.

Term defined:

Dictionary definition	
Comparison	
History	
Examples	

Forming a Topic Sentence

Once you have collected your support, write a topic sentence for your paragraph. The formula below shows the two main parts in a topic sentence.

Specific topic	an important feeling or part		topic sentence.
Pandemic	**+** strikes fear into people everywhere	**=**	"Pandemic" is a term that strikes fear into people everywhere.

Create Write a topic sentence for your paragraph using the formula above. If necessary, write two or three versions until your thesis says what you want it to say.

Specific topic	an important feeling or part		topic sentence.
	+	**=**	

LO7 Writing the First Draft

Writing a first draft is your first attempt to connect all of the thoughts you have gathered about your topic. Don't try to make everything perfect. Instead, simply get all your ideas on paper.

Read Carefully read the following paragraph about the word *pandemic*.

Spreading the Word

Topic Sentence

Pandemic is a medical term that strikes fear into people   *1*
everywhere. One news report might say, "The threat of a
pandemic flu hitting the United States exists"; another one
might say, "The World Health Organization has raised the
level of the influenza pandemic alert." Who wouldn't be scared   *5*
by threats such as these? So what exactly is a pandemic, and
where did this word come from? A pandemic is an "infectious
disease covering a wide geographic area and affecting a large
proportion of the population." Being "infectious" is a key
feature because a disease cannot be a pandemic unless it can   *10*

Body Sentences

be spread by humans over a very wide area. So influenza can
be pandemic, but cancer cannot. Some people use *pandemic*
interchangeably with *epidemic*. But an epidemic doesn't
become pandemic until it covers an extremely widespread
area, such as a series of countries. *Pandemic* comes from the *15*
Greek *pandemos*: The Greek root *pan* means "every" or "all"
and *demos* means "common people." Thus, *pandemos* means
"all the people," so the connection with pandemic is clear. Two
pandemics that are often cited are the Black Death during
the Dark Ages and the flu pandemic in 1918 that killed from   *20*

Closing Sentence

40 to 50 million people. Current pandemics include H1N1, an
infectious flu virus, and HIV. Here's a scary final thought:
Globetrotting provides an easy way for pandemics to occur.

Consider the Craft

1. What do you like best about this paragraph?
2. What types of details does the writer include about the main word?
3. Does the writer say just enough about the word, too much, or too little?
4. What did you learn about the word *pandemic*?

Drafting Tips

When you write a definition paragraph, you should give your readers a broad understanding of a word. Consider these tips for drafting a well-rounded paragraph.

- **To capture your reader's attention,** offer a surprising detail near the beginning of the paragraph, if possible in the topic sentence.

- **To add to your reader's understanding,** remember to offer historical information, example sentences using the word, and a quotation using the word.

- **To develop your definition fully,** add your own explanations and analogies to tie everything together. (The model on page 240 gives possible report headlines early on, and later it offers analogies of the definition.)

- **To help the paragraph move smoothly,** use transitional words to connect one point or detail to the next.

- **To bring your writing to an effective end,** focus on a key point about the term or stress the term's importance.

INSIGHT ——————————————————————————————————————

Every academic and professional discipline has a different vocabulary. Defining terms is an important starting point for any discussion about any text.

The Working Parts of a Paragraph

A paragraph consists of three main parts, and each has a special function. The information that follows explains each part.

Topic Sentence: A topic sentence names the term and a focus for your paragraph. (See page 239.)

Body Sentences: The body sentences present your support. (See your support chart from page 239.)

Closing Sentence: A closing sentence leaves the reader with a final thought about the term.

Write Develop your first draft using the information on this page and your planning on pages 238–239 as a guide.

LO8 Revising the Writing

Start the revising process by reading your first draft two or three times to get a feel for your work so far. Then have one of your classmates read and react to your work using a response sheet as a guide. (See page 428.)

Rewriting Confusing Sentences

Any time you come across a sentence in your first draft that doesn't sound right or causes you to stumble, you should rewrite it.

Confusing sentence: When people write *pandemic,* they think *epidemic* all over again.

Rewritten for clarity: Some people use *pandemic* interchangeably with *epidemic.*

Revising in Action

Read aloud the unrevised and then revised version of the following passage. Note that the second sentence has been rewritten because it was confusing.

> Ever since Carl Sagan's PBS special first aired, people have known that the word *cosmos* means "universe." ~~A different definition was once used for it to give it a different meaning.~~ The word comes from the Greek *kosmos,* which means "order." When the word is added to the Greek word *polis,* meaning "city," terms like *cosmopolitan* result. This term began, however, with a more down-to-earth definition.

Revise Improve your writing, using the following checklist and your partner's comments on the response sheet.

Using a Revising Checklist

Ideas

☐ 1. Do I state the topic and focus of my paragraph in the topic sentence?

☐ 2. Do I include different types of support (definitions, examples, and so on)?

☐ 3. Do I state all of my ideas clearly?

Organization

☐ 4. Does my paragraph have effective opening, body, and closing sentences?

☐ 5. Have I arranged the supporting details in an effective way?

Voice

☐ 6. Do I sound knowledgeable and interested?

LO9 Editing the Writing

The main work of editing is correcting your revised first draft. These next two pages cover the correct usage of apostrophes.

Using Apostrophes in Contractions

A contraction is a shortened form of a word or group of words with the missing letters replaced by an apostrophe. Here are some examples.

> **Common Contractions**
>
> **I'm** (I + am; the *a* is left out)
> **don't** (do + not; the *o* is left out)
> **they're** (they + are; the *a* is left out)
> **it's** (it + is; the *i* is left out)
> **should've** (should + have; the *h* and *a*
>   are left out)
>
> **wouldn't** (would + not; the *o* is left out)
> **they'd** (they + had; the *h* and *a* are left out)
> **must've** (must + have; the *h* and *a*
>   are left out)

Missing Letters or Numbers

Letters or numbers are left out in the following types of words and phrases. Apostrophes indicate where the omissions occur.

> **class of '10** (the number *20* is left out)
> **stop 'n' go traffic** (the letters *a* and *d* are omitted)

Apostrophe Practice Place an apostrophe as needed in the following sentences. If no apostrophe is needed, write "correct" on the blank next to the sentence.

1. Im sure that Jackson wouldve wanted to attend. _____
2. The menu listed "mac n cheese" and "ham n eggs." _____
3. The band was rockin way past midnight. _____
4. Its unfortunate that I lost my phone's protective case. _____
5. We're looking forward to the reunion of the class of 09. _____
6. You shouldnt stay up all night. I wouldnt. _____
7. Their flight might depart before theyre at the airport. _____

Additional Practice: For more practice see pages 608–609.

Apply Read the sentences in your definition paragraph, watching for contractions and special words with missing characters. Make sure these words have apostrophes in place to mark the missing letters or numbers.

Using Apostrophes to Show Basic Possession

Use apostrophes to show possession. Possession means "the act of having ownership." The placement of the apostrophe depends on whether the noun is singular or plural. Study the following examples.

Singular Possessives

■ The possessive form of singular nouns is usually made by adding an apostrophe and an *s*.

my computer**'s** virus	Elena**'s** latest hairstyle	last night**'s** storm

■ When a singular noun of more than one syllable ends with an *s* or *z* sound, the possessive may be formed by adding just an apostrophe, or an apostrophe and an *s*.

St. Louis**'** best park   or   St. Louis**'s** best park

Plural Possessives

■ The possessive form of plural nouns ending in *s* is made by adding just an apostrophe.

the instructors**'** offices   the Smiths**'** damaged car

■ For plural nouns not ending in *s,* add an apostrophe and *s*.

The men**'s** locker room   the children**'s** section of the library

Apostrophe Practice Indicate where apostrophes are needed in the following sentences. Add an apostrophe and an *s* for plural nouns not ending in *s*. If no apostrophe is needed, write "c" for "correct" on the blank line.

1. Carl car looks the same as Lois car. _____
2. The Kings house is smaller than the Davises house. _____
3. I like Wisconsin weather better than Texas weather. _____
4. The women organization donated to the childrens toy fund. _____
5. The alumni donation helped the childrens fund most. _____
6. The men suits use Sharissas design. _____

Additional Practice: For more practice see pages 608–609.

Apply Read the sentences in your definition paragraph, paying special attention to nouns that show possession. Be sure that you have correctly placed apostrophes in these words.

Marking a Paragraph

Edit the following model before you edit a revised version of your own paragraph.

Editing Practice   Carefully read the following paragraph, looking for problems listed in the checklist on the next page. Correct the model using the marks listed below.

A Cosmic Word

Ever since Carl Sagan's PBS special first aired people have known   *1*
that the word *cosmos* means "universe. This term began, however, with a
more down-to-earth definition. The word comes from the Greek *kosmos*,
which means "order." When this word is added to the Greek word *polis*,
meaning "city." Terms like *cosmopolitan* result. Even so, readers who pick   *5*
up the latest edition of *Cosmopolitan* aren't looking to find out about orderly
cities, but about fashion and fragrance—parts of the life of a cosmopolitan
woman. They certainly arent looking for stories about asteroids and other
cosmic phenomena. Knowing that, how is it that a word for "order" came to
be synonymous with the word four universe? Since the time of the ancient   *10*
Greeks many philosophers and theologians has noted that the universe is
orderly instead of chaotic. It follows certain laws. In fact, modern scientists
who seek to understand this orderly universe are called *cosmologists*.
Every resident of the cosmos can take comfort from the fact that such
thinkers arent called *chaos-ologists*.   *15*

Correction Marks

⌿ delete	⌃ add comma	⌃ add word (word)
d capitalize	? add question mark	⊙ add period
⌀ lowercase	⌄	⬭ spelling
⌃ insert	⌄ insert an apostrophe	⊓ switch

Using an Editing Checklist

Now it's time to correct your own definition paragraph.

Edit Prepare a clean copy of your revised essay and use the following checklist to edit it. Continue working until you can check off each item in the list.

Words

☐ 1. Have I used specific nouns and verbs? (See page 134.)

☐ 2. Have I used more action verbs than "be" verbs? (See page 536.)

Sentences

☐ 3. Have I used sentences with varying beginnings and lengths? (See pages 136–137.)

☐ 4. Have I avoided improper shifts in sentences? (See page 500.)

☐ 5. Have I avoided fragments and run-ons? (See pages 488–491, 494–495.)

Conventions

☐ 6. Do I use correct verb forms (*he saw,* not *he seen*)? (See pages 542, 544.)

☐ 7. Do my subjects and verbs agree (*she speaks,* not *she speak*)? (See pages 472–481.)

☐ 8. Have I used the right words (*their, there, they're*)?

☐ 9. Have I capitalized first words and proper nouns and adjectives? (See page 582.)

☐ 10. Have I used commas after long introductory word groups and to separate items in a series? (See pages 594, 596.)

☐ 11. Have I correctly punctuated any dialogue? (See pages 602–603.)

☐ 12. Have I used apostrophes correctly in contractions and to show possession? (See pages 608–609.)

Adding a Title

Make sure to add an attention-getting title. Here are three strategies to try.

- Highlight the main idea:

  A Cosmic Word

- Think creatively:

  Spreading the Word

Enrichment: Reading

On the following three pages you will find an essay entitled "Economics" from a textbook entitled *The Foundations of Business*. As you read and react to this essay, be sure to follow the steps in the reading process. The reading activities are followed by a number of writing ideas to choose from to write a definition paragraph or essay of your own.

> "Philosophy, rightly defined, is simply the love of wisdom."
> —Marcus Tullius Cicero

About the Authors

William M. Pride is professor of marketing, Mays Business School at Texas A&M University. He is author of *Marketing, 15th edition,* and has had many articles on marketing published in major journals. **Robert J. Hughes** specializes in business administration and college instruction. He has taught Introduction to Business for more than 35 years for Richland College and has authored a number of college textbooks. **Jack R. Kapoor** is a professor of business and economics at the College of DuPage. He has coauthored several textbooks and has served as a consultant on the television series *The Business File: An Introduction to Business.*

Prereading

College instructors often say that studying at the college level allows you to participate in the ongoing dialogue about important topics and issues. Reading helps you build a solid working knowledge of the issues so you can discuss them intelligently. What important topics are currently on your mind?

CONSIDER THE TRAITS

As you read the essay, focus first on the **ideas**—the concept that is being defined and the details that explain it. Then consider the **organization**—the way that the opening, middle, and closing parts are constructed.

What do you think?

Compare Cicero's definition of *philosophy* in the quotation at the top of the page with a dictionary definition. How are they similar and different? Share your thoughts with your classmates.

Identify   Before you read, answer these three questions.

1. What is your understanding of the topic, which is identified in the title?

_____

_____

2. Why would a business textbook address this topic?

_____

_____

3. What are two questions that you would like answered in your reading?

_____

_____

Reading and Rereading

You are familiar with the topic of this essay, and you know that it is important. But you may not have given it a great deal of careful thought. As you will see, the authors attempt to extend your understanding of the topic.

As you read, make it your goal to (1) identify the topic, (2) take special notice of the different definitions and explanations, and (3) decide if your questions have been answered.

Tip: You may find it helpful to take notes as you read (see page 22) because the essay contains many definitions and lists.

The Reading Process

Prereading   Rereading

Reading   Reflecting

Economics

Economics is the study of how wealth is created and distributed. By *wealth*, we mean "anything of value," including the products produced and sold by business. How wealth is distributed simply means "who gets what." Experts often use economics to explain the choices we make and how these choices change as we cope with the demands of everyday life. In simple terms, individuals, businesses, governments, and society must make decisions that reflect what is important to each group at a particular time. For example, suppose you want to take a weekend trip to some exotic vacation spot, and you also want to begin an investment program. Because of your financial resources, though, you cannot do both, so you must decide what is most important. Business firms, governments, and to some extent society face the same types of decisions. Each group must deal with

1

5

10

scarcity when making important decisions. In this case, scarcity means "lack of resources"—money, time, natural resources, and so on—that are needed to satisfy a want or need.   *15*

Today, experts often study economic problems from two different perspectives: microeconomics and macroeconomics. **Microeconomics** is the study of the decisions made by individuals and businesses. Microeconomics, for example, examines how the prices of homes affect the number of homes individuals will buy. On the other hand, **macroeconomics** *20* is the study of the national economy and the global economy. Macroeconomics examines the economic effects of national income, unemployment, inflation, taxes, government spending, interest rates, and similar factors on a nation and society.

The decisions that individuals, business firms, government, and   *25* society make and the way in which people deal with the creation and distribution of wealth determines the kind of economic system, or economy, that a nation has.

Over the years, the economic systems of the world have differed in essentially two ways: (1) the ownership of the factors of production and   *30* (2) how they answer four basic economic questions that direct a nation's economic activity.

Factors of production are the resources used to produce goods and services. There are four such factors.

- *Land and natural resources*—elements that can be used in the   *35* production process to make appliances, automobiles, and other products. Typical examples include crude oil, forests, minerals, land, water, and even air.
- *Labor*—the time and effort that we use to produce goods and services. It includes human resources such as managers and employees.   *40*
- *Capital*—the money, facilities, equipment, and machines used in the operation of organizations. Although most people think of capital as just money, it can also be the manufacturing equipment in a Pepperidge Farm production facility or a computer used in the corporate offices of McDonald's.   *45*
- *Entrepreneurship*—the activity that organizes land and natural resources, labor, and capital. It is the willingness to take risks and the knowledge and ability to use the other factors of production efficiently. An entrepreneur is a person who risks his or her time, effort, and money to start and operate a business.   *50*

A nation's economic system significantly affects all the economic activities of its citizens and organizations. This far-reaching impact becomes more apparent when we consider that a country's economic system determines how the factors of production are used to meet the

needs of society. Today, two different economic systems exist: capitalism   *55*
and command economics. The way each system answers the four basic
economic questions listed here determines a nation's economy.

1. What goods and services—and how much of each—will be
   produced?
2. How will these goods and services be produced?   *60*
3. For whom will these goods and services be produced?
4. Who owns and who controls the major factors of production?

From Pride/Hughes/Kapoor, *Foundations of Business*, 3E. © 2013 Cengage Learning

Reflecting

After you complete your reading, answer the following questions. Share your
responses with your classmates.

1. How do the authors define economics in this essay?

_____

_____

2. What other terms are defined in the essay? Name two.

_____

_____

3. What is one new thing that you have learned about economics in your
reading?

_____

_____

4. What questions, if any, do you still have about the topic?

_____

_____

_____

5. How would you rate this essay, and why?

Weak ★ ★ ★ ★ ★ Strong

_____

_____

Vocabulary Practice

Identify Define the word parts as indicated. Then try to explain the meaning of the complete word. (See pages 35–36 and 623–631 for help.)

1. **distributed** (line 1)   dis + trib(ut) + ed

_____

_____

2. **willingness** (line 47)   willing + ness

_____

_____

3. **capitalism** (line 55)   capital + ism

_____

_____

Drawing Inferences

Explain Answer these three questions to help you draw inferences about the text.

1. Why is the study of economics important?

_____

_____

_____

2. What observations can you make about your personal economy? Your family's economy?

_____

_____

_____

3. How will the economy affect your career choice?

_____

_____

LO3 Reading and Reacting to a Professional Paragraph

The process paragraph below explains how forensic scientists inspect a bloodstain. It comes from a textbook entitled *Forensic Science: Fundamentals and Investigations.* Use the reading process to help you gain a full understanding of the text.

Prereading Before you read, answer these three questions:

1. What do you learn from the title and first sentence?

_____

2. What do you already know about the topic?

_____

_____

3. What challenge might the text present as you read?

_____

_____

Reading and Rereading As you read, make it your goal to (1) identify the topic and main idea, (2) consider the supporting details, and (3) reread parts that you don't understand. Consider annotating the text (page 20) during your reading.

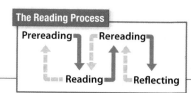

Crime-Scene Investigation of Blood

There are several steps used in processing a bloodstain, and each can provide a different kind of critical information. The first step is to confirm the stain is blood. Could ketchup, ink, or any other red substance cause the red stain? Before trying to collect the blood, it is necessary to confirm that the evidence is blood, either by using the Kastle-Meyer test or the Leucomalachite green test. If the substance proves to be blood, the second step is to confirm that the blood is human. One test that can be used to determine this is the ELISA test. The third step is to determine the blood type. Depending on the circumstances, blood typing may not be done at all, just DNA analysis.   1

    5

    10

"Crime-Scene Investigation of Blood" from BERTINO. *Forensic Science: Fundamentals and Investigations,* Copyright 2012 Wadsworth, a part Cengage Learning, Inc.

Reflecting   After you complete your reading, answer these questions. Share your responses with your classmates.

1. How many steps are provided in this process?

_____

2. What words or phrases are used to announce each new step?

_____

3. What questions does this text bring to mind? Name at least one.

_____

Vocabulary Practice

Identify   Use context clues to explain or define any two words in the paragraph other than the scientific tests. (See pages 33–34 for help.)

1. _____

clues: _____

definition: _____

2. _____

clues: _____

definition: _____

Drawing Inferences

Explain   Answer the following questions to help you draw inferences about the text. (See pages 35–36 for help.)

1. What does this paragraph tell you about the nature of a crime-scene investigation?

_____

2. How has the media glamorized investigations such as this one?

_____

3. Why do people enter professions related to safety and crime?

_____

LO4 Reading and Reacting to a Second Professional Paragraph

The paragraph below from a history textbook addresses a facet of modern urbanization. Use the reading process to help you understand the text.

About the Authors

Philip J. Adler taught courses in world history for nearly 30 years. He has published widely in the historical journals of this country and German-speaking Europe. **Randall L. Pouwels** has published widely. His book *Horn and Crescent: Cultural Change and Traditional Islam on the East African Coast, 800–1900* has become a standard work on African history.

Prereading Before you read, answer these questions:

1. What do the title and first sentence tell you about the text?

_____

2. What questions do you hope to have answered?

_____

Reading and Rereading As you read, make it your goal to (1) identify the topic, (2) locate the key supporting details, and (3) reread any parts that confuse you.

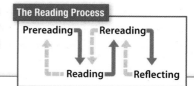

The Reading Process

Prereading   Rereading

Reading   Reflecting

The Human Face of Modern Urbanization

Megacities from Mexico City to Santiago, Chile, and Rio de Janeiro are the   *1*
result of massive, uncontrollable migrations from impoverished and strife-ridden
rural Latin America during the second half of the last century. The thousands
of newcomers who arrive daily depend at first on the hospitality of family or
friends who preceded them to the city. Then they scramble to find (or invent) jobs   *5*
as "informals" in the dynamic, unofficial informal economy (whose productivity
equals that of the official economy that is reflected in the statistics). Next, they
join others to build temporary huts on unoccupied lands in remote outskirts of
the city. After 10 or 20 years of persistent political activism and unrelenting
toil, the shantytown eventually becomes a settlement of owner-built houses   *10*
incorporated by the city, provided with water and utilities, and linked to the
urban public transportation system. The inhabitants must cobble together two
or three jobs as construction workers, street vendors or performers, or domestic
servants in the faraway city centers, commuting hours each way. Because they
are officially invisible, they have no benefits or employment guarantees.   *15*

From ADLER/POUWELS. *World Civilization*, 6E. Copyright 2008 Wadsworth, a part of Cengage Learning, Inc.

Reacting After you complete your reading, answer these questions. Share your responses with your classmates.

1. What process is explained in the paragraph?

   _____

   _____

   _____

2. How many steps in this process are included?

   _____

   _____

3. What words or phrases are used to signal different steps?

   _____

   _____

   _____

4. What are two key details you learned in your reading?

   _____

   _____

   _____

5. Has the text changed or expanded your understanding of the topic? If so, how?

   _____

   _____

   _____

6. How would you rate this paragraph, and why?

   Weak ★ ★ ★ ★ ★ Strong

   _____

   _____

Vocabulary Practice

Identify Use context clues to explain or define the following words. (See pages 33–34 for help.)

1. **outskirts** (line 8)

   clues: _____

   definition: _____

2. **unrelenting** (line 9)

   clues: _____

   definition: _____

3. **cobble** (line 12)

   clues: _____

   definition: _____

Drawing Inferences

Explain Answer these questions to help you draw inferences from the text. (See pages 29–31 for help.)

1. What do the "megacites" have to say about the state of affairs in the world now and for the future?

   _____

   _____

2. What is behind the "mass exodus" to the urban areas? And why is this the case?

   _____

   _____

3. What realistic alternatives are there to this development?

   _____

   _____

LO5 Practicing Reading Skills

Checking for Key Words

As you read, stay alert for key words that signal a process. Writers often indicate a new step by using transitional phrases like *first step, second phase, next stage,* or *final event.* Such words tell the order in which the steps occur. Here is a longer list of word clues that signal time order in process writing.

■ First	■ Second	■ Eventually
■ Start	■ Next	■ Last
■ Begin	■ Then	■ Final
	■ Third	■ End

In some process writing, dates (December 4, 1941), centuries (fourth century), decades (1980s), months (March), and days (Monday) are used to tell when a phase in a process begins or ends.

Understanding Patterns of Reasoning

Most of the paragraphs and essays that you read in your classes will follow either deductive or inductive reasoning. Deductive thinking moves from a topic sentence or thesis statement expressing a main idea to specific supporting details. Inductive thinking moves in the other direction, from specific facts to a general conclusion.

Use these questions to check for deductive thinking.

- Does the paragraph or essay start with a topic sentence (or thesis) that expresses the main idea of the writing?
- Do the details support or follow the topic sentence?
- Does the conclusion logically follow the ideas that come before it?

Use these questions to check for inductive thinking.

- Does the text start with a series of facts, examples, and explanations?
- Do they logically lead up to a general conclusion?
- Does the general conclusion support the evidence before it?

Apply Use the "critical questions" above to determine if the paragraphs on pages 258 and 260 follow deductive or inductive thinking.

Writing

In your own process paragraph, you will explain how something works or occurs or how to do or make something. Be sure to use the writing process to guide your work. (See pages 94–99.)

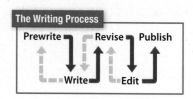

LO6 Planning Process Writing

The information on these two pages will help you complete the important first step—prewriting—before you start writing.

Selecting a Topic

Use the following ideas to generate possible process-paragraph topics.

> **Consider a process that . . .**
> - relates to your major or academic concentration.
> - demonstrates something you do well or want to learn more about.
> - has made the news recently.
> - impacts the world around you.
> - relates to your favorite entertainment—sports, music, the arts.

Select List four process topics that can be covered in one paragraph. They may be something you know a lot about or something you need to research. Then select one to write about.

1. _____
2. _____
3. _____
4. _____

Reviewing the Process

Once you have selected a process topic, review what you know about it, and if necessary, do some additional research.

Reflect Carefully consider these questions to plan your research and collecting of details.

1. How well do I know this process? _____
2. If needed, how can I learn more about it? _____
3. Do I have time to conduct enough research? _____

Gathering Details

Use a process analysis chart to organize the steps for your process paragraph. The example below lists the steps of tree decay.

Gather To complete a process analysis chart, first write down your subject and, if applicable, any materials needed. Then fill in the steps involved in the process.

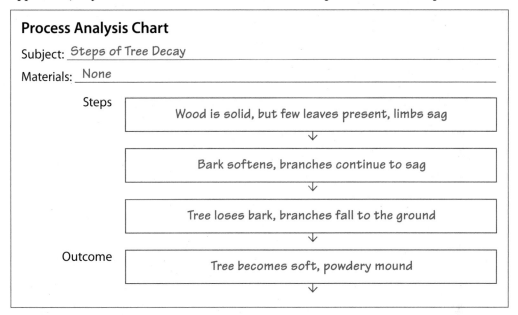

Process Analysis Chart

Subject: *Steps of Tree Decay*

Materials: *None*

Steps
> Wood is solid, but few leaves present, limbs sag
>
> ↓
>
> Bark softens, branches continue to sag
>
> ↓
>
> Tree loses bark, branches fall to the ground
>
> ↓

Outcome
> Tree becomes soft, powdery mound
>
> ↓

Using Transitions

Remember that transitions, or linking words, connect ideas by showing the relationship between them. In process paragraphs, time-order transitional words link the steps and add clarity to the writing. Refer to the following list as you write your paragraph. (Also see page 263.)

Transitions that show time order

before	during	after	next	finally
first	second	third	then	later
when	once	while	at	meanwhile

READING/WRITING CONNECTION

Transition words act as clue words for readers, signaling different steps in the process.

LO7 Writing the First Draft

Writing a first draft is your first attempt to connect all your ideas about a topic. While you write your first draft, don't worry about making everything right. Instead, focus on getting all your ideas on paper.

Read Carefully read and enjoy this student's paragraph about jump-starting a dead car battery.

Back from the Dead

Topic Sentence

One of the most frustrating situations to deal with is a car   1
with a dead battery. Fortunately, with a set of jumper cables and a
little help, you can get back on the road in no time. To jump-start
a car battery, you will need a set of jumper cables and a second
car with a fully charged battery. First, line both cars up so the   5
batteries are as close as they can be. Make sure both cars are
turned completely off. Next, familiarize yourself with the positive
(+) and negative (-) terminals of both car batteries. After you have
done so, connect one end of the positive jumper cable (usually

Body Sentences

red or orange) to the positive terminal of the dead battery. Then   10
connect the other end of the positive cable to the positive terminal
of the live battery. Next, connect the negative cable (usually black)
to the negative terminal of the live battery. Finally, clamp the
other end of the negative cable to a solid unpainted metal part of
the engine of the dead car. From there, stand back and start the   15
car that's providing the jump. Wait about five minutes, and then
try to start the car with the dead battery. If it starts up, your last

Closing Sentence

step is to remove the cables in the reverse order in which you put
them on. And then you can hit the road.

Consider the Craft

1. What do you like best about this paragraph?

2. Is the process easy to follow?

3. Does the writer use transitions to connect ideas? Which ones?

4. Could you complete the process by following the steps given in this paragraph?

Marking a Paragraph

The model that follows has a number of errors.

Punctuation Practice Correct the following paragraph, using the corrections marks below.

Proposing a New Amendment

Did you know their are two ways to propose a new amendment to the   *1*
Constitution?. The first method is the path each current amendment has
taken. For this process to work an amendment must be proposed by a
two-thrids vote in each house of Congress. Next, the proposed amendment
must be ratified by three-fourths of the states. Before it officially becomes   *5*
an amendment. The second way to amend the Constitution are to call for
a Constitutional Convention. For this to happen, two-thirds of the states
would have to demand that the convention take place. similar to the first
method, the proposed amendment would then have to be ratified by a
three-fourths vote of the states. To date, this method has never been used   *10*
it is unlikely we will see a constitutional Convention anytime soon.

Correction Marks

⌐	delete	⅄	add comma	word ∧	add word
d̲̲	capitalize	?	add question mark	⊙	add period
b̸	lowercase	∧		⌒	spelling
∧	insert	v̓	insert an apostrophe	⌐⌐	switch

INSIGHT ——————————————————————————————

Avoid using two negative words to express a single negative idea. Double negatives are not acceptable in academic writing.

Double Negative: I don't have no change for a $20 bill.

Standard: I don't have any change for a $20 bill.

I have no change for a $20 bill.

Using an Editing Checklist

Now it's time to correct your own paragraph.

Apply   Create a clean copy of your revised paragraph and use the following checklist to check for errors. Continue working until you can check off each item in the list.

Words

☐ 1. Have I used specific nouns and verbs? (See page 134.)

☐ 2. Have I used more action verbs than "be" verbs? *Is, are, was,* and *were* are examples of "be" verbs. (See page 536.)

Sentences

☐ 3. Have I varied the beginnings and lengths of sentences? (See pages 136–137.)

☐ 4. Have I combined short, choppy sentences? (See page 137.)

☐ 5. Have I avoided fragments, run-ons and comma splices? (See pages 136–137, 488–491, 494–495.)

Conventions

☐ 6. Do I use correct verb forms *(he saw,* not *he seen)*? (See pages 542, 544.)

☐ 7. Do my subjects and verbs agree *(she speaks,* not *she speak)*? (See pages 472–481.)

☐ 8. Have I used the right words *(their, there, they're)*?

☐ 9. Have I capitalized first words and proper nouns and adjectives?

☐ 10. Have I used commas after long introductory word groups? (See pages 592–595.)

☐ 11. Have I carefully checked my spelling?

Adding a Title

Make sure to add a title that calls attention to the topic. Here are two simple strategies for creating one.

- State the topic:

  Proposing a New Amendment

- Think creatively:

  Back from the Dead

Create   Prepare a clean final copy of your paragraph and proofread it before you share it.

Enrichment: Reading

On the following four pages you will find an essay entitled "Campus Racism 101" to read and react to. As you read this essay, be sure to follow the steps in the reading process. The reading activities are followed by a number of writing ideas to choose from to write a process paragraph or essay of your own.

> "Life is a lively process of becoming."
> —Douglas MacArthur

About the Author

Nikki Giovanni is a poet, essayist, and a University Distinguished Professor of English at Virginia Tech. She has received many honors and awards for her writing and has, over the years, become a valued spokesperson in the African-American community.

Prereading

Reading process essays can answer complicated questions: How does a nuclear fission reactor work? How do bacteria reproduce? Other times it can help you solve practical problems: What's the best way to cook an omelet? How do I tie a half-Windsor knot? No matter the topic, a process essay requires concentration and analysis. List a few complicated or practical processes that you wonder about:

CONSIDER THE TRAITS

As you read this essay, focus first on the **ideas**—the topic, main idea, and steps in the process. Then consider the **organization**—the way that the opening, middle, and closing parts are put together. Also notice the author's voice—or her writing personality. And finally, ask yourself if these traits combine to produce an enriching reading experience.

What do you think?

What point is Douglas McArthur trying to make in the quotation above?

Identify   Before you read, answer these three questions:

1. What do the title and the first two paragraphs tell you about the essay?

_____

2. What are your first thoughts about the author's purpose and audience?

_____

3. What questions would you like answered in your reading?

_____

Reading and Rereading

Read the following essay by Nikki Giovanni that first appeared in *Essence* in 1991. As you will see, she offers advice in her own wonderful way to one audience in particular. But is she also speaking to others in the university community?

As you read, make it your goal to (1) identify the topic and main idea, (2) pay careful attention to her rules (steps), and (3) consider her thoughts expressed in the ending part.

Tip: Consider annotating the text (page 20) and/or taking notes (page 22) during your reading.

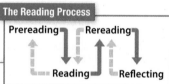

The Reading Process

Prereading   Rereading

Reading   Reflecting

Campus Racism 101

There is a bumper sticker that reads: *TOO BAD IGNORANCE ISN'T*   1
PAINFUL. I like that. But ignorance is. We just seldom attribute the pain to it or even recognize it when we see it. Like the postcard on my corkboard. It shows a young man in a very hip jacket smoking a cigarette. In the background is a high school with the American flag waving. The   5
caption says: "Too cool for school. Yet too stupid for the real world." Out of the mouth of the young man is a bubble enclosing the words "Maybe I'll start a band." There could be a postcard showing a jock in a uniform saying, "I don't need school. I'm going to the NFL or NBA." Or one showing a young man or woman studying and a group of young people saying, "So   10
you want to be white." Or something equally **demeaning**. We need to quit it.

I am a professor of English at Virginia Tech. I've been here for four years, though for only two years with academic rank. I am tenured, which means I have a teaching position for life, a rarity on a predominantly   15
white campus. Whether from **malice** or ignorance, people who think I

should be at a predominantly Black institution will ask, "Why are you
at Tech?" Because it's here. And so are Black students. But even if Black
students weren't here, it's painfully obvious that this nation and this
world cannot allow white students to go through higher education without   *20*
interacting with Blacks in authoritative positions. It is equally clear that
predominantly Black colleges cannot accommodate the numbers of Black
students who want and need an education.

    Is it difficult to attend a predominantly white college? Compared
with what? Being passed over for promotion because you lack credentials?   *25*
Being turned down for jobs because you are not college-educated? Joining
the armed forces or going to jail because you cannot find an alternative
to the streets? Let's have a little perspective here. Where can you go and
what can you do that frees you from interacting with the white American
mentality? You're going to interact; the only question is, will you be in   *30*
some control of yourself and your actions, or will you be controlled by
others? I'm going to recommend self-control.

    What's the difference between prison and college? They both prescribe
your behavior for a given period of time. They both allow you to read books
and develop your writing. They both give you time alone to think and time   *35*
with your peers to talk about issues. But four years of prison doesn't give
you a passport to greater opportunities. Most likely that time only gives
you greater knowledge of how to get back in. Four years of college gives you
an opportunity not only to lift yourself but to serve your people effectively.
What's the difference when you are called nigger in college from when you   *40*
are called nigger in prison? In college you can, though I admit with effort,
follow procedures to have those students who called you nigger kicked out
or suspended. You can bring issues to public attention without risking your
life. But mostly, college is and always has been the future. We, neither
less nor more than other people, need knowledge. There are discomforts   *45*
attached to attending predominantly white colleges, though no more so
than living in a racist world. Here are some rules to follow that may help:

    Go to class. No matter how you feel. No matter how you think the
professor feels about you. It's important to have a consistent presence in
the classroom. If nothing else, the professor will know you care enough and   *50*
are serious enough to be there.

    Meet your professors. Extend your hand (give a firm handshake)
and tell them your name. Ask them what you need to do to make an A.
You may never make an A, but you have put them on notice that you are
serious about getting good grades.   *55*

    Do assignments on time. Typed or computer-generated. You have the
syllabus. Follow it, and turn those papers in. If for some reason you can't
complete an assignment on time, let your professor know before it is due

and work out a new due date—then meet it.

Go back to see your professor. Tell him or her your name again. If an   *60*
assignment received less than an A, ask why, and find out what you need
to do to improve the next assignment.

Yes, your professor is busy. So are you. So are your parents who are
working to pay or help with your tuition. Ask early what you need to do if
you feel you are starting to get into academic trouble. Do not wait until you   *65*
are failing.

Understand that there will be professors who do not like you; there may
even be professors who are racist or sexist or both. You must discriminate
among your professors to see who will give you the help you need. You may
not simply say, "They are all against me." They aren't. They mostly don't   *70*
care. Since you are the one who wants to be educated, find the people who
want to help.

Don't defeat yourself. Cultivate your friends. Know your enemies.
You cannot undo hundreds of years of prejudicial thinking. Think for
yourself and speak up. Raise your hand in class. Say what you believe no   *75*
matter how awkward you may think it sounds. You will improve in your
articulation and confidence.

Participate in some campus activity. Join the newspaper staff. Run for
office. Join a dorm council. Do something that involves you on campus. You
are going to be there for four years, so let your presence be known, if not felt.   *80*

You will inevitably run into some white classmates who are troubling
because they often say stupid things, ask stupid questions—and expect an
answer. Here are some comebacks to some of the most common inquiries
and comments:

Q: What's it like to grow up in a ghetto?   *85*

A: I don't know.

Q: (from the teacher): Can you give us the Black perspective on Toni
Morrison, Huck Finn, slavery, Martin Luther King, Jr., and others?

A: I can give you my perspective. (Do not take the burden of 22 million
people on your shoulders. Remind everyone that you are an individual, and   *90*
don't speak for the race or any other individual within it.)

Q: Why do all the Black people sit together in the dining hall?

A: Why do all the white students sit together?

Q: Why should there be an African-American studies course?

A: Because white Americans have not adequately studied the   *95*
contributions of Africans and African-Americans. Both Black and white
students need to know our total common history.

Q: Why are there so many scholarships for "minority" students?

A: Because they wouldn't give my great-grandparents their forty acres
and the mule.   *100*

Q: How can whites understand Black history, culture, literature, and so forth?

A: The same way we understand white history, culture, literature, and so forth. That is why we're in school: to learn.

Q: Should whites take African-American studies courses?   *105*

A: Of course. We take white-studies courses, though the universities don't call them that.

Comment: When I see groups of Black people on campus, it's really intimidating.

Comeback: I understand what you mean. I'm frightened when I see   *110*
white students congregating.

Comment: It's not fair. It's easier for you guys to get into college than for other people.

Comeback: If it's so easy, why aren't there more of us?

Comment: It's not our fault that America is the way it is.   *115*

Comeback: It's not our fault, either, but both of us have a responsibility to make changes.

It's really very simple. Educational progress is a national concern; education is a private one. Your job is not to educate white people; it is to obtain an education. If you take the racial world on your shoulders, you   *120*
will not get the job done. Deal with yourself as an individual worthy of respect, and make everyone else deal with you the same way. College is a little like playing grown-up. Practice what you want to be. You have been telling your parents you are grown. Now is your chance to act like it.

demeaning
degrading or insulting

malice
desire to inflict injury, harm, or suffering

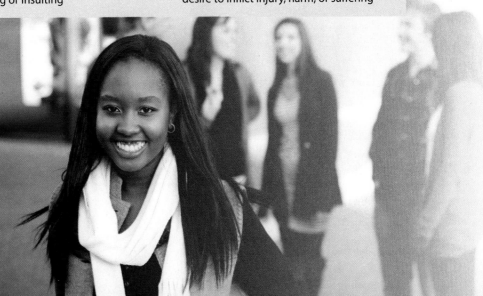

Reflecting

After your reading, answer the following questions:

1. What main idea is developed?

_____

_____

2. What audience can benefit from reading this essay?

_____

_____

3. Is this essay relevant today? It was written in 1991. Explain.

_____

_____

4. How would you describe the author's voice or writing personality?

_____

_____

5. What significance is there in the title?

_____

_____

6. What part of the essay do you like best (or the least)?

_____

_____

7. How would you rate this essay, and why?

Weak ★ ★ ★ ★ ★ **Strong**

_____

_____

Vocabulary Practice

Identify Define the word parts as indicated. Then try to explain the meaning of the complete word. (See pages 35–36 and 623–631 for help.)

1. **predominantly** (line 15) pre + domin + ant +ly

_____

_____

2. **discomforts** (line 45)   dis + comforts

_____

_____

3. **perspective** (line 87)   per + spect + ive

_____

_____

Drawing Inferences

Explain Draw inferences about the text by answering the questions below.

1. "But mostly, college is and always has been the future" is an idea in the essay. How would you explain it?

_____

_____

2. "Educational progress is a national concern; education is a private one" is another idea in the essay. How would you explain it?

_____

_____

3. Are you aware of other preconceived feelings such as the ones expressed in this essay?

_____

_____

Writing

What follows are possible writing activities to complete in response to the reading. Use the writing process (pages 94–99) to help you develop your writing.

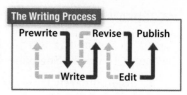

Prewriting

Choose one of the following writing ideas. Or decide upon an idea of your own related to the reading.

Writing Ideas

1. **Writing to Learn:** In the essay opening, Giovanni identifies the following bumper-sticker message: TOO BAD IGNORANCE ISN'T PAINFUL. Explore this idea in a personal journal or blog entry; base your thoughts on your own experiences and observations.

2. **Paragraph Writing:** Write a paragraph based on one of the topics you identified on pages 256 or 264.

3. In a paragraph, explain a process related to your job.

4. **Essay Writing:** Using Giovanni's essay as a model, provide the steps or rules to follow for another aspect of life (succeeding in the workplace, being gay and maneuvering in the straight world, etc.).

5. Explain a complicated process based on one of your personal interests or based on the course of study you would like to pursue.

When planning . . .

Refer to pages 264–265 to help you with your prewriting and planning. Also use the tips that follow.

- Make sure that you know the process well before you try to explain it.
- If necessary, carry out research to learn about the process.
- Create a visual representation of the steps in the process and decide if they are all there and in the correct order.
- Review the examples of process writing in this chapter to see what types of information they include.

Reading

Reading classification paragraphs helps you recognize the variety hidden in a complex topic.

LO2 Learning Reading Strategies

Analyzing the Categories

There are three basic questions to answer when reading a classification paragraph:

1. How does the writer break down the topic into categories?
2. How does the writer describe each category?
3. Are the categories equal?

> **INSIGHT**
>
> Certain phrases, like the ones below, signal a classification.
> - Four types
> - Separate classes
> - Different categories
> - Certain kinds

The Process in Action

Here is an analysis of a paragraph about basic taste sensations.

1. **How does the writer break down the topic into categories?**
   salty, sweet, sour, and bitter

2. **How does the writer describe each category?**
   A salty taste comes from substances that include sodium, such as potato chips. The sweet sensation comes from sugars, both processed and natural. Sour tastes come from acidic foods such as lemons, and bitter tastes come from alkaline foods such as coffee.

3. **Are the categories equal?**
   All of the categories seem related, and they are explained with the same type of details.

Diagramming the Key Parts

Classification paragraphs generally follow a similar pattern. The first sentence or two introduces the topic and categories. Then each category is addressed separately, including supporting details, which may involve a definition, examples, or traits.

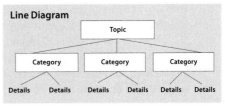

Line Diagram

To help you visualize the categories and supporting details, you can use a line diagram.

Practice Consider diagramming the key parts for the paragraph on the next page. Afterward, compare diagrams with your classmates.

LO3 Reading and Reacting to a Professional Paragraph

The classification paragraph below categorizes different methods of childhood discipline. It comes from a psychology textbook, *Psychology: A Journey* by Dennis Coon and John O. Mitterer. Use the reading process to help you gain a full understanding of the text. (See below.)

Prereading Before you read, answer these three questions:

1. What do the title and first sentence tell you about the topic?

   _____

2. Why might this topic be covered in a psychology textbook?

   _____

   _____

3. What do you expect to learn?

   _____

   _____

Reading and Rereading As you read, make it your goal to (1) identify the three ways of disciplining, (2) think about the author's purpose, and (3) the value of the information. Consider annotating the text as you read. (See page 20.)

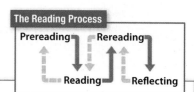

Effective Discipline

Parents typically discipline children in one of three ways. Power assertion refers to physical punishment or a show of force, such as taking away toys or privileges. As an alternative, some parents use withdrawal of love by refusing to speak to a child, threatening to leave, rejecting the child, or otherwise acting as if the child is temporarily unlovable. Management techniques combine praise, recognition, approval, rules, reasoning, and the like to encourage desirable behavior. Each of these approaches can control a child's behavior, but their side effects differ considerably.

1

5

From COON/MITTERER. *Psychology: A Journey*, 4E. © 2011 Wadsworth, a part of Cengage Learning, Inc.

Reflecting   After you complete your reading, answer these questions. Share your responses with your classmates.

1. What is the specific topic of the text?

2. How many supporting categories or types are provided? What are the categories?

3. What logical pattern of reasoning does the text follow—deductive or inductive? Explain. (See page 28 for help.)

4. Are signal words such as *first, second,* or *next* used in this paragraph?

5. How has the selection changed or expanded your understanding of the topic?

6. What questions do you still have about the topic?

7. How would you rate this paragraph, and why?

   Weak ★ ★ ★ ★ ★ Strong

Vocabulary Practice

Identify   Use context clues to explain or define the following words. (See pages 33–34 for help.)

1. **alternative** (line 3)

    clues: _____

    definition: _____

2. **withdrawal** (line 3)

    clues: _____

    definition: _____

3. **recognition** (line 6)

    clues: _____

    definition: _____

Critically Thinking

Explain   Freely explore your own thoughts about effective childhood discipline in the space below. How does your own thinking match up with the text on page 286?

_____

_____

_____

_____

_____

_____

_____

_____

LO4 Reading and Reacting to a Professional Classification

The selection below from *Media/Impact: An Introduction to Mass Media* classifies the typical roles in movie production. Use the reading process to help you gain a full understanding of the text.

About the Author

Shirley Biagi is a professor in the Department of Communication Studies at California State University, Sacramento. *Media/Impact* is in its tenth edition and is also published in Canadian, Greek, Spanish, and Korean editions.

Prereading Before you read, answer these questions:

1. What do the title and first paragraph tell you about the text?

_____

2. What is the significance of the list?

_____

3. What do you expect to learn in your reading?

_____

Reading and Rereading As you read, make it your goal to (1) identify the topic of the text, (2) locate each of the supporting categories, and (3) think about the author's purpose—to inform, to persuade, or to entertain. Consider annotating the text (page 20) and/or taking notes (page 22) as you read.

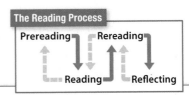

The Reading Process

Movies at Work

Today the center of the movie industry is movie production. Independent companies produce most of the movies that are distributed by the major studios and exhibited at your local theater under agreements with individual studios. Although these production companies work independently, and each company is organized differently, jobs in movie production fall mainly into the following categories:

1. Screenwriters
2. Producers

1

5

3. Directors
4. Actors   *10*
5. Technical production
6. Marketing and administration

Every movie begins with a story idea, and these ideas come from
screenwriters. Screenwriters work independently, marketing their story
ideas through agents, who promote their clients' scripts to the studios and   *15*
to independent producers.

Typically, producers are the people who help gather the funding to
create a movie project. Financing can come from banks or from individuals
who want to invest in a specific movies. Sometimes producers or actors
help finance the movies they make.   *20*

Once the funding for the story is in place, a director organizes all the
tasks necessary to turn the script into a movie. The director works with
the producer to manage the movie's budget.

Obviously, actors are important to any movie project. Sometimes the
producer and director approach particular stars for a project even before   *25*
they seek funding, to attract interest from the investors and also help
assure the investors that the movies will have some box office appeal.

Technical production includes all the people who actually create the
movie—camera operators, set designers, film editors, script supervisors,
and costumers, for example. Once the movie is finished, the marketing   *30*
people seek publicity for the project. They also design a plan to advertise
and promote the movie to the public.

As in any media industry, people who work in administration help
keep all the records necessary to pay salaries and track employees'
expenses, as well as keep track of the paperwork involved in organizing   *35*
any business.

From Biagi, *Media/Impact: An Introduction to Mass Media*, 10E. © 2012 Cengage Learning

Reflecting   After you complete your reading, answer the following questions about
the selection. Then discuss your responses with your classmates.

1. What is the topic of the text? _____

_____

2. How many supporting categories are provided? What are the categories?

_____

_____

3. What observations can you make about the organization of the text? Is it
   easy or hard to follow, and why? _____

_____

LO7 Writing the First Draft

After you are done planning, you are ready to write the first draft of your paragraph. Provided below is another sample classification paragraph.

Read Read the paragraph, noting how the writer classified the topic, mustard, into four distinct subgroups.

My Condiments to the Chef

Topic Sentence / Category 1 / Category 2 / Category 3 / Category 4 / Closing Sentence

When most Americans talk about mustard, they mean a type of bright-yellow goo that the rest of the world hardly recognizes. Actually, there are four basic types of mustard. Yellow mustard is the most common in America, made from finely ground mustard seeds, vinegar, and a bright yellow coloring called turmeric. Yellow mustard is mild and is a common seasoning on hot dogs. For a spicier type of mustard, people enjoy brown mustard, which is made from coarse-ground mustard seeds and looks yellow and brown. For an even stronger flavor, mustard lovers turn to the famous mustard called Dijon, named after the French city where it was first processed. Dijon mustard is finely ground and is usually mixed with wine instead of vinegar. Finally, there are many hybrid mustards categorized as specialty mustards, including everything from honey to jalapeños. When it comes to taste, there's a mustard for just about everybody.

Consider the Craft

1. What do you like best about this paragraph?
2. What are two of your favorite details?
3. What is the reason behind the arrangement of the categories?

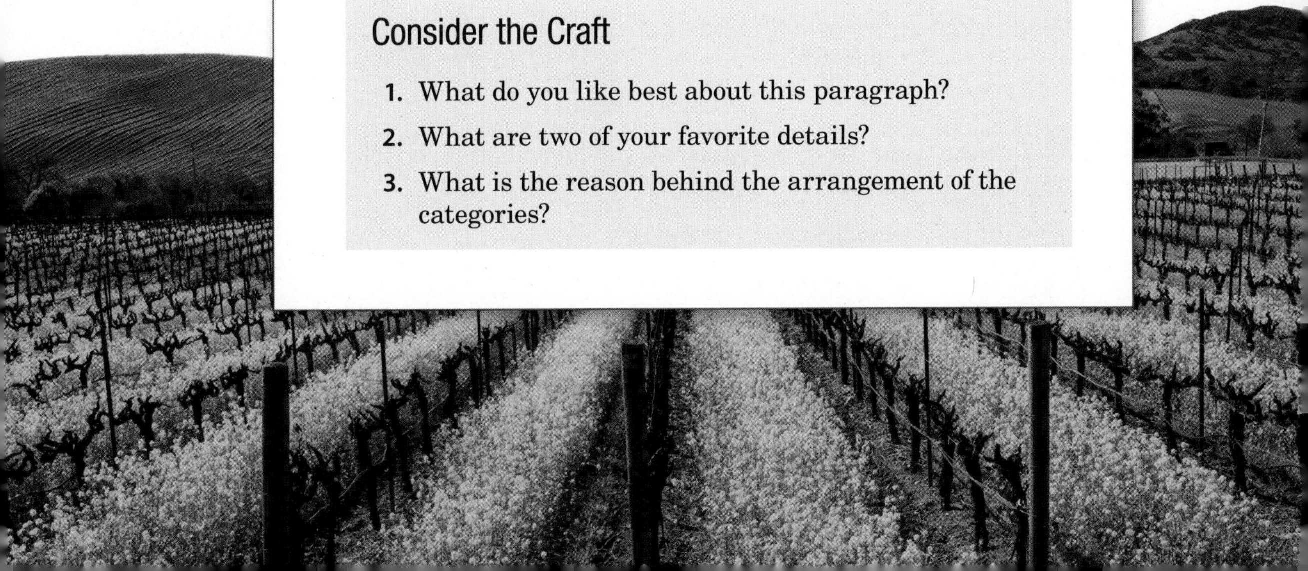

Harris Shiffman, 2013 / Used under license from Shutterstock.com

Drafting Tips

When you write a classification, your goal is to share information in a clear, organized manner. To that end, consider the following tips as you write your first draft.

- **To make your beginning clear,** make sure that your topic sentence identifies your topic and introduces your categories.
- **To help your readers follow your classification,** decide on an effective and consistent (similar) way to introduce each category. Also decide on a logical arrangement of the categories.
- **To make sure that your writing has balance,** provide an equal number of details for each category.
- **To emphasize your purpose,** use language that reflects your goal—to inform, to entertain, or so on.

INSIGHT ——————————————————————————————

Remember that a paragraph is a limited unit of writing, so restrict yourself to just a few supporting details for each category. (If you have a lot to say about each category, perhaps you should develop a classification essay. See pages 303–307.)

The Working Parts of a Paragraph

A paragraph consists of three main parts, each of which has a special function. The information that follows explains each part.

Topic Sentence:	The topic sentence introduces the subject and refers to the types or categories. (See page 294.)
Body Sentences:	The body sentences name and describe each category and, if possible, provide examples.
Closing Sentence:	The closing sentence leaves the reader with an interesting final thought.

Write Develop your first draft using the information on this page and your planning on pages 293–394 as a guide.

LO8 Revising the Writing

Start the revising process by reading your first draft two or three times to get a feel for your work so far. Then have one of your classmates read and react to your work using a response sheet as a guide. (See page 428.)

Using Transitions

Transition words and phrases can help you identify each type or category and rank them, perhaps by age, importance, rarity, and so on.

One type	The simplest	The most common	The earliest
A second	A more complex	A less common	A later
A third	An advanced	A rare	A recent
▼ The last	▼ The most complex	▼ A very rare	▼ The newest

Revising in Action

Read aloud the unrevised and then revised version of the following excerpt. Note how the transition words identify and rank the categories.

> The simplest form of solar energy is
> . . . people are discovering more and more ways to use the free energy of the
>   which
> sun. Solar lighting means designing buildings to take advantage of natural
> A more advanced form is   or
> light. Solar heating is gathering the sun's warmth and using it to heat a
> A third use of solar energy is
> building. Solar cooking is a new reality for many. Box cookers are insulated
>
> boxes with clear tops, and parabolic cookers use solar rays to boil water or cook
>
> food. . . .

Revise Improve your writing, using the following checklist and your classmate's comments on the response sheet. Continue working until you can check off each item in the list.

Using a Revising Checklist

Ideas

☐ 1. Do I identify my subject?

☐ 2. Do I name and describe the types or categories?

Organization

☐ 3. Do I have an effective topic sentence, body sentences, and a closing sentence?

☐ 4. Do I use transition words and phrases to identify and rank the types?

Voice

☐ 5. Does my voice sound knowledgeable and interested?

LO9 Editing the Writing

Subjects and verbs must agree in number. These two pages cover basic subject-verb agreement and agreement with compound subjects.

Basic Subject-Verb Agreement

A singular subject takes a singular verb, and a plural subject takes a plural verb:

One percussion instrument is the drums.
            singular subject singular verb

Two percussion instruments are drums and cymbals.
          plural subject   plural verb

In order to identify the actual subject, disregard any words that come between the subject and verb, such as words in a prepositional phrase:

One of the types of instruments is percussion.
singular subject   singular verb

(The words *types* and *instruments* are not subjects; both are objects of the prepositions.)

Agreement Practice   Correct the following sentences so that the subjects and verbs agree. The first sentence has been done for you.

1. Percussion instruments ~~makes~~ make a noise by striking something.

2. Pianos, by that definition, is percussion instruments.

3. The hammers inside a piano strikes the strings to make a sound.

4. Of course, drums is also a type of percussion.

5. The drumsticks, made of hardwood, hits the skin of the drumhead to create the sound.

6. Another of the instrument types are winds.

7. This family of instruments include flutes, clarinets, and even brass.

8. Wind produce the sound in these instruments.

Additional Practice: For additional practice, see pages 472–473.

Apply   Read your classification paragraph, making sure that your subjects and verbs agree.

Agreement with Compound Subjects

A compound subject is made of two or more subjects joined by *and* or *or*. When the subjects are joined by *and,* they are plural and require a plural verb:

A baritone and a trombone play the same range.
plural subject   plural verb

When the subjects are joined by *or,* the verb must match the number of the last subject:

Either the woodwinds or the trumpet plays the main theme.
singular subject singular verb

Either the trumpet or the woodwinds play the main theme.
plural subject   plural verb

Agreement Practice Correct the following sentences so that the subjects and verbs agree. The first sentence has been done for you.

1. Stringed instruments and their players ~~fills out~~ fill out the orchestra.
2. Violins and violas plays the higher notes.
3. A cello or bass handle the lower notes.
4. The horsehair bow and the string makes the sound.
5. Either music or screeches emerges, depending on the player's talent.
6. A soloist or all the violins carries the melody.
7. The conductor or the concertmaster indicate when to bow.
8. The concertmaster and the strings sits closest to the audience.

Additional Practice: For additional practice, see pages 474–475.

Write Write the end of each sentence, matching the verb to the compound subject.

1. The director and the orchestra _____
2. The orchestra or the director _____

Apply Read your classification paragraph, making sure that your compound subjects agree with their verbs.

Marking a Paragraph

The model that follows has a number of errors.

Editing Practice   Correct the following paragraph, using the correction marks below. One correction has been done for you.

A Question of Taste

    All the flavors that a person can taste ~~is~~ *are* made up of a few basic taste   *1*
sensations. In the Western world, people are used to thinking about four
tastes: salty, sweet, sour, and bitter The salty taste come from substances
that include sodium, such as snacks like potato chips or pretzels. The sweet
sensation comes from sugars, whether in processed foods like sweetened   *5*
cereals or naturally occurring in fruit or honey. Sour tastes come from
acidic foods (pH below 7) such as lemons and grapefruit, and bitter tastes
come from alkaline foods (pH above 7) such as coffee or dark chocolate. But
in the world Eastern, two other taste sensations are recognized. A savory
taste (umami) comes from amino acids, which are a basic part of meats   *10*
and proteins. And a spicy taste (piquancy) comes from substances like
the capsaicin in hot peppers. Given the savory and spicy nature of Indian,
Thai, chinese, and other Eastern foods, it's no wonder that these tastes are
recognized. With all of the senses to consider chefs can make every dish a
unique work of art.   *15*

Correction Marks

✄	delete	⅄	add comma	ʌ *word*	add word
d̲̲	capitalize	?	add question mark	⊙	add period
Ø	lowercase	ʌ		⌒	spelling
ʌ	insert	ᵛ	insert an apostrophe	⌐⌐	switch

INSIGHT

In academic writing, the pronouns *I* and *you* have special rules for subject-verb agreement:

- *I* takes the verb *am* instead of *is*: I *am* (**not** I *is*).
- *I* also takes plural action verbs: I *sit* (**not** I *sits*).
- *You* always takes a plural verb: You *are*; you *sit* (**not** You *is*; you *sits*).

Using an Editing Checklist

Now it's time to correct your own paragraph.

Apply   Create a clean copy of your revised paragraph and use the following checklist to check for errors. Continue working until you can check off each item in the list.

Words

☐ **1.** Have I used specific nouns and verbs? (See page 134.)

☐ **2.** Have I used more action verbs than "be" verbs? (See page 536.)

Sentences

☐ **3.** Have I combined short, choppy sentences? (See page 137.)

☐ **4.** Have I avoided shifts in sentences? (See page 500.)

☐ **5.** Have I avoided fragments and run-ons? (See pages 488–491, 494–495.)

Conventions

☐ **6.** Do I use correct verb forms (*he saw*, not *he seen*)? (See pages 542, 544.)

☐ **7.** Do my subjects and verbs agree (*she speaks*, not *she speak*)? (See pages 472–481.)

☐ **8.** Have I used the right words (*their, there, they're*)?

☐ **9.** Have I capitalized first words and proper nouns and adjectives? (See page 582.)

☐ **10.** Have I used commas after long introductory word groups? (See pages 652–655.)

☐ **11.** Have I punctuated dialogue correctly? (See pages 602–603.)

☐ **12.** Have I carefully checked my spelling?

Adding a Title

Make sure to add a title to your paragraph. Here are some simple strategies for coming up with a catchy one.

- Use a number:

  Four Types of Mustard

- Use an expression:

  A Question of Taste

- Think outside the box:

  Plugging into Sunlight

- Be clever:

  My Condiments to the Chef

Create   Prepare a clean final copy of your paragraph and proofread it.

"I find that different types of music are good
for certain activities."
—Peter Steele

Enrichment: Reading

On pages 303–307 you will find the essay "No Wonder They Call Me Bitch" to read and respond to. As you read, use the steps in the reading process as your guide. Your reading activities here are followed by a number of ideas for writing a classification paragraph or essay of your own.

CONSIDER THE TRAITS

As you read this classification, focus first on the **ideas**—the topic that is being classified, the categories, and the details that support and explain each category. Then consider the **organization**—the way that the opening, middle, and closing parts are constructed. Also pay special notice to the author's **voice** (tone)—or writing personality. Ask yourself if these traits combine to produce an enjoyable reading experience.

About the Author

Ann Hodgman has authored many books, from children's books to cook books to vampire novels. Her essay on the next page, which was included in "Best American Essays," appeared in *Spy* magazine. When in print, the magazine was known for its witty and well-researched articles.

Prereading

A famous classification system is the Myers-Briggs Type Indicator that was created during World War II. Today, the Myers-Briggs test has become the most widely used tool for personality assessment. The test classifies people as either extroverted (*outgoing*) or introverted (*shy, inner-directed*). Do you consider yourself extroverted or introverted? Explain.

_____

_____

_____

What do you think?

Do you agree with the quotation at the top of the page? How do certain activities influence the type of music you listen to?

Q. Are those little cans of Mighty Dog actually branded with the 140
sizzling word BEEF, the way they show in the commercials?

A. You should know by now that that kind of thing never happens.

Q. Does chicken-flavored dog food taste like chicken-flavored cat food?

A. To my surprise, chicken cat food was actually a little better—
more chickeny. It tasted like inferior canned pâté. 145

Q. Was there any dog food that you just couldn't bring yourself to try?

A. Alas, it was a can of Mighty Dog called Prime Entree with Bone
Marrow. The meat was dark, dark brown, and it was surrounded by
gelatin that was almost black. I knew I would die if I tasted it, so I put it
outside for the raccoons. 150

extruded	**discernible**	**semiotics**
forced out	knowledgable, identifiable	the study of symbols
palpated	**imperious**	**duped**
explored through touch	commanding, domineering	tricked
callous	**arcane**	
hard, tough	mysterious, hard to understand	

GLYPHstock, 2013 / Used under license from Shutterstock.com

Reflecting

After you complete your reading, answer the following questions. Afterward, share your responses with your classmates.

1. What is the topic of the selection?

_____

_____

2. Who might be the intended audience?

_____

_____

3. What categories are provided?

_____

_____

4. Does the writing follow a logical pattern of reasoning? If so, which one? (See page 28.)

_____

_____

5. Is the writer's voice academic or personal? How can you tell? (See pages 78–79.)

_____

_____

6. What part do you find especially entertaining, and why?

_____

_____

7. How would you rate this selection, and why?
   Weak ★ ★ ★ ★ ★ Strong

_____

_____

Vocabulary Practice

Identify   For each of the following words, create an entry for a vocabulary notebook. Identify the pronunciation, helpful word parts, a primary definition, and the word used in a sentence. (Refer to a dictionary and pages 32–36 in this book for help.)

1. **rivulets** (line 45)

_____

_____

2. **unsavory** (line 51)

_____

_____

3. **palatable** (line 115)

_____

_____

4. **emphatic** (line 127)

_____

_____

Thinking Critically

Explain   Answer these questions to help you think critically about the text.

1. Can there be a serious side to the essay? If so, what is it?

_____

_____

2. What does this essay say about pets and the pet industry?

_____

_____

3. What, if anything, does this essay say about pet owners?

_____

_____

Writing

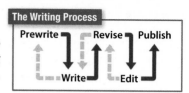

The Writing Process

Prewrite · Revise · Publish · Write · Edit

What follows are possible writing activities to complete in response to the reading. Use the writing process (pages 94–99) to help you develop your writing.

Prewriting

Choose one of the following writing ideas. Or decide upon an idea of your own that is related to the reading.

Writing Ideas

1. **Writing to Learn:** Observe a public place (public park, dog park, bus stop, or so on) over a series of days, and record what you see or hear. Afterward, create a personal blog that categorizes and summarizes what you observed. Use a personal voice as was used in the essay on pages 303–307.

2. **Paragraph Writing:** Write an essay in which you classify the habits or actions of your pet.

3. Write a classification paragraph based on another subject that you identified on page 293.

4. **Essay Writing:** In an essay, categorize the street foods (fast foods) that you and your friends enjoy. Or try out new street foods and categorize them.

5. Or write a classification essay stemming from your responses to the "What do you think?" question on page 283.

> ## When planning . . .
> Refer to pages 293–294 to help you with your prewriting and planning. Also use the tips that follow.
>
> - Choose a topic that you understand well or can easily learn about.
> - If necessary, research your topic to find all the major categories or parts.
> - Collect similar types of details for each category.
> - Decide on a logical way to order your categories.
> - Review the classification writing examples in this chapter to see how they are developed.

Humannet, 2013 / Used under license from Shutterstock.com

Writing and Revising

Use the tips that follow and the information on pages 295–297 to help you with your drafting and revising.

When writing . . .

- Include an opening, a middle, and a closing part in your classification writing. Each part has a specific role. (See page 296.)
- Follow your planning notes, but also consider new ideas as they come to mind.
- Introduce each new category in the same basic way.
- Use transitions to shift from one category to the next.

When revising . . .

- Check that the order of your categories is logical and clear.
- Make sure the categories are exclusive, consistent, and equal.
- Decide if your classification will interest the reader. If not, improve your essay by adding new details, trying a different opening or closing strategy, and so on.
- Ask a trusted peer to react to your classification.

Editing

Refer to the checklist on page 301 when you are ready to edit your classification for style and correctness.

Carlos E. Santa Maria, 2013 / Used under license from Shutterstock.com

Reflecting on Classification Writing

Answer the following questions about your classification reading and writing experiences in this chapter.

1. Why do writers and researchers classify information?

   _____

2. What is your favorite selection in this chapter? Explain.

   _____

3. What reading strategy in this chapter seems most helpful? Explain.

   _____

4. What is the main benefit of reading a classification text?

   _____

5. What is the easiest thing about classification writing? The hardest?

   _____

6. What do you like best about your classification?

   _____

7. What is one thing you would like to change in it?

   _____

8. What are some transitional words or phrases that are common in a classification?

   _____

Key Terms to Remember

When you read and write classification writing, it's important to understand the following terms.

- **Classification**—the act of arranging or organizing according to categories, or subgroups
- **Categories**—specifically defined divisions; general types or classes of ideas
- **Line diagram**—a graphic organizer that can be used to show main categories and supporting details
- **Classification factors**—the qualities the writer uses to divide a topic into categories

12

"Shallow men believe in luck, believe in circumstances. Strong men believe in cause and effect."
—Ralph Waldo Emerson

Cause-Effect

Flip a switch; a light comes on. The relationship is obvious.

Make a joke; a friend laughs. The reason may be less obvious. *Was it the joke itself or your delivery? Is your friend just being polite or reacting to your attempt at humor?*

These are simple examples of cause-effect relationships. More complex examples include the causes and effects of a disease, the causes and effects of interest rates on consumer spending, and the causes and effects of solar flares.

This chapter deals with the cause-effect form of thinking and writing. First, you will learn about the basics related to this form. Then you will read and react to two professional examples of cause-effect writing before writing a cause-effect text of your own. The strategies you learn in this chapter will apply to cause-effect assignments in all of your classes.

Learning Outcomes

LO1 Understand cause-effect.

LO2 Learn reading strategies (studying the topic sentence and using a cause-effect organizer).

LO3 Read and react to a professional paragraph.

LO4 Read and react to a professional cause-effect essay.

LO5 Practice reading skills (considering the evidence and purpose).

LO6 Plan cause-effect writing.

LO7 Write the first draft.

LO8 Revise the writing.

LO9 Edit the writing.

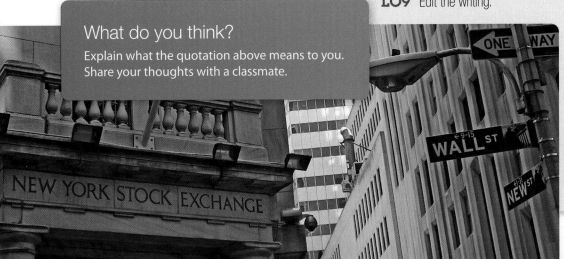

What do you think?

Explain what the quotation above means to you. Share your thoughts with a classmate.

Vladislav Gajic, 2013 / Used under license from Shutterstock.com

LO1 Understanding Cause-Effect

In a chemistry class, you learn that combining certain chemicals results in a particular reaction. "Results in" is another way of saying "causes." A history text may explain the reasons behind a particular event and the consequences of that event. "Reasons" is another way of saying "causes," and "consequences" another way of saying "effects."

> " . . . no thought or action is without its effects, present or ultimate, seen or unseen, felt or unfelt."
> —Norman Cousins

These two examples indicate how central cause-effect analysis is in your classes. The body of knowledge in all disciplines is expanded largely by seeking to discover how things work, and that means finding out what causes what. This knowledge is then passed along by explaining the cause-effect relationship related to new situations and circumstances. Understanding this relationship can be more beneficial than memorizing facts.

Much of your college reading will involve cause-effect analysis. Often, the word "cause" or "effect" (or a similar term) will be mentioned in the text itself. Even if these words aren't used, you can recognize a cause-effect explanation by its two-part structure. The explanation will either introduce various causes and then conclude with the main effect, or it will begin with a single cause and then explain its many effects. In a few cases, cause-effect writing may begin with multiple causes and then discuss their many effects. Keep this two-part structure in mind as you read the cause-effect paragraphs in this chapter.

INSIGHT

Finding cause-effect relationships is a way of analyzing a topic, as are classifying and comparing. Each type of analysis requires that you examine a topic closely, consider it deeply, and refine your understanding of it in the process.

Identify Name two or three recent news stories that explain a cause-effect relationship. Provide a one- or two-sentence summary of each example. Share your summaries with your classmates.

1. _____

_____

2. _____

_____

3. _____

_____

Reading

Reading cause-effect paragraphs will introduce you to one of the more common tasks of college assignments—finding the reasons and results resting beneath the surface of complex topics.

LO2 Learning Reading Strategies

These two strategies—studying the topic sentence and using a cause-effect organizer—will help you read cause-effect texts.

Studying the Topic Sentence

By definition, a topic sentence introduces the reader to the topic of the paragraph and the key part of it that will be emphasized. So if you study the topic sentence in most cause-effect paragraphs, you should be able to learn a lot about the information that will follow. Here's an example:

> **Topic sentence:** Though the fighting ceased in 1953, the effects of the Korean War are still felt today.

Discussion: The topic of the paragraph is the Korean War. As the topic sentence states, the paragraph will focus on the remaining effects of the war. The causes will not be a major emphasis.

Remember that some paragraphs will not begin with a clearly defined topic sentence. So this strategy won't work for all cause-effect paragraphs. **Note:** In an essay, a thesis statement directs the information that follows.

Using a Cause-Effect Organizer

Part of understanding a cause-effect paragraph is keeping track of the important details. Completing a cause-effect organizer will help you do so.

Subject	
Causes (Because of . . .)	Effects (. . . these conditions resulted.)
-	-
-	-
-	-

LO3 Reading and Reacting to a Professional Paragraph

This cause-effect paragraph, which comes from a science textbook entitled *Living in the Environment* by G. Tyler Miller, Jr., and Scott E. Spoolman, explores a serious environmental problem. Remember to use the reading process to help you gain a full understanding of the text.

Prereading Before you read, answer these three questions:

1. What do the title and first sentence tell you about the text?

2. What do you already know about this topic?

3. What questions would you like answered in this reading?

Reading and Rereading As you read, make it your goal to (1) understand the importance of the topic, (2) consider the value of the supporting details, and (3) study the cause-effect relationship that is developed. Consider annotating the text (page 20) as you read.

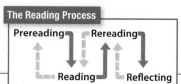

The Reading Process

Burning Tropical Forests and Climate Change

The burning of tropical forests releases CO_2 into the atmosphere.   1
Rising concentration of this gas can help warm the atmosphere, which is projected to change the global climate during this century. Scientists estimate that tropical forest fires account for at least 17 percent of all human-created greenhouse gas emissions, and that each year they emit   5
twice as much CO_2 as all of the world's cars and trucks emit. The large-scale burning of the Amazon rain forest accounts for 75 percent of all of Brazil's greenhouse gas emissions, making Brazil the world's fourth largest emitter of such gases, according to the National Inventory of Greenhouse Gases. And with these forests gone, even if savannah or   10
second-growth forests replace them, far less CO_2 will be absorbed for photosynthesis, resulting in even more atmospheric warming.

From MILLER. *Living in the Environment,* 17E. © 2012 Brooks/Cole, a part of Cengage Learning, Inc.

Reflecting After you complete your reading, answer these questions. Share your responses with your classmates.

1. What is the main idea of the paragraph?

   _____

2. Does the paragraph focus more attention on causes or effects?

   _____

3. What new things did you learn about the topic?

   _____

4. What questions do you still have about it?

   _____

Vocabulary Practice

Identify Define the word parts as indicated. Then try to explain the meaning of the complete word. (See pages 35–36 and 623–631 for help.)

1. **projected** (line 3) pro + ject + ed

   _____

   _____

2. **emissions** (line 5) (e)miss + ions

   _____

   _____

3. **photosynthesis** (line 12) photo + synthesis

   _____

   _____

Drawing Inferences

Explain Answer these questions to help you draw inferences from the text.

1. Does the supporting evidence (the effects) seem believable in the paragraph? Why or why not?

   _____

2. What part of the text seems especially important, and why?

   _____

LO4 Reading and Reacting to a Professional Cause-Effect Essay

This essay, which comes from a textbook entitled *American Government and Politics Today*, examines wealth in the United States. Remember to use the reading process to help you gain a full understanding of the text.

About the Authors

Steffen W. Schmidt is a professor of political science at Iowa State University. Mack C. Shelley II is a professor of political science and statistics at Iowa State University. **Barbara A. Bardes** is a professor emerita of political science at the University of Cincinnati. **Lynn E. Ford** is a professor of political science at the College of Charleston.

Prereading Before you read, answer these three questions:

1. What do the title and any boldfaced words tell you about the text?

2. Why types of causes and/or effects might be addressed?

3. What questions do you have about the topic?

Reading and Rereading As you read, make it your goal to (1) identify the main idea or focus, (2) consider the value of the supporting details, and (3) understand the cause-effect relationship that is developed.

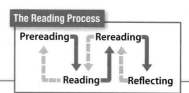

The Reading Process

Prereading   Rereading

Reading   Reflecting

How Unequal Is American Society?

In the early days of the American nation, the distribution of wealth   1
among the people was, of course, unequal. Relatively few large landholders owned large farms and plantations, and relatively few wealthy merchants owned ships and traded in goods. There were, of course, craftspeople, lawyers, and other professionals who were better off than the rest of the citizens.   5
Most of the free people of the United States were farmers or craftspeople working in their own communities. They probably owned their land, tools, furnishings, and products, but nothing more. In the southern states, most of the free individuals owned no slaves or only a few. Only a very few wealthy

individuals owned a large number of enslaved persons. Wealth, at the levels 10
known today, was unheard of. As the United States developed economically,
many individuals did well enough to form a strong middle class.

Many commentators and economists believe that the United States
today is a much less equal society than it was only a few decades ago. Due to
the recession, the median income today for American families, in inflation- 15
adjusted dollars, is less than it was 10 years ago. Many families have lost
their savings or their homes due to unemployment. On the other hand, the
wealthiest Americans have continued to increase their worth due both to
their ability to keep their tax bills relatively low and their ability to earn
more wealth through investments, even during a recession. Technological 20
developments have created many billionaires. Among those are Mark
Zuckerberg, founder of Facebook, and the creators of Instagram, a smart-
phone app that was sold to Facebook for more than $1 billion only two years
after it entered the business scene. While it is true that the wealthiest 1
percent of Americans pay a **proportionately** large share of income taxes, 25
about 38 percent of all taxes paid, their average income is 18 times the
median, and their wealth is growing.

How does the United States compare to the rest of the world in terms of
this income inequality? We all know large numbers of truly impoverished
individuals exist in many nations, but is overall income equality more 30
likely in those nations? The Organization for Economic Cooperation and
Development (OECD), an international agency dedicated to improving
conditions in all nations, publishes an annual report on income inequality
based on a statistic called the "the **Gini Index**." The index is named after the
Italian statistician who created the measure, and it measures the degree of 35
income equality in a nation by looking at the proportions in different income
categories. A Gini Index score of zero means that there is perfect equality
among all incomes in a nation. The larger the score, the further the nation
is from equality in incomes.

If we compare the score of the United States to those of all of the nations of 40
the world, our ranking is not too low: In 2011, the United States ranked 43rd
in income inequality among the 104 nations for which data were available.[a]
The nation with the most inequality was Namibia, and that with the least
was Sweden. Most of the nations with higher levels of income inequality
were underdeveloped nations that may have a small group of very wealthy 45
households and a multitude of very poor citizens. However, the OECD also
published the index only for its own members, mostly developed Western
nations. Among this group of 22 nations, the United States is the third most
unequal nation, although its ranking is close to those of Israel, the United
Kingdom, Italy, and Australia. Mexico has the highest Gini score in this 50
group and Denmark the lowest.

The issue of income inequality in America has also been the subject of the
research of two French economists who currently teach in the United States.[b]
Both Emmanuel Saez and Thomas Piketty claim to love the United States

and admire greatly the free and **entrepreneurial** nature of the country. What 55
they find in their research is that the United States is quickly becoming
more unequal than at any time in its history. Piketty says, "The United
States is getting accustomed to a completely crazy level of inequality."[c] He
continues, "The United States is becoming like Old Europe, which is very
strange in historical perspective . . . [it] used to be very **egalitarian**, not just 60
in spirit but in actuality." The work of these two economists, according to the
New York Times, is being read in Washington, D.C., as well as in economic
journals.

[a] Organization for Economic Development and Cooperation, "Divided We 65
    Stand: Why Inequality Keeps Rising," 2011.
[b] Emmanuel Saez and Thomas Piketty, cited in "Income Distribution in the
    U.S.," www.wealthandwant.com/income/income_distribution.html.
[c] Annie Lowry, "French Duo See (Well) Past Tax Rise for the Richest," *New York
    Times*, April 17, 2012, A1.

From Schmidt/Shelley/Bardes/Ford, *American Government and Politics Today*, 2013-2014 Edition,
16E. © 2014 Cengage Learning

proportionately
having the correct relationship of size or
quantity

Gini Index
A statistical measure of the distribution
of income in a nation. A higher number

indicates more inequality in incomes within
a nation.

entrepreneurial
the quality of business risk-taking

egalitarian
believing in equality

Reflecting   After you complete your reading, answer these questions. Share your
responses with your classmates.

1. What is the main idea of the text? Is it directly stated or implied?

2. What supporting details support the main idea? Name two.

3. Are both causes and effects discussed? Explain.

4. What questions, if any, do you still have about the topic?

5. How would you rate the essay, and why?
   Weak ★ ★ ★ ★ ★ Strong

Vocabulary Practice

Identify Define the word parts as indicated for each word below. Then try to explain the meaning of the complete word. (See pages 35–36 and 623–631 for help.)

1. **recession** (line 15)   re + cess + ion

   _____

   _____

2. **median** (line 15)   medi + an

   _____

   _____

3. **inequality** (line 29)   in + equal + ity

   _____

   _____

Drawing Inferences

Explain Answer the following questions to help you draw an inferences about the text.

1. What observations can you make about areas in the world that might offer a decent quality of life for most people?

   _____

   _____

   _____

2. What thoughts do you have about the income distribution in the United States?

   _____

   _____

   _____

LO5 Practicing Reading Skills

Often in a cause-effect paragraph, you run into unfamiliar terms, and you have to make sure that the causes described are really causes.

Considering the Evidence

People used to think that ice floats because it's thin. After all, needles and razor blades float, and they're made of metal, which is heavier than water. Then someone demonstrated that when you push a needle, a razor blade, and a thin piece of ice to the bottom of a basin of water, the ice will return to the top while the other two remain at the bottom.

This demonstration shows how important it is to be sure about a cause-effect relationship. Just because something seems to cause something else doesn't mean it actually does.

When studying the causes and effects in a paragraph, always judge the value of the evidence. It's important to know if the causes and effects seem reliable and reasonable.

Considering the Purpose

Sometimes writers use cause-effect reasoning to convince you to take an action. In that case, ask yourself the following questions.

1. What does the author hope to gain by convincing me of this cause-effect relationship?
2. What is the author's background related to the subject?
3. What other explanations might there be?
4. What evidence might be missing?

INSIGHT

Never reject a point of view just because it doesn't match up to your own thinking. Remember, people used to quite reasonably believe that ice floats because it's thin. If they hadn't been prepared to entertain a better explanation, we might still be puzzled by ice cubes, which float despite being shaped like chunky rocks.

Review   Reread the essay on pages 318–320. Then discuss it with your classmates using the "purpose" questions above as a guide.

Writing

Beginning on this page, you will plan and write a cause-effect paragraph about a topic of your choice. Use the writing process to help you produce your best work. (See pages 94–99.)

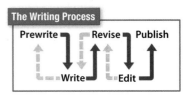

LO6 Planning Cause-Effect Writing

To begin, you must choose a topic that both interests you and involves a cause-effect relationship.

Selecting a Topic

Think about the classes you are currently taking. What cause-effect ideas have you encountered in your studies? Also consider topics derived from the following categories.

- Family Life
- Politics
- Society

- Environment
- Entertainment
- Workplace

Select   List four cause-effect topics that interest you. Then circle the one you would like to write about.

1. Benefits of vegetarianism
2. Why people save things
3. Results of the 2009 jet landing on the Hudson River
4. How superhero movies affect our culture

Researching the Causes and Effects

Once you have selected a topic, research the causes and effects involved and list them for further use.

Identify   Use a cause-effect organizer to list possible causes and effects of your topic.

Subject	
Causes	Effects
-	-
-	-
-	-

Gathering and Evaluating Details

Effective cause-effect writing includes strong evidence. This means you must use trustworthy sources of information. Avoid sources that seem to approach your topic in a questionable way. Watch for sources that include the following types of information.

- **Broad generalization:** A statement that is based on too little evidence or allows no exceptions

  > Video games are the reason that today's youth have a shorter attention span.
  > *(This claim ignores the possibility of other reasons.)*

- **Straw man:** A claim that exaggerates or misinterprets an opponent's position

  > If you cause deforestation, you hate the planet.

- **False cause:** A claim that confuses sequence with causation (If A comes before B, A must have caused B.)

  > Since that new skate park opened, vandalism among young people has increased.
  > *(The two factors may have no real connection.)*

Creating Your Topic Sentence

Your topic sentence should name your topic and identify what you plan to emphasize about it. Use the following formula.

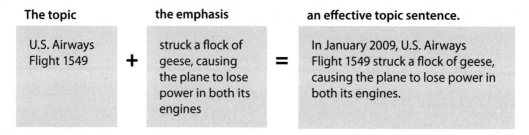

The topic

U.S. Airways Flight 1549

+

the emphasis

struck a flock of geese, causing the plane to lose power in both its engines

=

an effective topic sentence.

In January 2009, U.S. Airways Flight 1549 struck a flock of geese, causing the plane to lose power in both its engines.

Create Write your own topic sentence, following the example above.

The topic

+

the emphasis

=

an effective topic sentence.

LO7 Writing the First Draft

Your first draft is a first attempt to get your thoughts on paper in a reasonable order. It doesn't have to be perfect. You'll have time to polish it later.

Read Carefully read the following cause-effect paragraph about the emergency landing of Flight 1549.

Emergency Landing

Topic Sentence

In January 2009, U.S. Airways Flight 1549 struck a flock of geese, causing the plane to lose power in both its engines. The situation forced pilot Chesley "Sully" Sullenberger to perform an emergency landing on the Hudson River outside of New York City. Not only did he land safely, but all 150 passengers survived without a single serious injury. The event had many meaningful effects. Massive media coverage of the landing made "Sully" a household name. Many hailed him as

Body Sentences

an American hero. Meanwhile the passengers on the flight, though safe, suffered emotional trauma from the landing. Many refuse to step back onto a plane. Maybe the greatest effect, however, was the impact on the airline industry. The emergency landing led to a greater awareness of the dangers of bird populations near airways. Government agencies have gone so far as to wipe out geese populations in the proximity of airports. In the end, a tragic collision and remarkable

Closing Sentence

emergency landing may result in safer air travel for years to come.

1

5

10

15

Consider the Craft

1. What do you like best about this paragraph?
2. What are two of your favorite details?
3. Does the paragraph focus more on causes or effects?
4. What is the value of this paragraph?

Drafting Tips

When you write a cause-effect paragraph, try to be both clear and interesting. To accomplish this, consider the following strategies.

In the topic sentence . . .
- Introduce the topic in a dramatic way that captures your reader's interest.
- State the main cause-effect connection clearly.

In the middle . . .
- Make sure that your cause-effect details follow logically and make sense.
- Use chronological order if the events follow a clear time sequence.
- Use order of importance (either most to least important or least to most important) if time sequence doesn't apply.
- Include enough details to explain each cause or effect.

In the closing sentence . . .
- End by reflecting on the main cause-effect connection.
- Leave the reader with an interesting idea to think about.
- Consider suggesting possibilities for further study or investigation.

INSIGHT

Journalism, the sciences, and even the arts often use the cause-effect approach when exploring a topic. Mastering this form will serve you well in all your college classes.

The Working Parts of a Paragraph

As you can see from the previous page, a paragraph has three main parts, each with its own specific purpose.

Topic Sentence:	A topic sentence introduces your reader to your topic and identifies the main point about it that you want to stress.
Body Sentences:	The body sentences support the topic sentence, adding specific details to make the causes and effects clear to the reader.
Closing Sentence:	A closing sentence (or two) often summarizes the topic or may offer an interesting final idea.

Tip

Transition words that show cause-effect relationships: accordingly / as a result / because / consequently / for this purpose / for this reason / hence / just as / since / so / such as / therefore / thus / to illustrate / whereas

---

Write   Prepare your first draft using the information on this page and your planning on pages 323–324 as a guide.

LO8   Revising the Writing

Start the revising process by reading your first draft two or three times to get a feel for your work so far. Then have one of your classmates read and react to your work using a response sheet as a guide. (See page 428.)

Using an Academic Style

Cause-effect paragraphs often require an academic style. Consider the quick tips below as you revise your paragraph.

Quick Tips for Academic Style

- **Avoid personal pronouns.** Avoid using personal pronouns such as *I, we,* and *you* in your cause-effect paragraph.
- **Define technical terms.** If your readers are not experts on your topic, define the specialized vocabulary or technical words you use.
- **Beware of unnecessary intensifiers.** Words such as *really, totally,* and *completely* are usually associated with a personal style.

Revising in Action:

Read aloud the unrevised and then the revised version of the following excerpt. Note how the changes improved the excerpt's academic style.

> Maybe the greatest effect, however, was the impact on the airline industry.
> ~~I think the greatest effect was the impact on aviation.~~ The emergency
> landing led to a ~~completely and totally~~ greater awareness of the dangers of bird
> populations near ~~air hubs. You see~~ airways. government agencies have . . .

Revise   Use the following checklist and your classmate's comments on the response sheet to improve your writing. Continue working until you can check off each item in the list.

Using a Revising Checklist

Ideas

☐   1. Does the topic sentence clearly introduce the topic and focus (causes, effects, or both) of the paragraph?

☐   2. Do the causes and effects seem important and reliable?

☐   3. Are all the links between the causes and effects clear and logical?

Organization

☐   4. Do I include a topic sentence, body sentences, and a closing sentence?

☐   5. Have I used transitions to show cause-effect relationships?

Voice

☐   6. Have I used an appropriate voice—serious and academic or relaxed and personal?

LO9 Editing the Writing

Pronouns and their antecedents, the words that are replaced by the pronouns, must agree in three ways: in number, in person, and in gender. This page covers basic pronoun-antecedent agreement.

Basic Pronoun-Antecedent Agreement

Number

Somebody needs to bring his or her laptop to the meeting.

(The singular pronouns *his or her* agree with the singular antecedent *somebody*.)

Person

If students want to do better research, they should talk to a librarian.

(The third-person pronoun *they* agrees with the antecedent *students*.)

Gender

Chris picked up his lawn mower from his parents' garage.

(The masculine pronoun *his* agrees with the antecedent *Chris*.)

Practice   Read the sentences below. Correct the pronouns so that they agree with their antecedents in number, person, and gender.

1. The musicians strummed his guitars.
2. After Shauna finished washing the dishes, it sparkled.
3. If the waitress wants a better tip, he should be more polite.
4. As the basketball players walked onto the court, he waved to the crowd.
5. Mrs. Jackson started their car.
6. Everyone can attend the extra study session if they need help.
7. Eric poured root beer in their favorite mug.

Additional Practice: For additional practice, see pages 524–525.

Apply   Read your cause-effect paragraph, watching for agreement issues with your pronouns and their antecedents. Correct any pronoun-antecedent agreement errors that you find.

Case of Pronouns

The case of a pronoun tells what role it can play in a sentence. There are three cases: *nominative, possessive,* and *objective.* Review the information below, which explains each case.

The nominative case is used for subjects and predicate nouns.
I, you, he, she, it, we, they

She walked to the bank. It was she who needed more money.

The possessive case shows possession or ownership.
my, mine, our, ours, his, her, hers, their, theirs, its, your, yours

The jacket is his. This jacket is mine. Your jacket is gone.

The objective case is used for direct or indirect objects and for objects of prepositions or infinitives.
me, us, you, him, her, it, them

Reid told her that going to the movie was fine with him.

Practice In each sentence below, select the correct pronoun in parentheses based on the case of the word.

1. Frank said that (he, him) needed someone to pick (his, him) up.
2. I looked over (their, them) expense report, and (they, them) went way over budget.
3. (She, her) worked on (she, her) new project.
4. The judge commended the competitor on (he, his) speed and agility.
5. (Their, them) lawn service is better than (our, ours) service.
6. It was (him, he) who spotted the bird.
7. The CEO increased (she, her) pay.
8. My brother and (I, me) attended the film festival.
9. (We, us) learned quickly how to recognize each other's voice.
10. On account of (I, me), my little brother does a lot of texting.

Additional Practice: For additional practice, see pages 522–523.

Apply Read your cause-effect paragraph, checking the pronouns you've used. Make sure each pronoun is in the correct case.

Marking a Paragraph

The model that follows has a number of errors.

Editing Practice   Correct the following paragraph, using the marks below. One correction has been done for you.

Divided Along the 38th Parallel

Though the fighting ceased in 1953 the effects of the Korean War are   *1*

still felt today. The war began in 1950 when communist-occupied North

Korea. Waged war with south Korea. In a larger context, the war was

caused by the United States' desire to stop the spread of communism.

The effects of the conflict were considerable. Both sides suffered massive   *5*

casualties, and the Battle sparked the start of the cold war between the

United States and the Soviet Union. Today, Korea remain divided along

the 38th parallel. North Korea has a heavy military presence and has

suffered much poverty South Korea has thrived economically. Though the

countries have taken smalls steps toward political piece, the war has not   *10*

ended

Correction Marks

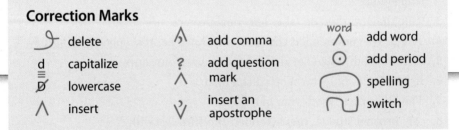

ꝰ delete	⅄ add comma	^word add word
d̲ capitalize	? add question mark	⊙ add period
ⱷ lowercase	∧	⬭ spelling
∧ insert	⩔ insert an apostrophe	⌒ switch

INSIGHT

When checking for errors, it helps to use specific editing strategies. For example, to check for punctuation, you can circle all of the marks in your paper and check each one for correctness. To check for spelling, you should work from the bottom up in your writing. This strategy will help you focus on each word for spelling and usage. (See page 99 for more of these strategies.)

Using an Editing Checklist

Now it's time to correct your own paragraph.

Apply   Create a clean copy of your revised paragraph and use the following checklist to check for errors. Continue working until you can check off each item in the list.

Words

☐ **1.** Have I used specific nouns and verbs? (See page 134.)

☐ **2.** Have I used more action verbs than "be" verbs? (See page 536.)

Sentences

☐ **3.** Have I varied the beginnings and lengths of sentences? (See pages 136–137.)

☐ **4.** Have I combined short, choppy sentences? (See page 137.)

☐ **5.** Have I avoided sentence errors such as fragments and comma splices? (See pages 488–493.)

Conventions

☐ **6.** Do I use correct verb forms (*he saw,* not *he seen*)? (See pages 542, 544.)

☐ **7.** Do my subjects and verbs agree (*she speaks,* not *she speak*)? (See pages 472–481.)

☐ **8.** Do my pronouns and antecedents agree?

☐ **9.** Have I capitalized first words and proper nouns and adjectives? (See page 582.)

☐ **10.** Have I carefully checked my spelling?

Adding a Title

Make sure to add an effective title. Here are two strategies for creating one.

■ Grab the reader's attention:

Emergency Landing

■ Use an idea from the paragraph:

The Changing Family

> "Life is a perpetual instruction in cause and effect."
> —Ralph Waldo Emerson

Enrichment: Reading

On pages 333–335 you will find the essay "The Pros and Cons of Gambling" from a textbook devoted to the hospitality business. As you read this essay, use the steps in the reading process as your guide. The reading activities are followed by a number of writing ideas to choose from for a cause-effect paragraph or essay of your own.

About the Authors

Kaye Chon, PhD, is the Chair Professor and Director of Hotel and Tourism Management at the Hong Kong Polytechnic University. He has published more than 200 articles on hospitality tourism issues. **Thomas A. Maier**, PhD, is an International Professor of Service Leadership and Innovation at the Rochester Institute of Technology in Dubai. He is also president of TAM—Global Services, Inc.

Prereading

The actions of people provide a common starting point for cause-effect essays and articles. Cause-effect writing often examines what we do and why we do it. The paragraph on page 316 examines the causes and effects of people burning the tropical forests, and the essay on pages 318–320 examines the causes and effects of the inequality in America. The essay that follows examines the causes and effects of gambling. List two or three actions you have observed, experienced, or read about that have a cause-effect element.

CONSIDER THE TRAITS

As you read this selection, focus first on the **ideas**—the topic, main idea, and causes and effects. Then consider the **organization**—the way that the opening, middle, and closing parts are constructed.

What do you think?

How would you explain the quotation above? (Perpetual means "lasting forever.")

Identify Before you read the essay, answer these three questions:

1. What do the title, opening paragraph, and the beginning of other paragraphs tell you about the text?

   _____

2. What do you already know about the topic?

   _____

3. What questions would you like answered?

   _____

Reading and Rereading

Read the following essay from *Welcome to Hospitality: An Introduction.* The authors examine the pros and cons and the causes and effects of gambling.

As you read, make it your goal to (1) study the causes and effects of the topic, (2) decide if your questions have been answered, and (3) consider additional questions that come to mind.

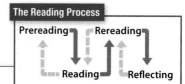

The Pros and Cons of Gambling

Because of the large amounts of money generated, gaming has **inherent**   *1*
bonuses and risks. When politicians see the amount of money generated
by the gaming industry, everyone wants a piece of the action. From a local
perspective, it begins with the construction trade, since a construction
company (or companies) will be selected to build the casino. Then, as the   *5*
hiring begins, people move to the area for the jobs. They need to buy or
rent homes, and then they need banks, grocery stores, drugstores, and
other retailers to supply their day-to-day living needs. The expansion of
the local population increases the need for public facilities like schools and
hospitals, infrastructure development like roads, and other public projects.   *10*
All of these people and businesses pay taxes both directly and indirectly.
The government takes the taxes and prospers.

In addition, tourists coming to gamble need hotels, restaurants,
shopping complexes, spas, and world-class entertainment venues. In
fact, many casino visitors say they come for the food, shows, and other   *15*
entertainment than come for the gaming alone.[a] This creates jobs for the
locals and generates many different tax bases for the government. To
meet the needs of the visitors, the new tax revenues are used to improve
and further expand local infrastructures that support the traffic. As the

commercial base continues to expand, more new businesses open to support   *20*
the growing number of tourists and locals. As a result, gaming is a very
strong economic development tool. Casino development creates an upward
spiral that increases jobs, adds more taxes from businesses and tourists,
and decreases taxes for the townspeople. When residents see the projected
economic impact, they are likely to agree that the positive aspects of   *25*
gaming are impressive.

However, as with any growth in tourism, this expansion comes with
costs. The main problem is rooted in the business itself. Casinos generate
millions of dollars a day in hard currency. For example, to convert the
customers' paper money to chips and back again, the casinos have many   *30*
areas called cages. They act as mini-banks. At any given moment, the
average cage may hold five million dollars in cash. That figure does not
even include all the money that is on the tables, in the slot machines, or in
the patrons' possession at that moment.

Think about being around that kind of money! Does it make you   *35*
contemplate some different ideas? It does for everyone. This leads us to the
negative aspects of the industry. It is perfectly normal to watch millions
of dollars changing hands and think what it would be like to have some
of it for your very own. Politicians, employees, customers, and local people
are not exempt from this fantasy. This has sometimes led to bribery, graft,   *40*
money laundering, and other illegal and/or criminal operations and has
given gambling its negative image. In addition, because enormous amounts
of money are located in one place, organized crime has always been
reputed to be a part of the gambling industry. However, when respected
businesspeople like Howard Hughes and Baron Hilton invested their   *45*
money in casinos, gambling gained social acceptance. Although gambling's
criminal background will always be part of the excitement of a casino,
strict government regulation of casino employees and owners, as well as the
formation of large business **conglomerates**, has helped to alter the reality.

There are two main problems for casino employees and players: *50*
wanting the casino's money and spending too much of their own.
Understanding both sides of these issues is important so that you, as an
individual, can decide how you stand on each issue.

The first issue is that some people want the cash they see in the
casinos. If they cannot win it, they may want to steal it. This is one of the   *55*
arguments that many anti-gaming advocates use to deter people from
voting to allow gaming in their community. They speculate that crime will
increase in the areas where casinos operate. On one hand, this is a simple,
logical argument. With any increase in population density, problems are
going to arise. On the other hand, you can argue that a casino-related   *60*
crime increase is **counterintuitive**. Newer **longitudinal** studies show that

crime increases during the introductory phases of casino development, but crime rates actually decrease over the long term. Casino owners understand that the open display of cash is a temptation. The casinos do not want big winners to be robbed, because it is bad for business. People who do not feel secure are not going to come back. Therefore, security and surveillance are a major part of any casino operation. Good security deters people from thinking about theft too long or too seriously.

65

The second issue is that people become obsessed with trying to win the jackpot and stay at a casino too long. A select few will become problem gamblers. Problem gamblers tend to follow similar patterns. Usually, they win big early in their careers, and then they chase their losses. This means that if they lose, they double the bet to get money back. This is a bad strategy and rapidly increases gambling debts. However, less than 2 percent of gambling players are at risk of becoming addicted to gambling. Some researchers have stretched this statistic to 40 or 50 percent of the population.

70

75

The key point to remember is that there are many ways to define "problem." Do you become a problem gambler when you spend $10 more than you budgeted, or when you steal to get money to gamble? Keep in mind that problem gamblers are a very small percentage of players overall. On the whole, over 98 percent of the people who come to a casino will not suffer any ill effects from the experience.

80

[a] MGM Mirage home page. Retrieved July 4, 2008. http://www.mgmmirage.com/companyoverview.asp.

From Chon/Maier, *Welcome to Hospitality*, 3E. © 2010 Cengage Learning

inherent
basic, part of the very nature of something

conglomerates
business organizations involved in many areas

counterintuitive
different from what would be expected

longitudinal
extending over time

Paher, 2013 / Used under license from Shutterstock.com

Reflecting

After you complete your reading, answer these questions. Share your responses with your classmates.

1. What is the main idea of the essay?

   _____

   _____

2. Does the essay focus more attention on causes or effects? Or does it give equal attention to both? Explain.

   _____

   _____

   _____

3. What is one cause of gambling that is identified? One effect?

   _____

   _____

   _____

4. What is the purpose of the reading—to inform, to entertain, or to persuade? Explain.

   _____

   _____

5. Has this essay confirmed or changed your understanding of the topic? Explain?

   _____

   _____

   _____

6. How would you rate this reading, and why?
   Weak ★ ★ ★ ★ ★ Strong

   _____

   _____

Vocabulary Practice

Identify Use context clues to help you explain or define the following words. (See pages 33–34 for help.)

1. **infrastructures** (lines 19)

   clues: _____

   definition: _____

2. **graft** (line 40)

   clues: _____

   definition: _____

3. **surveillance** (line 67)

   clues: _____

   definition: _____

Thinking Critically

Explain Answer these questions to help you think critically about the text.

1. What parts of the text seem especially important, and why?

   _____

   _____

   _____

2. Why is gambling so popular? What does this say about human nature?

   _____

   _____

   _____

3. Is legalized gambling limited to casinos? Explain.

   _____

   _____

   _____

Writing

What follows are possible writing activities to complete in response to the reading. Use the writing process (pages 94-99) to help you develop your writing.

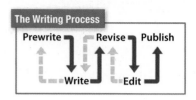

Prewriting

Choose one of the following writing ideas. Or decide upon another idea of your own related to the reading.

Writing Ideas

1. **Writing to Learn:** In one or more personal blogs or journal entries, explore your own experiences with gambling.

2. **Paragraph Writing:** Write a cause-effect paragraph about another topic that you identified on page 323.

3. Write a paragraph explaining the effects of an important decision you have made.

4. **Essay Writing:** Explore the causes and/or effects related to one of your "vices," such as your addiction to junk food, devotion to TV, excessive shopping, etc.

5. Develop a cause-effect essay about a topic related to current events or a subject you are studying.

When planning . . .

Refer to pages 323–324 to help with your prewriting and planning. Also use the tips below.

- Choose a topic you care about. Writing about something you find interesting is always the best choice. Make sure it will interest your readers as well.

- Make certain your listed causes and effects are clearly related and will make sense to your readers.

- Research any fuzzy areas so all the cause-effect connections are plain.

- If necessary, change your thesis or your topic sentence to match what you learn from your research.

Writing and Revising

Use the tips that follow and the information on pages 325–327 to help you with your drafting and revising.

When writing . . .

- Include an opening, a middle, and a closing part in your cause-effect piece. Each part has its own role to play. (See page 326.)
- Write your first draft freely, using your notes as a guide but allowing yourself to explore new connections and explanations as they come to mind.
- If questions arise as you are writing the draft, make a note to return to these parts later.

When revising . . .

- Let your first draft sit unread for a while. Then read it critically, with fresh eyes. Also, reading a printed copy can help you see it differently.
- Ask a classmate or another writer to review and critique your writing. Use a peer-review sheet to guide the critique. (See page 622.)
- Make sure you have included enough details to explain the causes and effects.
- Consider the style of your writing. For most cause-effect writing, an academic style is appropriate. (See page 132.)

Editing

Refer to the checklist on page 331 when you are ready to edit your cause-effect writing for style and correctness.

Reflecting on Classification Writing

Answer the following questions about your cause-effect reading and writing experiences in this chapter.

1. Why is cause-effect such a common structure in textbooks?

    _____

    _____

2. What is the most important thing you learned about reading a cause-effect paragraph or essay?

    _____

    _____

3. What reading strategy in this chapter do you find most helpful? Explain.

    _____

    _____

4. What is your favorite cause-effect piece in this chapter? Why?

    _____

    _____

5. What do you like most about your own cause-effect writing? Why?

    _____

    _____

6. What is one thing you would like to change in it?

    _____

Key Terms to Remember

Whenever you read and write cause-effect paragraphs and essays, it's important to understand the following terms.

- **Causes**—the reasons for an action or a condition
- **Effects**—the results of a cause or an action
- **Cause-effect organizer**—a graphic organizer used to list causes in one column and effects in another
- **Evidence**—the facts and details that support or explain the main points in writing

13

> "Another possible source of guidance for teenagers is television, but television's message has always been that the need for truth, wisdom, and world peace pales by comparison with the need for a toothpaste that offers whiter teeth and fresher breath."
>
> —Dave Barry

Comparison

Take a close look at the photograph below. It is full of contrasts. A tree is contrasted with a man-made power station. The dark green foreground is contrasted with the light blue background. And even the vertical stature of the tree and power station contrasts with the horizontal field and sky.

But the photo also contains some interesting comparisons. The water vapor from the power plant looks similar to the clouds overhead. The green leaves of the tree match the green grass. And the vegetation and the power station are both involved with energy use and production.

Texts that examine similarities and differences are comparing and contrasting topics. In this chapter, you will read and react to two professional comparison-contrast texts and learn how to write one of your own.

Learning Outcomes

LO1 Understand comparison.

LO2 Learn reading strategies (recognizing patterns and transitions).

LO3 Read and react to a professional paragraph.

LO4 Read and react to a professional comparison.

LO5 Practice reading skills (using graphic organizers).

LO6 Plan a comparison.

LO7 Write the first draft.

LO8 Revise the writing.

LO9 Edit the writing.

What do you think?

What contrast is illustrated in the quotation above? Hint: The word *pales* means "to lack, or to be short of."

Hervé Hughes/Hemis/Corbis

LO1 Understanding Comparison

Creating a ranking requires you to make comparisons. A food critic ranking the "5 Best Pizzerias in Town" would need to compare different pizza places to come up with an appropriate list. This same type of thinking is required to evaluate a ranking. If you disagreed with the food critic's list, you would need to make your own comparison: *The crust at La Familia's Pizza sets it apart from Ann's Pizza.*

The effectiveness of a ranking depends on the points of comparison that are made. In the example above, crust is used to compare two different pizzerias. The sauce, the toppings, or the staff's attentiveness could also serve as valuable points of comparison. As you study a ranking, always ask yourself if it is the result of a meaningful comparison. Ask the same question as you read and respond to a comparison text.

> "There are dark shadows on the earth, but its lights are stronger in the contrast."
> —Charles Dickens

Comparing vs. Contrasting

Comparing means to look for similarities between subjects. Contrasting means to look for differences. The term *comparison* in this chapter refers to both comparing and contrasting. Some comparisons focus more on the similarities, while others may focus more on the differences. Still others may present a balanced analysis— equal numbers of similarities and differences. It all depends on the information the writer has discovered—and the points of comparison she or he intends to make.

INSIGHT

Related types of analysis include cause-effect and classification. These two forms require you to carefully examine the subjects, just as making comparisons requires. (See pages 283–312 and 313–340.)

Identify   Write down a general field of study. Then write down jobs for people who graduate with that major. Finally, write two or three points of comparison for the jobs.

1. Field of study _____

2. Jobs in that field _____

   _____

3. Points of comparison _____

   _____

Reading

Comparison texts involve two primary subjects, which must be evaluated equally.

LO2 Learning Reading Strategies

Recognizing Common Patterns

Knowing the different patterns of organization used in comparison texts will help you follow the main ideas.

- **Point-by-point:** Some comparison writing is organized point-by-point. That is, each subject is addressed according to different points of comparison.
- **Subject-by-subject:** Other comparison writing discusses one subject in the first part and the other subject in the second part.
- **Similarities & differences:** Still other pieces address the similarities between the subjects in the first part and the differences in the second part.

INSIGHT

A writer may use a variation on one of the patterns, following it in general, but not exactly, from start to finish.

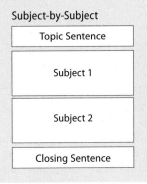

Recognizing Common Transitions

As you read comparison texts, watch for transitions or linking words that alert you to specific comparisons and contrasts.

Transitions that show comparisons				
also	both	in the same way	much as	likewise
much like	one way	similarly	another way	as
Transitions that show contrasts				
although	even though	by contrast	but	however
on the one hand	on the other hand	otherwise	though	

LO3 Reading and Reacting to a Professional Paragraph

The following comparison paragraph comes from *Cultural Anthropology: An Applied Perspective*, a college textbook by Gary Ferraro and Susan Andreatta that examines the cultural differences among humans.

Prereading Before you read, answer these three questions:

1. What do the title and first sentence tell you about this comparison?

2. What do you think is meant by the word "miscues"?

3. What do you expect to learn in this reading?

Reading and Rereading As you read, make it your goal to (1) recognize the organizational pattern, (2) identify the specific examples, and (3) judge the information's value. Consider annotating the text (page 20) as you read.

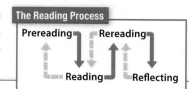

The Reading Process

Prereading · Rereading · Reading · Reflecting

Cross-Cultural Miscues

Although both New Yorkers and Londoners speak English, there are enough differences between American English and British English to cause communication miscues. Speakers of English on opposite sides of the Atlantic often use different words to refer to the same thing. To illustrate, Londoners put their trash in a dustbin, not a garbage can; they take a lift, not an elevator; and they live in flats, not apartments. To further complicate matters, the same word used in England and the United States can convey very different meanings. For example, in England the word "homely" (as in the statement "I think your wife is very homely") means warm and friendly, not plain . . . as in the United States; for the British, the phrase "to table a motion" means to give an item a prominent place on the agenda rather than to postpone taking action on an item, as in the United States; and a rubber in British English is an eraser, not a condom. These are just a few of the linguistic pitfalls that North Americans and Brits may encounter when they attempt to communicate using their own version of the "same" language.

1

5

10

15

Reflecting After you complete your reading, answer these questions. Share your responses with your classmates.

1. What is the purpose of this paragraph?

   _____

2. What two things are being compared?

   _____

3. What pattern of organization is used? (See page 343.)

   _____

4. What questions, if any, do you still have about the topic?

   _____

5. How would you rate the paragraph, and why?
   Weak ★ ★ ★ ★ ★ Strong

   _____

Vocabulary Practice

Identify Are the phrases "communication miscues" (line 3) and "linguistic pitfall" (line 13) close in meaning (synonyms) or greatly different in meaning (antonyms)? Explain your choice.

_____

_____

Drawing Inferences

Explain Answer the following questions to help you draw inferences from the text. (See pages 29–31 for help.)

1. Why are there differences between the two types of English?

   _____

   _____

2. What do these differences tell you about languages?

   _____

   _____

LO4 Reading and Reacting to a Professional Comparison

This comparison appeared in an essay about book censorship. Use the reading process to help you gain a full understanding of the text.

About the Author

Rudolfo Anaya is a Mexican-American author best known for his novel *Bless Me*. He is considered one of the leading voices in modern Chicano literature.

Prereading Before you read, answer these questions:

1. What do the title and first paragraph tell you about the text?

_____

2. Who is Salman Rushdie?

_____

3. What do you expect to learn?

_____

Reading and Rereading As you read, make it your goal to (1) identify the subjects of the comparison, (2) decide how they are compared, and (3) judge the value of the text. Consider annotating the text (page 20) during your reading.

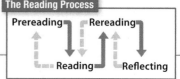

The Reading Process

Prereading → Rereading → Reading → Reflecting

From "Take the Tortillas Out of Your Poetry"

In a recent lecture, "Is Nothing Sacred?", Salman Rushdie, one of the   1
most censored authors of our time, talked about the importance of books.
He grew up in a household in India where books were as sacred as bread.
If anyone in the household dropped a piece of bread or a book, the person
not only picked it up, but also kissed the object by way of apologizing for   5
clumsy disrespect.

He goes on to say that he had kissed many books before he had
kissed a girl. Bread and books were for his household, and for many like
his, food for the body and the soul. This image of the kissing of the book
one had accidentally dropped made an impression on me. It speaks to the   10
love and respect many people have for them.

I grew up in a small town in New Mexico, and we had very few books in our household. The first one I remember reading was my **catechism** book. Before I went to school to learn English, my mother taught me catechism in Spanish. I remember the questions and answers I had to *15* learn, and I remember the well-thumbed, frayed volume, which was sacred to me.

Growing up with few books in the house created in me a desire and a need for them. When I started school, I remember visiting the one-room library of our town and standing in front of the dusty shelves. In *20* reality there were only a few shelves and not over a thousand books, but I wanted to read them all. There was food for my soul in the books, that much I realized.

The Anaya Reader, copyright 1995 by Rudolfo Anaya, published by Warner Books, New York. Originally published in *Censored Books, Critical Viewpoints*. Eds. Karolides, Burres, Kean, Scarecrow Press, May 1993, Metuchen, N.J.

catechism
instruction in principles of Christianity

Reflecting   After you complete your reading, answer the following questions about the selection. Then discuss your responses with your classmates.

1. What is the main idea of the selection? Is it directly stated or implied?

   _____

   _____

2. Are the two subjects more alike or more different in this comparison?

   _____

   _____

3. What pattern of organization is used? (See page 343.)

   _____

   _____

4. How would you rate this comparison, and why?
   Weak ★ ★ ★ ★ ★ Strong

   _____

Vocabulary Practice

Identify   Create a vocabulary entry for the word *censored* (line 2) and two other words that may be new to you. Identify the pronunciation, helpful word parts, and a primary definition, and use the word in a sentence. (Refer to a dictionary and pages 32–36 in this book for help.)

_____

_____

_____

_____

Drawing Inferences

Explain   Answer these questions to help you draw inferences from the text. (See pages 29–31 for help.)

1. What cultural conclusions, if any, can you draw from this text?

_____

_____

_____

2. Why are books and reading so valued by many people?

_____

_____

_____

3. What value do they hold for you?

_____

_____

4. What does the future hold for books?

_____

_____

LO5 Practicing Reading Skills

Comparison texts focus on details that show similarities and differences. To identify and organize such details, consider using one of the graphic organizers that follow.

Comparison T-Chart

A T-chart helps you identify the details about the two topics being compared. On one side of the chart, write details relating to the first subject, and on the second side, write details relating to the second subject.

> **CONSIDER THE READING-WRITING CONNECTION** ——
>
> Graphic organizers like the ones here help you analyze the details in a comparison text. They will also help you gather details for your own comparison writing.

Subject A	Subject B
Details	Details

Venn Diagram

A Venn diagram is a useful graphic organizer for any type of comparison writing. It is especially helpful for complex comparisons that examine both similarities and differences.

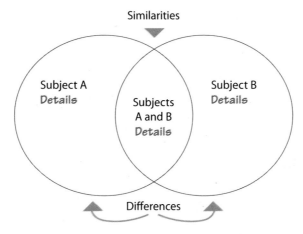

Similarities

Subject A
Details

Subjects
A and B
Details

Subject B
Details

Differences

Graph Use one of the graphic organizers from above to identify the details in one of the comparisons you have just read.

Writing

Starting on this page, you will plan and write a comparison paragraph about two people. Follow the writing process to help you do your best work. (See pages 94–99.)

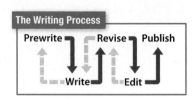

LO6 Planning a Comparison

These two pages will help you gather your thoughts about your topic before you actually begin writing.

Selecting a Topic

Choose two people that interest you for your paragraph. They could be people you know well or complete strangers; people who are dead or alive; famous people or unknowns. You can even include yourself in the comparison.

Select For each heading below, identify two people you would like to compare and contrast. Then select the two people you would most like to write about in your paragraph.

Family   1._____   2._____

Friends   1._____   2._____

Role Models   1._____   2._____

Famous People   1._____   2._____

Experts in Your   1._____   2._____
Academic Major

Describing the People

Select Decide on three points of comparison to compare and contrast the two people. Consider the suggestions that follow.

- **Appearance:** Think of size, shape, hair color, eye color, skin color, gender, clothing, and so on.
- **Personality:** Think of attitude, outlook, feelings, actions, and so on.
- **Background:** Think of birthplace, schooling, hometown, family, and so on.
- **Interests:** Think of favorite activities, hobbies, friends, food, music, and so on.
- **Other**

LO9 Editing the Writing

Commas tell the reader when to pause, making the writing easy to follow.

Commas After Introductory Words

Many sentences naturally start with the subject. Some sentences, however, start with an introductory phrase or clause. A comma is used to separate a long introductory word group from the rest of the sentence. When you read sentences like these out loud, you will naturally pause after the introductory words. That tells you that a comma is needed to separate these words from the rest of the sentence. See the examples that follow.

Introductory Word Groups:

After my third birthday, my brother was born. (prepositional phrase)

When he arrived on the scene, life changed for me. (dependent clause)

Punctuation Practice   Read the sentences below, out loud. Listen for the natural pause after an introductory phrase or clause. Place a comma to set off the introductory words.

1. When my younger brother was born I was jealous.
2. Before he showed up I had Mom all to myself.
3. At the beginning of our relationship we didn't get along very well.
4. As the years passed my brother stopped being a pest and became a friend.
5. As a matter of fact we both came to love basketball.
6. Without my younger brother I wouldn't have anyone to push my basketball skills.
7. Taking that into account our long rivalry has helped us both.
8. Since our teenage years we've become best friends.
9. Although we still tease each other we're not being vicious.
10. When we bump fists I sometimes remember when we bumped heads.

Apply   Read your comparison paragraph and look for sentences that begin with introductory phrases or clauses. If you do not find any, add an introductory phrase or clause to a few sentences to vary their beginnings. Does this help your writing read more smoothly? Remember to use a comma to separate a long introductory word group from the rest of the sentence. (For more information, see pages 592 and 594.)

Commas with Extra Information

Some sentences include phrases or clauses that add information in the middle or at the end of sentences. This information should be set off with commas. You can recognize this extra information because it can be removed without changing the basic meaning of the sentence. When you read the sentence out loud, there's a natural pause before and after the phrase or clause. This indicates where you are to place the commas.

Extra Information:

I have a tough time waking up, not surprisingly.

My mother, who works two jobs, makes me breakfast every morning.

Punctuation Practice   In each sentence, use a comma or commas to separate extra information. Listen for the natural pause. Some sentences may not contain examples of extra information.

1. My mother works as a waitress which is a tough job.
2. She also works as a licensed practical nurse which is an even tougher job.
3. The nursing home the one on Main and 7th is strict.
4. A time card punched one second late is docked fifteen minutes an unfair policy.
5. A time card punched ten minutes early does not earn overtime.
6. The restaurant job pays minimum wage which is not much.
7. Tips from a good lunch not the busiest time can double Mom's pay.
8. What I've learned about determination real grit I learned from Mom.
9. She wants to help me qualify for a better job a selfless goal.
10. I want exactly the same thing no surprise there.

Apply   Read your comparison paragraph and look for sentences that have extra information. If you haven't included any, add some extra information in a sentence or two. Do these additions make your writing more interesting? Remember to use commas to set off extra information in your sentences. (For more on comma use, see page 598.)

INSIGHT ———————————————————————————————

Commas are very important in written English. For more practice with comma use, see pages 591–600.

Marking a Paragraph

The model that follows has a number of errors.

Editing Practice Correct the following paragraph, using the correction marks below. One correction has been done for you.

Into the Spotlight

My wife and I love each other, but it's hard to imagine how we could be   *1*
more different. Lupe's a social butterfly. She been always meeting people
for coffee or talking to people on the phone. By contrast, I'm private. I
work at U.S. steel and come home. The only person I really want to be
with is Lupe, but she's always dragging me out to partys. Their is another   *5*
big difference. Lupe who is a great singer and dancer loves theater. She's
been in a dozen plays. When it come to me, the idea of being on stage is
terrifying. She convinced me once to be in a play I forgot my one line. so,
is there anything Lupe and I have in common? We love each other. Lupe
needs me to keep her grounded, and I need her to pry me out of the house.   *10*
We've even figured out a way to work around the theater thing. The next
play she is in. I'll work set crew. That's how we get along so well. I will
work backstage, setting props for her, and getting what she needs. Then
she will walk into the spotlight and performs.

Correction Marks

ꟾ delete	⅄ add comma	*word* ∧ add word
d̲ capitalize	? add question	⊙ add period
₫ lowercase	∧ mark	spelling
∧ insert	ᵛ insert an apostrophe	switch

INSIGHT

As you've seen, commas are needed to set off extra information in a sentence. Sometimes the extra information comes between the subject and the verb:

Lupe, who is a great singer and dancer, loves theater.

But when there is no extra information to set off, do not separate the subject and verb with a comma.

Incorrect: Lupe, loves theater.   **Correct:** Lupe loves theater.

Using an Editing Checklist

Now it's time to correct your own paragraph.

Edit Prepare a clean copy of your revised writing and use the following checklist to look for errors. Continue working until you can check off each item in the list.

Words

☐ **1.** Have I used specific nouns and verbs? (See page 134.)

☐ **2.** Have I used more action verbs than "be" verbs? (See page 536.)

Sentences

☐ **3.** Have I varied the beginnings and lengths of sentences? (See pages 136–137.)

☐ **4.** Have I combined short, choppy sentences? (See page 137.)

☐ **5.** Have I avoided shifts in sentences? (See page 500.)

☐ **6.** Have I avoided fragments and run-ons? (See pages 488–491, 494–495.)

Conventions

☐ **7.** Do I use correct verb forms (*he saw,* not *he seen*)? (See pages 542, 544.)

☐ **8.** Do my subjects and verbs agree (*she speaks,* not *she speak*)? (See pages 472–481.)

☐ **9.** Have I capitalized first words and proper nouns and adjectives? (See page 582.)

☐ **10.** Have I used commas after long introductory word groups? (See pages 652–655.)

☐ **11.** Have I punctuated dialogue correctly? (See pages 189–190.)

☐ **12.** Have I carefully checked my spelling?

Adding a Title

Make sure to add an attention-getting title. Here are three simple strategies for creating one.

- Use a phrase from the paragraph:

  Into the Spotlight

- Point to a similarity or difference:

  We Can Dance

- Use the word "versus":

  Old Versus New

Create Prepare a clean final copy of your paragraph and proofread it before sharing it.

> "What makes the universe so hard to comprehend is that there's nothing to compare it with it."
> —Scott Adams

Enrichment: Reading

On the following four pages, you will find a comparison essay entitled "The Brain Game." As you read this essay, use the steps in the reading process as your guide. The reading activities are followed by a number of writing ideas to choose from to write a comparison paragraph or essay of your own.

About the Author

Since 2006, Nancy Snyderman, a physician and journalist, has frequently appeared on NBC's *Today* and MSNBC to examine medical issues. She is on the staff in the Department of Otolaryngology—Head and Neck Surgery at the University of Pennsylvania and is the author of four books.

CONSIDER THE TRAITS

As you read the report, focus first on the **ideas**—the topic, main idea, and comparisons. Then consider the **organization**—the comparison-contrast pattern used to structure the text (see page 343). Also take special notice of the **voice,** or overall tone, of the text. And finally, ask yourself if these traits combine to produce a worthy reading experience.

Prereading

Many comparisons can be made between different classifications of people. For example, interesting comparisons can be made between men and women, husbands and wives, parents and their children, Democrats and Republicans, chefs and cooks, etc. Think of interesting pairs that could be compared and contrasted. List two or three possible choices below.

_____

_____

_____

_____

What do you think?

What does the quotation at the top of the page have to say about the value of comparisons?

Identify   Before you read "The Brain Game," answer these three questions.

1. What do the title, beginning two paragraphs, and the headings tell you about the text?

   A story told about the brain game b/w men and women

2. What do you already know about the topic?

   The Brain Games test the brain

3. What questions do you hope to have answered?

   What is the story about

Reading and Rereading

In the 2002 ABC News special *The Brain Game*, Nancy Snyderman reported on the differences between men and women based on brain development. The research she cites is enlightening and thoughtful.

As you read, make it your goal to (1) identify the focus of the comparison, (2) note the types of comparisons made, and (3) study the specific comparative details. Use a graphic organizer to help you keep track of the comparative details. (See page 349.) Also consider annotating the text (page 20) during your reading.

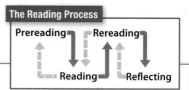

The Reading Process

Prereading ⟶ Reading ⟶ Rereading ⟶ Reflecting

The Brain Game

When Lori and Rich Boulware of Kendall Park, N.J., hit the road   1
recently, their navigational radars were tuned into different frequencies.
Rich used a mental map, while Lori used landmarks to get around. As the
couple tried to get around a tricky area of town, Rich said, "Turn left on
Webster," while Lori said, "You have to turn before the ice cream cone." Dr.   5
Helen Fisher, an expert in gender differences, says the Boulwares are not
unusual in their navigational skills. "Women go from one object to another.
. . . A man will say, go two miles down the road and then head east. That's
very different from saying go down to the shoe store and take a left at the
high stone wall."   10

But these differences begin long before people get their driver's
licenses. The Boulwares are already observing major differences in the
way their three children communicate, particularly their two eldest—
Jordan, 11, and Jerika, 9. Lori Boulware says her daughter Jerika
describes her day with a lot more drama than her son. "Everything is   15
about relationships," she said. "I know who was whose best friend today
and who fought with who and what boy likes who. Jordan has no interest
in that kind of stuff at all. Jordan would be happy to just say, 'My day was

fine.'" Do the Boulwares' family stories sound familiar? If so, you're not
alone. Fact is, men and women are very different in the way they speak,   *20*
behave, solve problems, and even remember where the car keys are.

Size Isn't Everything

The reasons behind these differences have fueled arguments for
generations and continue to do so today. Is it our biology or our culture?
Many scientists say it's all in our heads or, more precisely, in the way men's   *25*
and women's brains are designed and the way they function. A century ago,
the discovery that female brains were about 10 percent smaller than male
brains was cited as proof that women could never be as smart as men—
contributing to their status as second-class citizens. We now know that size
isn't everything when it comes to brainpower. Our I.Q.s are the same. In   *30*
fact, the highest recorded I.Q. belongs to a woman, a writer named Marilyn
vos Savant.

There are other, perhaps more significant differences that distinguish
male and female brains. Male brains are wired to move information
quickly within each side—or hemisphere—of the brain. This gives them   *35*
better **spatial** abilities. They can see an object in space and react quickly.
In women's brains, areas of the cerebral cortex—linked to language,
judgment, and memory—are more densely packed with nerve cells than
men's brains are. This allows them to process that information more
effectively. Fisher explained that the corpus callosum, which she describes   *40*
as a "big highway between the two sides of the brain," is larger in women
toward the rear than it is in men. "Hence," she said, "the two sides of
the brain are better interconnected" in women. This means that women
can absorb and analyze all sorts of information from the environment
simultaneously. This makes women more adept at multitasking, while men   *45*
tend to do better tackling one thing at a time. . . .

An Old Brain in a Modern Culture

The degree to which individuals' behavior is determined by their
physiological makeup remains a hotly debated question. [Michael] Lewis,
points out that children grow up in a world that reinforces boy and girl   *50*
differences—through cartoons, commercials, clothing—and their behavior
as adults will be shaped by these social cues. Ann Fausto-Sterling, a
biologist at Brown University, thinks these external influences are so
substantial that we shouldn't study the brain in isolation. "I **balk** at the
notion that our brains are hard-wired," Fausto-Sterling said. "Our brains   *55*
develop, and they develop new connections. So, you never have development
outside of culture and experience," she said. Fausto-Sterling, like Lewis,
pointed out that children are bombarded with "heavily gendered messages."
Fausto-Sterling said these messages "start earlier than we can imagine."

Some researchers say the perception that men excel in motor and   *60*
spatial skills while women are stronger in the verbal department is not just
an **overparodied** stereotype. Evolutionary scientists claim it all began with
our ancient ancestors. Fisher said it all goes back to the hunter-gatherer
days. Women needed verbal and emotional skills to **cajole**, educate, and

discipline their babies, while men needed spatial skills out on the hunt.   *65*
"We've got an old brain in a very modern culture."

From the Classroom to Career Choices

Researchers are also trying to understand why boys and girls often
show **stark** differences in academic performance. In grade school, girls
usually outshine the boys in every subject, including math. In high school,   *70*
however, it's a different subject altogether. Lewis noted that "early math
really isn't math. It's really more language problems." Once puberty hits,
boys get a second surge of **testosterone**, and their math and spatial abilities
climb dramatically—but some researchers don't exactly know what the
connection is. By the time high school kids take their SATs, boys outscore   *75*
girls in the math section by 7 percent. Fisher said, "It's quite remarkable
how much better boys become at all kinds of spatial skills, mechanical
skills, engineering skills, when that surge of testosterone comes on them."
Meanwhile, **estrogen** starts flooding the girls' bodies, and experts think
that helps them develop stronger verbal and memory skills. According to   *80*
Fisher, a woman's verbal ability climbs rapidly during the middle of the
monthly menstrual cycle, when estrogen levels peak.

Some researchers say these physiological differences may **predispose**
men and women to gravitate toward certain careers. Fisher notes that
despite the move toward equal employment opportunity in the U.S. job   *85*
market, some 85 percent of the architects in America are still men, and 90
percent of the mechanics are still men. She said she's not at all surprised
that men gravitate to those jobs that need and require mechanical spatial
skills. Meanwhile, 94 percent of all speech therapists are women, and 99
percent of all pre-school and kindergarten teachers are female.   *90*

Fausto-Sterling cautions that an over-emphasis on innate brain
differences may unfairly limit an individual's opportunities. "By saying
something is innate we shut doors and say, 'Well, this is just the way it
is.' We close down possibilities. For every woman I think of who's sort of
stereotypically female, I can think of one who isn't, and the same for men."   *95*
Michael Lewis agrees. "Even if there are dispositions we're born with, it
doesn't mean environments can't alter them. The thing we know about
brains now, [which] we didn't know ten years ago, is that the brain is not a
static organ. It's changing throughout our lives," Lewis said.

Beauty and the Brain   *100*

Differences in the way male and female brains work don't just affect
our career choices or academic **aptitudes**; they control the way we perceive
beauty, and they may affect how our bodies deal with stress and disease.
While romantics believe love comes from the heart, scientists know it
starts with the brain. When the brain sees something it likes—a very   *105*
distinct message is transmitted throughout the body. Researchers have
learned that beauty taps into a part of the brain called the limbic system,
which deals with craving and reward. Dr. Nancy Etcoff, a Harvard
psychologist, has been studying how the brain responds to beauty. She

observed that the so-called reward area in men's brains lit up when they   *110*
were shown pictures of beautiful women. The same reward circuitry is
triggered for many different pleasures, researchers say. Some people
will respond similarly to a good meal, and cocaine will trigger the same
reaction in addicts. When men were shown photos of attractive men,
however, there was no activity in the brain's reward center at all. Women   *115*
responded differently to the photos. "They wanted to get a second look, not
only at the beautiful men, but at the beautiful women," Etcoff said.

Depression and Women

Because the two halves of their brains are better connected, women
may be more prone to emotional problems. Women make up some two-   *120*
thirds of those who suffer from depression. Some researchers say the root
of this may lie in the balance of estrogen and other chemicals in the female
brain. Depression in females usually begins after age 13, when puberty
and estrogen kick in. It is most prevalent during a woman's childbearing
years, and drops off after menopause.   *125*

Autoimmune diseases also affect more women than men. Dr. Esther
Sternberg of the National Institutes of Health said women sufferers of these
diseases outnumber men by a two-to-one ratio. Again, researchers think that
estrogen is behind it. The hormone plays a major role in the immune system.
When released, it acts in delicate balance with other hormones in the brain,   *130*
including those that fight stress. When estrogen and other hormones are
in **equilibrium**, the immune system fights off disease. If the balance is off,
however, the immune system can fall asleep at the switch, making you
vulnerable to colds and flu, or it can become hyper-alert and begin attacking
your own body. This can lead to **autoimmune diseases**.   *135*

But researchers are working on new medicines that may target the
root of the problem. They're working to develop drugs that focus on the
brain to control illnesses that devastate the body. Sternberg said, "We have
a whole new category of drugs that we can begin to develop and test, and
use to treat . . . a whole host of autoimmune diseases."   *140*

"The Brain Game" from SNYDERMAN. *ABCNews.com*, July 31, 2002. Reprinted by permission of ABC News.

spatial
relating to space

balk
to hesitate

overparodied
made fun of or ridiculed excessively

cajole
urge with gentle and repeated pleading or teasing

stark
bare and plain

testosterone
a hormone responsible for male characteristics

estrogen
a hormone responsible for female characteristics

predispose
influence or persuade

aptitudes
abilities

equilibrium
balance, stability

autoimmune diseases
illnesses that cause the immune system to attack the person's own body

Reflecting

After you complete your reading, answer the following questions. Afterward share your responses with your classmates.

1. What is the main idea in this essay? When in the essay is it stated?

   _____

   _____

2. What information is presented in the first paragraph? What does this paragraph accomplish?

   _____

   _____

   _____

3. Which questions does this text address?

   _____

   _____

   _____

4. Which comparisons surprise you?

   _____

   _____

   _____

5. What additional questions does it bring to mind?

   _____

   _____

   _____

6. How would you rate this reading, and why?
   Weak ★ ★ ★ ★ ★ Strong

   _____

   _____

Vocabulary Practice

Identify   For each word below, define the word parts as indicated. Then try to explain the meaning of the complete word. (See pages 623-631 and a dictionary for help.

   1. navigational (line 2) navigat(e) + ional

   _____

   _____

   2. multitasking (line 45) multi + task + ing

   _____

   _____

   3. transmitted (line 106) trans + mit + (t)ed

   _____

   _____

Drawing Inferences

Explain   Answer these questions to help you draw inferences from the text.

   1. What is meant by the following idea: "We've got an old brain in a very modern culture"?

   _____

   _____

   2. Is intelligence inherent or environmental?

   _____

   _____

   3. What is the ultimate value in "The Brain Game"?

   _____

   _____

Writing

What follows are possible comparison writing activities to complete in response to the reading.

The Writing Process

Prewrite → Write → Revise → Edit → Publish

Prewriting

Choose one of the following ideas. Or decide upon another idea of your own related to the reading.

Writing Ideas

1. **Writing to Learn:** In a personal blog or journal entry, consider how your own behaviors and problem-solving abilities match the findings in "The Brain Game."

2. **Paragraph Writing:** Compare your approach to a particular task or two with the approach of a brother or sister.

3. Write a paragraph about one of the topics you identified on page 350.

4. **Essay Writing:** Compare the effects of testosterone and estrogen. (This may require some research.)

5. Write a review comparing two of your favorite restaurants. (Consider two or three points of comparison during your planning.)

When planning . . .

Refer to pages 350–351 to help you with your prewriting and planning. Also use the tips that follow.

- Choose subjects that are specific enough for a paragraph or an essay and that you know a lot about or can research effectively.

- Choose appropriate points of comparison and a pattern of organization. (See pages 343 and 349.)

- Collect plenty of details relating to those points of comparison. Use a graphic organizer to collect and organize the details. (See page 349.)

- Review the examples of comparison writing in this chapter to see how they are developed.

Writing and Revising

Refer to pages 352–354 to help you write and revise your first draft. Also use the tips that follow.

When writing . . .

- Include opening, middle, and closing parts in your writing. Each part has a specific role. (See page 353.)
- Follow the pattern of organization and points of comparison you chose during your planning, but be open to making changes in organization or content if the writing is not logically coming together.
- Use transitional words to help the reader follow your ideas. (See page 343.)

When revising . . .

- Ask yourself if your paragraph or essay contains any dead spots that either need more details or should be cut back.
- Decide if any parts are confusing or cause you to stumble. Rewrite these parts as needed.
- Determine if you have organized your details in the best way.
- Have at least one trusted peer react to your writing.

Editing

Refer to the checklist on page 358 when you are ready to edit your comparison-contrast writing for style and correctness.

Reflecting on Comparison Writing

Answer the following questions about your reading and writing experiences in this chapter.

1. What makes a comparison enjoyable to read?

   _____

2. What is your favorite selection in this chapter?

   _____

3. Which reading strategy in this chapter seems the most helpful? Explain.

   _____

   _____

4. What do you like most about the comparison that you wrote in this chapter? Explain.

   _____

   _____

5. What is one thing that you would like to change in your text?

   _____

   _____

6. What is the hardest thing about this type of writing? The easiest?

   _____

   _____

   _____

Key Terms to Remember

When you read and write comparisons, it's important to understand the following terms.

- **Comparing**—showing how two or more subjects are similar
- **Contrasting**—showing how two or more subjects are different
- **Points of comparison**—the special elements or features used to make a comparison (size, strength, appearance, and so on)
- **Patterns of organization for comparison writing**—point-by-point, subject-by-subject, or similarities and differences (See page 343.)

14

> "Use soft words and hard arguments."
> —English Proverb

Argumentation

Have you ever wondered why political candidates participate in debates? It's no accident. Argumentation plays a central role in any civilization. Given our variety of personalities, backgrounds, values, and assumptions, the only way of coming to a consensus is to discuss our opinions. That discussion requires the ability to argue in its original sense: to clearly state a position, to back it up with reasonable support, and to address any arguments against it.

Of course, argumentation plays its daily role outside of politics, as well. Every day in school, at work, and at home, we present our opinions and the reasons to support them. In this chapter, you will learn to refine your own ability to present arguments through a series of reading and writing activities.

Learning Outcomes

LO1 Understand argumentation.
LO2 Learn reading strategies (separating facts and opinions).
LO3 Read and react to a professional paragraph.
LO4 Read and react to a professional argument.
LO5 Practice reading skills (identifying claims and considering objections).
LO6 Plan an argument.
LO7 Write the first draft.
LO8 Revise the writing.
LO9 Edit the writing.

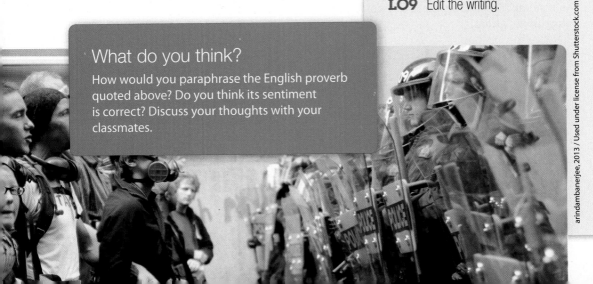

arindambanerjee, 2013 / Used under license from Shutterstock.com

What do you think?

How would you paraphrase the English proverb quoted above? Do you think its sentiment is correct? Discuss your thoughts with your classmates.

LO1 Understanding Argumentation

As the quotation below shows, the word "argument" is commonly misused. It doesn't mean to bicker, squabble, or fight. Those things happen when people don't engage in honest debate.

To argue means to present and support a disputable position. It assumes first considering all sides of a situation and then coming to an opinion. This is why Andre Maurois says, "The difficult part in an argument is not to defend one's opinion, but rather to know it."

Once you've done your research, you will be prepared to argue a position convincingly. It's simply a matter of organizing and presenting the support that led you to your conclusion. As Dale Carnegie puts it, "The best argument is that which seems merely an explanation."

> "People generally quarrel because they cannot argue."
> —Gilbert K. Chesterton

Argumentation Versus Persuasion

The main purpose of persuasion is to be convincing. A campaigning politician trying to gain votes through persuasion will very likely appeal more to the voters' personal interests—"Follow me. I can fix the economy!"—than to logic and reason. A thorough, logical argument may be persuasive, but that is not its main purpose. Its real intent is to prove the strength of a certain line of thinking.

Identify Brainstorm a list of debatable topics you would like to know more about. (Avoid topics on which you already have a firm opinion, unless you are honestly prepared to have that opinion challenged.) Compare your list with those of your classmates, and chose an interesting topic to explore in a paragraph of argumentation.

INSIGHT

In order to be convincing, you must be aware of opposing viewpoints on your topic and either counter them directly or present a weight of evidence that overshadows them. Notice how the examples in this chapter address counterarguments.

_____

_____

_____

_____

_____

Reading

Reading argument paragraphs requires a close examination of the main claim and supporting details.

LO2 Learning Reading Strategies

As you read an argument, watch for the difference between facts and opinions. This page will help you understand the difference.

Separating Facts and Opinions

A fact is a statement that can be directly proven to be true. An opinion is a personal belief that is disputable because it cannot be directly proven. Opinions often present the meaning of facts, give suggestions for policies, or predict what might happen in the future. Note how a fact (shown below in the center) can spawn opposite opinions.

Opinions ◄———	Facts ———►	Opinions
We need to build many more wind farms.	Wind energy currently accounts for only 1 percent of power supplied in the country.	Wind energy will never be able to replace fossil fuels.
Wind farms should be built in forests to double the carbon savings.	A single wind turbine can displace 2,000 tons of carbon dioxide, the same amount as 1 square mile of forest.	Trees should never be felled to make room for wind farms.

Identify Tell whether each piece of text below is an opinion or a fact.

1. Text messaging while driving should be banned. _____

2. Mobile devices contribute to 2,600 deaths per year. _____

3. Thirty-four states have banned texting while driving. _____

4. Teenagers are the problem. _____

5. Twenty percent of adults admit to texting while driving. _____

6. The time has come to outlaw texting while driving. _____

Write For each fact listed below, write two opposite opinions.

Opinions ◄———	Facts ———►	Opinions
	Writing tutors have their hours posted in the Writing Lab.	
	Online assistance is also available.	

LO3 Reading and Reacting to a Professional Paragraph

The argumentation paragraph below discusses the benefits of wind farming. Use the reading process to help you gain a full understanding of the text.

Prereading Before you read, answer these three questions:

1. What does the title and first sentence tell you about the text?

2. What do you already know about the topic?

3. What questions would you like to be answered?

Reading and Rereading As you read, make it your goal to (1) identify the main idea (opinion) and (2) locate the supporting facts and details. Consider annotating the text (page 20) as you go along.

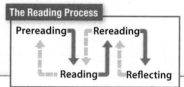

The Reading Process

Support Wind Farm Energy

To counteract its dependence on fossil fuels, the United States must invest   1
in wind farms for its energy needs. A wind farm is made up of a group of large
wind turbines, which convert wind into electric energy. The benefits of wind
farms are numerous. First, wind is a free and renewable source of energy. In
comparison, fossil fuels like oil and coal are limited in supply and cost money   5
to extract from the earth. Secondly, wind farms are a clean energy source.
Unlike power plants, which emit dangerous pollutants, wind farms release no
pollution into the air or water, meaning less smog, less acid rain, and fewer
green house emissions. And then there's this: The National Wind Resource
Center reports that running a single wind turbine has the potential to displace   10
2,000 tons of carbon dioxide, or the equivalent of one square mile of forest
trees ("The Opportunity"). But despite being the fastest growing energy source
in the U.S., wind energy accounts for only 1 percent of power supplied in the
country ("Renewable"). If the United States wants to limit carbon emissions
and lessen its dependence on fossil fuels, it must act now and invest more   15
money in wind farms. The answer is in the air.

Works Cited

"The Opportunity." *Windcenter.com.* NWRC, n.d. Web. 31 Jan. 2012.
"Renewable Energy Sources in the United States." *nationalatlas.gov.* National Atlas of
the United States, 26 Jan. 2011. Web. 31 Jan. 2012.

Reflecting   After you complete your reading, answer these questions. Then share your responses with your classmates.

1. What is the main idea or opinion developed in the paragraph?

_____

_____

_____

2. How many key supporting points are provided?

_____

_____

_____

3. Does the support seem convincing? Explain.

_____

_____

_____

4. Are any objections to this argument raised? (*Objections* are points against the argument.) If so, what are they?

_____

_____

_____

5. How would you rate this paragraph, and why?
   Weak ★ ★ ★ ★ ★ Strong

_____

_____

_____

Vocabulary Practice

Identify Use context clues to explain or define the following words. (See pages 33–34 for help.)

1. **dependence** (line 1)

   clues: _____

   definition: _____

2. **emissions** (line 9)

   clues: _____

   definition: _____

3. **displace** (line 10)

   clues: _____

   definition: _____

Thinking Critically

Identify Answer these questions to help you think critically about the text.

1. What logical pattern of reasoning does the paragraph follow? (See page 28.)

   _____

   _____

2. Why do you think that wind energy "accounts for only 1 percent of power supplied in this country" if it is so cost effective?

   _____

   _____

   _____

3. What other questions do you have about the topic?

   _____

   _____

   _____

LO4 Reading and Reacting to a Professional Argument

The essay below appeared on "About.com Animal Rights." Use the reading process to help you gain a full understanding of the text.

About the Author

Doris Lin is an animal rights attorney and has been a vegan for more than 20 years. She holds a J.D. from the University of Southern California Law Center.

Prereading Before you read, answer these three questions:

1. What do the title and first paragraph tell you about the topic?

_____

2. What do you already know about the topic?

_____

3. What do you expect to learn?

_____

Reading and Rereading As you read, make it your goal to (1) identify the writer's main opinion (claim), (2) locate the main supporting facts and details (evidence), and (3) identify any objections to the position. Consider annotating the text (page 20) and/or taking notes (page 22) as you read.

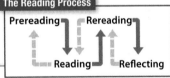

Veganism Is Not a Sacrifice

Many consider **veganism** to be an exercise in self-denial and self-sacrifice, but the opposite is true: Using animals and consuming animal products is an unjust and often violent taking. To consider veganism a sacrifice is to believe that we have a right to use and abuse animals any way we choose. Veganism cannot be a sacrifice because it's not about giving up meat, eggs, or dairy; it's about not taking someone else's life and liberty.

More simply, it's not a sacrifice to give up something that wasn't ever rightfully yours.

1

5

Dictionary.com defines sacrifice as "the surrender or destruction *10* of something prized or desirable for the sake of something considered as having a higher or more pressing claim." The implication is that the prized or desirable thing being surrendered belongs to the person making the sacrifice. It can't be a sacrifice to surrender someone else's prized or desirable possession. *15*

No one claims that obeying that law is a sacrifice. Refraining from assaulting, raping, or murdering people is never considered a sacrifice. Similarly, refraining from taking another **sentient** being's life or liberty is not a sacrifice.

There are other reasons veganism cannot be considered a sacrifice. *20* Some believe that being vegan is difficult, but as Professor Gary Francione explains, veganism is not a sacrifice because it's easy:

"I became a vegan 24 years ago. It was not particularly difficult back then, but it is absolutely absurd to characterize it as difficult today. It is easy to be a vegan. Sure, you are more limited in your restaurant *25* choices, particularly if you do not live in or near a large city, but if this inconvenience is significant to you and keeping you from being vegan, then you probably were not serious about the issue anyway."

Veganism is also healthy, so one's health is not sacrificed. The American Dietetic Association supports vegan diets: *30*

"It is the position of the American Dietetic Association that appropriately planned vegetarian diets, including total vegetarian or vegan diets, are healthful and nutritionally adequate and may provide health benefits in the prevention of certain diseases."

Vegans also do not sacrifice delicious foods. A plant-based diet can *35* include fruits, vegetables, beans, and grains from all over the world. If one is interested in vegan meats, cheeses, ice creams, and other sweets, there are more and more of these types of products hitting the market every day. It might take some time and effort to learn about vegan products, but any change in routine requires an adjustment period. *40*

Vegans give up little or nothing in terms of convenience, health, and gastronomy, but most importantly, veganism in not a sacrifice to give up something that never belonged to you.

veganism
the practice of not using animal products, especially in the diet

sentient
capable of feeling and perceiving

Reflecting   After you complete the reading, answer the questions below. Afterward share your responses with your classmates.

1. What is the writer's main idea or opinion?

_____

2. What is one essential fact provided in support?

_____

_____

3. Does the essay address any objections to this claim? If so, what are they?

_____

_____

4. How would you rate the strength of this argument, and why?
    Weak ★ ★ ★ ★ ★ Strong

_____

_____

Vocabulary Practice

Identify   Create vocabulary entries for the three words below. Identify the pronunciation, helpful word parts, and a primary definition, and use the word in a sentence. (Refer to pages 32–36 in this book and a dictionary for help.)

1. **implication** (line 12)

_____

2. **inconvenience** (line 27)

_____

3. **gastronomy** (line 42)

_____

Personal Response

Explore   Write freely about veganism, exploring what it means to you, what values it holds, and what experiences you have had with it.

LO5 Practicing Reading Skills

When reading argumentative texts, it is important to keep an open mind but also to watch for bias. (*Bias* is "the unfair approval or dislike of something.") To do so, consider the writer's treatment of the claim.

Identifying Claims

To help you consider the claims in an argument, list each one separately, and then write any evidence that explains it.

Main opinion (claim): Text messaging while driving should be banned in all states because it is dangerous.

First supporting fact: Studies by the National Highway Traffic Safety Administration show that texting while driving is six times more likely to cause an accident than drunk driving.

Second supporting fact: A driver whose eyes are concentrating on a phone are obviously not giving the necessary attention to the road.

Considering Objections

Also consider any objections (opposing viewpoints) to the problem. List each one separately, along with the details that show how the writer concedes (admits the value) or counters (opposes) it.

Objection 1: Critics say teenage drivers are the problem.

Concession: Yes, teens do most of the texting, but also know that many adults do, too.

Objection 2: Laws banning it would be difficult to enforce.

Counter: Seat-belt laws met the same objections, but they are now commonly enforced.

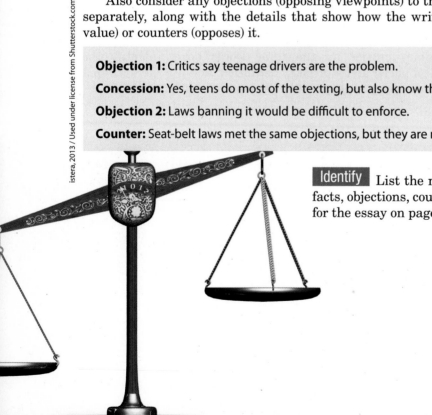

istera, 2013 / Used under license from Shutterstock.com

Identify List the main opinion, supporting facts, objections, counters, and/or concessions for the essay on pages 375–376.

Writing

In your own argument paragraph, you will develop a claim about a debatable topic. Be sure to write about a topic that you truly care about. Use the writing process to help you do your best work. (See pages 94–99.)

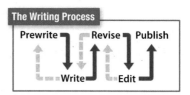

LO6 Planning an Argument

Your prewriting begins by selecting a topic that interests you, developing a position about it, and refining that position.

Selecting a Topic

Will began his topic search by browsing newspapers, magazines, and the Internet for current issues that people have strong feelings about. When a friend of his almost ran off the road because of texting, Will had found his topic.

Select List three or four debatable issues you could write about in an argument paragraph. Choose your favorite topic.

_____   _____

_____   _____

Stating a Position (Opinion)

Once you decide on a topic, you need to state a preliminary position about it. In one sentence, write a defensible position statement using the formula below.

Topic		Position		Position Statement
Text messaging while driving	**+** *would, should, must, ought to, needs*	be banned in all states	**=**	Text messaging while driving should be banned in all states.

Create Write a position statement by providing the topic, selecting a verb, and indicating your position.

Topic: _____ **+** *would, should, must, ought to, needs* **+**

Position: _____ **=**

Position Statement: _____

Refining Your Position

With your initial position written, use the following strategies to develop and refine your opinion on the issue:

- **Research** all possible positions on the issue. Who supports each position, and why? Who opposes your position, and why?
- **Gather** solid evidence regarding your issue. Does the most compelling evidence support or oppose your position?
- **Refine** your position. At this point, you may have new convictions about your position, or you may have changed your mind about it. Before you are ready to write, clarify your position statement.

Gathering Details

When you take a stand on an issue, you must gather convincing support to defend your position. Using a variety of supporting details will strengthen your position. Four common types of support are **facts**, **statistics**, **testimonials**, and **predictions**.

Support Chart

Fact	At least 34 states and the District of Columbia have passed laws against text messaging while driving.
Statistic	According to the U.S. Department of Transportation, mobile devices contribute to 2,600 deaths per year.
Testimony	In the words of U.S. Secretary of Transportation Ray LaHood, "This is an important safety step, and we will be taking more to eliminate the threat of distracted driving."
Prediction	Roads will be safer if texting while driving is banned in all states.

Gather   Create a support chart with the research you have gathered about your issue. Try to include at least one fact, statistic, piece of testimony, and prediction. If you have not found supporting details for each category, consider doing additional research.

facts
details that offer statements or claims of verified information

statistics
details that offer concrete numbers about a topic

testimonials
details that offer insight from an authority on the topic

predictions
details that offer insights into possible outcomes or consequences by forecasting what might happen under certain conditions

LO7 Writing the First Draft

Let your first draft be an experiment to get your thoughts and research down on paper. Don't worry about trying to get everything perfect.

Read Read and consider the following argument for a mandatory public service program.

Citizen Service

Topic Sentence

Our country and our youth would benefit from a one- or *1* two-year period of national service after high school. Democracy has a long history of service by private citizens. Think of the citizen soldiers of Ancient Greece or the Minutemen of colonial America. Consider today's National Guard members, *5* Reservists, and Peace Corps volunteers. Ask most people who have served, and they will tell you the experience helped them grow up and discover their potential. It also made them more

Body Sentences

conscious of their responsibility to their nation. Of course, some may object that mandatory service would violate our *10* liberties. However, we already require public education from kindergarten through high school. Adding another year or two shouldn't matter, especially since people would have a choice of how they wished to serve. The military's various branches would offer possibilities, as would the Peace Corps, Americorps, *15* and other civilian volunteer organizations. In these various services, people would learn life and career skills, and under a bill currently going through Congress, they could also earn grants for college ("Mandatory"). A nation is only as good as its

Closing Sentence

people. Adding a year or two of public service to our educational *20* track would benefit us all.

Works Cited

"Mandatory Public Service." *FactCheck.org*. U. of Penn., 21 Apr. 2009. Web. 31 Jan. 2012.

Consider the Craft

1. How effectively does the paragraph make its claim?
2. How effectively does it address counterclaims?
3. What do you like most about this paragraph?
4. What improvements might you suggest?

Drafting Tips

When writing an argument paragraph, appeal to the reader with logical reasoning and compelling evidence.

In the opening...

- Lead up to your claim, if necessary, by providing reasonable background.
- Make your claim firmly but respectfully.

In the middle...

- Give the reader plenty of solid reasons to adopt your point of view.
- Use valid research to back up your position.
- Address any counterclaims politely, providing a convincing argument against them.

In the closing...

- Restate your position in light of the reasons you have provided.
- If appropriate, give your reader a call to action.

TRAITS

Transition words that show importance: first of all / to begin / secondly / another reason / the best reason / also / in addition / more importantly / most importantly / finally

The Working Parts of a Paragraph

As the previous page shows, a paragraph has three main parts, each with its own purpose.

Topic Sentence:	The topic sentence states your position (opinion).
Body Sentences:	The body sentences support the position using logical reasoning and reliable details. These sentences also address counterclaims.
Closing Sentence:	A closing sentence (or two) reinforces your argument and (if appropriate) encourages your reader to adopt it.

Write Prepare the first draft of your argument paragraph using the information on this page and the planning on pages 379–390 as a guide.

LO8 Revising the Writing

Start the revising process by reading your first draft two or three times to get a feel for your work so far. Then have one of your classmates read and react to your work using a response sheet as a guide. (See page 428.)

Five Common Logical Fallacies

A logical fallacy is a false assertion that weakens an argument. Below are five common logical fallacies that should be removed from your writing.

- A **bare assertion** denies that an issue is debatable, claiming, "That's just how it is."

  Withdrawal of troops is our only option for peace.

  (The claim discourages discussion of other ways to promote peace.)

- A **threat** is a simple way to sabotage an argument, claiming, "If you don't agree with me, you'll regret it."

  If you don't accept alternative fuel sources, get ready to move back to the Stone Age.

- A **slippery slope** fallacy argues that a single step will start an unstoppable chain of events.

  If we build a skate park, vandalism is going to run rampant in our city.

- An **unreliable testimonial** is a statement made by a biased or unqualified source. A testimonial has force only if it is made by an authority.

  As TV's Dr. Daniels, I recommend Xanax for all my patients.

- A **half-truth** contains part of but not the whole truth.

  Three out of five doctors recommend ibuprofen, according to a recent study.

  (This may be true in this one study but not universally.)

Revise   Improve your writing using the following checklist and your partner's comments on the response sheet. Continue until you can check off each item.

Using a Revising Checklist

Ideas
- [ ] 1. Does my topic sentence identify an issue and my position?
- [ ] 2. Do I include a variety of supporting details?
- [ ] 3. Do I avoid errors in logic?

Organization
- [ ] 4. Do I have a topic sentence, body sentences, and a closing sentence?
- [ ] 5. Have I used transitions to connect my ideas?

Voice
- [ ] 6. Do I sound knowledgeable and passionate about the issue?

LO9 Editing the Writing

"Mechanics" refers to the standards of presenting written language; capitalization and number use are two of the mechanics issues writers encounter.

Capitalization Errors

Capitalizing proper nouns and proper adjectives (adjectives derived from proper nouns) is a basic rule of capitalization. There are times, however, when certain words are capitalized in one instance but not in another. The quick guide below refers to a number of these special cases. (Also see pages 582–590.)

Capitalize	Do Not Capitalize
American	un-American
January, **M**ay	winter, spring
The **S**outh is quite conservative	Turn south at the stop sign.
Duluth City **C**ollege	a Duluth college
Chancellor John Bohm	John Bohm, our chancellor
President Obama	the president of the United States
Earth (planet name)	the earth
Internet	electronic communications network

Proofreading Practice In each sentence below, indicate which words should be capitalized, using the correction mark (≡).

1. with november around the corner, it's only so long until winter engulfs minnesota.

2. Flag burning is the definition of an un-american activity.

3. I caught up with chancellor Greg Williams of the university of pittsburgh.

4. I used the internet to find out that Missouri is nicknamed the show-me state.

5. My favorite french restaurant rests in a quiet neighborhood off college avenue.

6. The west coast is known for its laid-back lifestyle.

7. Does the winter sports season begin before or after december?

8. The president of the united states lives in the white house.

INSIGHT

Different languages use capitalization differently. Even different Englishes (U.S. and British, for example) treat capitals differently. For more practice see pages 582–590.

Apply As you edit your paragraph, be careful to discern common nouns from proper nouns. Remember: Do not capitalize common nouns and titles that appear near, but are not part of, a proper noun.

Using Numbers

When a paragraph includes numbers or statistics, you will have to know whether to write them as words or as numerals. Below are three basic rules to follow.

Numerals or Words

Numbers from one to one hundred are usually written as words; numbers 101 and greater are usually written as numerals.

two	seven	twenty-five	103	1,489

Numerals Only

Use numerals for the following forms: decimals, percentages, pages, chapters, addresses, dates, telephone numbers, identification numbers, and statistics.

13.1	**20** percent	Highway **41**	chapter **6**
February **12, 2010**	**(273) 289-2288**	**2.4** feet	

Words Only

Use words to express numbers that begin a sentence.

Thirteen players suffered from food poisoning.

Proofreading Practice In each sentence below, cross out any incorrect numbers and write the correct form above.

1. My 2 cousins, Braden and Candace, live 4 miles apart on Highway Eleven.

2. 300 raffle tickets were bought at the gates.

3. The results showed twenty-five percent of participants were born before January first, 1985.

4. Please review chapter seventeen for the test on Monday.

5. The coastal reef is two point eight knots away.

6. 15 of us are hoping to complete the three point one-mile race.

Apply Read your argument paragraph, paying special attention to sentences that include numbers and statistics. Present numbers in the correct way: either as numerals or as words.

Marking a Paragraph

Before you finish editing your revised paragraph, you can practice by editing the following model.

Editing Practice   Correct the following paragraph, using the marks below. One correction has been done for you.

A Super Blow to Roscoe

For the good of the local economy the Roscoe City Council must vote   *1*
down a proposal to build a SuperMart store on Highway Thirty-One.
The discount chain may slash prices, it will slash local businesses in the
process. a University of Iowa study showed a group of small towns lost up
to 47 percent of they're retail trade after ten years of a SuperMart moving   *5*
in nearby. Grocery stores and retail businesses were hit the hardest. If a
SuperMart comes to Roscoe, local grocers like Troyer's will have to lower
wages or risk clozing. A 2007 study showed how a SuperMart caused
a one point five percent reduction in earnings for local grocery stores.
Proponents of a SuperMart expansion says the store will bring new jobs,   *10*
more sales taxes, and great bargains. But all SuperMart will accomplish
is reallocating where existing income is spent. The Roscoe City Council
should look for alternatives to jump-start the community's economy vote no
for SuperMart.

Correction Marks

⊰ delete	⅄ add comma	^word^ add word
d̲ capitalize	? add question	⊙ add period
Ø̲ lowercase	∧ mark	◯ spelling
∧ insert	⌄ insert an apostrophe	⌒ switch

INSIGHT

On the previous page, you learned some basic rules for using numbers in your writing. Here is another useful guideline:

- Use numerals when the time of day is expressed with an abbreviation; spell out the number when time is expressed in words.

    6:00 p.m. or **six o'clock** (not *6 o'clock*)

    the **2:15** p.m. train (not *two-fifteen p.m. train*)

    an **eleven o'clock** wake-up call (not *an 11 o'clock wake-up call*)

Using an Editing Checklist

Now it's time to correct your own paragraph.

Apply Create a clean copy of your paragraph and use the following checklist to check for errors. When you can answer *yes* to a question, check it off. Continue working until all items are checked.

Words
- ☐ **1.** Have I used specific nouns and verbs? (See page 134.)
- ☐ **2.** Have I used more action verbs than "be" verbs? (See page 536.)

Sentences
- ☐ **3.** Have I varied the beginnings and lengths of sentences? (See pages 136–137.)
- ☐ **4.** Have I combined short, choppy sentences? (See page 137.)
- ☐ **5.** Have I avoided shifts in sentences? (See page 500.)
- ☐ **6.** Have I avoided fragments and run-ons? (See pages 488–491, 494–495.)

Conventions
- ☐ **7.** Do I use correct verb forms (*he saw*, not *he seen*)? (See pages 542, 544.)
- ☐ **8.** Do my subjects and verbs agree (*she speaks*, not *she speak*)? (See pages 472–481.)
- ☐ **9.** Have I used the right words (*their, there, they're*)?
- ☐ **10.** Have I capitalized first words and proper nouns and adjectives? (See page 582.)
- ☐ **11.** Have I used commas after long introductory word groups? (See pages 652–655)
- ☐ **12.** Have I carefully checked my spelling?

Adding a Title

Make sure to add an attention-getting title. Here are three simple strategies for creating one.

- Create a slogan:

  Support Wind Farm Energy

- Sum up your argument:

  Texting and Driving Don't Mix

- Use a play on words:

  A Super Blow to Roscoe

Create Prepare a clean final copy of your paragraph and proofread it.

> "When I'm getting ready to reason with a man, I spend one-third of my time thinking about myself and what I am going to say—and two-thirds thinking about him and what he is going to say."
> — Abraham Lincoln

Enrichment: Reading

On pages 389–391 you will find the argumentative essay "What Exactly Is a Frivolous Lawsuit?" to read and respond to. As you read this essay, use the steps in the reading process to help you gain a full understanding of the author's argument. The reading activities are followed by a number of writing ideas to choose from to write an argumentative paragraph or essay of your own.

CONSIDER THE TRAITS

As you read the essay, consider the development of the **ideas**—including the position (main opinion), evidence, and any objections to the position. Then note the essay's **organization**—the way in which the argument is developed from start to finish.

About the Author

Laraine Flemming is a textbook writer as well as an experienced instructor. Her first teaching experience was in a psychiatric hospital in Vinita, Oklahoma. It was there that she became convinced of the transformative power of reading. Flemming has a PhD from State University of New York in Buffalo.

Prereading

Social issues can be complicated. Each of us comes to an issue with our own beliefs based on our backgrounds, needs, and desires. Argumentation is a process that allows us to present and support our positions (opinions) on issues in a thoughtful way. Think of a local or national issue that matters to you: the shortage of student parking spaces, gender or race issues in employment, the use of drones, etc. Then freely write for five minutes about the issue.

_____

_____

_____

What do you think?

What does the Lincoln quotation tell you about presenting an effective argument? Discuss your thoughts with your classmates.

Identify   Before you read the essay, answer these questions.

1. What do the title, beginning two paragraphs, and the first sentence of other paragraphs tell you about the text?

_____

2. What do you already know about this topic?

_____

3. What claim do you think the author will make? Why?

_____

Reading and Rereading

The court system in this country is a common topic of discussion. Essays are written about the unfairness of the courts, the selection of judges, and fair representation. "What Exactly Is a Frivolous Lawsuit?" examines another common topic: lawsuits (actions brought before the courts to recover something or to seek a settlement). Pay careful attention to the position that the author develops in the essay.

As you read, make it your goal to (1) identify the author's claim, (2) locate the key supporting facts and details, and (3) note any objections to the claim. Consider annotating the text (page 20) and/or taking notes (page 22) as you read.

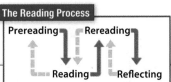

What Exactly Is a **Frivolous** Lawsuit?

The lawsuit of seventy-nine-year-old Stella Liebeck, launched against   *1*
McDonald's in 1994 after spilling hot coffee on herself as she went through
the drive-through lane, immediately became the stuff of comedy. A *Seinfeld*
episode even used it, making one of the characters sue for damages after
he spilled coffee on himself. But the general attitude toward the suit, on   *5*
television and off, was summed up in the response of another *Seinfeld*
character, Elaine, who expressed puzzlement at the very idea of a lawsuit
involving hot coffee being spilled and McDonald's being somehow liable.
"Who ever heard of this anyway? Suing a company because their coffee
is too hot? Coffee is supposed to be hot." In other words, the suit was a   *10*
ridiculous joke.

What got left out of all the jokes, though, were the actual details of
the case. Liebeck suffered third-degree burns. Third-degree burns are the
most serious kind, especially for a woman of her age. Plus, there had been
at least 700 previous cases of people being scalded by McDonald's coffee   *15*
before Liebeck went to court. McDonald's had settled other claims but did

not want to give Liebeck the $20,000 compensation she had requested. So she sued and the case went to court.

What Liebeck's lawyers proved was that McDonald's was making its coffee 30 to 50 degrees hotter than other restaurants. In fact, the Shriner Burn Institute had already warned McDonald's not to serve coffee above 130 degrees. Yet the liquid that burned Liebeck was the usual temperature for McDonald's brew—about 190 degrees. As a result of Liebeck's suit, McDonald's coffee is now sold at the same temperature as most other restaurants.

Yes, there probably are trivial lawsuits filed on a regular basis. But Liebeck's wasn't one of them. It's actually ironic that the "hot coffee" lawsuit, as it's come to be called, is often cited as an illustration of why the country desperately needs **tort reform**. Yet a closer examination of this issue suggests that citizens might want to think twice before joining in the chorus of calls to enact tort reform.

Tort reform legislation, in place or pending, differs from state to state. Thus one of the questions involved in the debate is how tort reform should go forward. Should it be on a state or federal level?

In general, though, the tort reform movement focuses on three goals: (1) the need to limit the circumstances under which injured people may file a lawsuit after being injured by a product or procedure, (2) the goal of making it more difficult for people injured by a product or procedure to obtain a trial by jury, and (3) the desire to place limits on the amount of money injured parties may be awarded.

In the eyes of some, like political activist and organizer Jon Greenbaum, the idea that the country is desperately in need of tort reform is a myth. From his perspective, the right to sue corporations or companies if their products were defective or their procedures badly managed or fraudulent was a consumer victory won in the 1950s. In his eyes, now is not the time to abandon that right. He thinks implementing tort reform would be a step backward for consumers, not a step forward: "It will limit our ability to hold corporations accountable for their misdeeds. Corporate America has succeeded to a great extent by buying up our legislators and capturing regulatory bodies. We must not let them wrest control of the judicial system as well."

That, however, would not be the position of Court Koenning, the president of Citizens Against Lawsuit Abuse of Houston. For him, lawsuits demanding compensation for injury due to defective products or procedures reveal a growing canker on American society—the **abdication** of personal responsibility. As he writes, "The somebody's gotta pay attitude is pervasive, and that does not bode well for future generations. We need to reacquaint ourselves with personal responsibility and stop playing the blame game. We need to realize that every dilemma or personal

disappointment is not **fodder** for a lawsuit and does not warrant a treasure   *60*
trove of cash."

These are all stirring sentiments. But they need to be viewed in the
light of what consumers "playing the blame game" in court have actually
tried to accomplish. In Los Angeles, California, consumers have gone
to court to stop health insurers from canceling policies of people newly   *65*
diagnosed with a serious illness. The insurance cancellations, usually
based on technicalities, seem to target people who will require long-term
and expensive care, for which the insurance companies would have to pay if
the policies weren't cancelled.

In Harrisburg, Pennsylvania, consumers turned to the courts to take   *70*
action against "mortgage rescue" companies who, for a fee, claimed they
could help those falling behind on their payments. But after the fee was
paid, no help was forthcoming. In Hartford, Connecticut, consumers also
went to court against a pharmaceutical company that was blocking generic
alternatives to the high-priced drugs on which the company's profits were   *75*
based.

This is not to say that all personal injury complaints taken to court
are worthy of respect. Did anyone really want to see the woman who
sued a cosmetics company for changing the shade of her hair become
a millionaire? But many of the personal injury lawsuits brought by   *80*
consumers do real good, helping not just the **litigant** but the public in
general. We might want to consider that fact next time we hear or read
another argument in favor of tort reform because what we might be
reforming is our own right to seek justice by legal means.

Sources: Court Koenning, "Starbucks 'Hot Tea' Lawsuit Highlights a Void in Personal
Responsibility," www.setexasrecord.com; Jon Greenbaum, "McDonald's Hot Coffee Lawsuit and
Beyond: The Tort Reform Myth Machine," CommonDreams.org

From Flemming, *Reading for Thinking*, 7E. © 2012 Cengage Learning.

frivolous
not worth taking seriously

tort reform
laws passed to place limits on the types
or amounts of awards or compensation in
personal injury lawsuits

abdication
to give something up

fodder
material for creating a response or reaction

litigant
someone involved in a lawsuit

Reflecting

After you complete your reading, answer the following questions. Then share your responses with your classmates.

1. What main claim or opinion is developed in the essay?

   _____

   _____

2. Who is cited in support of this position? Why does he support it?

   _____

   _____

   _____

3. Who is cited in opposition of the position? Why does this person oppose it?

   _____

   _____

   _____

4. Does the author counter or concede this person? Explain. (See page 378.)

   _____

   _____

   _____

5. What point does the author make in the final few lines?

   _____

   _____

   _____

6. What is something that you have learned from this reading?

   _____

   _____

   _____

Vocabulary Practice

Identify Define the word parts for each word as indicated below. Then try to explain the meaning of the complete word. (See pages 35–36 and 623–631 for help.)

1. **misdeeds** (line 48)   mis + deeds

_____

_____

2. **defective** (line 54)   de + fect + ive

_____

_____

3. **consumers** (line 64)   con + sum(e) + ers

_____

_____

Drawing Inferences

Explain Answer the following questions to help you draw inferences from the text. (See pages 29–31 for help.)

1. How would you explain the purchasing term *caveat emptor* (buyer beware) after reading this essay?

_____

_____

2. What does "justice" mean to you?

_____

_____

3. Should we put limits on seeking justice? Explain.

_____

_____

Writing

What follows are possible writing activities to complete in response to the reading. Use the writing process (pages 94–99) to help you develop your writing.

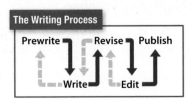

Prewriting

Choose one of the following writing ideas. Or decide upon anther idea of your own related to the reading.

Writing Ideas

1. **Writing to Learn:** Think about an important person in your life. Write a thoughtful email message or letter to this person, arguing for or against an opinion that this person holds dearly. (Whether you send the message is up to you.)

2. **Paragraph Writing:** Write a paragraph about one of the debatable topics you brainstormed on page 370 or another one of the issues you identified on page 378.

3. Think of one of your strongly held beliefs and argue against it.

4. **Essay Writing:** Think about a problem you would like to see fixed. In an essay, argue in favor of a particular solution.

5. Write an essay supporting the following idea: "We need to stop playing the blaming game."

When planning . . .

Refer to pages 379–380 to help with your prewriting and planning. Also use the tips below.

- State your main idea clearly, so that you can remain focused during writing.
- Consider your reader. What opinion will that person likely have about the subject? What questions or objections might your reader have?
- Consider your purpose. If your reader's opinion matches your own, your purpose will be to further the reader's understanding of the topic and any counterarguments. If your reader's opinion is contrary to yours, your purpose will be to soothe any objections and provide convincing support for yours.
- Consider your voice. For a paragraph or an essay of argument, your voice should usually be respectful but confident.

Writing and Revising

Refer to pages 381–383 to help you write and review your first draft. Also use the tips below to help with your drafting and revising.

When writing . . .

- Include an opening, a middle, and a closing in your argument. Each part has a specific role to play. (See page 382.)
- Follow your planning notes, but remain free to expand upon new ideas.
- If you encounter a claim or counterclaim that you have not researched, note it in your text and keep on writing. Research that claim or counterclaim after finishing your first draft rather than getting sidetracked during writing.
- Try to keep your intended audience in mind. Picture someone in particular, and keep your voice appropriately confident and respectful.

When revising . . .

- Be prepared to reorganize your ideas for better impact. Often a new arrangement will suggest itself as you reread your first draft.
- Make sure your writing doesn't antagonize the reader by taking on a negative or condescending tone.
- Also make sure your writing sounds confident, not apologetic.
- Watch for spots where your argument seems "thin." If a point needs more support, find it. If an important counterclaim has not been mentioned, address it.
- Ask a classmate or another writer to review and critique your writing. Use a peer-review sheet to guide the critique. (See page 622.)

Editing

Refer to the checklist on page 387 when you are ready to edit your argument for style and correctness.

Monkey Business Images, 2013 / Used under license from Shutterstock.com

Reflecting on Argument Writing

Answer the following questions about your argumentation reading and writing experience in this chapter.

1. Why is argumentation so important?

   _____

2. What is your favorite sample argument in this chapter? Why?

   _____

3. What reading strategy in this chapter do you find most helpful? Explain.

   _____

   _____

4. What do you like most about the argument you developed in this chapter? Why?

   _____

   _____

5. What is one thing you would like to change in it?

   _____

6. What is the most important thing you have learned about writing paragraphs and essays of argumentation?

   _____

   _____

Key Terms to Remember

Whenever you read and write argumentation, it's important to understand the following terms.

- **Claim**—main opinion that is supported in an argument.
- **Evidence**—facts and details that support the claims. Facts and details can be checked for accuracy and authenticity.
- **Objections**—criticism of a claim. Objections can be countered (opposed) or conceded (admitted as valuable).
- **Logical fallacies**—false assertions. These actually weaken an argument by making it seem less than carefully considered.

15

"If you can't explain it simply, you don't understand it well enough."
—Albert Einstein

Summarizing

Longer forms of academic reading and writing, like essays, are often packed with important information. For a reader, memorizing all the key details in longer texts can be a tall order. Summarizing the writing is a more effective way to learn the information. Summarization is the process of identifying and explaining the key ideas of a reading in your own words.

Writing a summary is one of the best ways of becoming actively involved in your reading. Summarizing a text also helps you to evaluate how much you know about the material and to remember what you read. If you have trouble explaining any ideas, then you know you need to reread the passage.

In this chapter, you will read and summarize a number of academic passages. You will also learn strategies for identifying key ideas and explaining them in your own words.

Learning Outcomes

LO1 Understand summarizing.

LO2 Learn reading strategies (using a table diagram and understanding the structure of writing).

LO3 Read and react to a summary.

LO4 Write a summary.

LO5 Practice additional summary writing.

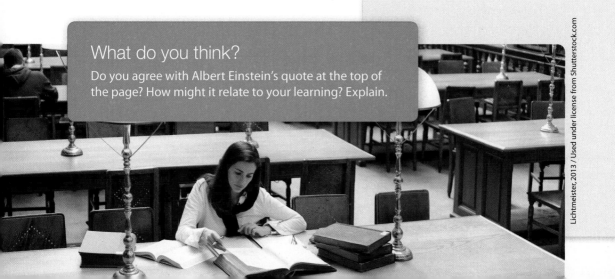

What do you think?

Do you agree with Albert Einstein's quote at the top of the page? How might it relate to your learning? Explain.

LO1 Understanding Summarizing

In some ways you practice summarizing every day in conversations with your friends, family members, and co-workers. For example, when someone asks you what you did over the weekend, you wouldn't tell every detail about it. Instead you would summarize or highlight the most important points in your own words.

When you write a summary, you should use your own words, except for any specific, essential words for ideas from the text. The key is to share only the main ideas of the text, rather than every last detail. Your goal is to provide a glimpse of the whole text, not a detailed look at the parts.

> "The simpler you say it, the more eloquent it is."
> —August Wilson

Summary Versus Paraphrase

A paraphrase, also written in your own words, does not reduce a text to its basic meaning. Rather, it explains the full meaning of a challenging reading. Because a paraphrase often includes explanations or interpretations, it can actually be longer than the original. A summary, by contrast, provides a brief explanation of the main ideas in the text and should be about one-third the length of the original.

Identify Telling friends about a movie is one example of informal summarizing. List three or four other examples of summaries that commonly occur in your conversations.

INSIGHT

A typical one- or two-page essay can be summarized in one well-formed paragraph. The first sentence in a summary is the topic sentence. The sentences that follow must support the topic sentence.

1. _Recapping a television episode for a friend is one example of informal summarizing_

2. _____

   _____

3. _____

   _____

4. _____

   _____

Reading

Summarizing is an important learning tool in all of your class work, especially for report and research assignments. But to summarize a text, you need to understand it in its original form. The strategies below will help.

LO2 Learning Reading Strategies

Using a Table Diagram

Part of the challenge when reading a text is keeping track of the main idea and key supporting details. A graphic organizer called a table diagram works well for this purpose. Identify the thesis, or main idea, of the reading on the table top, and list the key supporting details underneath. Then refer to this information as you write a summary of the text.

Table Diagram

Thesis or main idea

supporting details	supporting details	supporting details	supporting details

ajt, 2013 / Used under license from Shutterstock.com

Understanding the Structure of Writing

Most informational texts are shaped in the following way: The first part introduces the topic and states the thesis or main idea. The middle paragraphs support and develop the thesis. The closing part usually reviews what has been said and may offer an additional idea or two. Keeping this structure in mind should help you find the key information in a text.

Beginning

Middle

Ending

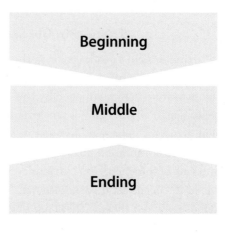

LO3 Reading and Reacting to a Summary

The passage below comes from an article entitled "How Our Skins Got Their Color" by Marvin Harris. Use the reading process to help you gain a full understanding of the text.

About the Author

Dr. Marvin Harris (1927–2001) was chair of the Anthropology Department at Columbia University, then Graduate Research Professor at the University of Florida. During his life he published 16 books and a series of essays entitled *Our Kind*.

Prereading Before you read, answer these three questions:

1. What do the title and boldfaced words tell you about the topic?

_____

2. What do you already know about the topic?

_____

3. What questions would you liked answered?

_____

Reading and Rereading As you read, make it your goal to (1) identify the topic, (2) study the supporting details, and (3) decide if your questions have been answered. Consider annotating the text (page 20) as you read.

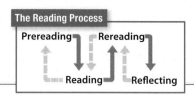

The Reading Process

Prereading ⟶ Rereading

Reading   Reflecting

From "How Our Skins Got Their Color"

Human skin owes its color to the presence of particles known as   *1*
melanin. The primary function of melanin is to protect the upper levels of
the skin from being damaged by the sun's ultraviolet rays. This radiation
poses a critical problem for our kind because we lack the **dense** coat of hair
that acts as a sunscreen for most mammals. . . . Hairlessness exposes us to   *5*
two kinds of radiation hazards: ordinary sunburn, with its blisters, rashes,
and risk of infection; and skin cancers, including malignant melanoma,
one of the deadliest diseases known. Melanin is the body's first line of
defense against these afflictions. The more melanin particles, the darker

the skin, and the lower the risk of sunburn and all forms of skin cancer. *10*
This explains why the highest rates for skin cancer are found in sun-
drenched lands such as Australia, where light-skinned people of European
descent spend a good part of their lives outdoors wearing scanty attire.
Very dark-skinned people such as heavily **pigmented** Africans of Zaire
seldom get skin cancer, but when they do, they get it on depigmented parts *15*
of their bodies—palms and lips.

If exposure to solar radiation had nothing but harmful effects,
natural selection would have favored inky black as the color for all human
populations. But the sun's rays do not present an **unmitigated** threat. As it
falls on the skin, sunshine converts a fatty substance in the **epidermis** into *20*
vitamin D. The blood carries vitamin D from the skin to the intestines,
where it plays a vital role in the absorption of calcium. In turn, calcium
is vital for strong bones. Without it, people fall victim to the crippling
diseases **rickets** and **osteomalacia**. In women, calcium deficiencies can
result in a deformed birth canal, which makes childbirth lethal for both *25*
mother and fetus.

Vitamin D can be obtained from a few foods, primarily the oils and
livers of marine fish. But inland populations must rely on the sun's rays
and their own skins for this crucial substance. The particular color of a
human population's skin, therefore, represents in large degree a trade-off *30*
between the hazards of too much versus too little solar radiation: acute
sunburn and skin cancer on the one hand, and rickets and osteomalacia on
the other. It is this trade-off that largely accounts for the **preponderance**
of brown people in the world and for the general tendency for skin color to
be darkest among **equatorial populations** and lightest among populations *35*
dwelling at higher latitudes.

dense
thick

pigmented
colored by pigment

unmitigated
not made less severe

epidermis
uppermost layer of skin

rickets
softening of bones in the
young

osteomalacia
softening of bones in adults

preponderance
majority

equatorial populations
people who live close to the
earth's equator

Reflecting   After you complete your reading, answer these questions. Then share your responses with your classmates.

1. What is the main idea or focus of this text?

   _____

2. What supporting evidence seems especially important? (Name two key details.)

   _____

   _____

3. How would you rate this passage, and why?
   Weak ★ ★ ★ ★ ★ Strong

   _____

   _____

Vocabulary Practice

Identify   Create a vocabulary entry for the three words below. Identify the pronunciation, helpful word parts, and a primary definition, and use the word in a sentence. (Refer to pages 32–36 in this book and a dictionary for help.)

1. ultraviolet (line 3)

   _____

2. malignant (line 7)

   _____

3. deficiencies (line 24)

   _____

Drawing Inferences

Explain   Answer the following question to help you draw an inference from the text. (See pages 29–31 for help.)

- What can you infer about your own skin color after reading this selection?

   _____

   _____

Reading   Carefully read the following summary of the text about skin and sunlight. Notice that it is not more than one-third the length of the original text.

Summary of the Text

> In the passage from "How Our Skins Got Their Color," Marvin Harris explores the impact of sunlight on skin health and skin color. There are two main dangers caused by overexposure to the sun. They are sunburn and skin cancer. The presence of melanin particles protects skin from these dangers. Melanin also influences skin color—the more melanin particles present, the darker the skin. But while too much sunlight can cause health problems, so too can lack of sunlight, since sunlight provides the body with vitamin D. Lack of vitamin D can cause a person's bones to soften. The author concludes that this balancing act between too much and too little sun exposure is why a large percentage of the world's population has brown skin.

Reflecting   Answer the following questions about the summary. Then share your responses with your classmates.

1. What information is provided in the topic sentence of the summary?

   _____

   _____

   _____

2. What information is provided in the body or middle sentences? Name three ideas.

   _____

   _____

   _____

3. What information is provided in the closing sentence?

   _____

   _____

   _____

INSIGHT

When you are writing a summary for a report or research paper, note the source of the text (title of the text, author, page number, and so on). This will make it easier for you to acknowledge or cite the source in your actual report.

Writing

LO4 Writing a Summary

In this part of the chapter, you will write a summary of your own following the guidelines presented in this section. To get started, read the text on the next page from a business textbook entitled *Foundations of Business*. Use the reading process to help you gain a full understanding of the text. (See below.)

About the Authors

William M. Pride is professor of marketing, Mays Business School at Texas A&M University. He is author of *Marketing, 15th edition,* and has had many articles on marketing published in major journals. **Robert J. Hughes** specializes in business administration and college instruction. He has taught Introduction to Business for more than 35 years for Richland College and has authored a number of college textbooks. **Jack R. Kapoor** is a professor of business and economics at the College of DuPage. He has coauthored several textbooks and has served as a consultant on the television series *The Business File: An Introduction to Business.*

Prereading   Before you read, answer these questions.

1. What do the title, first paragraph, and first sentences of other paragraphs tell you about the text?

_____

_____

2. What do you know about purchasing furniture?

_____

_____

3. What questions come to mind? (List at least two.)

_____

_____

Reading and Rereading   As you read, make it your goal to (1) identify the main idea, (2) find the key supporting details, and (3) decide if your questions were answered.

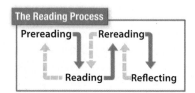

The Reading Process

Prereading → Rereading → Reading → Reflecting

From "Artistic Roots, Blu Dot Styles Marketing Strategy"

When a trio of college friends with backgrounds in art and architecture 1
started moving into their first apartments in the late 1990s, they were
frustrated to find that when it came to furniture, they couldn't afford what
they liked and didn't like when they could afford. Happily for many future
furniture shoppers, however, this frustration led the three to found Blu Dot, 5
a Minneapolis-based furniture design and manufacturing company that
has flourished and grown.

Blu Dot specializes in the creation of furniture that is attractive, high
quality, and affordable. Its modern, streamlined pieces use off-the shelf
materials and simple manufacturing processes that keep the company's 10
costs and prices down. The company also contracts with suppliers that make
industrial rather than consumer products because they use more efficient
and cost-effective processes and technology. These strategies, plus designs
that pack flat and are easy to ship, allow the firm to combine what Maurice
Blanks, one of the founders, describes as the affordability of the low end of 15
the market and the craftsmanship of the high end. Anyone can design a
$600 or $700 coffee table, Blu Dot believes. It's the $99 one the company is
aiming for that's more of a challenge.

The company sells seven product lines—tables, storage, accessories,
desks, beds, seating, and shelving. Its pricing strategy for each of these 20
is straightforward. Managers add their fixed and **variable** costs, plus the
markup they believe they'll need to keep the business functioning. They
then usually look at what competitors are doing with similar products and
try to identify three or four different pieces of pricing information to help
them settle on a profitable price. The company also uses some creative 25
pricing strategies to make its margins. For instance, one coffee table in a
set might have a higher markup, whereas another has a slightly lower one
for more **price-conscious** customers. Overall, then the target margins are
often met. . . .

In an interesting recent promotion that flirted with the price of zero, Blu 30
Dot celebrated the opening of its new store in New York's hip Soho district
by leaving 25 brand-new units of its **iconic** "Real Good Chair," normally
priced at $129, on various street corners in the city. Most of the chairs were
equipped with GPS devices that allowed the company's marketing agency
to trace the chairs to those who "rescued" them and brought them home. 35
The company's Web site proclaims that all the chairs found good homes,
and those "scavengers" who agreed to chat with the firm about its products
received a second free chair in thanks.

From Pride/Hughes/Kapoor, *Foundations of Business*, 3E. © 2013 Cengage Learning

variable
subject to change

price-conscious
avoiding buying expensive things

iconic
important, enduring, classic

Reflecting   After you complete your reading, answer these questions. Then share your responses with your classmates.

1. What is the main idea of the selection?

   _____

2. What types of furniture does Blu Dot specialize in? Why?

   _____

   _____

3. What supporting details do you find most important?

   _____

   _____

Vocabulary Practice

Identify   Use context clues to explain or define the following words. (See pages 33–34 for help.)

1. **flourished** (line 7)

   clues: _____

   definition: _____

2. **accessories** (line 19)

   clues: _____

   definition: _____

Drawing Inferences

Explain   Answer this question to help you draw an inference from the text. (See pages 29–31 for help.)

- What value does a story like this have for someone interested in business?

   _____

   _____

   _____

Writing Guidelines

The following guidelines will help you write a paragraph summary of an essay or extended passage.

Planning Your Summary

Most of your prewriting and planning will occur when you read and react to the text. During your planning . . .

- Name the thesis or main idea of the text.
- Identify the key details that support the thesis.

Writing the First Draft

Remember that you are writing a paragraph, starting with a topic sentence and following with supporting ideas. As you write your first draft . . .

- Use your own words as much as possible.
- Start with a topic sentence, naming the title, author, and topic of the text.
- Continue with the key points that explain the thesis. (Avoid specific details.)
- Arrange your ideas in the most logical order.
- Add a closing sentence, if one seems necessary.

Revising the Writing

Remember that your summary should address just the key information from the original text. As you review your first draft . . .

- Determine if it identifies the main idea of the text.
- Decide if you've limited yourself to key supporting details.
- See if your summary reads smoothly and logically.
- Determine if you've used your own words, except for key ideas.

Editing the Writing

Be sure that your summary is clear and accurate if you are turning it in for evaluation. As you edit your revised summary . . .

- Check that you've used complete sentences.
- Check for spelling, capitalization, and punctuation errors. Pay special attention to titles and quoted material. (See the next page.)
- Check for proper usage and grammar.

Write Write a paragraph summary of the text on page 405 using the information above as a guide. Be prepared to refer to the original text many times as you develop your writing.

A CLOSER LOOK at Revising and Editing

Revising

The information that follows will help you check your summary for (1) recognizing the source and (2) identifying exact ideas from the text.

Recognizing the Source Follow your instructor's guidelines for identifying the source of your summary (if you are turning it in for evaluation). The following example shows you how to identify the title and author in the topic sentence of your summary.

- In this passage from "Religious Faith Versus Spirituality," author Neil Bissoondath explores spirituality. . . .

Identifying Exact Ideas from the Text In your summary, you may find it necessary to include a few exact ideas or specialized words from the original text. When this type of information is taken directly from the text, enclose it within quotation marks.

- **Exact idea:** The author describes himself as "soaring with a lightness I'd never known before" after the ceremony.
- **Specialized word:** One teacher recognized as a master teacher serves as a "standard-bearer" for all great teachers.

Editing

This information will help you correctly capitalize and punctuate titles and quoted materials.

Capitalizing Titles Capitalize the first and last words in a title and all important words in between. Do not capitalize words such as *a, for, by, in, and,* and *the* if they occur within the title. (See pages 586–587 for more.)

- **Title:** Chinese Space, American Space *(All the words are important, so they are all capitalized.)*
- **Title:** Catcher in the Rye *("In" and "the" occur within the title, so they are lowercased.)*

Punctuating Titles Use quotation marks to set off the titles of chapters, essays, articles, and so on. Italicize or underline the titles of books, magazines, newspapers, Web sites, and so on.

- **Title of an Essay:** "Chinese Space, American Space"
- **Title of a Book:** Catcher in the Rye

Placement of Other Punctuation Place commas and periods inside quotation marks. Place question marks or exclamation marks inside the quotation marks when they punctuate the quotation and outside when they punctuate the sentence.

- **Placement of a Comma:** In this passage from "Religious Faith Versus Spirituality," author Neil Bissoondath explores spirituality. *(Commas and periods are always placed inside the quotation marks.)*

- **Placement of a Question Mark:** The essay "Yes, Accidents Happen. But Why?" analyzes the causes of accidents. *(The question mark punctuates the quotation, so it is placed inside the quotation marks.)*

- Have you read "Spanglish Spoken Here"? *(The question mark punctuates the entire sentence, so it is placed outside the quotation marks.)*

Check Be sure to use the information on these two pages to help you revise and edit your summary, correctly capitalizing and punctuating titles and quoted material.

LO5 Practicing Additional Summary Writing

This section includes two texts that you can use for additional summary-writing practice. Always read and react to the text before writing your summary.

First Text

This selection, which comes from a textbook entitled *Living in the Environment*, discusses the protection of wilderness areas in this country. Use the reading process to help you gain a full understanding of the text.

> **About the Authors**
>
> **G. Tyler Miller, Jr.,** has a PhD from the University of Virginia and has written 59 textbooks on environmental science. Before devoting his time to writing, he taught for 20 years and created one of this nation's first environmental programs. **Scott E. Spoolman** is a textbook writer and editor and has worked with Miller since 2003. He holds a master's degree in science journalism from the University of Minnesota and is the author of many articles on science, engineering, business, and politics.

Prereading Before you read, answer these three questions:

1. What do the title and opening paragraph tell you about the topic?

   _____

   _____

2. What do you know about wilderness areas in the United States?

   _____

   _____

3. What questions do you have about the topic? (List at least two.)

   _____

   _____

Reading and Rereading As you read, make it your goal to (1) identify the topic and main idea, (2) study the supporting details, and (3) judge the impact of the final paragraph. Consider annotating the text (see page 20) and/or filling in a table diagram as explained on page 399.

Controversy over Wilderness Protection in the United States

In the United States, conservationists have been trying to save wild areas from development since 1900. Overall, they have fought a losing battle. Not until 1964 did Congress pass the Wilderness Act. It allowed the government to protect undeveloped tracts of public land from development as part of the National Wilderness Preservation System. Such lands get the highest level of protection from human activities such as logging, mining, and motor vehicle use.

The area of protected wilderness in the United States increased tenfold between 1979 and 2010. Even so, only about 4.7 percent of the U.S. land is protected as wilderness—almost three-fourths of it in Alaska. Only about 2 percent of the land area of the lower 48 states is protected, most of it in the West.

However, in 2009 the U.S. government granted wilderness protection to over 800,000 hectares (2 million acres) of public land in nine of the lower 48 states. It was the largest expansion of wilderness lands in 15 years. The new law also increased the total length of wild and scenic rivers (treated as wilderness areas) by 50 percent—the largest such increase ever.

One problem is that only four of the 413 wilderness areas in the lower 48 states are large enough to sustain all of the species they contain. Some species, such as wolves, need large areas in which to roam as packs, to find prey, and to mate and rear young. Also, the system includes only 81 of the country's 233 distinct ecosystems. Most wilderness areas in the lower 48 states are threatened habitat islands in a sea of development.

Scattered blocks of public lands with a total area roughly equal to that of the U.S. state of Montana could qualify for designation as wilderness. About 60 percent of such land is in the national forest. But for decades, the politically powerful oil, gas, mining, and timber industries have sought entry to these areas—owned jointly by all citizens of the United States—in hopes of locating and removing valuable resources. Under the law, as soon as such an area is accessed in this way, it automatically becomes disqualified for wilderness protection.

From Miller, *Living in the Environment*, 17E. © 2012 Cengage Learning

Reflecting   After you complete your reading, answer these questions. Then share your responses with your classmates.

1. What is the main idea?

   _____

   _____

2. What supporting details stand out?

   _____

   _____

3. What have you learned in this reading?

   _____

   _____

Vocabulary Practice

Identify   Use context clues to explain or define the following two words. (See pages 33–34 for help.)

1. **expansion** (line 15)

   clues: _____

   definition: _____

2. **sustain** (line 20)

   clues: _____

   definition: _____

Thinking Critically

Explain   Answer these two questions to help you think critically about the selection.

1. How will you use this information?

   _____

2. What questions do you still have about the topic?

   _____

Second Text

The selection below, which comes from the textbook *Sociology: Your Compass for a New World*, explores an interesting topic—the links between people. Use the reading process to help you gain a full understanding of the text.

About the Authors

Robert J. Brym is a professor of sociology at the University of Toronto. He has won numerous awards for his teaching and scholarly work. **John Lie** is a professor of social theory and political economy at the University of California, Berkeley.

Prereading Before you read, answer these three questions:

1. What do the title and first few sentences tell you about the topic?

2. What do you know about Kevin Bacon?

3. What do you expect to learn about him?

Reading and Rereading As you read, make it your goal to (1) identify the topic and main idea, (2) locate the supporting details, and (3) consider what you have learned. Consider annotating the text (page 20) as you read.

Six Degrees of Kevin Bacon

The Internet Movie Database (2003) contains information on the half   *1*
million actors who have ever performed in a commercially released movie.
While this number is large, you might be surprised to learn that, socially,
they form a small world. We can demonstrate this fact by first selecting an
actor who is not an especially big star—someone like Kevin Bacon. We can   *5*
then use the Internet Movie Database to find out which other actors have
ever been in a movie with him (University of Virginia, 2003). Acting in a
movie with *another* actor constitutes a link. Actors two links away from
Bacon have never been in a movie with him but have been in a movie with
another actor who has been in a movie with him. Remarkably, more than   *10*
85 percent of the half million actors in the database have one, two, or three
links to Bacon. We conclude that although film acting stretches back more
than a century and has involved people in many countries, the half million
people who have ever acted in films form a pretty small world.

What is true for the world of film actors turns out to be true for the *15* rest of us, too. Jeffrey Travers and Stanley Milgram (1969) conducted a famous study in which they asked 300 randomly selected people to mail a document to a complete stranger. However, the people could not mail the document directly to [the strangers]. They had to mail it to a person they knew on a first-name basis, who, in turn, could send it only to a person *20* he or she knew on a first-name basis, and so forth. Travers and Milgram defined this passing of a letter from one person to another as a link, or a "degree of separation." Remarkably, it took only six links on average for the document to reach the stranger. The idea soon became widespread that there are no more than six degrees of separation between any two people in *25* the United States.

From BRYM/LIE, *Sociology*, 2E. © 2007 Cengage Learning

Reflecting   After you complete your reading, answer these questions. Then share your responses with your classmates.

1. What is the main idea of the text?

   _____

   _____

2. What examples are used to developed this idea?

   _____

   _____

3. What have you learned in this reading? (Name two things.)

   _____

   _____

4. How would you rate this selection, and why?
   Weak ★ ★ ★ ★ ★ Strong

   _____

   _____

Life Stages

Even though individuals differ greatly, each person passes through *1*
certain stages of growth and development from birth to death. These
stages are frequently called life stages. A common method of classifying
life stages is as follows:
- Infancy: birth to 1 year   *5*
- Early childhood: 1-6 years
- Late childhood: 6-12 years
- Adolescence: 12-18 years
- Early adulthood: 19-40 years
- Middle adulthood: 40-65 years   *10*
- Late adulthood: 65 years and older

As individuals pass through these life stages, four main types of
growth and development occur: physical, mental or cognitive, emotional,
and social. Physical refers to body growth and includes height and weight
changes, muscle and nerve development, and changes in body organs.   *15*
Mental or cognitive refers to intellectual development and includes
learning how to solve problems, make judgments, and deal with situations.
Emotional refers to feelings and includes dealings with love, hate, joy, fear,
excitement, and other similar feelings. Social refers to interactions and
relationships with other people.   *20*

Each stage of growth and development has its own characteristics
and has specific developmental tasks that an individual must master.
These tasks progress from the simple to the more complex. For example,
an individual first learns to sit, then crawl, then stand, then walk, and
then, finally, run. Each stage establishes the foundation for the next stage.   *25*
In this way, growth and development proceeds in an orderly pattern. It is
important to remember, however, that the rate of progress varies among
individuals. Some children master speech early, others master it later.
Similarly, an individual may experience a sudden growth spurt and then
maintain the same height for a period of time.   *30*

Erik Erikson, a psychoanalyst, has identified eight states of
psychosocial development. His eight stages of development, the basic
conflict or need that must be resolved at each stage, and ways to resolve
the conflict are shown in [the] table [below]. Erikson believes that if an
individual is not able to resolve a conflict at the appropriate stage, the   *35*
individual will struggle with the same conflict later in life. For example,
if a toddler is not allowed to learn and become independent by mastering
basic tasks, the toddler may develop a sense of doubt in his or her abilities.
This sense of doubt will interfere with later attempts at mastering
independence.   *40*

Health care providers must understand that each life stage creates
certain needs in individuals. Likewise, other factors can affect life stages

and needs. An individual's sex, race, heredity (factors inherited from parents, such as hair color and body structure), culture, life experiences, and health status can influence needs. Injury or illness usually has a negative effect and can change needs or impair development.

45

Erikson's Eight Stages of Psychosocial Development*		
Stage of Development	*Basic Conflict*	*Major Life Event*
Infancy: Birth to 1 Year; Oral-Sensory	Trust vs. Mistrust	Feeding
Toddler: 1-3 Years; Muscular-Anal	Autonomy vs. Shame/Doubt	Toilet Training
Preschool: 3-6 Years; Locomotor	Initiative vs. Guilt	Independence
School-Age: 6-12 Years; Latency	Industry vs. Inferiority	School
Adolescence: 12-18 Years	Identity vs. Role Confusion	Peer
Young Adulthood: 19-40 Years	Intimacy vs. Isolation	Love Relationships
Middle Adulthood: 40-65 Years	Generativity vs. Stagnation	Parenting
Older Adulthood: 66 Years to Death	Ego Identity vs. Despair	Reflection on and Acceptance of Life

*Table adapted from *Diversified Health Occupations,* minus the "Ways to Resolve Conflict" column.

From Simmers, Diversified Health Occupations, 7E. © 2009 Cengage Learning

Reflecting   After you complete your reading, answer these questions. Then share your responses with your classmates.

1. What is the main idea of the selection?

_____

2. What are two supporting details that you find important and/or interesting?

_____

_____

3. What questions about the topic still remain unanswered?

_____

_____

4. How would you rate the selection, and why?
   Weak ★ ★ ★ ★ ★ Strong

_____

_____

Vocabulary Practice

Identify Use context clues to explain or define the following words. (See pages 33–34 for help.)

1. cognitive (line 13)

clues: _____

definition: _____

2. master (line 28)

clues: _____

definition: _____

3. impair (line 46)

clues: _____

definition: _____

Summarizing to Understand

In your own words, write a one-paragraph summary of the essay. (See page 25.) If you outlined the essay, use it as a general guide. Compare your summary with those of your classmates.

Topic Sentence: _____

_____

Support: _____

_____

_____

_____

_____

_____

Conclusion: _____

_____

_____

Writing

Starting on this page, you will plan and write an essay of definition about a topic you are studying. Be sure to use the writing process to do your best work. (See pages 94–99.)

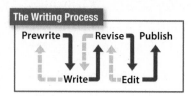

The Writing Process

Prewrite ▸ Revise ▸ Publish

Write ▸ Edit

LO4 Planning an Essay of Definition

While an essay of definition can change its readers, it can also change its writer. Writing an essay of definition is a chance to explore a topic more fully than you have before. As a result, your understanding of the topic will deepen. At the same time, your writing skills will improve.

Selecting a Topic

Below are listed four topics Azzie listed as possible topics for definition, using the categories from page 418. She decided to write about marriage.

- Arts: _Self-expression_
- Journalism: _Slanted language_
- History: _(Marriage)_
- Nutrition: _Vegetarianism_

Select On page 418 you listed a topic for each of the categories of arts, journalism, history, and nutrition. Choose one of the topics you listed and use it for your own essay of definition.

"The point of the essay is to change things."
—Edward Tufte

hektor2, 2013 / Used under license from Shutterstock.com

Using Resources to Gather Details

There are many resources you can use to begin developing your essay of definition. Here are a few of the most helpful.

- **Dictionary:** Often, your term will have a specific definition in a dictionary. This can be a good starting place for understanding the term. Just make sure to use the correct definition—many words have several possible meanings.
- **Thesaurus:** A thesaurus lists synonyms—words with similar meanings. It also lists antonyms—words with opposite meanings. A synonym or an antonym may be useful in your opening statement.
- **Negative definition:** Sometimes explaining what a term is not can help to reveal what it is.
- **Examples:** Specific examples or instances can help your reader to understand your definition.
- **Function or purpose:** Explaining what something does can help to define that thing.
- **Description:** If what you are defining can be divided into parts, a description of those parts can help make it clear.

The writer of the essay on the next page started a sheet to gather details about marriage from various resources.

Dictionary:	"1 a (1) : the state of being united to a person of the opposite sex as husband or wife in a consensual and contractual relationship recognized by law" *Merriam-Webster's Dictionary*
Thesaurus:	"wedding, matrimony, nuptials" Microsoft Word
Negative definition:	In my opinion, marriage is not just a contract between people. Nor is it always feelings of love.
Examples:	My parents have been married for 35 years. I still see them talking and laughing a lot. Sometimes they also argue.
Function/purpose:	A way of protecting children while they grow. (But what about after children are grown and gone?)
Description:	Joy and passion come and go. So do pain and disappointment. A good marriage seems to be about care and respect beneath it all.

Collect   Use a table like the one above to gather your own details about your topic.

LO5 Writing the First Draft

When writing your first draft, don't worry about making everything perfect. Just get your thoughts down on paper.

Read   Carefully read and consider the following definition essay about marriage.

Let's Talk Marriage

The thesis statement introduces the topic.

Weddings are great, but marriages can be tough. Many marriages end early, and divorces can be ugly. We might wonder why anyone bothers to get married in the first place. Still, something about marriage keeps people coming back for more.   1

The author builds upon a dictionary definition.

Historically, marriage has been a public contract between two people, promising to support each other until death. In many cultures, it has also been a contract between two families, each giving something to help launch the new couple. Biologically, marriage has also provided a safe haven for children to grow to adulthood.   5   10

Negative definitions put the topic in a new perspective.

However, nowadays that contract and safe haven seem to matter less. Our society has less of a stigma about divorce than in previous decades. Many people argue that it is better for children to grow up with separated parents than with parents who argue all the time. The topic of "being in love" seems to be most important. People say, "I love you. Let's get married," then, "I don't love you anymore. Let's get divorced." That seems a pretty narrow definition of love.   15

Examples are used to round out the definition.

My parents have been married for 35 years, and I think they know true love. Sometimes they argue. I've seen my mom cry over some of their fights. I've seen my dad cry, too. Often their fights have been over how to raise their children. I've also seen my parents support each other through tough times, like when my dad had to have back surgery, or when my mom lost her favorite job. The most important thing is, I see how much they like to spend time together, even just sitting and talking. I see how they still make each other laugh.   20   25

The author uses further examples to discuss one aspect of the definition.

As for raising children, I'm starting to think that never ends. My brothers and I are all out of the house, but our mom and dad still help out when we need something. Also, when I think about it, I can remember hearing my mom or dad on the phone asking their own parents for advice.   30

The closing paragraph gives a final thought about the topic.

All things considered, successful marriages seem to be about respect and care. Joy comes and goes. Passion comes and goes. Pain comes and goes. Disappointments come and go. Good marriages show a type of love that outlasts them all.   35

schools give women's sports the same treatment as men's games receive. That meant that in schools and colleges across the United States, for every boys' varsity soccer team, there must be a girls' varsity soccer team; for every male basketball scholarship, there must be a female basketball scholarship of equal dollars. Since the early 1970s, the law has increased money for new equipment, coaches, and travel for women's teams. More college scholarships have translated into more diplomas and better jobs for women. Thomas earned a partial academic scholarship when she applied to Berkeley, one of the country's top universities, but without an additional basketball scholarship awarded in her junior and senior years, she would have had a hard time paying for the education.

Girls' participation in high school sports has spiked from about 300,000 in 1971 to 2.4 million in 1996. At the college level, where competition is tougher, the number of female athletes has increased to 123,832 from 80,040 in 1982, says the National Collegiate Athletic Association.

"No other experience I know of can prepare you for the high-level competition of business," says Anh Ngyuen, 25, a former Carnegie Mellon University varsity soccer star. She should know. Now she battles Microsoft as a product manager for Netscape Communications. "My colleagues can't believe how aggressive I am," she says.

Sports helped these women master the interpersonal skills, like teamwork, that many men take for granted. "I've seen firsthand hundreds and hundreds of times that one person can't win a soccer or softball game," says Maria Murnane, a 28-year-old senior account executive for a San Francisco public relations firm. "Same goes for work. You have to learn to trust the people on your team, let them run with projects," the former Northwestern soccer center midfielder says. Her boss, William Harris, the president of Strategy Associates, agrees: "We don't want Lone Rangers. She's a team player—a captain and cheerleader."

Playing team sports helps with the little things, too. Women learn to speak in sports metaphors, as many men do. Lisa Delpy, professor of sports management at George Washington University in Washington, D.C., also notes that in many companies a lot of business is conducted on the golf course, at ballgames, or at other sports events. Women who know the difference between a slide tackle and a sweeper at a World Cup soccer match can fit right in.

Stephanie Delaney, now 31, captained the varsity soccer team at Franklin and Marshall College in Lancaster, Pennsylvania, when it won the Mid-Atlantic Conference championship her senior year. Now the sales manager for the Caribbean and Latin American division of ConAgra's Lamb-Weston, one of the world's largest frozen french fry producers, she was the only woman to play a game of basketball with potential clients at a big food conference last year in Jamaica. "I was the high scorer," she notes.

And yes, it helped sell french fries. "I didn't close the deal on the court, but afterward when we were hanging out drinking water and shooting the breeze, they agreed to test my product. Now we have Kentucky Fried Chicken's business in Jamaica," says Delaney.

Female executives say that Title IX had another subtle but important effect. For the first time, many boys, coaches, and parents opened their eyes to the fact that their sisters and daughters could be just as strong, fast, and nimble on the field as their brothers and sons. Likewise, girls whose talents had formerly gone *70* unnoticed under driveway basketball nets and on back lots began realizing their own power—that they could compete with boys and win. "When my girlfriends and I formed a softball team back in college, we were dreadful—like the Keystone Kops," recalls Penny Cate, 45, now a vice president at Quaker Oats. "There'd be four of us in the outfield and the ball would go through our legs. But *75* after a few years, we became very good. It built my confidence, made me realize I could accomplish anything in sports or out," she says.

That point is repeatedly brought home when Nike executives ask schoolgirls what they think of one of the company's TV ads. The ad begins with the voice of a young girl saying, "If you let me play . . ." The phrase is finished *80* by other little girls saying things like "I will have greater self-confidence" or "I will be more likely to stay in school."

The girls often reply, in a tone of genuine befuddlement, "If who lets me play?" They don't see any barriers between themselves and America's playing fields. Twenty years from now, might they say, "What glass ceiling?" *85*

Reflecting

After your reading, answer the following questions. Then share your responses with your classmates.

1. What is the main idea in the text? How far into the essay did you read to be able to identify it?

_____

2. How is the essay organized—spatially, logically, or chronologically? (See page 71 for help.)

_____

3. What effect did the athletic experiences have on the women discussed in the essay? Cite two specific examples.

_____

4. How would you rate this essay, and why?

Weak ★ ★ ★ ★ ★ Strong

_____

Parts III–IV:

Sentence, Word, and Punctuation Workshops

Part III: Sentence Workshops

17

"Grasp the subject; the words will follow."
—Cato the Elder

Sentence Basics

All right, soldiers, fall in for basic training. Of course, you've studied all of this before, so the following pages will be a review. And the basics of sentences really are basic. A sentence is the connection between a noun and a verb (or a subject and a predicate), with all of the other words modifying those two parts. These are the building blocks of thought.

In the pages that follow, you will explore the ins and outs of subjects and predicates, as well as the words, phrases, and clauses that describe them. Fear not. These are sentence basics, and we'll make sure they are easy to understand.

Learning Outcomes

LO1 Subjects and Verbs (Predicates)

LO2 Special Types of Subjects

LO3 Special Verbs (Predicates)

LO4 Adjectives

LO5 Adverbs

LO6 Prepositional Phrases

LO7 Clauses

LO8 Real-World Application

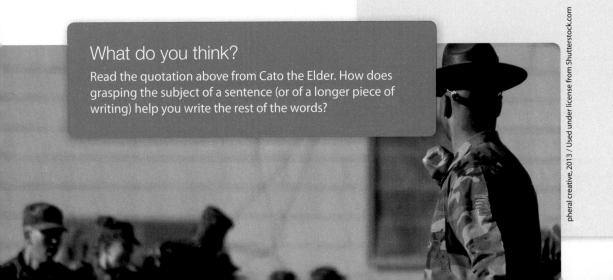

What do you think?

Read the quotation above from Cato the Elder. How does grasping the subject of a sentence (or of a longer piece of writing) help you write the rest of the words?

pheral creative, 2013 / Used under license from Shutterstock.com

LO1 Subjects and Verbs (Predicates)

The subject of a sentence tells what the sentence is about. The verb (predicate) of a sentence tells what the subject does or is.

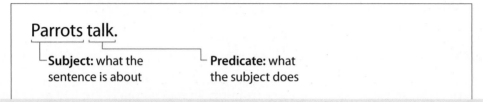

Parrots talk.

Subject: what the sentence is about

Predicate: what the subject does

Simple Subject and Simple Predicate

The **simple subject** is the subject without any modifiers, and the **simple predicate** is the verb and any helping verbs without modifiers or objects.

The red and black parrot sang the song all day.
        simple subject   simple predicate

Complete Subject and Complete Predicate

The **complete subject** is the subject with modifiers, and the **complete predicate** is the predicate with modifiers and objects.

The red and black parrot sang the song all day.
        complete subject   complete predicate

Implied Subject

In commands, the subject *you* is implied. Commands are the only type of sentence in English that can have an **implied subject**.

(You)   Stop singing!
implied subject   complete predicate

Inverted Order

Most often in English, the subject comes before the predicate. However, in questions and sentences that begin with *here* or *there*, the subject comes after the predicate.

            subject   subject
Why are you so loud?   Here is a cracker.
    predicate   predicate

Creating Subjects and Verbs (Predicates)

Identify/Write For each sentence below, identify the simple subject (SS) and simple predicate (SP). Then write a similar sentence of your own and identify the simple subject and simple predicate in the same way.

1. In the wild, parrots gather in large groups.

2. In a person's home, a parrot needs constant companionship.

3. Without enough attention, some parrots pluck their feathers.

4. A caring pet owner understands the parrot's need for attention.

Identify/Write For each sentence below, identify the complete subject (CS) and complete predicate (CP). Then write a similar sentence of your own and identify the complete subject and complete predicate in the same way.

1. A typical pet parrot can live to be eighty years old.

2. A baby parrot could outlive the person.

3. Parrot owners often place their parrots in their wills.

4. Why do parrots live so long?

5. There must be an explanation.

simple subject the subject without any modifiers **simple predicate** the verb and any helping verbs without modifiers or objects	**complete subject** the subject with modifiers **complete predicate** the predicate with modifiers and objects	**implied subject** the word *you* implied in command sentences

LO2 Special Types of Subjects

As you work with subjects, watch for these special types.

Compound Subjects

A **compound subject** is two or more subjects connected by *and* or *or*.

My brother and sister swim well. Dajohn, Larinda, and I love to dive.
         compound subject   compound subject

"To" Words (Infinitives) as Subjects

An **infinitive** can function as a subject. An infinitive is a verbal form that begins with *to* and may be followed by objects or modifiers.

To complete a one-and-a-half flip is my goal.
         infinitive subject

"Ing" Words (Gerunds) as Subjects

A **gerund** can function as a subject. A gerund is a verb form that ends in *ing* and may be followed by objects or modifiers.

Swimming is his favorite sport.   Handing him the goggles would be nice.
gerund subject   gerund subject

Noun Clause as Subject

A **noun clause** can function as a subject. The clause itself has a subject and a verb but cannot stand alone as a sentence. Noun clauses are introduced by words like *what, that, when, why, how, whatever,* or *whichever*.

Whoever wants to go swimming must remember to bring a swimsuit.
         noun clause subject

Whatever remains of the afternoon will be spent at the pool.
         noun clause subject

CONSIDER THE TRAITS

Note that each of these special subjects still functions as a noun or a group of nouns. A sentence is still, at root, the connection between a noun and a verb.

Say It

Pair up with a partner and read each sentence aloud. Take turns identifying the type of subject—compound subject, infinitive subject, gerund subject, or noun-clause subject. Discuss your answers.

1. Swimming across the pool underwater is challenging.
2. To get a lifesaving certificate is hard work.
3. Whoever gets a certificate can be a lifeguard.
4. You and I should go swimming sometime.

Creating Special Subjects

Identify/Write   For each sentence below, identify the complete subject as a compound subject (CS), infinitive (I), gerund (G), or noun clause (NC). Then write a similar sentence of your own and identify the complete subject in the same way.

1. To clean the car thoroughly requires a vacuum.

2. Wishing for better weather won't stop the rain.

3. The river and the lake are flooding into the streets.

4. Whoever needs to set the table should get started now.

5. Shoes, shirts, and pants are required in this restaurant.

6. Reading us the riot act is not the best way to win us over.

7. To reassure your boss about the expenditures is your first priority.

8. Whatever you plan needs to be simple and affordable.

9. Are Jason, Micah, and Eli in the play?

10. Helping us change the tire will speed everything along.

compound subject two or more subjects connected by *and* or *or* infinitive a verb form that begins with *to* and can be used as a noun (or as an adjective or adverb)	gerund a verb form that ends in *ing* and is used as a noun	noun clause a group of words beginning with words like *that, what, whoever,* and so on; containing a subject and a verb but unable to function as a sentence

LO3 Special Verbs (Predicates)

As you work with predicates, watch for these special types.

Compound Predicates

A **compound predicate** consists of two or more predicates joined by *and* or *or*.

I sang and danced. The audience laughed, clapped, and sang along.
compound predicate   compound predicate

Predicates with Direct Objects

A **direct object** follows a transitive verb and tells what or who receives the action of the verb.

I sang a song. I danced a few dances. I told a joke or two.
direct object   direct object   direct objects

Predicates with Indirect Objects

An **indirect object** comes between a transitive verb and a direct object and tells to whom or for whom an action was done.

I sang Jim his favorite song. I told Ellen her favorite joke.
indirect object   indirect object

Passive Predicates

When a predicate is **passive**, the subject of the sentence is being acted upon rather than acting. Often, the actor is the object of the preposition in a phrase that starts with *by*. To make the sentence **active**, rewrite it, turning the object of the preposition into the subject.

Passive

Teri was serenaded by Josh.
subject   passive verb   object of the preposition

Active

Josh serenaded Teri.
subject   active verb   direct object

Rob Byron, 2013 / Used under license from Shutterstock.com

Say It

Pair up with a partner and read each sentence aloud. Take turns identifying the sentence as active or passive. If the sentence is passive, speak the active version out loud.

1. I threw out my back.
2. My friends were warned by the bouncer.
3. A camera crew was escorted to the exit by the guard.
4. I plan to go.

Creating Special Predicates

Identify/Write For each sentence below, identify any compound predicate (CP), direct object (DO), and indirect object (IO). Then write a similar sentence of your own and identify the compound predicate and direct or indirect object.

1. Everyone at the party danced and sang.

2. The DJ played dance music.

3. I gave him a request.

4. The crowd twisted and shouted.

5. I gave my date a kiss.

6. The music rattled and boomed.

7. The DJ provided everyone some awesome entertainment.

Identify/Write For each passive sentence below, identify the simple subject (SS), the simple predicate (SP), and the object of the preposition *by* (O). Then rewrite each sentence, making it active.

1. Many songs were played by the DJ. _____

2. A good time was had by the partygoers. _____

3. My friend was asked by Sarah to the next party. _____

---

compound predicate
two or more predicates joined by *and* or *or*
direct object
a word that follows a transitive verb and tells what or who receives the action of the verb

indirect object
a word that comes between a transitive verb and a direct object and tells to whom or for whom an action was done
passive
the voice created when a subject is being acted upon

active
the voice created when a subject is acting

LO4 Adjectives

To modify a noun, use an adjective or a phrase or clause acting as an adjective.

Adjectives

Adjectives answer these basic questions: *which, what kind of, how many, how much.*

To modify the noun **books,** ask . . .

Which books? ⟶ hardbound books

What kind of books? ⟶ old books

How many books? ⟶ five books

five old hardbound books

Adjective Phrases and Clauses

Phrases and clauses can also act as adjectives to modify nouns.

To modify the noun **books,** ask . . .

What kind of books? ⟶ books about women's issues

⟶ books showing their age

Which books? ⟶ books that my mother gave me

Showing their age, the books that my mother gave me about women's issues rest on the top shelf.

INSIGHT

It's less important to know the name of a phrase or clause than to know how it functions. If a group of words answers one of the adjective questions, the words are probably functioning as an adjective.

> ## Say It
>
> Pair up with a classmate to find adjectives—words, phrases, or clauses—that modify the nouns below. Take turns asking the questions while the other person answers.
>
> 1. **Cars**
>   *Which* cars?
>   *What kind of* cars?
>   *How many* cars?
>
> 2. **Trees**
>   *Which* trees?
>   *What kind of* trees?
>   *How many* trees?

Use Adjectives

Answer/Write For each noun, answer the questions using adjectives—words, phrases, or clauses. Then write a sentence using two or more of your answers.

1. **Dogs**

   Which dogs? _____

   What kind of dogs? _____

   How many dogs? _____

   Sentence: _____

   _____

2. **Classes**

   Which classes? _____

   What kind of classes? _____

   How many classes? _____

   Sentence: _____

   _____

3. **Ideas**

   Which ideas? _____

   What kind of ideas? _____

   How many ideas? _____

   Sentence: _____

   _____

LO5 Adverbs

To modify a verb, use an adverb or a phrase or clause acting as an adverb.

Adverbs

Adverbs answer these basic questions: *how, when, where, why, how long,* and *how often.*

To modify the verb **jumped,** ask . . .

How did they jump? ⟶	jumped exuberantly
When did they jump? ⟶	jumped today
Where did they jump? ⟶	jumped there
How often did they jump? ⟶	jumped often

The children jumped exuberantly and often today, there on the pile of old mattresses.

Adverb Phrases and Clauses

Phrases and clauses can also act as adverbs to modify verbs.

To modify the verb **jumped,** ask . . .

How did they jump? ⟶	jumped with great enthusiasm
When did they jump? ⟶	jumped before lunchtime
Where did they jump? ⟶	jumped on the trampoline
Why did they jump? ⟶	jumped to get some exercise
⟶	jumped because it's fun
How long did they jump? ⟶	jumped for an hour

To get some exercise before lunchtime, the children jumped on the trampoline with great enthusiasm. I think, though, that they jumped for an hour just because it's fun!

CONSIDER SPEAKING AND LISTENING

Read the last two sentences aloud. Though they may look imposing on the page, they sound natural, probably because adverbs and adjectives are a common part of our speech. Experiment with these modifiers in your writing as well.

18

"A complex system that works is invariably found to have evolved from a simple system that works."
—John Gaule

Simple, Compound, and Complex Sentences

A two-by-four is a simple thing—a board with standard dimensions. But two-by-fours can be used to create everything from a shed to a mansion. It's the way that the boards are connected and combined that determines the proportions of the final structure.

A sentence can be a simple thing as well, just a subject and a verb. But sentences can also be connected to become compound or complex sentences. The way in which writers use simple, compound, and complex sentences determines the maturity of their writing.

Learning Outcomes

LO1 Simple Sentences
LO2 Simple Sentences with Compound Subjects
LO3 Simple Sentences with Compound Verbs
LO4 Compound Sentences
LO5 Complex Sentences
LO6 Complex Sentences with Relative Clauses
LO7 Real-World Application

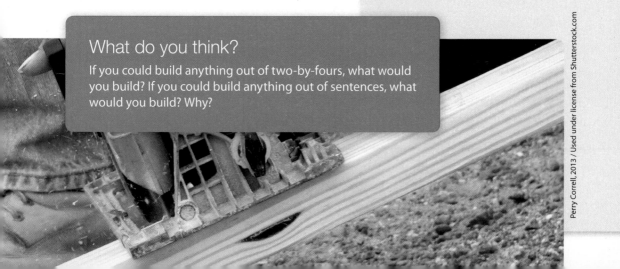

What do you think?

If you could build anything out of two-by-fours, what would you build? If you could build anything out of sentences, what would you build? Why?

LO1   Simple Sentences

A **simple sentence** consists of a subject and a verb. The subject is a noun or pronoun that names what the sentence is about. The verb tells what the subject does or is.

Terrance played.
subject   verb

Modifiers

Other words can modify the subject. Words and phrases that modify the subject answer the adjective questions: *which, what kind of, how many, how much.*

My longtime friend Terrance played.
(The phrase tells *which Terrance.*)

Other words can also modify the verb. These words and phrases answer the adverb questions: *how, when, where, why, how long,* and *how often.*

Terrance played all afternoon and into the evening.
(The phrases tell *when Terrance played.*)

Direct and Indirect Objects

The verb may also be followed by a **direct object**, a noun or pronoun that receives the action of the verb. The direct object answers the question *what* or *whom.*

Terrance played basketball.
(*Basketball* tells *what Terrance played.*)

A noun or pronoun that comes between the verb and its direct object is called an **indirect object**. The indirect object answers the question *to whom* or *for whom* an action is done.

Terrance passed me the basketball.
(*Me* tells *to whom Terrance passed the basketball.*)

Creating Simple Sentences

Create Provide a noun for a subject and a verb for a predicate. Then write a sentence with the noun and verb, adding details that answer the questions asked. The first question has been done for you.

1.

Subject	Verb

Which? _____

Simple Sentence: _____

2.

Subject	Verb

What kind of? _____

Simple Sentence: _____

3.

Subject	Verb

When? _____

Simple Sentence: _____

4.

Subject	Verb

Where? _____

Simple Sentence: _____

5.

Subject	Verb

How? _____

Simple Sentence: _____

---

simple sentence
a subject and a verb that together form a complete thought

direct object
a noun or pronoun that follows a verb and receives its action

indirect object
a noun or pronoun that comes between a verb and a direct object, telling *to whom* or *for whom* an action is done

LO2 Simple Sentences with Compound Subjects

A simple sentence can have a **compound subject** (two or more subjects).

A Simple Sentence with Two Subjects

To write a simple sentence with two subjects, join them using *and* or *or*.

One Subject: Chan collected donations for the animal shelter.

Two Subjects: Chan and Lynn collected donations for the animal shelter.
Chan or Lynn collected the most donations.

One Subject: The president of the shelter gave Lynn an award.

Two Subjects: The president and vice president of the shelter gave Lynn an award.
The president or the vice president of the shelter thanked her for her hard work.

A Simple Sentence with Three or More Subjects

To write a simple sentence with three or more subjects, create a series, using *and* or *or* before the last one.

Three Subjects: Chan, Lynn, and I went out to celebrate.

Five Subjects: Chan, Lynn, the president, the vice president, and I were interviewed by a reporter.

NOTE: When a compound subject is joined by *and,* the subject is plural and requires a plural verb. When a compound subject is joined by *or,* the verb should match the last subject.

Chan and Lynn plan to help out again next year.

Chan or Lynn plans to help out again next year.

CONSIDER THE TRAITS

Using a compound subject in a simple sentence does not make the sentence compound. As long as the subjects connect to the same verb, the sentence is still considered simple.

Say It

Speak each of the following sentences out loud.
1. Chan *volunteers* regularly.
2. Chan *and* Lynn *volunteer* regularly.
3. Chan *or* Lynn *volunteers* once a month.
4. Chan, Lynn, *and* Dave *help* at the shelter each week.
5. Chan, Lynn, *or* Dave *helps* at the shelter each week.

Using Compound Subjects

Create For each item below, write subjects in the boxes provided. Then connect the subjects using *and* or *or* and use the compound subject in a simple sentence.

1.
Subject	Verb

Simple Sentence: _____

2.
Subject	Verb

Simple Sentence: _____

3.
Subject	Verb

Simple Sentence: _____

4.
Subject	Verb

Simple Sentence: _____

5.
Subject	Verb

Simple Sentence: _____

compound subject
two or more subjects joined by the
conjunction *or* or *and*

LO3 Simple Sentences with Compound Verbs

A simple sentence can have a **compound verb** (two or more verbs).

A Simple Sentence with Two Verbs

To write a simple sentence with two verbs, join them using *and* or *or*.

One Verb: The tornado roared.

Two Verbs: The tornado roared and twisted.

Remember that the predicate often includes words that modify or complete the verbs.

One Verb: A tornado tore through our town.

Two Verbs: A tornado tore through our town and damaged buildings.

A Simple Sentence with Three or More Verbs

To write a simple sentence with three or more verbs, create a series, using *and* or *or* before the last one.

Three Verbs: The tornado roared, twisted, and shuddered.

Five Verbs: People shouted, ran, gathered, hid, and waited.

Each verb in a series can also include modifiers or completing words (direct and indirect objects).

The tornado tore apart a warehouse, ripped the roofs from homes, and flattened trailers in a local park.

solarseven, 2013 / Used under license from Shutterstock.com

CONSIDER THE TRAITS

Using a compound verb in a simple sentence does not make the sentence compound. As long as the verbs connect to the same subject, the sentence is still considered simple.

Using Compound Verbs

Create For each subject below, write verbs, along with modifiers or completing words, in the boxes provided. (See page 462.) Then create a compound verb using *and* or *or* and write the complete simple sentence on the lines.

1. The hailstorm

Verb

Verb

Simple Sentence: _____

2. Driving rain

Verb

Verb

Simple Sentence: _____

3. A news crew

Verb

Verb

Simple Sentence: _____

4. Many homes

Verb

Verb

Simple Sentence: _____

compound verb
two or more subjects joined by the
conjunction *or* or *and*

LO4 Compound Sentences

A **compound sentence** is made out of simple sentences joined by a coordinating conjunction: *and, but, or, nor, for, so,* or *yet*.

Compound of Two Sentences

Most compound sentences connect two simple sentences, or independent clauses. Connect the sentences by placing a comma and a coordinating conjunction between them.

Two Sentences: We drove all night. The sun rose behind us.

Compound Sentence: We drove all night, and the sun rose behind us.

You can also join two sentences with a semicolon.

Compound Sentence: We drove all night; the sun rose behind us.

Compound of Three or More Sentences

Sometimes, you may want to join three or more short sentences to form a compound sentence.

Three Sentences: I drove. Janice navigated. Paulo slept.

Compound Sentence: I drove, Janice navigated, and Paulo slept.

You can also join the sentences with semicolons. This approach works well for sharing a long, involved process or a flurry of activity.

I took the shift from Williamsburg to Monticello; Janice drove from Monticello to Louisville; Paulo brought us from Louisville to Indianapolis.

NOTE: Remember that a compound sentence is made of two or more simple sentences, each containing its own subject and verb.

Create Compound Sentences

Write   Write a simple sentence for each prompt; then combine them into a compound sentence.

1. What did you do on a road trip? _____

    What did a different person do? _____

    Compound sentence: _____

    _____

2. What do you like to eat? _____

    What does a friend like to eat? _____

    Compound sentence: _____

    _____

3. What did you do last weekend? _____

    What did a friend do? _____

    What did a relative do? _____

    Compound sentence: _____

    _____

4. Where do you want to go? _____

    Where does a friend want to go? _____

    Where does a relative want to go? _____

    Compound sentence: _____

    _____

5. What is your favorite place? _____

    What is a friend's favorite place? _____

    What is a relative's favorite place? _____

    Compound sentence: _____

    _____

compound sentence
two or more simple sentences joined with a
coordinating conjunction

LO5 Complex Sentences

A **complex sentence** shows a special relationship between two ideas. Instead of connecting two sentences as equal ideas (as in a compound sentence), a complex sentence shows that one idea depends on the other.

Using a Subordinating Conjunction

You can create a complex sentence by placing a subordinating conjunction before the sentence that is less important. Here are common subordinating conjunctions:

after	before	so that	when
although	even though	that	where
as	if	though	whereas
as if	in order that	till	while
as long as	provided that	'til	
because	since	until	

The subordinating conjunction shows that the one sentence depends on the other and cannot stand on its own.

Two Sentences:	We searched the package. We found no instructions.
Complex Sentence:	Though we searched the package, we found no instructions.
	We found no instructions though we searched the package.

NOTE: The subordinating conjunction begins the dependent clause, but the two clauses can be in either order. When the dependent clause comes second, it is usually not separated by a comma.

Compound-Complex

You can also create a **compound-complex sentence** by placing a subordinating conjunction before a simple sentence and connecting it to a compound sentence.

Simple Sentence:	I wouldn't give up.
Compound Sentence:	Jan went to watch TV, and Bill joined her.
Compound-Complex:	Although I wouldn't give up, Jan went to watch TV, and Bill joined her.

Create Complex Sentences

Write   Write a simple sentence for each prompt. Then select a subordinating conjunction from the facing page, place it at the beginning of one sentence, and combine the two sentences into a single complex sentence.

1. What did you look for? _____

   What did you find? _____

   Complex sentence: _____

2. Who helped you? _____

   Who did not help? _____

   Complex sentence: _____

3. What do you need? _____

   What did you get? _____

   Complex sentence: _____

4. What did you see? _____

   What did a friend see? _____

   Complex sentence: _____

5. Whom did you meet? _____

   Whom did you avoid? _____

   Complex sentence: _____

6. What did you win? _____

   What did you lose? _____

   Complex sentence: _____

CONSIDER SPEAKING AND LISTENING

Read the example complex and compound-complex sentences aloud. Despite their daunting names, these sentences aren't that complicated and are used often in speech. Experiment with them in your writing.

WilleeCole, 2013 / Used under license from Shutterstock.com

LO6 Complex Sentences with Relative Clauses

In a complex sentence, one idea depends on the other. You've seen how a dependent clause can start with a subordinating conjunction. Another type of dependent clause starts with a relative pronoun.

Relative Clauses

A **relative clause** is a group of words that begins with a **relative pronoun** (*that, which, who, whom*) and includes a verb and any words that modify or complete it.

Relative Clauses:	that celebrates my promotion
	which is very generous
	who comes to the party

Each relative clause above has a subject and a verb, but none of the clauses is a complete sentence. All need to be connected to independent clauses to complete their meaning.

Complex Sentences:	I hope you come to the party that celebrates my promotion.
	My boss gave me an office, which is very generous.
	I'll have a gift for everyone who comes to the party.

That and *Which*

The pronoun *that* signals information that is necessary to the meaning of the sentence. The pronoun *which* signals information that is not necessary, so the clause is set off with a comma.

That:	Please reserve the room **that** we will use. (The clause beginning with *that* defines the room.)
Which:	We'll have cheesecake, **which** I love. (The clause beginning with *which* just adds information about the cake.)

Who and *Whom*

The pronoun *who* is the subject of the relative clause that it introduces. The pronoun *whom* is a direct object in the clause it introduces.

Who:	I spoke to the woman **who** baked the cake. (*Who* is the subject.)
Whom:	I greeted the Joneses, **whom** I invited. (*Whom* is the direct object.)

20

"Another way to look at sentences is to see them as carriers of 'news.'"
—Scott Rice

Sentence Problems

Mathematics is full of problems. The whole point of math is to puzzle out a solution. And for each problem, there should be only one or, occasionally, a small set of right answers.

Writing is different. Sentences should not be full of problems. If a reader has to puzzle out the meaning of a sentence, the sentence *is* a problem. Sometimes a shift has occurred in person, tense, or voice. At other times, a modifier is misplaced or dangling. The result can be a sentence that confuses instead of communicates.

This chapter focuses on correcting these additional sentence problems. You'll find exercises for each type of problem as well as a real-world application.

Learning Outcomes

LO1 Common Fragments

LO2 Tricky Fragments

LO3 Comma Splices

LO4 Run-On Sentences

LO5 Rambling Sentences

LO6 Misplaced and Dangling Modifiers

LO7 Shifts in Sentence Construction

LO8 Real-World Application

LO9 Real-World Application

LO10 Real-World Application

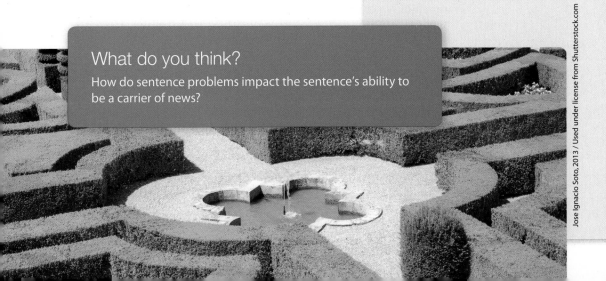

What do you think?

How do sentence problems impact the sentence's ability to be a carrier of news?

Jose Ignacio Soto, 2013 / Used under license from Shutterstock.com

LO1 Common Fragments

In spoken communication and informal writing, sentence fragments are occasionally used and understood. In formal writing, fragments should be avoided.

Missing Parts

A sentence requires a subject and a predicate. If one or the other or both are missing, the sentence is a **fragment**. Such fragments can be fixed by supplying the missing part.

Fragment:	Went to the concert.
Fragment + Subject:	We went to the concert.
Fragment:	Everyone from Westville Community College.
Fragment + Predicate:	Everyone from Westville Community College may participate.
Fragment:	For the sake of student safety.
Fragment + Subject and Predicate:	The president set up a curfew for the sake of student safety.

Incomplete Thoughts

A sentence also must express a complete thought. Some fragments have a subject and a verb but do not express a complete thought. These fragments can be corrected by providing words that complete the thought.

Fragment:	The concert will include.
Completing Thought:	The concert will include an amazing light show.
Fragment:	If we arrive in time.
Completing Thought:	If we arrive in time, we'll get front-row seats.
Fragment:	Which opened the concert.
Completing Thought:	I liked the bluegrass band which opened the concert.

Say It

Read these fragments aloud. Then read each one again, but this time supply the necessary words to form a complete thought.

1. The student union building.
2. Where you can buy used books.
3. Walked to class every morning.
4. When the instructor is sick.
5. The cop was.

Correct Add words to correct each fragment below. Write the complete sentence on the lines provided.

1. Groceries for our special meal.

_____

2. While I made the pasta, Maya prepared.

_____

3. Finished everything within forty-five minutes.

_____

4. Easily, the best meal ever.

_____

5. Not everyone likes.

_____

Correct The following paragraph contains numerous fragments. Either add what is missing or combine fragments with other sentences to make them complete. Use the correction marks shown below.

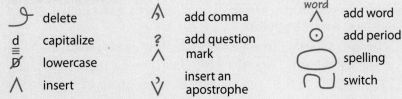

> The kitchen truly needs a new coat of paint. Everyone who uses the   *1*
> kitchen. Should help out. Need lots of help. If you have next Saturday
> afternoon to spare, plan to paint. Ben and I will provide. We'll try to pick
> a color that goes with the cabinets. When we are finished. The kitchen will
> be more pleasant for everyone to use. However, we won't guarantee that   *5*
> the food will taste any better.

Correction Marks

			word
⌐⎺ delete	⋏ add comma	∧ add word	
d̳ capitalize	? add question	⊙ add period	
∅̸ lowercase	∧ mark	⟲ spelling	
∧ insert	⌄ insert an apostrophe	⎌ switch	

Correct On your own paper or orally, correct the following fragments by supplying the missing parts. Use your imagination.

1. The front hall of the dorm.
2. When I arrived.
3. Was filled with new students.
4. Worked hard all morning.
5. Which was more than most people had done.

fragment
a group of words that is missing a subject or a predicate (or both) or that does not express a complete thought

LO2 Tricky Fragments

Some fragments are more difficult to find and correct. They creep into our writing because they are often part of the way we communicate in our speaking.

Absolute Phrases

An **absolute phrase** looks like a sentence that is missing its helping verb. An absolute phrase can be made into a sentence by adding the helping verb or by connecting the phrase to a complete sentence.

Absolute Phrase (Fragment):	Our legs trembling from the hike.
Absolute Phrase + Helping Verb:	Our legs were trembling from the hike.
Absolute Phrase + Complete Sentence:	We collapsed on the couch, our legs trembling from the hike.

Informal Fragments

Fragments that are commonly used in speech should be eliminated from formal writing. Avoid the following types of fragments unless you are writing dialogue.

Interjections:	Hey! Yeah!	**Questions:**	How come? Why not? What?
Exclamations:	What a nuisance! How fun!		
Greetings:	Hi, everybody. Good afternoon.	**Answers:**	About three or four. As soon as possible.

NOTE: Sentences that begin with *here* or *there* have a **delayed subject**, which appears after the verb. Other sentences (commands) have an **implied subject** (*you*). Such sentences are not fragments.

Delayed Subject:	Here are some crazy fans wearing wild hats.
Implied Subject:	Tackle him! Bring him down!

Say It

Read these fragments aloud. Then add words to form a complete thought.

1. Are three types of laptop computers.
2. Our instructor explaining the assignment.
3. About three in the morning.
4. Is my favorite Web site.
5. My friend working at a half-priced disk shop.

Fixing Tricky Fragments

Practice A   Rewrite each tricky fragment below, making it a sentence.

1. Their hearts melting at the sight of the orphaned pets.

   _____

2. The dogs yelping hellos and wagging their tails.

   _____

3. Our cats and dogs chasing each other and playing together.

   _____

4. Are many benefits to pet ownership.

   _____

5. The vet's office teeming with a variety of pets.

   _____

Practice B   The following paragraph contains a number of informal fragments. Identify and delete each one. Reread the paragraph and listen for the difference.

> Both dogs and cats have long been companions to humans. Awesome!   *1*
> Dogs started off as wolves at the end of the last Ice Age. What then?
> Human hunters killed off wolves that tried to take their food, but a wolf
> that was neither afraid of humans nor aggressive toward them might
> be spared. Living alongside people meant wolves were beginning to be   *5*
> domesticated, or comfortable in a human environment.
>   Cats, however, came a bit later, when humans had become farmers.
> Yeah. Ancient "barn cats" were probably the first kind. They loved to eat
> the mice and rats that fed on stored grains, and farmers let them. Perfect!
> If kittens are handled by humans, they become tame. If they are not, they   *10*
> stay wild.
>   That's why dogs like walks and cats like to stay home. Dogs joined us
> when we were walking everywhere, and cats arrived when we were staying
> put. Yessir.

absolute phrase a group of words with a noun and a participle (a word ending in *ing* or *ed*) and the words that modify them	**delayed subject** a subject that appears after the verb, as in a sentence that begins with *here* or *there* or a sentence that asks a question	**implied subject** the word *you*, assumed to begin command sentences

LO3 Comma Splices

Comma splices occur when two sentences are connected with only a comma. A comma splice can be fixed by adding a coordinating conjunction (*and, but, or, nor, for, so,* or *yet*) or a subordinating conjunction (*while, after, when,* and so on). The two sentences could also be joined by a semicolon (;) or separated by a period.

Comma Splice: The winners were announced, we were not mentioned.

Corrected by adding a coordinating conjunction:	The winners were announced, but we were not mentioned.
Corrected by adding a subordinating conjunction:	When the winners were announced, we were not mentioned.
Corrected by replacing the comma with a semicolon:	The winners were announced; we were not mentioned.

INSIGHT

A comma is not strong enough to join sentences without a conjunction. A semicolon can join two closely related sentences. A period or question mark can separate two sentences.

Comma Splice: Our instructor praised our efforts, he thought we deserved an award.

Corrected by adding a coordinating conjunction:	Our instructor praised our efforts, and he thought we deserved an award.
Corrected by adding a subordinating conjunction:	Our instructor praised our efforts because he thought we deserved an award.
Corrected by replacing the comma with a period:	Our instructor praised our efforts. He thought we deserved an award.

Correcting Comma Splices

Practice A Correct the following comma splices by adding a coordinating conjunction (*and, but, yet, or, nor, for, so*), adding a subordinating conjunction (*when, while, because,* and so on), or replacing the comma with a semicolon or period. Use the approach that makes the sentence read most smoothly.

1. Contests are set up to have many participants very few actually win.
2. Businesses run contests to stir up buzz, they are trying to advertise.
3. The business gives away a few prizes, it brings in many names and addresses.
4. Most people enter a contest for one reason, they want the prize, of course.
5. A business should follow up with entrants, they provide a marketing opportunity.
6. Both Bill and I entered the contest, we both were disappointed.
7. Then we received discount coupons, we were happy to get them.
8. Winning is a long shot, there are other benefits to entering.
9. We each used our coupons, the discount was significant.
10. We're on the lookout for another contest, maybe we'll have better luck in the future.

Practice B Rewrite the following paragraph, correcting any comma splices that you find.

Braille is a system of communication used by the blind. It was developed by Louis Braille in 1824. The system uses combinations of small raised dots to create an alphabet, the dots are imprinted on paper and can be felt. A blind person reads the page by running his or her fingers across the dots. The basic unit is called a cell, a cell is two dots wide and three dots high. Numbers, punctuation marks, and written music can be expressed with this system. Braille has allowed the blind to read, it is truly a great invention.

comma splice
a sentence error that occurs when two sentences are connected with only a comma

LO4 Run-On Sentences

A **run-on sentence** occurs when two sentences are joined without punctuation or a connecting word. A run-on can be corrected by adding a comma and a conjunction or by inserting a semicolon or period between the two sentences.

Run-On: I was feeling lucky I was totally wrong.

Corrected by adding a comma and coordinating conjunction:	I was feeling lucky, but I was totally wrong.
Corrected by adding a subordinating conjunction and a comma:	Although I was feeling lucky, I was totally wrong.
Corrected by inserting a semicolon:	I was feeling lucky; I was totally wrong.

INSIGHT

As you can see, run-ons and comma splices are very similar. As such, they can be corrected in the same basic ways.

Run-On: I signed up for the contest I had to write a story about robotic life.

Corrected by adding a comma and a coordinating conjunction:	I signed up for the contest, so I had to write a story about robotic life.
Corrected by adding a subordinating conjunction and a comma:	When I signed up for the contest, I had to write a story about robotic life.
Corrected by inserting a period:	I signed up for the contest. I had to write a story about robotic life.

Correcting Run-On Sentences

Correct   Correct the following run-on sentences. Use the approach that makes the sentence read most smoothly.

1. John McCarthy coined the term *artificial intelligence* this field deals with the intelligence of machines.

2. Thinking machines first appeared in Greek myths they have been a common feature in fiction since the 1800s.

3. True artificial intelligence could become a reality an electronic brain could be produced.

4. Scientists had computers solving algebra word problems people knew these machines could do incredible things.

5. Reports criticized the artificial intelligence movement funding for research stopped.

6. Funding is again very strong today artificial intelligence plays an important role in the technology industry.

7. Computers solve problems in one way human beings solve them in other ways.

8. People acquire a great deal of basic knowledge it would not be so easy to build this knowledge into machines.

Rewrite   Rewrite the following paragraph, correcting any run-on sentences that you find.

Smart Cars look like little water bugs on the road. They are only *1* about eight feet long they are less than five feet wide. You can fit two or three Smart Cars in a typical parking space. Smart Cars have been quite popular in Europe it remains to be seen how they will be received in the United States. By the way, the two co-stars in *The Da Vinci Code* raced *5* around Rome in one of these cars. Some versions of the Smart Car run on a three-cylinder engine they still can go from zero to 60 in about 15 seconds. They can get about 33 miles per gallon in the city and 41 miles per gallon on the highway.

run-on sentence
a sentence error that occurs when two sentences are joined without punctuation *or* a connecting word

LO5 Rambling Sentences

A rambling sentence occurs when a long series of separate ideas are connected by one *and, but,* or *so* after another. The result is an unfocused sentence that goes on and on. To correct a rambling sentence, break it into smaller units, adding and cutting words as needed.

Rambling: When we first signed up for the contest, I had no thought that we would win, but then my brother started talking about how he would spend the money and he asked me if he could have my share of it, so we were counting on winning even though we really had no chance and as it turned out we of course didn't win.

Corrected: When we first signed up for the contest, I had no thought that we would win. Then my brother started talking about how he would spend the money. He even asked for my share. Soon, we were counting on winning even though we had no chance. As it turned out, we didn't win.

Say It

Read the following rambling sentences aloud. Afterward, circle all of the connecting words (*and, but, so*), and be prepared to suggest different ways to break each rambling idea into more manageable units.

1. I enjoyed touring the hospital and I would enjoy joining the nursing staff and I believe that my prior work experience will be an asset but I also know that I have a lot more to learn.

2. The electronics store claims to offer "one-stop shopping" and they can take care of all of a customer's computer needs and they have a fully trained staff to answer questions and solve problems so there is really no need to go anywhere else.

Correct Correct the following rambling sentences by dividing some of the ideas into separate sentences.

1. The cat entered silently through the window and next he jumped onto a chair and darted behind the curtain so he could hide from everyone and then he curled up and relaxed for a while.

_____

_____

_____

2. I went to the dentist yesterday and when I got there, I had to wait forever to see him and when he finally examined my teeth, he found two cavities and now I have to go back next week to get fillings and I don't want to go.

_____

_____

_____

3. We use trampolines for entertainment but they were used for other purposes a long time ago and Eskimos once used a form of a trampoline made from skins to watch for whales and seals and I think that is a much better use of a trampoline than to just jump up and down on it so I wonder what practical way we can use them today.

_____

_____

_____

_____

_____

Correct In the space provided below, write a rambling sentence or idea about a topic of your own choosing. Afterward, exchange your work with a classmate, and correct each other's rambling idea.

_____

_____

_____

_____

LO6 Misplaced and Dangling Modifiers

Dangling Modifiers

A modifier is a word, phrase, or clause that functions as an adjective or adverb. When the modifier does not clearly modify another word in the sentence, it is called a **dangling modifier**. This error can be corrected by inserting the missing word and/or rewriting the sentence.

Dangling Modifier: After buckling the fancy red collar around his neck, my dog pranced proudly down the street. *(The dog could buckle his own collar?)*

Corrected: After I buckled the fancy red collar around his neck, my dog pranced proudly down the street.

Dangling Modifier: Trying desperately to chase a rabbit, I was pulled toward the bushes. *(The person was chasing the rabbit?)*

Corrected: Trying desperately to chase a rabbit, my dog pulled me toward the bushes.

Misplaced Modifiers

When a modifier is placed beside a word that it does not modify, the modifier is misplaced and often results in an amusing or **illogical** statement. A **misplaced modifier** can be corrected by moving it next to the word that it modifies.

Misplaced Modifier: The dog was diagnosed by the vet with mange. *(The vet has mange?)*

Corrected: The vet diagnosed the dog with mange.

Misplaced Modifier: The vet gave a chewable pill to the dog tasting like liver. *(The dog tastes like liver?)*

Corrected: The vet gave my dog a pill tasting like liver.

INSIGHT ——————————————————————————————

Avoid placing any adverb modifiers between a verb and its direct object.

Misplaced: I will throw quickly the ball.

Corrected: I will quickly throw the ball.

Also, do not separate two-word verbs with an adverb modifier.

Misplaced: Please take immediately out the trash.

Corrected: Please immediately take out the trash.

Say It

Read the following sentences aloud, noting the dangling or misplaced modifier in each one. Then tell a classmate how you would correct each error.

1. The new dog park makes good use of vacant property called Dog Heaven.
2. You will usually find an old basset hound running around the park with extremely stubby legs.

Correcting Dangling and Misplaced Modifiers

Rewrite Rewrite each of the sentences below, correcting the misplaced and dangling modifiers.

1. We saw a buck and a doe on the way to marriage counseling.

2. The car was reported stolen by the police.

3. We have new phones for hard-of-hearing people with loud ring tones.

4. Please present the proposal that is attached to Mr. Brumbly.

5. I drove with Jennie to the place where we live in a Buick.

6. I found some moldy cheese in the fridge that doesn't belong to me.

7. I bought a parrot for my brother named Squawky.

Correct For each sentence, correct the placement of the adverb.

1. Provide promptly the form to Human Resources.

2. We will initiate immediately your new insurance.

3. Please fill carefully out the form.

dangling modifier	**illogical**	**misplaced modifier**
a modifying word, phrase, or clause that appears to modify the wrong word or a word that isn't in the sentence	without logic; senseless, false, or untrue	a modifying word, phrase, or clause that has been placed incorrectly in a sentence, often creating an amusing or illogical idea

LO7 Shifts in Sentence Construction

Shift in Person

A **shift in person** is an error that occurs when first, second, and/or third person are improperly mixed in a sentence.

> **Shift in person:** Once you feel better, you can do everything an individual loves to do. (The sentence improperly shifts from second person—*you*—to third person—*individual*.)
>
> **Corrected:** Once you feel better, you can do everything you love to do.

Shift in Tense

A **shift in tense** is an error that occurs when more than one verb tense is improperly used in a sentence. (See pages 542–549 for more about tense.)

> **Shift in tense:** I searched everywhere before I find my essay. (The sentence improperly shifts from past tense—*searched*—to present tense—*find*.)
>
> **Corrected:** I searched everywhere before I found my essay.

Shift in Voice

A **shift in voice** is an error that occurs when active voice and passive voice are mixed in a sentence.

> **Shift in voice:** As you search for your essay, your keys may also be found. (The sentence improperly shifts from active voice—*search*—to passive voice—*may be found*.)
>
> **Corrected:** As you search for your essay, you may also find your keys.

Say It

Read the following sentences aloud, paying careful attention to the improper shift each contains. Then tell a classmate how you would correct each error.

1. Margo drinks plenty of fluids and got plenty of rest.
2. Landon is running again and many new routes are being discovered by him.
3. When you are ready to work, a person can search for jobs online.
4. Charley served as a tutor in the writing lab and helps English language learners with their writing.

Correcting Improper Shifts in Sentences

Rewrite   Rewrite each sentence below, correcting any improper shifts in construction.

1. I jogged along the wooded path until I feel exhausted.

_____

2. As we drove to the movie theater, favorite comedies had been discussed by us.

_____

3. When you drop off my toolbox, can he or she also return my grill?

_____

Correct   Correct the improper shifts in person, tense, or voice in the following paragraph. Use the correction marks below when you make your changes.

> When you think about today's technology, the first word that comes to mind was convenience. For instance, if you traveled before the creation of the Internet, printed maps were used by you. And if you were traveling out of state, a person needed to purchase other state maps from a gas station or convenience store. You would unfold each map, and the best possible route was planned by you. Now you have access to digital maps, personal navigation systems, and Web sites to find your way. You probably enjoy the ease and speed of the new technology and thought the old methods are tiresome.

1

5

Correction Marks

⟋ delete	⅃ add comma	word ∧ add word
d̲ capitalize	? add question mark	⊙ add period
ø̸ lowercase		⌒ spelling
∧ insert	ⱽ insert an apostrophe	∿ switch

person	voice of verb	shift in tense
first person (*I* or *we*—the person speaking), second person (*you*—the person spoken to), or third person (*he, she, it,* or *they*—the person or thing spoken about)	whether the subject is doing the action of the verb (active voice) or is being acted upon (passive voice) (See page 540.)	an error that occurs when more than one verb tense is improperly used in a sentence
	shift in person	**shift in voice**
	an error that occurs when first, second, and third person are improperly mixed in a sentence	an error that occurs when active voice and passive voice are mixed in a sentence

LO8 Real-World Application

Correct Correct any sentence fragments in the following business memo. Use the correction marks below.

3041 45th Avenue
Lake City, WI 53000
November 14, 2010

1

Ms. Colleen Turner
Human Resource Director
Western Printing Company
100 Mound Avenue
Racine, WI 53001

5

Dear Ms. Turner:

In response to your advertisement in the *Racine Standard Press* on
November 12, I am writing to apply for the position of Graphic Designer.
Have worked as a designer for Alpha Publications in Brookfield, Wisconsin,
for the past three years.

10

I worked with a team of talented designers to create business handbooks
and workbooks, including the award-winning handbook *Write for Business.*
Our team each product from early design ideas to preparation of the final
disk. My special skills include coloring illustrations and incorporating
graphics in page design.

15

My experience with design software packages includes Adobe InDesign,
Photoshop, and Illustrator.

20

Enclosed is my résumé. Gives more information about my qualifications
and training. I look forward to hearing from you and can be reached at
(200) 555-6655 or at aposada@atz.com. Thank you for your consideration.

Sincerely,

Anna Posada

25

Anna Posada
Encl. résumé

Correction Marks

✄ delete	⌃ add comma	word ⌃ add word
d̲ capitalize	? add question mark	⊙ add period
D̸ lowercase	⌃ insert	⌣ spelling
⌃ insert	⌄ insert an apostrophe	⌇ switch

LO9 Real-World Application

Correct Correct any comma splices or run-on sentences in the following sales letter.

Dale's Garden Center
405 Cherry Lane
Flower City, IL 53185

> NOTE: An *ing* or *ed* phrase is called a participial phrase and serves as an adjective in a sentence. (See page 550 for more information.)

February 1, 2011

Dear Gateway College Student:

Did one of your science instructors ever tell you that plants can talk? Well, they can.Dale's flowers speak the language of romance.   *1*

With Valentine's Day just two weeks away, let Dale's flowers give you the words to share with your sweetheart. Red roses share your love in the traditional way, a Southern Charm Bouquet says the same thing with a   *5* little more class. Or send "poetry" by choosing our Valentine Special in a porcelain vase!

Check out the enclosed selection guide then place your order by phoning 1-800-555-LEAF. If you call by February 13, we promise delivery of fresh flowers on Valentine's Day.   *10*

Let Dale's flowers help you start a conversation that could last a lifetime!

Sincerely,

Dale Brown

P.S. Long-distance romances are not a problem, we deliver flowers anywhere in the world.   *15*

Extend Correct each of the following comma splices or run-on sentences by changing one of the sentences into an *ing* or *ed* phrase and connecting it to the other sentence. The first one has been done for you.

1. Carnations are a very popular flower they show love and wonder.

   _____

2. The iris is an elegant flower, it is distinguished by its special blue color.

   _____

LO10 Real-World Application

Correct Correct any dangling modifiers, misplaced modifiers, or shifts in construction in the following message. (Only one sentence is free of errors.) Use the correction marks below.

 Home Builders

1650 Northwest Boulevard • St. Louis, MO 63124
314-555-9800 • FAX 314-555-9810 • www.homebuilders-stl.org

February 15, 2010   *1*

Philip Tranberg
1000 Ivy Street
St. Louis, MO 63450

Dear Philip: *5*

You show a strong interest in Home Builders and the desire to provide people with affordable housing is expressed by you.

First review the enclosed list in Missouri of Home Builders affiliates. Each affiliate handles your own assignments and work groups. Then check the enclosed brochure for additional affiliates on Home Builders campus   *10* chapters. This brochure shows you how to join or start a campus chapter and explained service learning for academic credit. Ben Abramson, the Campus Outreach Coordinator, would love to talk with you, and he can be contacted by you at the address printed on the brochure.

Again, thank you for your interest in providing affordable housing with   *15* Home Builders.

Sincerely,

Matthew Osgoode

Matthew Osgoode

Enclosures   *20*

Correction Marks

℘	delete	⌃	add comma	*word* ⌃	add word
d̲	capitalize	?	add question	⊙	add period
ȼ	lowercase	⌃	mark	⌒	spelling
⌃	insert	⌄	insert an apostrophe	⌣	switch

Using Different Classes of Nouns

Identify In each sentence below, identify the underlined nouns as common (C) or proper (P).

1. Waterfalls capture the imagination.

2. Niagara Falls is the most powerful set of falls in North America.

3. Niagara Falls is nearly 4,400 feet wide, but Victoria Falls is well over 5,500 feet wide.

4. Every second, 85,000 gallons of water rush over Niagara Falls.

Identify In each sentence below, identify the underlined nouns as individual (I) or collective (CL).

1. The tallest cascade is Angel Falls in Venezuela at 3,212 feet.

2. A team of explorers led by Ruth Robertson measured the height of Angel Falls in 1949.

3. In 1937, Jimmie Angel crash-landed on the falls; a crew had to bring the plane down.

4. The company that made *Up* drew inspiration for Paradise Falls from Angel Falls.

Identify In each sentence below, identify the underlined nouns as concrete (CT) or abstract (A).

1. Iguazu Falls is at the border of Argentina and Brazil.

2. Tourists gaze with wonder and amazement at 275 falls spread over 1.9 miles.

3. The largest fall, Devil's Throat, roars like a devil full of rage.

4. When Eleanor Roosevelt saw them, she said in awe, "Poor Niagara!"

---

common noun
noun referring to a general person, place, thing, or idea; not capitalized as a name

proper noun
noun referring to a specific person, place, thing, or idea; capitalized as a name

individual noun
noun referring to one person or thing

collective noun
noun referring to a group of people or animals

concrete noun
noun referring to something that can be sensed

abstract noun
noun referring to an idea, a condition, or a feeling—something that cannot be sensed

LO2 Singular and Plural Nouns

The **number** of a noun indicates whether it is singular or plural. A **singular** noun refers to one person, place, thing, or idea. A **plural** noun refers to more than one person, place, thing, or idea. For most words, the plural is formed by adding *s*. For nouns ending in *ch, s, sh, x,* or *z,* add an *es*.

	Most Nouns Add *s*		Nouns Ending in *ch, s, sh, x,* or *z* Add *es*	
	Singular	Plural	Singular	Plural
Person:	sister	sisters	coach	coaches
Place:	park	parks	church	churches
Thing:	spoon	spoons	kiss	kisses
Idea:	solution	solutions	wish	wishes

Same in Both Forms or Usually Plural

Some nouns are the same in both forms, and others are usually plural:

Same in Both Forms		Usually Plural	
Singular	Plural	Plural	
deer	deer	clothes	series
fish	fish	glasses	shears
moose	moose	pants	shorts
salmon	salmon	proceeds	species
sheep	sheep	savings	tongs
swine	swine	scissors	trousers

Irregular Plurals

Irregular plurals are formed by changing the words themselves. That is because the plural form comes from Old English or Latin.

From Old English		From Latin	
Singular	Plural	Singular	Plural
child	children	alumnus	alumni
foot	feet	axis	axes
goose	geese	crisis	crises
man	men	datum	data
mouse	mice	millennium	millennia
person	people	medium	media
tooth	teeth	nucleus	nuclei
woman	women	phenomenon	phenomena

Using Singular and Plural Nouns

Identify   For each word, fill in the blank with either the singular or plural form, whichever is missing. If the word usually uses the plural form or is the same in both forms, write an X on the line.

1. boy   _____
2. _____ girls
3. child   _____
4. man   _____
5. _____ women
6. deer   _____
7. _____ clothes
8. _____ species
9. swine   _____
10. axis   _____
11. _____ teeth
12. _____ millennia
13. automobile   _____
14. tree   _____
15. _____ pants
16. _____ moose
17. phenomenon   _____
18. crisis   _____
19. _____ mice
20. _____ savings
21. _____ data
22. alumnus   _____
23. goose   _____
24. fish   _____
25. _____ shears

number	**plural**	**irregular plural**
whether a word is singular or plural	referring to more than one thing	a plural noun formed by changing the word rather than by adding *s*
singular		
referring to one thing		

LO3 Tricky Plurals

Some plural nouns are more challenging to form. Words ending in *y, f,* or *fe* and certain compound nouns require special consideration.

Nouns Ending in *y*

If a common noun ends in *y* after a consonant, change the *y* to *i* and add *es*. If the noun ends in *y* after a vowel, leave the *y* and add *s*.

y After a Consonant		*y* After a Vowel	
Singular	Plural	Singular	Plural
fly	flies	bay	bays
lady	ladies	key	keys
penny	pennies	toy	toys
story	stories	tray	trays

Nouns Ending in *f* or *fe*

If a common noun ends in *f* or *fe,* change the *f* or *fe* to a *v* and add *es*—unless the *f* sound remains in the plural form. Then just add an *s*.

v Sound in Plural		*f* Sound in Plural	
Singular	Plural	Singular	Plural
calf	calves	belief	beliefs
life	lives	chef	chefs
self	selves	proof	proofs
shelf	shelves	safe	safes

Compound Nouns

A **compound noun** is made up of two or more words that function together as a single noun. Whether the compound is hyphenated or not, make it plural by placing the *s* or *es* on the most important word in the compound.

Important Word First		Important Word Last	
Singular	Plural	Singular	Plural
editor in chief	editors in chief	bird-watcher	bird-watchers
mother-in-law	mothers-in-law	human being	human beings
professor emeritus	professors emeritus	test tube	test tubes
secretary of state	secretaries of state	well-wisher	well-wishers

Forming Tricky Plurals

Form Plurals For each word below, create the correct plural form.

1. ray _____
2. elf _____
3. high school _____
4. bunny _____
5. boy _____
6. leaf _____
7. reef _____
8. calf _____
9. guy _____
10. credit card _____

11. brother-in-law _____
12. day _____
13. patty _____
14. café _____
15. sister-in-law _____
16. fife _____
17. rear guard _____
18. jury _____
19. power of attorney _____
20. poppy _____

Form Plurals In the sentences below, correct the plural errors by writing the correct forms.

1. I read two different storys about ladys who swallowed flys.
2. The toies on the shelfs belong to my stepchilds.
3. The cheves served salmon pattys with the soup of the days.
4. After a few daies, the daisys sprouted in the flowers box.
5. The secretary of states from both countrys discussed the treatys.
6. I saw mud puppys and rivers otter on my hike.
7. He gave me four pennys, which I divided between the two take-a-penny traies.
8. The keis for my carries-on are missing.
9. Why is "elfs" spelled one way and "dwarves" spelled the other?
10. The crys of babys usually alert parents.

compound noun
noun made up of two or more words

LO4 Count and Noncount Nouns

Some nouns name things that can be counted, and other nouns name things that cannot. Different rules apply to each type.

Count Nouns

Count nouns name things that can be counted—*pens, people, votes, cats,* and so forth. They can be singular or plural, and they can be preceded by numbers or articles (*a, an,* or *the*).

Singular	Plural
grape	grapes
dog	dogs
car	cars
idea	ideas

INSIGHT

Many native English speakers aren't even aware of count and noncount nouns, though they use them correctly out of habit. Listen for their use of count and noncount nouns.

Noncount Nouns

Noncount nouns name things that cannot be counted. They are used in singular form, and they can be preceded by *the,* but not by *a* or *an*.

This semester, I'm taking **mathematics** and **biology** as well as **Spanish**.

Substances	Foods	Activities	Science	Languages	Abstractions
wood	water	reading	oxygen	Spanish	justice
cloth	milk	boating	weather	English	harm
ice	wine	smoking	heat	Mandarin	publicity
plastic	sugar	dancing	sunshine	Farsi	advice
wool	rice	swimming	electricity	Greek	happiness
steel	meat	soccer	lightning	Latin	health
aluminum	cheese	hockey	biology	French	joy
metal	flour	photography	history	Japanese	love
leather	pasta	writing	mathematics	Afrikaans	anger
porcelain	gravy	homework	economics	German	fame

Two-Way Nouns

Two-way nouns can function as count or noncount nouns, depending on their context.

Please set a **glass** in front of each place mat. (count noun)

The display case was made of tempered **glass**. (noncount noun)

Using Count and Noncount Nouns

Sort Read the list of nouns below and sort the words into columns of count and noncount nouns.

door	wool	vacation	happiness	sunshine
heat	tablecloth	wagon	photography	flour
swimming	cherry	French	ruler	tablespoon

Using Count and Noncount Nouns

Correct Read the following paragraph and correct the noun errors. Write down the line number and any words you would change. Then show what changes you would make. The first line has been done for you.

There are different activities for ~~four~~ different weathers. For days   *1*

with sunshines, outdoor activities are best. Some people enjoy swimmings,

others like boatings, and even more play soccers. For days in the

spring or fall, quieter activities work well. Writing poetries and enjoying

photographies are good pastimes, as well as dancings. During the winter,   *5*

there are readings and homeworks to do. The key to happinesses is to enjoy

whatever you are doing.

Correction Marks

୬	delete	⅄	add comma	word ∧	add word
d̿	capitalize	?	add question mark	⊙	add period
D̸	lowercase	∧		⌒	spelling
∧	insert	⌄	insert an apostrophe	⌌⌍	switch

count noun	**noncount noun**	**two-way noun**
noun naming something that can be counted	noun naming something that cannot be counted	noun that can function as either a count or a noncount noun

LO6 Other Noun Markers

Other words help provide information about nouns.

Possessive Adjective

A **possessive adjective** is the possessive form of a noun or pronoun. Possessive adjectives can be formed by adding *'s* to singular nouns and *'* to plural nouns.

Dave's email came back, but **Ellen's** didn't.

Milwaukee's harbor is usually calm.

The **Smiths'** house needs painting.

That is **my** car. That car is **mine**.

It's **your** book. The book is **yours**.

Possessive Pronouns

	Singular		Plural	
	Before	After	Before	After
First Person	my	mine	our	ours
Second Person	your	yours	your	yours
Third Person	his	his	their	theirs
	her	hers	their	theirs
	its	its	their	theirs

Indefinite Adjectives

An **indefinite adjective** signals that the noun it marks refers to a general person, place, thing, or idea. Some indefinite adjectives mark count nouns and others mark noncount nouns.

All people are welcome to join. **Much** celebrating will be done.

With Count Nouns			With Noncount Nouns	With Count or Noncount		
each	either	every	much	all	any	more
few	many	neither		most	some	
several						

Demonstrative Adjectives

A **demonstrative adjective** marks a specific noun. The words *this* and *that* (singular) or *these* and *those* (plural) demonstrate exactly which one is meant.

These songs are by **that** artist.   **This** song includes **those** lyrics.

Quantifiers

A **quantifier** tells *how many* or *how much* there is of something.

With Count Nouns		With Noncount Nouns		With Count or Noncount		
each	a couple of	a bag of	a little	no	a lot of	most
several	every	a bowl of	much	not any	lots of	all
a number of	many	a piece of	a great deal of	some	plenty of	
both	a few					
nine						

Using Noun Markers

Identify   Indicate the appropriate noun marker in parentheses for each sentence.

1. Please leave (*your, yours*) phone number after the beep.
2. Is this phone number (*your, yours*)?
3. How (*many, much*) students are allowed in the class?
4. The professor did not give us (*any, each*) homework.
5. I want to buy (*this, these*) shirts.
6. The resident assistant didn't like (*that, those*) idea.
7. After making the dough, we had (*several, a little*) flour left.
8. I liked (*a number of, much*) the suggestions.
9. The proposal was originally (*her, hers*).
10. Let's make sure to return (*their, theirs*) pillows.

Correct   In the following paragraph, delete or replace any noun markers that are incorrectly used. Write down the line number and any words you would change. Then show what changes you would make. The first line has been done for you.

> your
> What is ~~yours~~ major? You probably have heard that ~~much~~ many times. But   *1*
> taking a little courses in one area does not mean it is yours major. Much
> students don't choose a major until theirs junior year. This students have
> to explore theirs options before making up theirs minds. Those delay isn't
> a problem. Those exploration is the point of undergraduate study. Until you   *5*
> know for sure a major is your, you should taste-test much fields. In mine
> junior year, I was told I would not graduate unless I picked mine major. I
> added up mine hours, and that total showed I was
> closest to English. Two weeks later, the head of the
> English Department called and said, "I thought we   *10*
> should meet since you are one of mine majors."

Correction Marks

✄	delete
d̲̲	capitalize
ȸ	lowercase
∧	insert
⌄	add comma
?	add question
∧	mark
word ∧	add word
⊙	add period
◯	spelling
∿	switch

possessive adjective
the possessive form of a noun or pronoun, showing ownership of another noun

indefinite adjective
an indefinite pronoun (*many, much, some*) used as an adjective to mark a nonspecific noun

demonstrative adjective
a demonstrative pronoun (*this, that, those*) used as an adjective to mark a specific noun

quantifier
a modifier that tells *how many* or *how much*

LO7 Real-World Application

Correct In the following letter, correct any errors with nouns, articles, or other noun markers. Write down the line number and any words you would change. Then show what changes you would make.

Dale's Garden Center
405 Cherry Lane • Flower City, IL 53185

February 1, 2010   *1*

Dear Student:

Did one of yours science professors ever tell you that plants can talk?
Well, they can. Dale flowers speak a language of love to the womans or
mans in your life.   *5*

If you're at an loss for words with valentine's day just two weeks away,
let Dale's flowers give you the words. Red roses share yours love in the
language of Romance. A Southern charm bouquet says it with class and
a added touch of Magnolias. Or send poetries by choosing our Valentine's
Day special in a porcelain vase!   *10*

Come browse our shelfs. Or check out the enclosed catalog and place
yours order by phoning 1-800-555-LEAF. If you call by february 13,
we guarantee delivery of fresh flowers on Valentine's Day. Order by
Februaries 10, and you'll receive an 20 percent discount.

Let Dales' flowers help you start a conversation that could last a lifetime!   *15*

Sincerely,

Jerilynn Bostwick

Jerilynn Bostwick
Sales Manager

P.S. Is your a long-distance romance? Remember, we deliver flowers   *20*
anywhere in the world through the telefloral network.

22

Pronoun

"The personal pronoun in English has three cases, the dominative, the objectionable, and the oppressive."
—Ambrose Bierce

Mannequins are everywhere—trying to sell this dress or that shirt, trying to show you a suit or a pair of shorts. The reason mannequins are everywhere is that it would be too expensive and boring for real people to stand around all day showing off clothing.

Pronouns are like mannequins—they are stand-ins for nouns. They aren't nouns, but they refer back to them. Writing that has no pronouns quickly becomes overloaded with nouns, repetitive and hard to read. So a pronoun can take the noun's place.

This chapter will show you how to make sure your pronoun stand-ins work well.

Learning Outcomes

LO1 Personal Pronouns
LO2 Pronoun-Antecedent Agreement
LO3 Other Pronoun Problems
LO4 Indefinite Pronouns
LO5 Relative Pronouns
LO6 Other Pronoun Types
LO7 Real-World Application

What do you think?

Have you ever confused a mannequin for a real person?
What was the result?

LO1 Personal Pronouns

A **pronoun** is a word that takes the place of a noun or another pronoun. The most common type of pronoun is the **personal pronoun**. Personal pronouns indicate whether the person is speaking, is being spoken to, or is being spoken about.

Person	Singular			Plural		
	Nom.	**Obj.**	**Poss.**	**Nom.**	**Obj.**	**Poss.**
First (speaking)	I	me	my/mine	we	us	our/ours
Second (spoken to)	you	you	your/yours	you	you	your/yours
Third (spoken about) masculine	he	him	his	they	them	their/theirs
feminine	she	her	her/hers	they	them	their/theirs
neuter	it	it	its	they	them	their/theirs

Nom. = nominative case / **Obj.** = objective case / **Poss.** = possessive case

Case of Pronouns

The **case** of a personal pronoun indicates how it can be used.

- **Nominative** pronouns are used as the subjects of sentences or as subject complements (following the linking verbs *am, is, are, was, were, be, being,* or *been*).

  I was nominated, but the person selected was she.

- **Objective** pronouns are used as direct objects, indirect objects, or objects of prepositions.

  The professor lectured them about it.

- **Possessive** pronouns show ownership and function as adjectives.

  My notebook has fewer notes than hers.

Gender

Pronouns can be **masculine**, **feminine**, or **neuter**.

She helped him with it.

Say It

Read the following aloud.
1. *I* am / *You* are / *He* is / *She* is / *It* is / *We* are / *They* are
2. Help *me* / Help *you* / Help *him* / Help *her* / Help *it* / Help *us* / Help *them*

Using Personal Pronouns

Select   For each sentence below, select the correct personal pronoun in parentheses.
1. The dorm cafeteria is where *(I, me, my)* friends gather.
2. *(We, Us, Our)* talk about classes and also about each other.
3. I told Emily that I would help *(she, her, hers)* with her homework.
4. I have a heavy schedule, but not as heavy as *(she, her, hers)* is.
5. *(I, Me, My, Mine)* 18 credits require less work than *(she, her, hers)* 20.

Correct   In the following paragraph, correct the pronouns. Write the line number and any incorrect pronoun. Cross it out and write a correction beside it.

> I asked me sons if them would like to take a walk around Lake   *1*
> Geneva. Them asked how us could walk around the lake. I told they that
> a path goes all the way around the lake, and its is open to the public. My
> sons said that them wanted to go, but them wondered how far the walk
> was. Me told they that it was about 30 miles. They mouths dropped open.   *5*
> Them couldn't figure out what to say to I. My sons and me looked at each
> other. Then I said them needed to get theirs backpacks and shoes. They
> told me that I should get a life. But I convinced they, and us hiked all the
> way around Lake Geneva. When it was over, I wished I had listened to
> they. My legs hurt so much!   *10*

pronoun a word that takes the place of a noun or other pronoun **personal pronoun** a pronoun that indicates whether the person is speaking, is spoken to, or is spoken about	**case** whether a pronoun is used as a subject, an object, or a possessive **nominative** used as a subject or subject complement **objective** used as a direct object, an indirect object, or an object of a preposition	**possessive** used to show ownership **masculine** male **feminine** female **neuter** neither male nor female

LO2 Pronoun-Antecedent Agreement

The **antecedent** is the word that a pronoun refers to or replaces. A pronoun must have the same person, number, and gender as the antecedent, which is called **pronoun-antecedent agreement**.

> **third-person**   **singular feminine**
>
> Linda asked to borrow a pen but then found hers.

Agreement in Person

A pronoun needs to match its antecedent in **person** (first, second, or third).

> **third person**   **second person**
>
> **Incorrect:** If people look hard, you might find some good deals.
> **Correct:** If you look hard, you might find some good deals.
> **Correct:** If people look hard, they might find some good deals.

Agreement in Number

A pronoun needs to match its antecedent in **number** (singular or plural).

> **singular**   **plural**
>
> **Incorrect:** Each student should bring their assignment.
> **Correct:** Students should bring their assignments.
> **Correct:** Each student should bring her or his assignment.

Agreement in Gender

A pronoun needs to match its antecedent in **gender** (masculine, feminine, or neuter).

> **feminine**   **masculine**
>
> **Incorrect:** Janae will share his project.
> **Correct:** Janae will share her project.

Correcting Agreement Errors

Correct Person   Rewrite each sentence to correct the person error.

1. If both of you go to the job fair, they will probably find job opportunities.

   _____

2. We went to the fair last year, and they landed some good jobs.

   _____

3. If the graduates fill out applications, you may find jobs.

   _____

4. One considers the future when you attend the fair.

   _____

Correct Number   Rewrite each sentence to correct the number error.

5. Each applicant should put down their name.

   _____

6. An employee will greet you, and they will interview you.

   _____

7. Applicants should supply his contact information.

   _____

Correct Gender   Rewrite each sentence to correct the gender error.

8. If Lionel goes, she can drive others.

   _____

9. Tawny said he was going.

   _____

10. Ask David if she is planning to attend.

   _____

11. The hall is big, and she sits at a major intersection.

   _____

antecedent	**person**	**gender**
the word that a pronoun refers to or replaces	whether the pronoun is speaking, being spoken to, or being spoken about	whether the pronoun is masculine, feminine, or neuter
pronoun-antecedent agreement		
matching a pronoun to its antecedent in terms of person, number, and gender	**number** whether the pronoun is singular or plural	

LO3 Other Pronoun Problems

Pronouns are very useful parts of speech, but if they are mishandled, they can cause problems.

Vague Pronoun

Do not use a pronoun that could refer to more than one antecedent.

> **Unclear:** Lupe spoke to her roommate and her sister.
> **Clear:** Lupe spoke to her roommate and her roommate's sister.

Missing Antecedent

Avoid using *it* or *they* without clear antecedents.

> **Unclear:** It says in the tabloid that a donkey-boy was born.
> **Clear:** The tabloid says that a donkey-boy was born.
>
> **Unclear:** They have found one of the causes of arthritis.
> **Clear:** Scientists have found one of the causes of arthritis.

Double Subjects

Do not place a pronoun right after the subject. Doing so creates an error called a **double subject**, which is not a standard construction.

> **Incorrect:** Kyle and Jules, they went to the movies.
> **Correct:** Kyle and Jules went to the movies.

Usage Errors *(They're, You're, It's)*

Do not confuse possessive pronouns (*your, their, its*) with contractions (*you're, they're, it's*). Remember that contractions use apostrophes in place of missing letters.

> **Incorrect:** Please place you're plastic bottles in they're recycling bin.
> **Correct:** Please place your plastic bottles in their recycling bin.

CONSIDER SPEAKING AND LISTENING

The pronoun problems on this page may not cause confusion in spoken English. In written English, these problems can derail meaning. Correct them in your writing.

Correcting Other Pronoun Problems

Rewrite Rewrite each sentence to correct the pronoun-reference problems.

1. Raul asked his father and his friend to help him move.

_____

2. It says in the article that three people are trapped.

_____

3. They are proposing an amendment to the Constitution.

_____

4. Shakira wants her sister and her friend to help.

_____

5. It says in the news report that stocks are down.

_____

6. They have a new cure for baldness.

_____

Correct In the following paragraph, correct the pronoun errors. Write the line number and any words you would change. Then show how you would change them.

> It says on the Internet that many major companies have pulled April   _1_
> Fool's Day pranks. They replaced the name "Google" with the name
> "Topeka," for one. It says also that a rare baby skeksis was born in a
> zoo, but it exists only in the film _The Dark Crystal_. One classical music
> station, it claimed that a British billionaire was sending a violinist to   _5_
> the moon in a special spaceship. It's console had a button to make the
> ship's cockpit sound like the Royal Albert Hall. They had a lot of fun
> with they're gags, but gullible people kept getting tripped up all day. It
> also claims that in the UK, Australia, and South Africa, the gags stop
> at noon, but they're citizens, they still get pranked by Americans all day.   _10_

vague pronoun	missing antecedent	double subject	usage error
using a pronoun that could refer to more than one antecedent	using a pronoun that has no clear antecedent	error created by following a subject with a pronoun	using the wrong word (e.g., _they're_ instead of _their_)

LO4 Indefinite Pronouns

An **indefinite pronoun** does not have an antecedent, and it does not refer to a specific person, place, thing, or idea. These pronouns pose unique issues with subject-verb and pronoun-antecedent agreement.

Singular Indefinite Pronouns

Some indefinite pronouns are singular. When they are used as subjects, they require a singular verb. As antecedents, they must be matched to singular pronouns.

each	anyone	anybody	anything
either	someone	somebody	something
neither	everyone	everybody	everything
another	no one	nobody	nothing
one			

Someone is supposed to empty the dishwasher.

No one has said he will do it.

Plural Indefinite Pronouns

Some indefinite pronouns are plural. As subjects, they require a plural verb, and as antecedents, they require a plural pronoun.

both	few	several	many

A few of the housemates leave dirty dishes everywhere.

Several of their friends said they are fed up.

Singular or Plural Indefinite Pronouns

Some indefinite pronouns can be singular or plural, depending on the object of the preposition in the phrase that follows them.

all	any	most	none	some

All of the pies were eaten.

All of the pie was eaten.

INSIGHT ——————————————————————

For more practice with indefinite pronouns, see pages 478–481.

Correcting Agreement

Correct Rewrite each sentence to correct the agreement errors. (Hint: The sentences are about a group of male campers.)

1. Everyone needs to wash their own dishes.

2. No one are exempt.

3. Anyone not washing their dishes must wash everyone else's.

4. Nothing short of illness are an excuse.

5. Few is arguing with the new policy.

6. Several says it is about time.

7. Many expresses their appreciation.

8. For a week, all of the dishes has been washed.

9. Ted made sure all of his plates was washed and put away.

10. Most of the roommates agrees that this works.

11. Most of the morning are spent cleaning up.

12. None of the dishes is left lying about.

13. None of the food are left to eat either, since everybody have forgotten to go shopping.

indefinite pronoun
a pronoun that does not refer to a specific person, place, thing, or idea

LO5 Relative Pronouns

A **relative pronoun** introduces a dependent clause and relates it to the rest of the sentence.

who	whom	which	whose
whoever	whomever	that	

relative clause

I would like to meet the person who invented the World Wide Web.

Who/Whoever and Whom/Whomever

Who, whoever, whom, and *whomever* refer to people. *Who* or *whoever* functions as the subject of the relative clause, while *whom* or *whomever* functions as the object of the clause.

I would like to thank whoever chose the playlist for this party.

The person whom I thanked had terrific taste in music.

relative clause   **relative clause**

NOTE: In the second **relative clause**, *whom* introduces the clause even though it is the direct object, not the subject *(I thanked whom).*

That and Which

That and *which* usually refer to things. When *that* introduces the clause, the clause **is not** set off with commas. When *which* introduces the clause, the clause **is** set off with commas.

I read the book that told of Teddy Roosevelt's journey down the Amazon.

I enjoyed *The River of Doubt,* which was a $29 hardback.

relative clause   **relative clause**

Whose

Whose shows ownership or connection.

relative clause

The mechanic whose hand got cut was fixing our car.

NOTE: Do not confuse *whose* with the contraction *who's* (who is).

Using Relative Pronouns

Select For each sentence, select the correct relative pronoun.

1. Theo Jansen is an engineer and artist *(who, whom)* is creating new life.

2. He builds sculptures *(that, which)* harness the wind to walk.

3. Theo refers to his sculptures as animals, *(that, which)* is unusual for an engineer.

4. These animals are built of plastic pipe, *(that, which)* is inexpensive and strong.

5. Another engineer and artist *(who, whom)* Jansen admires is Leonardo da Vinci.

6. Theo's creations are on display for *(whoever, whomever)* is on the beach.

7. His most famous creation is the Strandbeest, *(that, which)* has wings on top.

8. The wings pump air into plastic bottles, *(that, which)* store it up.

9. The air powers "muscles" *(that, which)* are made of sliding tubes.

10. Muscles open taps that activate other muscles, *(that, which)* makes the beast walk.

11. Theo Jansen, *(who, whose)* creations are spellbinding, hopes these "animals" will roam on their own one day.

12. Theo feels that the boundary between art and engineering is only in our minds, *(that, which)* allows him to create such creatures.

Write Write a relative clause for each of these relative pronouns:

1. who	3. whom	5. which
2. whoever	4. whomever	6. that

Write a sentence including one of your clauses.

relative pronoun a pronoun that begins a relative clause, connecting it to a sentence	**relative clause** a type of dependent clause that begins with a relative pronoun that is either the subject or the direct object of the clause

INSIGHT

For more practice with relative pronouns, see pages 468–469.

LO6 Other Pronoun Types

Other types of pronouns have specific uses in your writing: asking questions, pointing to specific things, reflecting back on a noun (or pronoun), or intensifying a noun (or pronoun).

Interrogative Pronoun

An **interrogative pronoun** asks a question—*who, whose, whom, which, what.*

Who will help me make the salads? What is your favorite dressing?

Demonstrative Pronoun

A **demonstrative pronoun** points to a specific thing—*this, that, these, those.*

This is the best of times! These are wonderful days!

Reflexive Pronoun

A **reflexive pronoun** reflects back to the subject of a sentence or clause—*myself, ourselves, yourself, yourselves, himself, herself, itself, themselves.*

I emailed myself the file. You can send yourself the vacation photos.

Intensive Pronoun

An **intensive pronoun** emphasizes the noun or pronoun it refers to—*myself, ourselves, yourself, yourselves, himself, herself, itself, themselves.*

I myself will be there. You yourself will see me.

Reciprocal Pronoun

A **reciprocal pronoun** refers to two things in an equal way—*each other, one another.*

We should apologize to each other. We should love one another.

Say It

Speak the following words aloud.
1. Interrogative: *Who* is? / *Whose* is? / *Which* is? / *What* is? / *Whom* do you see?
2. Demonstrative: *This* is / *That* is / *These* are / *Those* are
3. Reflexive: I helped *myself.* / You helped *yourself.* / They helped *themselves.*
4. Intensive: I *myself* / You *yourself* / She *herself* / He *himself* / They *themselves*
5. Reciprocal: We helped *each other.* / We helped *one another.*

Using Other Types of Pronouns

Identify   Indicate the type of each underlined pronoun: *interrogative, demonstrative, reflexive, intensive,* or *reciprocal.*

1. <u>That</u> is the reason we should fill the tank. _____

2. <u>What</u> should we use to pay for gas? _____

3. I <u>myself</u> expected you to bring money. _____

4. You should pat <u>yourself</u> on the back. _____

5. <u>That</u> is all the money you have? _____

6. The change <u>itself</u> won't be enough. _____

7. <u>Who</u> gets $1.73 worth of gas? _____

8. <u>That</u> won't get us far. _____

9. <u>This</u> is ridiculous. _____

10. <u>What</u> should we do? _____

11. I <u>myself</u> am prepared to push. _____

12. We should be ashamed of <u>ourselves</u>. _____

13. We shouldn't blame <u>each other</u>. _____

14. Let's help <u>one another</u> move this car. _____

15. Then let's get <u>ourselves</u> a soda. _____

Write   Create a sentence using *myself* as a reflexive pronoun, and a second using *myself* as an intensive pronoun.

1. _____

2. _____

LO7 Real-World Application

Correct | Correct any pronoun errors in the letter that follows. Write the line number and any words you would change. Cross out the word and show the change you would make.

⬛ Rankin Technologies
401 South Manheim Road, Albany, NY 12236 ▪ Ph: 708.555.1980 ▪ Fax: 708.555.0056

1   April 28, 2010

Mr. Henry Danburn
Construction Manager
Titan Industrial Construction, Inc.
5   P.O. Box 2112
Phoenix, AZ 85009-3887

Dear Mr. Danburn:

Thank you for meeting with I last week at the National Convention in Las Vegas. I want to follow up on ours discussion of ways in which
10   Rankin Technologies could work with Titan Industrial Construction.

Enclosed is the information that your requested. I believe this material demonstrates which Rankin Technologies would be a solid match for yours projects in western Illinois.

You yourselves are the construction manager for the Arrow Mills
15   renovation project in California. Rankin did the electrical installation on that project initially, and us would be very interested in working with you on the renovation. Someone whom is familiar with our work at Arrow Mills is Mike Knowlan. She is the plant manager and can be reached at 606-555-6328.

20   Us are excited about working with yous on any future projects and on the Arrow Mills project in particular. Please call I with any questions (708-555-1980).

Sincerely,

James Gabriel

25   James Gabriel
Vice President
Enclosures 5

Correction Marks

ℐ	delete
d̳	capitalize
l̸	lowercase
∧	insert
∧̖	add comma
?∧	add question mark
word ∧	add word
⊙	add period
◠	spelling
◡	switch

INSIGHT

In workplace documents, correct grammar is critical to creating a strong impression.

23

Verb

"I think I am a verb."
—R. Buckminster Fuller

Of course, we call ourselves human beings, but a few people have suggested we should think of ourselves as human doings. They would argue that our actions define us more than who we are.

Whether you are a human being or a human doing, you are thinking of yourself as a verb. Verbs express states of being and actions (doing). They give a sentence energy, movement, and meaning. This chapter provides practice working with these amazing words.

Learning Outcomes

What do you think?

Are you a human being or a human doing? Why?

Evgeniya Moroz, 2013 / Used under license from Shutterstock.com

LO1 Verb Classes

Verbs show action or states of being. Different classes of verbs do these jobs.

Action Verbs

Verbs that show action are called **action verbs**. Some action verbs are **transitive**, which means that they transfer action to a direct object.

Bill clutches the pillow.
(The verb *clutches* transfers action to the direct object *pillow*.)

Others are **intransitive**: They don't transfer action to a direct object.

Bill sleeps.
(The verb *sleeps* does not transfer action to a direct object.)

Linking Verbs

Verbs that link the subject to a noun, a pronoun, or an adjective are **linking verbs**. Predicates with linking verbs express a state of being.

Bill is a heavy sleeper.
(The linking verb *is* connects *Bill* to the noun *sleeper*.)

He seems weary.
(The linking verb *seems* connects *He* to the adjective *weary*.)

Linking Verbs

is	am	are	was	were	be	being	been	become
grow	feel	seem	look	smell	taste	sound	appear	remain

NOTE: The bottom-row words are linking verbs if they don't show action.

INSIGHT

If you are mathematically minded, think of a linking verb as an equal sign. It indicates that the subject equals (or is similar to) what is in the predicate.

Helping Verbs

A verb that works with an action or linking verb is a **helping** (or auxiliary) verb. A helping verb helps the main verb form tense, mood, and voice.

Bill has slept till noon before, and today he will be sleeping even longer.
(The helping verb *has* works with the main verb *slept;* the helping verbs *will be* work with *sleeping*. Both form special tenses.)

NOTE: Helping verbs work with verbs ending in *ing* or in past-tense form.

Helping Verbs

am	been	could	does	have	might	should	will
are	being	did	had	is	must	was	would
be	can	do	has	may	shall	were	

Using Verb Classes

Identify/Write For each sentence below, identify the underlined verbs as transitive action verbs (T), intransitive action verbs (I), linking verbs (L), or helping verbs (H). Then write your own sentence using the same class of verb.

1. I <u>need</u> eight hours of sleep per night, but I often <u>get</u> only six.

2. This weekend, I <u>will be</u> getting even less sleep.

3. One of my favorite bands is <u>playing</u> in town.

4. They <u>rock</u>, and whenever I <u>see</u> a concert of theirs, I hardly <u>sleep</u>.

5. I <u>am</u> eager, but after the weekend, I <u>will</u> be worn out.

6. The problem with having too much fun on the weekend <u>is</u> the week after.

7. Maybe I <u>should</u> go to bed earlier so that I <u>can</u> store up sleep.

8. I <u>feel</u> awake now, but next week I will <u>look</u> weary.

action verb	intransitive verb	helping (auxiliary) verb
word that expresses action	action verb that does not transfer action to a direct object	verb that works with a main verb to form some tenses, mood, and voice
transitive verb		
action verb that transfers action to a direct object	**linking verb**	
	verb that connects the subject with a noun, a pronoun, or an adjective in the predicate	

LO2 Number and Person of Verbs

Verbs reflect number (singular or plural) and person (first person, second person, or third person).

Number

The **number** of the verb indicates whether the subject is singular or plural. Note that most present-tense singular verbs end in *s,* while most present-tense plural verbs do not.

Singular: The Gettysburg Address speaks of those who "gave the last full measure of devotion."
Plural: Many historians speak of it as the greatest American speech.

Person

The **person** of the verb indicates whether the subject is speaking, being spoken to, or being spoken about.

	Singular	**Plural**
First Person:	(I) am	(we) are
Second Person:	(you) are	(you) are
Third Person:	(she) is	(they) are

Note that the pronoun *I* takes a special form of the *be* verb—*am.*

Correct: I am excited about going to Gettysburg.
Incorrect: I is excited about going to Gettysburg.

The pronoun *I* also is paired with plural-present tense verbs.

Correct: I want to go with you.
Incorrect: I wants to go with you.

In a similar way, the singular pronoun *you* takes the plural form of the *be* verb—*are, were.*

Correct: You are going to the Gettysburg National Military Park.
Incorrect: You is going to the Gettysburg National Military Park.

Correct: You were my first choice.
Incorrect: You was my first choice.

Using Number and Person

Provide For each sentence below, provide the correct person and number of the present-tense *be* verb *(is, am, are)*.

1. We _____ interested in going to Gettysburg.
2. It _____ a town in Pennsylvania where a great battle took place.
3. You _____ welcome to come on the trip with us.
4. Little Round Top _____ a hill where the fighting was focused.
5. The Union troops _____ memorialized in statues on the hill.
6. You _____ standing on a piece of American history.
7. Pickett's Charge _____ considered General Lee's greatest mistake.
8. Troops from both sides _____ buried in the cemetery.
9. I _____ eager to see where Lincoln gave the Gettysburg Address.
10. We _____ hoping to spend two days in Gettysburg.

Rewrite Rewrite each sentence below to fix the errors in the number and person of the verb.

1. I listens as the tour guide describe the last day of battle.

   _____

2. Rifle shots hails down on the Confederate soldiers.

   _____

3. General Pickett order them to charge Little Round Top.

   _____

4. Flying lead kill many Southern soldiers.

   _____

5. The Union troops repels the charge and wins the day.

   _____

6. President Lincoln deliver the Gettysburg Address.

   _____

number	person
singular or plural	whether the subject is speaking *(I, we)*, is being spoken to *(you)*, or is being spoken about *(he, she, it, they)*

LO3 Voice of the Verb

The **voice** of the verb indicates whether the subject is acting or being acted upon.

Voice

An **active voice** means that the subject is acting. A **passive voice** means that the subject is acted on.

Active: The usher led us to our seats.
Passive: We were led by the usher to our seats.

	Active Voice		Passive Voice	
	Singular	Plural	Singular	Plural
Present Tense	I see you see he/she/it sees	we see you see they see	I am seen you are seen he/she/it is seen	we are seen you are seen they are seen
Past Tense	I saw you saw he saw	we saw you saw they saw	I was seen you were seen it was seen	we were seen you were seen they were seen
Future Tense	I will see you will see he will see	we will see you will see they will see	I will be seen you will be seen it will be seen	we will be seen you will be seen they will be seen
Present Perfect Tense	I have seen you have seen he has seen	we have seen you have seen they have seen	I have been seen you have been seen it has been seen	we have been seen you have been seen they have been seen
Past Perfect Tense	I had seen you had seen he had seen	we had seen you had seen they had seen	I had been seen you had been seen it had been seen	we had been seen you had been seen they had been seen
Future Perfect Tense	I will have seen you will have seen he will have seen	we will have seen you will have seen they will have seen	I will have been seen you will have been seen it will have been seen	we will have been seen you will have been seen they will have been seen

Active voice is preferred for most writing because it is direct and energetic.

Active: We gave the band a standing ovation.
Passive: The band was given a standing ovation by us.

Passive voice is preferred when the focus is on the receiver of the action or when the subject is unknown.

Passive: A rose was thrown on stage.
Active: Someone threw a rose on stage.

Using Voice of a Verb

Rewrite Read each passive sentence below and rewrite it to be active. Think about what is performing the action and make that the subject.

1. The concert was attended by 3,000 fans.

2. A good time was had by everyone.

3. The ten greatest hits of the band were played by them.

4. Three concert T-shirts were bought by my friends and me.

5. The opening acts were tolerated by the crowd.

6. The air was electrified by the appearance of the main act.

7. I was not disappointed by their performance.

8. My short friend's view was blocked by a tall guy.

9. The guy was asked by my friend to switch seats.

10. Every new song was cheered by the crowd.

Write Using the chart on the facing page, write a sentence for each situation below.

1. (A present-tense singular active sentence) _____

2. (A past-tense plural passive sentence) _____

CONSIDER THE WORKPLACE

In workplace writing, use active voice for most messages. Use passive voice to deliver bad news.

voice	active voice	passive voice
active or passive	voice created when the subject is performing the action of the verb	voice created when the subject is receiving the action of the verb

LO4 Present- and Future-Tense Verbs

Basic verb tenses tell whether action happens in the past, in the present, or in the future.

Present Tense

Present-tense verbs indicate that action is happening right now.

A cruise ship arrives in Cabo San Lucas, Mexico.

Present-tense verbs also can indicate that action happens routinely or continually.

Every day, ships drop anchor outside of the harbor.

Present Tense in Academic Writing

Use present-tense verbs to describe current conditions.

Cabo San Lucas makes most of its income through tourism.

Use present-tense verbs also to discuss the ideas in literature or to use historical quotations in a modern context. This use is called the "historical present," which allows writers to continue speaking.

Some say that those who see Cabo do not truly see Mexico, or as G. K. Chesterton writes, "The traveler sees what he sees; the tourist sees what he has come to see."

NOTE: It is important to write a paragraph or an essay in one tense. Avoid shifting needlessly from tense to tense as you write.

Future Tense

Future-tense verbs indicate that action will happen later on.

Cruise ships will visit Cabo San Lucas for many years to come.

Using Present and Future Verb Tenses

Write   For each sentence below, supply the present-tense form of the verb indicated in parentheses.

1. Many visitors _____ in Cabo's warm waters. (snorkeled)

2. White, sandy beaches _____ many swimmers. (attracted)

3. Parasailors _____ overhead from parachutes. (flew)

4. Waves _____ if winds are strong. (picked up)

5. Boats _____ people from cruise ships to shore. (ran)

Change   Replace the verbs in the following paragraph, making them all present tense. Write the line number and the present-tense verb.

> We went to Lover's Beach in Cabo San Lucas. The beach was very   *1*
> busy. About a third of the people sunbathed, a third scuba dived, and a
> third just splashed in the waves. The waves were large because the wind
> was strong. We swam all afternoon until the water taxi returned for us.
> The day we spent in Cabo San Lucas was one of our favorite days of the   *5*
> trip.

Write   Write a sentence of your own, using each word below in the form indicated in parentheses.

1. enjoy (present) _____

2. swim (future) _____

3. realize (present) _____

4. complete (future) _____

present tense
verb tense indicating that action is happening now

future tense
verb tense indicating that action will happen later

LO5 Past-Tense Verbs

Past-tense verbs indicate that action happened in the past.

When referring to his campaign in England, Julius Caesar reported, "I came. I saw. I conquered."

Forming Past Tense

Most verbs form their past tense by adding *ed*. If the word ends in a silent *e*, just add *d*.

help ⟶ help**ed**   love ⟶ love**d**
look ⟶ look**ed**   hope ⟶ hope**d**

If the word ends in a consonant before a single vowel and the last syllable is stressed, double the final consonant before adding *ed*.

stop ⟶ stop**ped**   occur ⟶ occur**red**
plan ⟶ plan**ned**   refer ⟶ refer**red**

If the word ends in a *y* preceded by a consonant, change the *y* to *i* before adding *ed*.

study ⟶ stud**ied**   hurry ⟶ hurr**ied**
worry ⟶ worr**ied**   carry ⟶ carr**ied**

Irregular Verbs

Some of the most commonly used verbs form past tense by changing the verb itself. See the chart below:

Pres.	Past	Pres.	Past	Pres.	Past	Pres.	Past	Pres.	Past	Pres.	Past
am	was, were	come	came	find	found	hear	heard	see	saw	steal	stole
become	became	dig	dug	fly	flew	hide	hid	shake	shook	swim	swam
begin	began	do	did	forget	forgot	keep	kept	shine	shone	swing	swung
blow	blew	draw	drew	freeze	froze	know	knew	shrink	shrank	take	took
break	broke	drink	drank	get	got	lead	led	sing	sang	teach	taught
bring	brought	drive	drove	give	gave	pay	paid	sink	sank	tear	tore
buy	bought	eat	ate	go	went	ride	rode	sit	sat	think	thought
can	could	fall	fell	grow	grew	ring	rang	sleep	slept	throw	threw
catch	caught	feel	felt	hang	hung	rise	rose	speak	spoke	wear	wore
choose	chose	fight	fought	have	had	run	ran	stand	stood	write	wrote

Using Past-Tense Verbs

Write For each verb, write the correct past-tense form.

1. give _____
2. shop _____
3. trick _____
4. type _____
5. teach _____
6. cry _____
7. sing _____
8. soap _____

9. cap _____
10. cope _____
11. try _____
12. fly _____
13. think _____
14. grip _____
15. gripe _____
16. pour _____

Edit Make changes to the following paragraph, converting it from present tense to past tense. Write the line number and any word you would change. Cross it out and write the change.

> During my junior year of high school, I become a lifeguard at a   1
> campground pool. I think it is a cushy job, sitting poolside all summer.
> However, this pool hosts many day camps, meaning hundreds of little
> kids with little supervision. I quickly discover that the other guards and
> I are the supervision. It is hard to yell at kids all day, but it was more   5
> dangerous to stay silent. They run on the deck or dive into shallow water
> or jump into deep water when they don't know how to swim. Worse yet,
> families come, and when their kids do the same things and I yell, parents
> tell me their kids can run on deck if they want. Facing down adults at
> sixteen isn't easy. Still, my brother's summer job is mowing lawns at the   10
> same campground. When he walks by, drenched in sweat, my job sitting
> in my lifeguard chair suddenly seems cushy.

Correction Marks

⌐ delete	⅄ add comma	∧ add word (word)
d capitalize	? add question mark	⊙ add period
⌿ lowercase	∧	⬭ spelling
∧ insert	⌄ insert an apostrophe	⊓ switch

past tense
verb tense indicating that action happened previously

LO6 Progressive-Tense Verbs

The basic tenses of past, present, and future tell when action takes place. The progressive tense or aspect tells that action is ongoing.

Progressive Tense

Progressive tense indicates that action is ongoing. Progressive tense is formed by using a helping verb along with the *ing* form of the main verb.

Scientists are studying the growth of human populations.

There are past, present, and future progressive tenses. Each uses a helping verb in the appropriate tense.

In 1804, one billion people were sharing the globe.

Currently, about seven billion people are living on Earth.

In 2040, about nine billion people will be calling this planet home.

Forming Progressive Tense

Past:	was/were	+	main verb	+	ing
Present:	am/is/are	+	main verb	+	ing
Future:	will be	+	main verb	+	ing

INSIGHT

Avoid using progressive tense with the following:

- Verbs that express thoughts, attitudes, and desires: *know, understand, want, prefer*
- Verbs that describe appearances: *seem, resemble*
- Verbs that indicate possession: *belong, have, own, possess*
- Verbs that signify inclusion: *contain, hold*

     Correct: *I **know** your name.*
    Incorrect: *I **am knowing** your name.*

Using Progressive Tense

Form Rewrite each sentence three times, changing the tenses as requested in parentheses.

Epidemics drop populations, but vaccination leads to upswings.

1. (present progressive) _____

_____

2. (past progressive) _____

_____

3. (future progressive) _____

_____

Though food production grows by addition, population grows by multiplication.

4. (present progressive) _____

_____

5. (past progressive) _____

_____

6. (future progressive) _____

_____

Improved public-health programs lead to lower mortality rates.

7. (present progressive) _____

_____

8. (past progressive) _____

_____

9. (future progressive) _____

progressive tense
verb tense that expresses
ongoing action

_____

LO7 Perfect-Tense Verbs

The perfect tense tells that action is not ongoing but is finished, whether in the past, present, or future.

Perfect Tense

Perfect tense indicates that action is completed. Perfect tense is formed by using a helping verb along with the past-tense form of the main verb.

An estimated 110 billion people have lived on earth.

There are past, present, and future perfect tenses. These tenses are formed by using helping verbs in past, present, and future tenses.

By 1804, the world population had reached one billion.

We have added another billion people in the last 13 years.

In 13 more years, we will have welcomed another billion.

Forming Perfect Tense

Past:	had	+	past-tense main verb
Present:	has/have	+	past-tense main verb
Future:	will have	+	past-tense main verb

Perfect Tense with Irregular Verbs

To form perfect tense with irregular verbs, use the past-participle form instead of the past-tense form. Here are the past participles of common irregular verbs.

Pres.	Past Part.	Pres.	Past Part.	Pres.	Past Part.	Pres.	Past Part.	Pres.	Past Part.	Pres.	Past Part.
am, be	been	dig	dug	fly	flown	hide	hidden	see	seen	stand	stood
become	become	do	done	forget	forgotten	keep	kept	shake	shaken	steal	stolen
begin	begun	draw	drawn	freeze	frozen	know	known	shine	shone	swim	swum
blow	blown	drink	drunk	get	gotten	lead	led	show	shown	swing	swung
break	broken	drive	driven	give	given	pay	paid	shrink	shrunk	take	taken
bring	brought	eat	eaten	go	gone	prove	proven	sing	sung	teach	taught
buy	bought	fall	fallen	grow	grown	ride	ridden	sink	sunk	tear	torn
catch	caught	feel	felt	hang	hung	ring	rung	sit	sat	throw	thrown
choose	chosen	fight	fought	have	had	rise	risen	sleep	slept	wear	worn
come	come	find	found	hear	heard	run	run	speak	spoken	write	written

Using Perfect Tense

Form Rewrite each sentence three times, changing the tenses as requested in parentheses.

According to scientists, the earth circles the sun over 4.5 billion times.

1. (past perfect) _____

_____

2. (present perfect) _____

_____

3. (future perfect) _____

_____

The sun lives half of its lifetime.

4. (past perfect) _____

_____

5. (present perfect) _____

_____

6. (future perfect) _____

_____

Two stars within our galaxy go supernova.

7. (past perfect) _____

_____

8. (present perfect) _____

_____

9. (future perfect) _____

perfect tense
verb tense that expresses
completed action

_____

LO8 Verbals

A **verbal** is formed from a verb but functions as a noun, an adjective, or an adverb. Each type of verbal—gerund, participle, and infinitive—can appear alone or can begin a **verbal phrase**.

Gerund

A **gerund** is formed from a verb ending in *ing,* and it functions as a noun.

Swimming is my favorite pastime. (subject)
I love swimming. (direct object)

A **gerund phrase** begins with a gerund and includes any objects and modifiers.

Swimming laps at the pool builds endurance. (subject)
I prefer swimming laps in pools rather than in lakes. (direct object)

Participle

A **participle** is formed from a verb ending in *ing* or *ed,* and it functions as an adjective.

Excited, I received my lifesaving certification! (*excited* modifies *I*)
What an exciting day! (*exciting* modifies *day*)

A **participial phrase** begins with a participle and includes any objects and modifiers.

Exciting the crowd of young swimmers, I said we were diving today.

Infinitive

An **infinitive** is formed from *to* and a present-tense verb, and it functions as a noun, an adjective, or an adverb.

To teach is a noble profession. (noun)
This is an important point to remember. (adjective)
Students must pay attention to understand. (adverb)

An **infinitive phrase** begins with an infinitive and includes any objects or modifiers.

I plan lessons to teach an easy progression of swimming skills.

Using Verbals

Identify Identify each underlined verbal by selecting the correct choice in parentheses (gerund, participle, infinitive).

1. <u>Jogging</u> is another excellent exercise. (gerund, participle, infinitive)
2. You should plan <u>to jog</u> three times a week. (gerund, participle, infinitive)
3. <u>Jogging</u> with friends, you can also be social. (gerund, participle, infinitive)
4. Try <u>to wear</u> good shoes. (gerund, participle, infinitive)
5. <u>Avoiding</u> joint injury is important. (gerund, participle, infinitive)
6. <u>Toned</u> through exercise, your body will look better. (gerund, participle, infinitive)

Form Complete each sentence below by supplying the type of verbal (or verbal phrase) requested in parentheses.

1. The exercise I would choose is _____ . (gerund)
2. _____ , I would lose weight. (participle)
3. _____ is a good toning exercise. (infinitive)
4. I would also like to try _____ . (gerund)
5. When exercising, remember _____ . (infinitive)
6. _____ , I'll be in great shape. (participle)

Write For each verbal phrase below, write a sentence that correctly uses it.

1. to lift weights _____
2. preparing myself for a marathon _____
3. filled with anticipation _____

verbal
gerund, participle, or infinitive; a construction formed from a verb but functioning as a noun, an adjective, or an adverb

verbal phrase
phrase beginning with a gerund, a participle, or an infinitive

gerund
verbal ending in *ing* and functioning as a noun

gerund phrase
phrase beginning with a gerund and including objects and modifiers

participle
verbal ending in *ing* or *ed* and functioning as an adjective

participial phrase
phrase beginning with a participle and including objects and modifiers

infinitive
verbal beginning with *to* and functioning as a noun, an adjective, or an adverb

infinitive phrase
phrase beginning with an infinitive and including objects and modifiers

LO9 Verbals as Objects

Though both infinitives and gerunds can function as nouns, they can't be used interchangeably as direct objects. Some verbs take infinitives and not gerunds. Other verbs take only gerunds and not infinitives.

Gerunds as Objects

Verbs that express facts are followed by **gerunds**.

admit	deny	enjoy	miss	recommend
avoid	discuss	finish	quit	regret
consider	dislike	imagine	recall	

I enjoy playing cards.
not I enjoy to play cards.

I imagine winning a poker tournament.
not I imagine to win a poker tournament.

Infinitives as Objects

Verbs that express intentions, hopes, and desires are followed by **infinitives**.

agree	demand	hope	prepare	volunteer
appear	deserve	intend	promise	want
attempt	endeavor	need	refuse	wish
consent	fail	offer	seem	
decide	hesitate	plan	tend	

I attempt to win every hand.
not I attempt winning every hand.

I need to get a better poker face.
not I need getting a better poker face.

Gerunds or Infinitives as Objects

Some verbs can be followed by either a gerund or an infinitive.

begin	hate	love	remember	stop
continue	like	prefer	start	try

I love to play poker.
or I love playing poker.

Using Verbals as Objects

Select For each sentence below, select the appropriate verbal in parentheses.

1. I enjoy (to play, playing) canasta.
2. We should promise (to play, playing) canasta this weekend.
3. In canasta, you need (to get, getting) seven-card melds.
4. You and a partner endeavor (to meld, melding) suits.
5. You and your partner can discuss (to go, going) out.
6. The rules recommend (to keep, keeping) other table talk down.
7. I recall (to win, winning) three hands in a row.
8. If you lose a hand, you'll regret (to have, having) wild cards.
9. If you fail (to use, using) a wild card, it costs.
10. You'll dislike (to get, getting) penalized 50 points.

Write For each verb below, write your own sentence using the verb and following it with a gerund or an infinitive, as appropriate.

1. deny

   _____

2. promise

   _____

3. refuse

   _____

4. consider

   _____

5. recommend

   _____

6. avoid

   _____

| **gerund**
verbal ending in *ing* and functioning as a noun | **infinitive**
verbal beginning with *to* and functioning as a noun, an adjective, or an adverb |

LO10 Real-World Application

Revise Rewrite the following paragraph, changing passive verbs to active verbs.

> Your request to send all the sales reps to the Adobe training seminar in Cincinnati was reviewed by me. Your idea that this training would help your staff is agreed to by me. Our training budget was reviewed by me to see if the seminar could be afforded by us.

_____

_____

_____

Revise In the following paragraph, change future perfect verbs into past perfect verbs. Write the line number and the words you would change. Then show the change.

> We will have used a large portion of our budget to upgrade design   1
> software for the engineering staff. In addition, we will have made prior   2
> commitments to train office staff in August. As a result, we will not have   3
> reserved enough money to send all sales reps to Cincinnati.   4

Revise In the following paragraph, correct misused verbals. Write the line number and the words you would change. Then show the change.

> I want exploring other solutions with you. Do you recommend to send   1
> two reps who then could train others? I recall to do that in previous   2
> situations. I admit to agree that this isn't the optimal course, but I hope 3
> doing something.   4

24

> "We do our best that we know how at the moment, and if it doesn't turn out, we modify it."
> —Franklin Delano Roosevelt

Adjective and Adverb

All right, so you have a car. Lots of people have cars. It's a vintage Volkswagen beetle? Nice. And it's decked out with custom paint, toys, barrettes, and words like "smile," "laugh," and "let flow"? You call it your "crazy, lovey, hippy, dippy, vintage buggy"? Wow, do you have a car!

The owner of the car above has totally modified it and then has used strings of modifying words and phrases to describe it. That's what adjectives and adverbs do. They add color, texture, shape, size, and many more vivid details to each picture. Remember, though, that too many modifiers can overload a sentence—much as bric-a-brac can overwhelm a car.

Learning Outcomes

LO1 Adjective Basics
LO2 Adjective Order
LO3 Adjective Questions and Adjectivals
LO4 Adverb Basics
LO5 Placement of Adverbs
LO6 Adverbials
LO7 Real-World Application

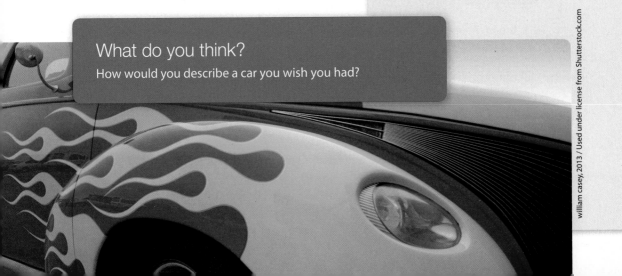

What do you think?
How would you describe a car you wish you had?

LO1 Adjective Basics

An **adjective** is a word that modifies a noun or pronoun. Even **articles** such as *a, an,* and *the* are adjectives, because they indicate whether you mean a general or specific thing. Adjectives answer these basic questions: *which, what kind of, how many/how much.*

Adjectives often appear before the word they modify.

You have a cute, fluffy dog.

A **predicate adjective** appears after the noun it modifies and is linked to the word by a linking verb.

Your dog is cute and fluffy.

Proper adjectives come from proper nouns and are capitalized.

He is a Yorkshire terrier.

Forms of Adjectives

Adjectives come in three forms: positive, comparative, and superlative.

- **Positive adjectives** describe one thing without making any comparisons.

Keats is a friendly dog.

- **Comparative adjectives** compare the thing to something else.

Keats is friendlier than our cat, Yeats.

- **Superlative adjectives** compare the thing to two or more other things.

He is the friendliest dog you will ever meet.

NOTE: For one- and two-syllable words, create the comparative form by adding *er,* and create the superlative form by adding *est.* For words of three syllables or more, use *more* (or *less*) for comparatives and *most* (or *least*) for superlatives. Also note that *good* and *bad* have special superlative forms:

Positive		Comparative		Superlative	
good	happy	better	happier	best	happiest
bad	wonderful	worse	more wonderful	worst	most wonderful
big		bigger		biggest	

Using the Forms of Adjectives

Identify/Write For each sentence below, identify the underlined adjectives as positive (P), comparative (C), or superlative (S). Then write a new sentence about a different topic, but use the same adjectives.

1. We once had a <u>beautiful</u> collie with a <u>long</u>, <u>shiny</u> coat.
2. She was <u>smarter</u> than our last dog, perhaps the <u>smartest</u> pet we've owned.
3. She thought she was the <u>alpha</u> female and my wife was the <u>beta</u> female.
4. My wife became even <u>more unhappy</u> when the dog tore up her <u>best</u> couch.
5. My wife was <u>happiest</u> on the day we gave the dog to a farmer.

Correct Read the paragraph below and correct adjective errors, using the correction marks below. The first one has been done for you.

      Did you know there is an Intelligence test for dogs? It includes Various   *1*
tasks to check the dog's Adaptive intelligence, or problem-solving ability.
The most smartest dogs can quickly find a treat under one of three
buckets, get a treat from under a piece of furniture, find its Favorite
spot after a room is rearranged, and gets a towel off its head. In tests,   *5*
border collies, poodles, and german shepherds have tested as the most
smartest, and afghan hounds, british bulldogs, and chow chows tested at
the most low end. Even if they aren't the intelligentest, these dogs might
still be the most cuddliest.

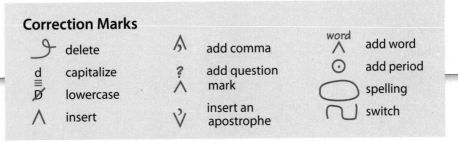

Correction Marks

⌔ delete	⋏ add comma	⌃ add word	
d̲ capitalize	? add question mark	⊙ add period	
⌀ lowercase		◯ spelling	
⌃ insert	⩒ insert an apostrophe	⌇ switch	

adjective word that modifies a noun or pronoun	**positive adjective** word that modifies a noun or pronoun without comparing it	**superlative adjective** word that modifies a noun or pronoun by comparing it to two or more things
articles the adjectives *a, an,* and *the*	**comparative adjective** word that modifies a noun or pronoun by comparing it to something else	
predicate adjective adjective that appears after a linking verb and describes the subject		

LO2 Adjective Order

Adjectives aren't all created equally. Native English speakers use a specific order when putting multiple adjectives before a noun, and all speakers of English can benefit from understanding this order.

InavanHateren, 2013 / Used under license from Shutterstock.com

Begin with . . .

1.	articles	a, an, the
	demonstrative adjectives	that, this, these, those
	possessives	my, our, her, their, Kayla's

Then position adjectives that tell . . .

2.	time	first, second, next, last
3.	how many	three, few, some, many
4.	value	important, prized, fine
5.	size	giant, puny, hulking
6.	shape	spiky, blocky, square
7.	condition	clean, tattered, repaired
8.	age	old, new, classic
9.	color	blue, scarlet, salmon
10.	nationality	French, Chinese, Cuban
11.	religion	Baptist, Buddhist, Hindu
12.	material	cloth, stone, wood, bronze

Finally place . . .

13.	nouns used as adjectives	baby [seat], shoe [lace]

Example:

> that gorgeous old French shrimp boat
> (**1** + **7** + **8** + **10** + **13** **noun**)

INSIGHT

As the introduction indicates, native English speakers use this order unconsciously because it sounds right to them. If you put adjectives in a different order, a native English speaker might say, "That's not how anybody says it." One way to avoid this issue is to avoid stacking multiple adjectives before nouns.

NOTE: Avoid using too many adjectives before a noun. An article and one or two adjectives are usually enough. More adjectives may overload the noun.

Too many:	my last three spiky old blue Cuban coral souvenirs
Effective:	my last three coral souvenirs

Placing Adjectives in Order

Order Rearrange each set of adjectives and articles so that they are in the correct order. The first one has been done for you.

1. purple   rectangular   this

    _____this rectangular purple_____   carton

2. your   Mexican   beautiful

    _____   guitar

3. wooden   worn-out   many

    _____   blocks

4. precious   the   Islamic

    _____   mosaic

5. traditional   several   Russian

    _____   dolls

6. stone   chess   Doug's

    _____   pieces

7. broken-down   that   old

    _____   sedan

8. felt   his   pin-striped

    _____   fedora

9. old   the   mossy

    _____   temple

10. original   three   piano

    _____   pieces

11. first   real   our

    _____   vacation

LO3 Adjective Questions and Adjectivals

Adjectives answer four basic questions: *which, what kind of, how many/how much.*

Children	
Which?	those children
What kind of?	smiling Indian children
How many/how much?	many children

those many smiling Indian children

Adjectivals

A single word that answers one of these questions is called an adjective. If a phrase or clause answers one of these questions, it is an **adjectival** phrase or clause.

Children	
Which?	children who were waiting to vote
What kind of?	children wanting to get photographed

Wanting to get photographed, the children who were waiting to vote crowded my camera.

The following types of phrases and clauses can be adjectivals:

Prepositional phrase:	from the school
Participial phrase:	standing in a line
Adjective clause:	who greeted me warmly

Say It

Partner with a classmate. One of you should say the noun, and the other should ask the adjective questions. Then the first person should answer each question with adjectives or adjectivals.

1. **mini-vans**
   Which mini-vans?
   What kind of mini-vans?
   How many mini-vans?

2. **shampoo**
   Which shampoo?
   What kind of shampoo?
   How much shampoo?

Using Adjectives and Adjectivals

Answer/Write For each word, answer the adjective questions using adjectives and adjectivals. Then write a sentence using two or more of your answers.

1. **Cats**

    Which cats? _____

    What kind of cats? _____

    How many cats? _____

    Sentence: _____

    _____

2. **Hobbies**

    Which hobbies? _____

    What kind of hobbies? _____

    How many hobbies? _____

    Sentence: _____

    _____

3. **Plans**

    Which plans? _____

    What kind of plans? _____

    How many plans? _____

    Sentence: _____

    _____

---

adjectival
phrase or clause that answers one of the adjective questions and modifies a noun or pronoun

prepositional phrase
phrase that starts with a preposition and includes an object and modifiers

participial phrase
phrase beginning with a participle (*ing* or *ed* form of verb) plus objects and modifiers; used as an adjective

adjective clause
clause beginning with a relative pronoun and including a verb, but not able to stand alone; functioning as an adjective

LO4 Adverb Basics

An **adverb** modifies a verb, a **verbal**, an adjective, an adverb, or a whole sentence. An adverb answers five basic questions: *how, when, where, why, to what degree, how often.*

He danced boldly.
(*Boldly* modifies the verb *danced.*)

He leaped very high.
(*Very* modifies the adverb *high,* which modifies *leaped.*)

Apparently, he has had dance training.
(*Apparently* modifies the whole sentence.)

NOTE: Most adverbs end in *ly.* Some can be written with or without the *ly,* but when in doubt, use the *ly* form.

loud ⟶ loudly   tight ⟶ tightly   deep ⟶ deeply

Forms of Adverbs

Adverbs have three forms: positive, comparative, and superlative.

- **Positive adverbs** describe without comparing.

  He danced skillfully.

- **Comparative adverbs** (*er, more,* or *less*) describe by comparing with one other action.

  He danced more skillfully than his brother.

- **Superlative adverbs** (*est, most,* or *least*) describe by comparing with more than one action.

  He danced most skillfully of any of those trying out.

AYAKOVLEV.COM, 2013 / Used under license from Shutterstock.com

NOTE: Some adverbs change form to create comparative or superlative forms.

well ⟶ better ⟶ best   badly ⟶ worse ⟶ worst

Using the Forms of Adverbs

Provide For each sentence below, provide the correct form of the adverb in parentheses—positive, comparative, or superlative.

1. I like to dance _____ (fast).

2. I dance _____ (fast) than any of my friends.

3. My moves are the _____ (fast) of anyone on the floor.

4. My brother moves _____ (well) for an older guy.

5. He eats _____ (well) than a spoiled child.

6. But I dance _____ (well) in my family.

7. I ask the band to play the song _____ (quickly).

8. They sometimes play it _____ (quickly) than I intended.

9. A thrash band played _____ (quickly) of any band I've heard.

10. That's when I danced _____ (badly) in my whole life.

Choose In each sentence, write the correct word in parentheses. If the word modifies a noun or pronoun, choose the adjective form (*good, bad*). If the word modifies a verb, a verbal, an adjective, or an adverb, choose the adverb form (*well, badly.*)

1. I hope this turns out to be a (good, well) movie.

2. Even if the actors do (good, well), the plot might not be (good, well).

3. I don't want to spend (good, well) money on a (bad, badly) movie.

4. I wanted to see this movie (bad, badly).

5. Every time Richard comes along, he behaves (bad, badly).

6. If I tell him to straighten up, he takes it (bad, badly).

7. That guy has a (bad, badly) attitude.

8. I have done (good, well) not to invite him.

adverb word that modifies a verb, a verbal, an adjective, an adverb, or a whole sentence **verbal** word formed from a verb but functioning as a noun, an adjective, or an adverb	**positive adverb** adverb that modifies without comparing **comparative adverb** adverb that modifies by comparing with one other thing	**superlative adverb** adverb that modifies by comparing to two or more things

LO5 Placement of Adverbs

Adverbs should be placed in different places in sentences, depending on their use.

How Adverbs

Adverbs that tell *how* can appear anywhere except between a verb and a direct object.

Furiously we paddled the raft.

We furiously paddled the raft.

We paddled the raft furiously.

not We paddled furiously the raft.

When Adverbs

Adverbs that tell *when* should go at the beginning or end of the sentence.

We ran the white water yesterday. Today we'll tackle the course again.

Where Adverbs

Adverbs that tell *where* should follow the verb they modify but should not come between the verb and the direct object. (NOTE: Prepositional phrases often function as *where* adverbs.)

Our guide shouted instructions from the back of the boat.

not Our guide shouted from the back of the boat instructions.

To What Degree Adverbs

Adverbs that tell *to what degree* go right before the adverb they modify.

I learned very quickly to hang on tight.

How Often Adverbs

Adverbs that tell *how often* should go right before an action verb, even if the verb has a helping verb.

I often dreamed about going white-water rafting.
Before that trip, I had never gotten to go.

Placing Adverbs Well

Place   For each sentence below, insert the adverb (in parentheses) in the most appropriate position. The first one has been done for you.

1. The instructor *often* ∧ reminded us to stay alert. (often)

2. He began our training by explaining the equipment. (thoroughly)

3. We got our paddles and helmets. (next)

4. The instructor was careful about safety. (very)

5. We took our positions. (in the raft)

6. The rapids chattered all around us. (soon)

7. We went over challenging rapids. (often)

8. No one fell out. (fortunately)

9. I would recommend that guide. (highly)

10. I hope to go rafting again. (someday)

Revise   Rewrite the paragraph below, moving adverbs that incorrectly come between a verb and a direct object to the correct position.

> Adrenaline junkies seek often thrills by putting themselves in   *1*
> danger. Dangerous situations trigger usually the release of adrenaline.
> Adrenaline is a hormone that causes typically the heart rate to increase.
> It triggers also the fight-or-flight response. Adrenaline junkies
> enjoy very much this feeling and seek often it out through high-risk   *5*
> activities. They try frequently skydiving or bungee jumping. Some
> use repeatedly white-water rafting to get their thrills.

LO6 Adverbials

Adverbs answer six basic questions: *how, when, where, why, to what degree,* and *how often.*

Yesterday, they repeatedly, spontaneously, and extremely joyously bounced around.

NOTE: Avoid this sort of adverb overload in your sentences.

They bounced.

How?	bounced joyously
When?	bounced yesterday
Where?	bounced around
Why?	bounced spontaneously
To what degree?	extremely joyously
How often?	bounced repeatedly

Adverbials

Often, the adverb questions are answered by **adverbial** phrases and clauses, which answer the same six questions.

They bounced.

How?	bounced doing the splits
When?	bounced during the Fun Day Festival
Where?	bounced in the inflatable castle
Why?	bounced because they had been studying too much
To what degree?	bounced until they got sick
How often?	bounced throughout the afternoon

Because they had been studying too much, they bounced in the inflatable castle throughout the afternoon until they got sick.

NOTE: Again, avoid this sort of adverbial overload in your sentences.

The following types of phrases and clauses can be adverbials:

Prepositional phrase:	in the inflatable castle
Participial phrase:	doing the splits
Dependent clause:	because they had been studying too much

Using Adverbials

Answer/Write For each sentence, answer the adverb questions using adverbs and adverbials. Then write a sentence using three or more of your answers.

1. **They ran.** _____

   How did they run? _____

   When did they run? _____

   Where did they run? _____

   Why did they run? _____

   To what degree did they run? _____

   How often did they run? _____

   Sentence: _____

   _____

2. **They laughed.**

   How did they laugh? _____

   When did they laugh? _____

   Where did they laugh? _____

   Why did they laugh? _____

   To what degree did they laugh? _____

   How often did they laugh? _____

   Sentence: _____

   _____

INSIGHT

The adverb questions can be memorized by turning them into a cheer:
how, when, where, why, to what degree, how often!

adverbial
phrase or clause that answers one of the
adverb questions

LO7 Real-World Application

Correct   In the following document, correct the use of adjectives and adverbs. Use the correction marks below.

 **Verdant Landscaping**

1500 West Ridge Avenue
Tacoma, WA 98466

1   January 6, 2012

Ms. Karen Bledsoe
Blixen Furniture
1430 North Bel Air Drive
5   Tacoma, WA 98466-6970

Dear Ms. Bledsoe:

We miss you! Verdant Landscaping has been scheduled not to care for your grounds since fall 2008. You were a valued customer. Did our service fall short in some way? Whatever prompted you to make a change, we would like to discuss
10   ways we could serve you gooder.

During the past year, Verdant has added important these new three services: A full-time landscape architect helps happily you improve your grounds with flower beds, hardy shrubs, and blooming trees. A tree surgeon can give at a moment's notice you help with diseased or damaged trees. And our lawn crews offer
15   now mulching services. We provide the most good service and value at the most good price!

I'd like to call next week you to discuss whatever concerns you may have and to offer you a 10 percent discount on a lawn-service new agreement. I can answer at that time any
20   questions you may have about our new services as they are described in the enclosed brochure.

Sincere,

Stephen Bates

Stephen Bates
25   Customer Service

Enclosure

Correction Marks

⌿	delete
d̲	capitalize
⌀	lowercase
∧	insert
⌃	add comma
?	add question mark
word ∧	add word
⊙	add period
◠	spelling
◡	switch

25

> "Take hold lightly; let go lightly. This is one of the great secrets of felicity in love."
> —Spanish Proverb

Conjunction and Preposition

Every relationship is different. A boyfriend and girlfriend will probably be equals, but a mother and daughter probably won't be. In fact, the daughter may be legally classified as a dependent.

Ideas have relationships, too. Sometimes ideas are equal—you can tell by the conjunction that connects them. At other times, one idea depends on another. There are conjunctions for that situation, too. And when words form a special relationship, prepositions are there to connect them.

Conjunctions and prepositions make connections in your writing and help your ideas relate to each other. This chapter shows how.

Learning Outcomes

LO1 Coordinating and Correlative Conjunctions
LO2 Subordinating Conjunctions
LO3 Common Prepositions
LO4 *By, At, On,* and *In*
LO5 Real-World Application

What do you think?
What kind of relationship does the photo suggest?

Cheryl Casey, 2013 / Used under license from Shutterstock.com

LO1 Coordinating and Correlative Conjunctions

A **conjunction** is a word or word group that joins parts of a sentence—words, phrases, or clauses.

Coordinating Conjunctions

A **coordinating conjunction** joins grammatically equal parts—a word to a word, a phrase to a phrase, or a clause to a clause. (A clause is basically a sentence.)

Coordinating Conjunctions						
and	but	or	nor	for	so	yet

Equal importance: A coordinating conjunction shows that the two things joined are of equal importance.

Ted and Jana like rhythm and blues.
(*And* joins words in an equal way.)

I have R&B songs on my iPod and on CDs.
(*And* joins the phrases *on my iPod* and *on CDs.*)

I want to download more, but I lost my USB cord.
(*But* joins the two clauses, with a comma after the first.)

Items in a series: A coordinating conjunction can also join more than two equal things in a series.

Ted, Jana, and I are planning to attend an R&B festival.
(*And* joins *Ted, Jana,* and *I.* A comma follows each word except the last.)

We will drive to the fest, check out the acts, and buy our tickets.
(*And* joins three parts of a compound verb.)

Correlative Conjunctions

Correlative conjunctions consist of a coordinating conjunction paired with another word. They also join equal grammatical parts: word to word, phrase to phrase, or clause to clause.

Correlative Conjunctions				
either/or	neither/nor	whether/or	both/and	not only/but also

Stressing equality: Correlative conjunctions stress the equality of parts.

I like not only rock but also classical.
(*Not only/but also* stresses the equality of *rock* and *classical.*)

Using Coordinating and Correlative Conjunctions

Correct For each sentence below, write the best coordinating conjunction in parentheses.

1. I should buy an MP3 player (but, for, or) an iPod.

2. Kelly, Eli, (and, nor, yet) I sometimes share music.

3. We have different tastes, (or, so, yet) we get to hear a variety.

4. Kelly likes hip-hop, (nor, but, for) I like Latin music.

5. Eli likes classic rock, (but, yet, so) he shares '70s bands.

6. Each week, Kelly, Eli, (and, but, or) I meet to talk about music.

7. We want to broaden our tastes, (and, or, yet) we don't like everything we hear.

8. I like rhythm, Kelly likes words, (and, nor, so) Eli likes melodies.

9. Ask us for recommendations, (and, for, so) we are committed fans.

10. We'll tell you what we like, (but, nor, for) you have to choose for yourself.

Write Create sentences of your own, using a coordinating conjunction (*and, but, or, nor, for, so, yet*) as requested.

1. joining two words: _____

2. joining two phrases: _____

3. creating a series: _____

4. joining two clauses (place a comma after the first clause, before the conjunction): _____

Write Create a sentence using a pair of correlative conjunctions:

_____

CONSIDER THE TRAITS
When two ideas correlate, they work together. They co-relate. Thinking in this way can help you remember the term *correlative conjunctions*.

conjunction	**coordinating conjunction**	**correlative conjunction**
word or word group that joins parts of a sentence	conjunction that joins grammatically equal components	pair of conjunctions that stress the equality of the parts that are joined

LO2 Subordinating Conjunctions

A **subordinating conjunction** is a word or word group that connects two clauses of different importance. (A clause is basically a sentence.)

Subordinating Conjunctions

after	as long as	if	so that	till	whenever
although	because	in order that	than	unless	where
as	before	provided that	that	until	whereas
as if	even though	since	though	when	while

Subordinate clause: The subordinating conjunction comes at the beginning of the less-important clause, making it subordinate (it can't stand on its own). The **subordinate clause** can come before or after the more important clause (the **independent clause**).

I go out to eat. I like to order Mexican food.
(two clauses)

Whenever I go out to eat, I like to order Mexican food.
(*Whenever* introduces the subordinate clause, which is followed by a comma.)

I like to order Mexican food whenever I go out to eat.
(If the subordinate clause comes second, a comma usually isn't needed.)

Special relationship: A subordinating conjunction shows a special relationship between ideas. Here are the relationships that subordinating conjunctions show:

Time	after, as, before, since, till, until, when, whenever, while
Cause	as, as long as, because, before, if, in order that, provided that, since, so that, that, till, until, when, whenever
Contrast	although, as if, even though, though, unless, whereas

Whenever Mexican food is on the menu, I will order it.
(time)

I order it extra spicy because I love to feel the burn.
(cause)

Even though I ask for extra heat, I often still have to add hot sauce.
(contrast)

Using Subordinating Conjunctions

Write For the blank in each sentence, provide an appropriate subordinating conjunction. Then write what type of relationship it shows.

1. _____ we washed the car, I got sprayed many times.
   (time, cause, contrast)

2. Car washing is work _____ it feels like play.
   (time, cause, contrast)

3. _____ the hoses go on, a splash fight is inevitable.
   (time, cause, contrast)

4. I usually don't start the fight _____ I'm willing to join in.
   (time, cause, contrast)

5. _____ people can't resist sudsy buckets, the fight begins.
   (time, cause, contrast)

6. The car may not get clean _____ the people do.
   (time, cause, contrast)

7. _____ I first get sprayed, I yell in shock.
   (time, cause, contrast)

8. _____ I get used to it, all bets are off.
   (time, cause, contrast)

9. I can be pretty ruthless _____ I have a hose in hand.
   (time, cause, contrast)

10. _____ people have such fun, not much washing gets done.
   (time, cause, contrast)

Write Create three of your own sentences using subordinating conjunctions, one for each type of relationship.

1. time: _____

2. cause: _____

3. contrast: _____

subordinating conjunction	subordinate clause	independent clause
word or word group that connects clauses of different importance	word group that begins with a subordinating conjunction and has a subject and verb but can't stand alone as a sentence	group of words with a subject and verb and that expresses a complete thought; it can stand alone as a sentence

LO3 Common Prepositions

A **preposition** is a word or word group that shows a relationship between a noun or pronoun and another word. Here are common prepositions:

Prepositions

aboard	back of	except for	near to	round
about	because of	excepting	notwithstanding	save
above	before	for	of	since
according to	behind	from	off	subsequent to
across	below	from among	on	through
across from	beneath	from between	on account of	throughout
after	beside	from under	on behalf of	'til
against	besides	in	onto	to
along	between	in addition to	on top of	together with
alongside	beyond	in behalf of	opposite	toward
alongside of	but	in front of	out	under
along with	by	in place of	out of	underneath
amid	by means of	in regard to	outside	until
among	concerning	inside	outside of	unto
apart from	considering	inside of	over	up
around	despite	in spite of	over to	upon
as far as	down	instead of	owing to	up to
aside from	down from	into	past	with
at	during	like	prior to	within
away from	except	near	regarding	without

Prepositional Phrases

A **prepositional phrase** starts with a preposition and includes an object of the preposition (a noun or pronoun) and any modifiers. A prepositional phrase functions as an adjective or adverb.

The store at the corner advertises in the newspaper.
(*At the corner* modifies *store*, and *in the newspaper* modifies *advertises*.)

Hand me the keys on the rack by the side of the door.
(*On the rack* modifies *keys*; *by the side* modifies *rack*; *of the door* modifies *side*.)

Using Common Prepositions

Create   For each sentence, fill in the blanks with prepositional phrases. Create them from the prepositions on the facing page and nouns or pronouns of your own choosing. Be creative!

1. This morning, I drove _____ .

2. Another driver _____ honked loudly.

3. I was so startled, I swerved _____ .

4. The other driver swerved _____ .

5. We both had looks of shock _____ .

6. I accelerated _____ .

7. Next thing I knew, I was _____ .

8. The incident _____ was a lesson.

9. The lesson was never to drive _____ .

Model   Read each sentence below and write another sentence modeled on it. Note how the writer uses prepositional phrases to create specific effects.

1. The boat went through the rapids, down a bowl, into the air, and over the falls.

   _____

2. I don't want to talk at you, nor to you—but with you.

   _____

3. After days of arguing and hours of negotiation, the Senate compromised.

   _____

4. Go through the back door, up the stairs, past the security guard, and into the party.

   _____

preposition	prepositional phrase
word or word group that creates a relationship between a noun or pronoun and another word	phrase that starts with a preposition; includes an object of the preposition (noun or pronoun) and any modifiers; and functions as an adjective or adverb

VR Photos, 2013 / Used under license from Shutterstock.com

LO4 *By, At, On,* and *In*

Prepositions often show the physical position of things—above, below, beside, around, and so on. Four specific prepositions show position but also get a lot of other use in English.

Uses for *By, At, On,* and *In*

By means "beside" or "up to a certain place or time."

> by the shed, by the road, by midnight, by April 15

At refers to a specific place or time.

> at the corner, at the station, at 4:35 p.m., at noon

On refers to a surface, a day or date, or an electronic medium.

> on the desk, on the cover
>
> on June 9, on Tuesday
>
> on the disk, on TV, on the computer

In refers to an enclosed space; a geographical location; an hour, a month, or a year; or a print medium.

> in the drawer, in the room, in Seattle, in Britain
>
> in an hour, in May, in 2012, in the book, in the newspaper

Say It

Team up with a partner. Have the first person read one of the words below, and have the second person use it in a prepositional phrase beginning with *by, at, on,* or *in.* The first person should check if the form is correct. (Some have more than one correct answer.) Then you should switch roles.

1. the living room
2. October 9
3. 11:15 a.m.
4. the cell phone
5. the edge
6. Chicago
7. the table
8. the restaurant
9. sunrise
10. the magazine

Using *By, At, On,* and *In*

`Circle`   For each sentence, circle the correct preposition in parentheses.

1. Please arrive (by, on, in) 11:55 p.m. because we will leave promptly (at, on, in) noon.

2. Make sure your carry-on fits (by, at, on, in) the overhead compartment or (by, at, on, in) the foot well in front of you.

3. I looked for a science article (by, at, on, in) the journal but could find only one (by, at, on, in) the Internet.

4. Though we sat (by, at, on, in) the waiting room, we weren't called (by, on, in) 3:15 p.m. for our appointment.

5. Four people standing (by, at, in) the corner reported a fire (at, on, in) a nearby garbage can.

6. (By, At, On, In) July 20, 1969, Neil Armstrong stepped (by, at, on, in) the surface of the moon.

7. I will meet you (by, at, on) the restaurant for our dinner reservation (by, at, on, in) 8:00 p.m.

8. Please place your check (by, at, on, in) the envelope, seal it, and write the following address (by, at, on, in) the envelope.

9. A parrot sat (by, at, on, in) the pirate's shoulder and looked me (by, at, on, in) the eye.

10. The song goes, "Under the boardwalk, down (by, at, on, in) the sea, (by, at, on, in) a blanket with my baby is where I'll be."

`Write`   Write a sentence that uses all four of these prepositions in phrases: *by, at, on, in.*

_____

_____

_____

LO5 Real-World Application

Revise Read the following email, noting how choppy it sounds because all of the sentences are short. Rewrite the email. Connect some of the sentences using a coordinating conjunction and a comma, and connect others using a subordinating conjunction. You can also change other words as needed. Reread the email to make sure it sounds smooth.

Subordinating Conjunctions

after	as long as	if	so that	till	whenever
although	because	in order that	than	unless	where
as	before	provided that	that	until	whereas
as if	even though	since	though	when	while

Coordinating Conjunctions

and	but	or	nor
for	so	yet	

Send	Attach	Fonts	Colors	Save As Draft

To: ESleightner@bramfeldpub.com

Subject: Update on Book Revision

Dear Ed: 1

Thank you for writing about the revision. It is going well. It should be complete in two weeks. I have finished most chapters. I have addressed the main points. It is easy to forget to apply a change throughout. I will read the whole book to watch for changes.   5

Some of the graphics are still rough. I will need to finalize them. The maps for the inside covers are drawn. They need to be professionally inked.

The permissions requests are still pending. I have gotten permissions for three of the five excerpts. The fee for using the material was reasonable. If the fees for the other two are not, I will replace them.   10

I will wrap up the revision in two weeks. You can plan to start editing then.

Thanks,

Maurice Williams
Author

Correcting Capitalization

Practice A In each sentence below, capitalize the appropriate words.

1. Singer jack johnson finds musical inspiration in his hometown of oahu, hawaii.

2. Hawaii is the only state made up entirely of islands and is located in the pacific ocean.

3. Known as the aloha state, it's home to the hawaii volcanoes national park.

4. Another national park, the U.S.S. *arizona* memorial, is dedicated to the navy members who were lost during the attack on pearl harbor.

5. On december, 7, 1941, the United States naval base at pearl harbor, Hawaii, was attacked by japan.

6. The attack triggered the united states' entry in world war II.

7. President franklin d. roosevelt declared December 7 as "a day that will live in infamy."

8. Hawaii's beautiful beaches and tropical temperatures attract tourists from the midwest to the far east.

Practice B Decide what words should be capitalized. Write them down.

> My favorite holiday is thanksgiving. every november, family members   *1*
> from illinois, indiana, and Michigan travel to my parents' house to
> celebrate the best thursday of the year. While Mom and my aunts work
> on the dressing and mashed potatoes, my cousins and I watch football on
> the fox network. it has long been a tradition for the Detroit lions to play a   *5*
> home game every thanksgiving. By the time the game is finished, the food
> is ready and the feast is on. Turkey, gravy, and green-bean casserole—you
> can't beat thanksgiving.

INSIGHT

Different languages use capitalization differently. For example, German capitalizes not just proper nouns but all important nouns. Compare and contrast capitalization styles between your heritage language and English.

LO2 Advanced Capitalization

Sentences in Parentheses

Capitalize the first word in a sentence that is enclosed in parentheses if that sentence is not combined within another complete sentence.

My favorite designer is hosting a fashion show for her new collection. (**Now** I just need a ticket.)

NOTE: Do *not* capitalize a sentence that is enclosed in parentheses and is located in the middle of another sentence.

Rachel's cousin (his name is Carl) can't make it tonight.

Sentences Following Colons

Capitalize a complete sentence that follows a colon when that sentence is a formal statement, a quotation, or a sentence that you want to emphasize.

I would like to paraphrase Patrick Henry: Give me chocolate or give me death.

Salutation and Complimentary Closing

In a letter, capitalize the first and all major words of the salutation. Capitalize only the first word of the complimentary closing.

Dear Dr. Howard: **Sincerely** yours,

Sections of the Country

Words that indicate sections of the country are proper nouns and should be capitalized; words that simply indicate directions are not proper nouns.

I'm thinking about moving to the **West Coast.** *(section of country)*
I'm thinking about driving **west** to California. *(direction)*

Languages, Ethnic Groups, Nationalities, and Religions

Capitalize languages, ethnic groups, nationalities, religions, Supreme Beings, and holy books.

African	Navajo	Islam	God	Allah
Jehovah	the Koran	the Book of Exodus		the Bible

Correcting Capitalization

Practice A   In each sentence below, capitalize the appropriate words.

1. The midwest region of the United States is made up of 12 states.

2. The bible and the koran are considered holy books.

3. The navajo indians of the southwest have significant populations in an area known as the Four Corners (arizona, new mexico, utah, and Colorado).

4. Mark Twain once said this about adversity: "it's not the size of the dog in the fight; it's the size of the fight in the dog."

5. My brother Phil is starting college today. (my mom finally has the house to herself.)

6. I'm a proud member of the latino community in Miami.

7. In Quebec, Canada, many citizens speak both english and french.

Practice B   Read the following paragraph. Then capitalize the appropriate words.

> I ate the best seafood of my life at a new england restaurant. The   *1*
> small coastal restaurant in Massachusetts features fresh seafood from
> the atlantic ocean. I ordered the maine lobster, and I have one impression:
> it was awesome. If you have never tried fresh lobster before, I highly
> recommend it. You won't be disappointed. (now I need to figure out when I   *5*
> can go back.)

Practice C   Decide what words should be capitalized. Write them down.

tomorrow   hanukah   wednesday   bank   frisbee

u.s. bank   flying disc   russia   tree

INSIGHT ———————————————————————————————————

Do not capitalize words used to indicate direction or position.

Turn **south** at the stop sign. *(South refers to direction.)*

The **South** is known for its great Cajun food. *(South refers to a region of the country.)*

LO3 Other Capitalization Rules I

Titles

Capitalize the first word of a title, the last word, and every word in between except articles *(a, an, the)*, short prepositions, *to* in an infinitive, and coordinating conjunctions. Follow this rule for titles of books, newspapers, magazines, poems, plays, songs, articles, films, works of art, and stories.

The Curious Case of Benjamin Button	*New York Times*
"Cry Me a River"	"Cashing in on Kids"
A Midsummer Night's Dream	*The Da Vinci Code*

Organizations

Capitalize the name of an organization or a team and its members.

American Indian Movement	Democratic Party
Lance Armstrong Foundation	Indiana Pacers
Susan G. Komen for the Cure	Boston Red Sox

Abbreviations

Capitalize abbreviations of titles and organizations.

M.D.	Ph.D.	NAACP	C.E.	B.C.E.	GPA

Letters

Capitalize letters used to indicate a form or shape.

U-turn	I-beam	V-shaped	T-shirt

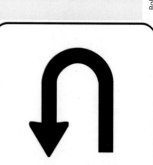

INSIGHT

Note that the American Psychological Association has a different style for capitalizing the titles of smaller works. Be sure you know the style required for a specific class.

Correcting Capitalization

Practice A   In the sentences below, capitalize the appropriate words.

1. I'm stopping by the gas station to pick up the sunday *Chicago tribune*.

2. The Los Angeles lakers play in the staples center.

3. At the next stoplight, you will need to take a u-turn.

4. My favorite author is Malcolm Gladwell, who wrote the best-sellers *blink* and *The tipping point*.

5. How many times have you heard the song "I got a feeling" by the Black-eyed peas?

6. The American cancer society raises money for cancer research.

7. I was happy to improve my gpa from 3.1 to 3.4 last semester.

8. Where did you buy that Seattle mariners t-shirt?

9. The doctor charted the growth of the tumor using an s-curve.

10. The man read a copy of *gq* magazine in New York City's central park.

11. Jill was promoted to chief operating officer (ceo) this july.

Practice B   Read the paragraph below. Then write down the words that need to be capitalized.

On our way to the Kansas city royals game, my friend Ted and I got   *1*

in an argument over our favorite music. He likes coldplay, while I prefer

radiohead. His favorite song is "Vida la viva." My favorite is "Fake plastic

trees." But as we argued about the merits of each band, we completely

missed our exit to the stadium. Ted suggested we perform a u-turn.   *5*

Instead, I used my gps to find a new route. Luckily, we made it to the

ballpark in time to grab a hot dog and coke before the opening pitch.

LO4 Other Capitalization Rules II

Words Used as Names

Capitalize words like *father, mother, uncle, senator,* and *professor* only when they are parts of titles that include a personal name or when they are substitutes for proper nouns (especially in direct address).

Hello, **Senator** Feingold. (*Senator* is part of the name.)

It's good to meet you, **Senator.** (*Senator* is a substitute for the name.)

Our **senator** is an environmentalist.

Who was your chemistry **professor** last quarter?

I had **Professor Williams** for Chemistry 101.

Good morning, **Professor.**

NOTE: To test whether a word is being substituted for a proper noun, simply read the sentence with a proper noun in place of the word. If the proper noun fits in the sentence, the word being tested should be capitalized. Usually the word is not capitalized if it follows a possessive—*my, his, our, your,* and so on.

Did **Dad** (Brad) pack the stereo in the trailer? (*Brad* works in the sentence.)

Did your **dad** (Brad) pack the stereo in the trailer?
(*Brad* does not work in the sentence; the word *dad* follows *your.*)

Titles of Courses

Words such as *technology, history,* and *science* are proper nouns when they are included in the titles of specific courses; they are common nouns when they name a field of study.

Who teaches **Art History 202**? (title of a specific course)

Professor Bunker loves teaching **history.** (a field of study)

Web Terms

The words *Internet* and *World Wide Web* are capitalized because they are considered proper nouns. When your writing includes a Web address (URL), capitalize any letters that the site's owner does (on printed materials or on the site itself).

When doing research on the **Internet**, be sure to record each site's **Web** address (URL) and each contact's **email** address.

Correcting Capitalization

Practice A   In each sentence below, capitalize the appropriate words.

1. I met mayor Greg Ballard by chance today at the daily brew, a coffee shop.

2. When I was a freshman, I studied the history of roman art in art history 101.

3. Ever since I gained wireless access to the internet, I've spent hours each day on YouTube.

4. Let's hope dad can make it in time for our tee time.

5. In a speech to his constituents, congressman Paul Ryan called for fiscal responsibility.

6. My favorite class this semester is advanced forensics 332 with dr. Charles Wendell, a well-known professor.

7. My uncle Brad has no clue how to navigate the world wide web.

8. Elizabeth attended the Wayne State University senior Banquet.

9. In searching for exercise routines, Jack bookmarked a web address (url) for *men's health* magazine.

10. You will need to contact commissioner Sheffield for permission.

Practice B   Read the paragraph below. Then write down the words that need to be capitalized.

Before Steve Jobs became ceo of apple Inc. and the brainchild behind   *1*

Macintosh, he attended high school in the San Francisco bay Area, a

region that is famously known as silicon valley. Jobs enrolled at Reed

College in portland, Oregon, but dropped out after the first semester to

return home to co-create apple. At the same time, other tech innovators   *5*

flooded the area to create companies such as Hewlett-packard and Intel.

It is also here that internet giants google and Yahoo! were founded. Today

Silicon valley remains a region of technological innovation.

LO5 Real-World Application

Correct   In the following basic letter, capitalize the appropriate words. Then lowercase the words that shouldn't be capitalized. (If a letter is capitalized and shouldn't be, put a lowercase editing mark through the letter.)

Ball State university Volunteer Center
7711 S. Hampton drive
Muncie, IN 47302
July, 5 2010

Mr. Ryan Orlovich
Muncie parks Department
1800 Grant Street
Muncie, IN 47302

Dear superintendent Orlovich:

Last Saturday, the Ball State volunteer center committee met to discuss new volunteer opportunities for the upcoming semester. We are interested in putting together a service event at big oak park for the incoming Freshmen.

We would like to get in contact with someone from your department to set up a time and date for the event. We would prefer the event to take place between thursday, August 23, and Sunday, August 26. Also, we hope to design t-shirts for the volunteers and are wondering if your office knows of any sponsors who might be interested in funding this expenditure.

When you have time, please contact me by phone at 317-555-3980 or Email at ehenderson@bs23u.edu. (you may also email the office at bsuvolunteerism@bs23u.edu.)

Yours Truly,

Liz Henderson

Liz Henderson

BSU Volunteer President

Special Challenge   Write a sentence that includes a colon followed by another sentence you want to emphasize. (See page 584).

27

> "The writer who neglects punctuation, or mispunctuates, is liable to be misunderstood for the want of merely a comma. "
> —Edgar Allan Poe

Comma

Commas divide sentences into smaller sections so that they may be read more easily and more precisely. They also show which words belong together and which line up in parallel. Of all the punctuation marks, commas are used most frequently—and oftentimes incorrectly.

This chapter will guide you in the conventional use of commas. Understanding correct comma usage is an important step in becoming a college-level writer. Applying these rules will make your writing clearer and easier to follow.

Learning Outcomes

LO1 In Compound Sentences and After Introductory Clauses

LO2 With Introductory Words and Equal Adjectives

LO3 Between Items in a Series and Other Uses

LO4 With Appositives and Other Word Groups

LO5 Real-World Application

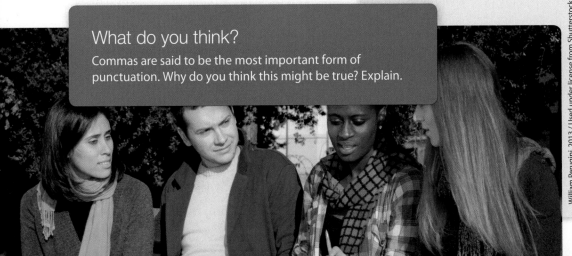

What do you think?

Commas are said to be the most important form of punctuation. Why do you think this might be true? Explain.

William Perugini, 2013 / Used under license from Shutterstock.com

LO1 In Compound Sentences and After Introductory Clauses

The following principles will guide the use of commas in your writing.

In Compound Sentences

Use a comma before the coordinating conjunction *(and, but, or, nor, for, yet, so)* in a compound sentence.

Heath Ledger completed his brilliant portrayal as the Joker in *The Dark Knight*, **but** he died before the film was released.

NOTE: Do not confuse a compound verb with a compound sentence.

Ledger's Joker became instantly iconic and won him the Oscar for best supporting actor. *(compound verb)*

His death resulted from the abuse of prescription drugs, but it was ruled an accident. *(compound sentence)*

After Introductory Clauses

Use a comma after most introductory clauses.

Although Charlemagne was a great patron of learning, he never learned to write properly. (adverb dependent clause)

When the clause follows the independent clause and is not essential to the meaning of the sentence, use a comma. This comma use generally applies to clauses beginning with *even though, although, while,* or some other conjunction expressing a contrast.

Charlemagne never learned to write properly, **even though he continued to practice.**

NOTE: A comma is *not* used if the dependent clause following the independent clause is needed for clarity.

CONSIDER THE TRAITS

Make sure to use both a comma and a coordinating conjunction in a compound sentence, or you will create a comma splice or a run-on.

Correcting Comma Errors

Correct   For each sentence below, add a comma before the coordinating conjunction (*and, but, or, nor, for, so, yet*) if the clause on each side could stand alone as a sentence. Write "correct" if the conjunction separates word groups that can't stand alone.

1. I was sick of sitting around on the couch so I drove over to the driving range.   _____

2. Her cell phone rang but she decided against answering it.   _____

3. Maria downloaded some new music and imported it on her iPod.   _____

4. I wanted to finish my assignment but I couldn't turn away from the *House* marathon.   _____

5. Should I put a down payment on a new car or should I save my money for a new apartment?   _____

6. Kelly is studying frog populations in the rain forest and she hopes to publish her work.   _____

7. Ryan wanted to make a new style of chili but he lost the recipe.   _____

8. Trisha was looking forward to the baseball game but it got rained out.   _____

Correct   For each sentence below, add a comma after any introductory clauses. If no comma is needed, write "correct" next to the sentence.

1. While Becca prefers grilled salmon Mia's favorite food is sushi.   _____

2. Although the water conditions were perfect I couldn't catch a wave to save my life.   _____

3. Perhaps I should rethink my major because I don't enjoy the classes.   _____

4. Even though the Cubs haven't won a World Series since 1901 I still cheer for them.   _____

5. While *American Idol* is popular in America *Britain's Got Talent* is the craze in England.   _____

LO2 With Introductory Phrases and Equal Adjectives

After Introductory Phrases

Use a comma after introductory phrases.

In spite of his friend's prodding, Jared decided to stay home and study.

A comma is usually omitted if the phrase follows an independent clause.

Jared decided to stay home and study **in spite of his friend's prodding.**

You may omit a comma after a short (four or fewer words) introductory phrase unless it is needed to ensure clarity.

At 10:32 p.m. he would quit and go to sleep.

To Separate Adjectives

Use commas to separate adjectives that equally modify the same noun. Notice in the examples below that no comma separates the last adjective from the noun.

You should exercise regularly and follow a **sensible, healthful** diet.

A good diet is one that includes lots of **high-protein, low-fat** foods.

To Determine Equal Modifiers

To determine whether adjectives modify a noun equally, use these two tests.

1. Reverse the order of the adjectives; if the sentence is clear, the adjectives modify equally. (In the example below, *hot* and *crowded* can be switched, but *short* and *coffee* cannot.)

   Matt was tired of working in the **hot, crowded** lab and decided to take a **short coffee** break.

2. Insert *and* between the adjectives; if the sentence reads well, use a comma when *and* is omitted. (The word *and* can be inserted between *hot* and *crowded,* but *and* does not make sense between *short* and *coffee.*)

Correcting Comma Errors

Correct If a comma is needed after the introductory phrase, write the words before and after the comma, with it between them. If no comma is needed, write "correct."

1. Before you can receive your diploma you will need to pay your unpaid parking tickets.   _____

2. At Central Perk Ross, Rachel, and the gang sipped coffee and exchanged barbs.   _____

3. In accordance with state law Hanna decided against sending a text message while driving on the interstate.   _____

4. The game was not cancelled despite heavy rain and muddy conditions.   _____

5. After handing in her paper Eva felt a great wave of relief.   _____

6. Eva felt a great wave of relief after handing in her paper.   _____

7. Based on his primary research Andy came up with a preliminary hypothesis.   _____

8. To save a few dollars Stephanie rode her bike to work.   _____

Correct For each sentence below, determine whether or not a comma is needed to separate the adjectives that modify the same noun. Add any needed commas. Write "no" next to the sentence if a comma is not needed.

1. The **long difficult** exam took a lot out of me.   _____

2. Last night I went to a **fun graduation** party.   _____

3. A good concert includes many **memorable hair-raising** moments.   _____

4. A **thoughtful considerate** friend goes an extra mile to make you smile.   _____

5. I could really use a **relaxing back** massage.   _____

6. When dressing for skiing, consider wearing a **thick well-insulated** jacket.   _____

LO3 Between Items in a Series and Other Uses

Between Items in Series

Use commas to separate individual words, phrases, or clauses in a series. (A series contains at least three items.)

Many college students must balance studying with **taking care of a family, working, getting exercise, and finding time to relax.**

Do not use commas when all the items are connected with *or, nor,* or *and.*

Hmm . . . should I study **or** do laundry **or** go out?

To Set Off Transitional Expressions

Use a comma to set off conjunctive adverbs and transitional phrases.

Handwriting is not**, as a matter of fact,** easy to improve upon later in life; **however,** it can be done if you are determined enough.

If a transitional expression blends smoothly with the rest of the sentence, it does not need to be set off.

If you are **in fact** coming**,** I'll see you there.

To Set Off Dialogue

Use commas to set off the words of the speaker from the rest of the sentence. Do not use a comma before an indirect quotation.

"Never be afraid to ask for help," advised Ms. Kane.

"With the evidence that we now have," Professor Thom said**, "many scientists believe there could be life on Mars."**

To Enclose Explanatory Words

Use commas to enclose an explanatory word or phrase.

Time management**, according to many professionals,** is an important skill that should be taught in college.

Correcting Comma Errors

Correct Indicate where commas are needed. Write the words before and after the comma, showing the comma between them.

1. I'm looking forward to graduation summer vacation and moving into a new apartment.

2. A new strain of virus according to biologists could cause future outbreaks of poultry disease.

3. "To confine our attention to terrestrial matters would be to limit the human spirit" said Stephen Hawking.

4. I need you to pick up two jars of peanut butter, a half-gallon of skim milk and snacks for the party.

5. I enjoy live music; however I don't like big crowds.

6. "With all the advancements in technology" Sara said, "you'd think we would have invented a quicker toaster by now."

7. Eighty percent of states as a matter of fact are in financial trouble.

8. We can meet up at either the library the student union or memorial hall.

9. The difference between perseverance and obstinacy according to Henry Ward Beecher is that one comes from strong will and the other from a strong won't.

10. Chicago, Detroit and Indianapolis are the most-populated cities in the Midwest.

Correct Indicate where commas are needed. Write the line number and the words before and after the comma, showing the comma between them.

> The Erie Canal is a man-made waterway that connects the Atlantic   *1*
> Ocean to Lake Erie. It was the first transportation system to connect the
> eastern seaboard and the Great Lakes was faster than carts pulled by
> animals and significantly cut transportation time. "The opening of the
> Erie Canal to New York in 1825 stimulated other cities on the Atlantic   *5*
> seaboard to put themselves into closer commercial touch with the West"
> said John Moody. Since the 1990s the canal is mostly home to recreational
> traffic; however some cargo is still transported down the waterway.

LO4 With Appositives and Nonrestrictive Modifiers

To Set Off Some Appositives

A specific kind of explanatory word or phrase called an **appositive** identifies or renames a preceding noun or pronoun.

Albert Einstein**, the famous mathematician and physicist,** developed the theory of relativity.

Do not use commas if the appositive is important to the basic meaning of the sentence.

The famous physicist **Albert Einstein** developed the theory of relativity.

With Some Clauses and Phrases

Use commas to enclose phrases or clauses that add information that is not necessary to the basic meaning of the sentence. For example, if the clause or phrase (in boldface) were left out of the two examples below, the meaning of the sentences would remain clear. Therefore, commas are used to set off the information.

The locker rooms in Swain Hall**, which were painted and updated last summer,** give professors a place to shower. (nonrestrictive clause)

Work-study programs**, offered on many campuses,** give students the opportunity to earn tuition money. (nonrestrictive phrase)

Do not use commas to set off necessary clauses and phrases, which add information that the reader needs to understand the sentence.

Only the professors **who run at noon** use the locker rooms. (necessary clause)

Using "That" or "Which"

Use *that* to introduce necessary clauses; use *which* to introduce unnecessary clauses.

Campus jobs **that are funded by the university** are awarded to students only. (necessary)

The cafeteria**, which is run by an independent contractor,** can hire nonstudents. (unnecessary)

Correcting Comma Errors

Correct Indicate where commas are needed in the following sentences. If no commas are needed, write "correct."

1. John D. Rockefeller the famous American philanthropist and oil executive is sometimes referred to as the richest person in history. _____

2. The new library which is scheduled to open in July will include three different computer labs. _____

3. The renowned trumpeter Louis Armstrong sang the song "What a Wonderful World." _____

4. Kansas City along with Memphis, Tennessee is known for its delicious barbecue. _____

5. Judge Sonya Sotomayer the first Hispanic Supreme Court justice was confirmed into office in 2009. _____

6. The book *The Notebook* which was later adapted into a movie was written by Nicolas Sparks. _____

Write The following sentences contain clauses using *that*. Rewrite the sentences with clauses using *which,* and insert commas correctly. You may need to reword some parts.

1. The road construction that delayed traffic yesterday should be completed by the end of the week.

   _____

   _____

2. The homework that Dr. Grant assigned yesterday will consume the next two weeks of my life.

   _____

   _____

3. The earplugs that we bought before the race made the deafening noise more bearable.

   _____

   _____

appositive
a noun or noun phrase that renames another noun right beside it

LO5 Real-World Application

Correct Indicate where commas are needed in the following email message. Write the line number and the words before and after the comma, showing it between them.

| Send | Attach | Fonts | Colors | Save As Draft |

To: Carrie Andritz <candritz@ucsc.edu>

Subject: Letter of Recommendation for Tyler Hoffman

Dear Professor Andritz: *1*

I enjoyed meeting with you today to discuss my letter of recommendation. You know the quality of my academic work my qualities as a person and my potential for working in the marketing industry.

As my professor for Marketing 303 and Economics 401 you have witnessed my   *5*
hardworking nature. As my adviser you know my career plans and should have a good sense of whether I have the qualities needed to succeed in the fast-paced competitive marketing industry.

Please send your letter to Craig Emmons human resources director at FastTech by April 14. If you have any questions please call me at (324) 472-3489.   *10*

Sincerely,

Tyler Hoffman

CONSIDER THE WORKPLACE ────────────

Correct comma use is critical for clear business communication.

28

> "A fine quotation is a diamond on the finger of a man of wit and a pebble in the hand of a fool."
> —Joseph Roux

Quotation Marks and Italics

Much of the time, language flows from us as naturally as breathing. We think; we speak; someone hears and responds—all without consciously thinking about the words.

Sometimes, however, we have need to note a word as a word, to call attention to a phrase in a special sense, to use an apt or time-honored quotation from someone else, or to mark the title of a work. In such cases, quotation marks and italics allow us to indicate this special use of language.

Learning Outcomes

LO1 Quotation Marks
LO2 Italics
LO3 Real-World Application

What do you think?
Study the image and quotation. What makes the gemstone in the photo valuable? In what way does this relate to the Joseph Roux quotation?

LO1 Quotation Marks

To Punctuate Titles (Smaller Works)

Use quotation marks to enclose the titles of smaller works, including speeches, short stories, songs, poems, episodes of audio or video programs, chapters or sections of books, unpublished works, and articles from magazines, journals, newspapers, or encyclopedias. (For other titles, see page 604.)

Speech:	"The Cause Endures"
Song:	"Head Like a Hole"
Short Story:	"Dark They Were, and Golden Eyed"
Magazine Article:	"The Moral Life of Babies"
Chapter in a Book:	"Queen Mab"
Television Episode:	"The Girl Who Was Death"
Encyclopedia Article:	"Cetacean"

Placement of Periods and Commas

When quoted words end in a period or comma, always place that punctuation inside the quotation marks.

"If you want to catch the train," Grace said, "you must leave now."

Placement of Semicolons and Colons

When a quotation is followed by a semicolon or colon, always place that punctuation outside the quotation marks.

I finally read "Heart of Darkness"; it is amazingly well written!

Placement of Exclamation Points and Question Marks

If an exclamation point or a question mark is part of the quotation, place it inside the quotation marks. Otherwise, place it outside.

Marcello asked me, "Are you going to the Dodge Poetry Festival?" What could I reply except "Yes, indeed"?

For Special Words

Quotation marks can be used (1) to show that a word is being referred to as the word itself; (2) to indicate that it is jargon, slang, or a coined term; or (3) to show that it is used in an ironic or sarcastic sense.

(1) Somehow, the term "cool" has survived decades.
(2) The band has a "wicked awesome" sound.
(3) I would describe the taste of this casserole as "swampy."

Using Quotation Marks

Correct   For the following sentences, insert quotation marks where needed.

1. Kamala loves to listen to the song I Take Time, over and over and over.

2. Ray Bradbury's short story A Sound of Thunder has been republished many times.

3. *Fast Company* published an article today called How Google Wave Got Its Groove Back.

4. Angelo told Arlena, I have a guy who can fix that fender.

5. Arlena asked, How much will it cost me?

6. Was she thinking, This car is driving me into bankruptcy?

7. This is the message of the article Tracking the Science of Commitment: Couples that enhance one another have an easier time remaining committed.

8. I love the article Tall Tales About Being Short; it challenged my preconceptions about the effect of height on a person's life.

9. How many examples of the word aardvark can you find on this page?

10. Is anyone else here tired of hearing about his bling bling?

Write   Write a sentence that indicates the actual meaning of each sentence below.

1. Hoyt's great Dane "skipped" across the floor and "settled" its bulk across his lap.

_____

_____

2. Our baked goods are always "fresh."

_____

_____

3. And so began another "wonderful" day of marching through a "fairyland" of bugs.

_____

_____

LO2 Italics

To Punctuate Titles (Larger Works)

Use italics to indicate the titles of larger works, including newspapers, magazines, journals, pamphlets, books, plays, films, radio and television programs, movies, ballets, operas, long musical compositions, CDs, DVDs, software programs, and legal cases, as well as the names of ships, trains, aircraft, and spacecraft. (For other titles, see page 602.)

Magazine: *Wired*

Play: *Night of the Iguana*

Film: *Bladerunner*

Book: *Moby Dick*

Newspaper: *Washington Post*

Journal: *Journal of Sound & Vibration*

Software Program: *Paint Shop Pro*

Television Program: *The Prisoner*

For a Word, Letter, or Number Referred to as Itself

Use italics (or quotation marks—see page 602) to show that a word, letter, or number is being referred to as itself. If a definition follows a word used in this way, place that definition in quotation marks.

The word *tornado* comes to English from the Spanish *tronar,* which means "to thunder." I can't read your writing; is this supposed to be a *P* or an *R*?

For Foreign Words

Use italics to indicate a word that is being borrowed from a foreign language.

Je ne sais pas is a French phrase that many English speakers use as a fancy way of saying "I don't know what."

For Technical Terms

Use italics to introduce a technical term for the first time in a piece of writing. After that, the term may be used without italics.

The heart's *sternocostal* surface—facing toward the joining of sternum and ribs—holds the heart's primary natural pacemaker. If this sternocostal node fails, a lower, secondary node can function in its place.

NOTE: If a technical term is being used within an organization or a field of study where it is common, it may be used without italics even the first time in a piece of writing.

Using Italics

Correct For the following sentences, underline words that should be in italics.

1. I almost couldn't finish Stephenie Meyer's second book, New Moon, because of its deep emotion.

2. What is your favorite part of the movie Avatar?

3. The Spanish say duende to describe a transcendent, creative passion.

4. Was the aircraft carrier Enterprise named after the vessel from the Star Trek series or the other way around?

5. You might use the term bonhomie to describe our relationship.

6. One thing I love about the MS Word program is its "Track Changes" feature.

7. In this course, we will use the term noetics as an indication of deep-felt self-awareness, beyond mere consciousness.

8. How am I supposed to compete at Scrabble when all I have is an X and a 7?

9. Wait, that's not a 7; it's an L.

10. That, ladies and gentleman, is what we in show business call a finale!

Write Write three sentences, each demonstrating your understanding of one or more rules for using italics.

1. _____

_____

_____

2. _____

_____

_____

3. _____

_____

_____

LO3 Real-World Application

In the following business letter, underline any words that should be italicized and add quotation marks where needed.

Brideshead Publishing
1012 Broadway
New York, New York 10011

May 13, 2010   *1*

Neva Konen
4004 W. Obleness Parkway
Hollenshead, New Hampshire 03305

Dear Neva Konen: *5*

Thank you for your recent novel submission entitled A Time of Dimly Perceived Wonders, which I read with great interest. The setting is richly portrayed, and the main characters are at the same time both mysterious and familiar, conveying a certain je ne sais quas about themselves. For example, although his words land strangely on my ear, still I am overwhelmed with feelings of kinship for Anibal when he cries out, I could've et 'em up   *10* right there 'n' then! Similarly, when at the end Kandis softly croons the words of Come One, Come All, to the Family Reunion, I feel I'm being called home myself, although I've never actually seen the Appalachians.

While I greatly enjoyed the novel, and it would certainly receive an "A" in my Creative Writing Seminar at Midtown College, I do have a few concerns. For one thing, the title   *15* seems long and somewhat vague; I'd recommend Foggy Mountain Memories, instead. Also, it seems unnecessary to print the full text of Abraham Lincoln's Gettysburg Address and Martin Luther King, Jr.'s, I Have a Dream speech in the chapter entitled A Few Words of Hope. Modern readers are certainly familiar with both speeches. It should be enough to merely include a few phrases, such as Four score and seven years ago and Let   *20* freedom ring from Lookout Mountain of Tennessee.

If you are willing to accept changes such as these, I believe we can work together to make your novel a commercial success. Please review the enclosed contract and return it to me at your earliest convenience.

Sincerely,   *25*

Christene Kaley

Christene Kaley

29

"If the English language made any sense,
a catastrophe would be an apostrophe with fur."
—Doug Larson

Other Punctuation

You may be surprised to discover that the words *catastrophe* and *apostrophe* have something in common. Both come from the Greek word for "turn." An apostrophe simply turns away, but a catastrophe overturns.

Sometimes the use of apostrophes becomes a catastrophe. Apostrophes shouldn't be used to form plurals of words. Their main use is to form possessives and contractions. The rules and activities in this chapter will help you understand their usage and avoid an apostrophe catastrophe.

This chapter also provides guidelines for the rules and correct usage of semicolons, colons, hyphens, and dashes.

Learning Outcomes

LO1 Contractions and Possessives

LO2 Semicolons and Colons

LO3 Hyphens

LO4 Dashes

LO5 Real-World Application

LO6 Real-World Application

What do you think?

Why do you think *apostrophe* comes from the word "to turn away?"

LO1 Apostrophes for Contractions and Possessives

Apostrophes are used primarily to show that a letter or number has been left out or that a noun is possessive.

Contractions

When one or more letters are left out of a word, use an apostrophe to form the **contraction**.

> **INSIGHT**
> Pronoun possessives *do not use* apostrophes: *its, whose, hers, his, ours*

don't	he'd	would've
(*o* is left out)	(*woul* is left out)	(*ha* is left out)

Missing Characters

Use an apostrophe to signal when one or more characters are left out.

class of '16	rock 'n' roll	good mornin'
(*20* is left out)	(*a* and *d* are left out)	(*g* is left out)

Possessives

Form possessives of singular nouns by adding an apostrophe and an *s*.

Sharla's pen	the man's coat	*The Pilgrim's Progress*

Singular Noun Ending in *s* (One Syllable)

Form the possessive by adding an apostrophe and an *s*.

the boss's idea	the lass's purse	the bass's teeth

Singular Noun Ending in *s* (Two or More Syllables)

Form the possessive by adding an apostrophe and an *s*—or by adding just an apostrophe.

Kansas's plains	*or*	Kansas' plains

Plural Noun Ending in *s*

Form the possessive by adding just an apostrophe.

the bosses' preference   the Smiths' home

the girls' ball
(*girls* are the owners)

> **INSIGHT**
> The word before the apostrophe is the owner.

Plural Noun Not Ending in *s*

Form the possessive by adding an apostrophe and an *s*.

the children's toys   the women's room

Forming Contractions and Possessives

Write   For each contraction below, write the words that formed the contraction. For each set of words, write the contraction that would be formed.

1. they're _____

2. you've _____

3. Charlie is _____

4. wouldn't _____

5. we have _____

6. have not _____

7. I would _____

8. I had _____

9. won't _____

10. will not _____

Rewrite   Rework the following sentences, replacing the "of" phrases with possessives using apostrophes.

1. The idea of my friend is a good one.

_____

2. I found the flyer of the orchestra.

_____

3. The foundation of the government is democracy.

_____

4. He washed the jerseys of the team.

_____

5. I went to the house of the Kings.

_____

6. The plan of the managers worked well.

_____

7. I like the classic albums of Kiss.

_____

8. I graded the assignment of Ross.

_____

9. The pastries of the chef were delicious.

_____

10. The books of the children covered the floor.

_____

contraction
word formed by joining two words, leaving out one or more letters (indicated by an apostrophe)

LO2 Semicolons and Colons

Semicolons and colons have specific uses in writing.

Semicolon

A **semicolon** can be called a soft period. Use the semicolon to join two sentences that are closely related.

The job market is improving; it's time to apply again.

Before a Conjunctive Adverb

Often, the second sentence will begin with a conjunctive adverb *(also, besides, however, instead, meanwhile, therefore)*, which signals the relationship between the sentences. Place a semicolon before the conjunctive adverb, and place a comma after it.

I looked for work for two months; however, the market is better now.

With Series

Use a semicolon to separate items in a series if any of the items already include commas.

I should check online ads, headhunting services, and position announcements; compile a list of job openings; create a résumé, an e-résumé, and a cover letter; and apply, requesting an interview.

Colon

The main use of a **colon** is to introduce an example or a list.

I've forgotten one other possibility: social networking.
I'll plan to use the following: LinkedIn, Twitter, and Facebook.

After Salutations

In business documents, use a colon after **salutations** and in memo headings.

Dear Mr. Ortez: To: Lynne Jones

Times and Ratios

Use a colon to separate hours, minutes, and seconds. Also use a colon between the numbers in a ratio.

7:35 p.m.   6:15 a.m.   The student-teacher ratio is 30:1.

Using Semicolons and Colons

Correct Add semicolons and commas as needed in the sentences below.

1. Searching for a job is nerve-wracking however it's also about possibilities.

2. Don't think about rejections think about where you could be working.

3. Each résumé you send is a fishing line then you wait for a nibble.

4. Put out dozens of lines also give yourself time.

5. Make sure that you have a strong résumé e-résumé and cover letter that you consult social networks local newspapers and friends and that you keep your spirits up.

6. It doesn't cost much to send out résumés therefore send out many.

7. Job searching can feel lonely and frustrating rely on friends and family to help you through.

8. Ask people if you can use them as references don't provide the list of references until requested.

9. When you interview, wear professional clothing show up at the right place at the right time and armed with any information you need and be confident.

10. Try to enjoy the process it is the gateway to your future.

Correct Add colons where needed in the sentences below.

1. Use your social resources contacts, references, and organizations.

2. Call for an appointment between 9 00 a.m. and 4 00 p.m.

3. Remember, a response rate of 1 10 is good for résumés submitted.

4. Politely start your cover letter with a salutation "Dear Mrs. Baker."

5. For an interview, remember these three keys Be punctual, be polite, and be professional.

6. Here's one last piece of advice Be yourself.

---

semicolon
a punctuation mark (;) that connects sentences and separates items in some series

colon
a punctuation mark (:) that introduces an example or list and has other special uses

salutation
the formal greeting in a letter; the line starting with "Dear"

LO3 Hyphens

A **hyphen** joins words to letters or to each other to form compounds.

Compound Nouns

Use hyphens to create **compound nouns**.

city-state	fail-safe	fact-check	one-liner	mother-in-law

Compound Adjectives

Use hyphens to create **compound adjectives** that appear before the noun. If the adjective appears after, it usually is not hyphenated.

peer-reviewed article   an article that was peer reviewed

ready-made solution   a solution that is ready made

NOTE: Don't hyphenate a compound made from an -*ly* adverb and an adjective, or a compound that ends with a single letter.

newly acquired songs (*ly* adverb)   grade B plywood (ending with a letter)

Compound Numbers

Use hyphens for **compound numbers** from twenty-one to ninety-nine. Also use hyphens for numbers in a fraction and other number compounds.

twenty-two	fifty-fifty	three-quarters	seven thirty-seconds

With Letters

Use a hyphen to join a letter to a word that follows it.

L-bracket	U-shaped	T-shirt	O-ring	G-rated	x-ray

With Common Elements

Use hyphens to show that two or more words share a common element included in only the final term.

We offer low-, middle-, and high-coverage plans.

Using Hyphens

Correct Rewrite the following sentences. Add hyphens as needed.

1. The secretary treasurer recorded the vote as four five.

   _____

2. We had to x ray twenty one people today.

   _____

3. Cut each board at seven and three sixteenths inches.

   _____

4. The statistics on low , middle , and high income households are ready.

   _____

5. A double insulated wire should be used for high voltage applications.

   _____

6. The x axis shows months, and the y axis shows dollar amounts.

   _____

7. The tax rate table shows I should pay twenty eight cents.

   _____

8. My mother in law thinks I am quite a fine son in law.

   _____

9. The L bracket measured eleven sixteenths by twenty seven thirty seconds.

   _____

| **hyphen** a short horizontal line (-) used to form compound words **compound noun** a noun made of two or more words, often hyphenated or spelled closed | **compound adjective** an adjective made of two or more words, hyphenated before the noun but not afterward | **compound numbers** two-word numbers from twenty-one to ninety-nine |

sfam_photo, 2013 / Used under license from Shutterstock.com

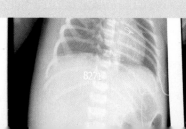
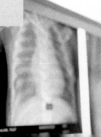

LO4 Dashes

Unlike the hyphen, the **dash** does more to separate words than to join them together. A dash is indicated by two hyphens with no spacing before or after. Most word-processing programs convert two hyphens into a dash.

For Emphasis

Use a dash instead of a colon if you want to emphasize a word, phrase, clause, or series.

Ice cream—it's what life is about.

I love two things about ice cream—making it and eating it.

Ice cream is my favorite dessert—cold, sweet, and flavorful.

To Set Off a Series

Use a dash to set off a series of items.

Rocky road, moose tracks, and chocolate-chip cookie dough—these are my favorite flavors.

Neapolitan ice cream—chocolate, strawberry, and vanilla—is my sister's favorite.

With Nonessential Elements

Use a dash to set off explanations, examples, and definitions, especially when these elements already include commas.

Ice milk—which, as you might guess, is made of milk instead of cream—provides a light alternative.

To Show Interrupted Speech

Use a dash to show that a speaker has been interrupted or has started and stopped while speaking.

"Could you help me crank this—"

"I've got to get more salt before—"

"It'll freeze up if you don't—Just give me a hand, please."

Using Dashes

Correct   In the sentences below, add a dash where needed.

1. Which dessert would you prefer brownies, apple pie, or ice cream?

2. I love the triple brownie surprise a brownie with vanilla and chocolate ice cream covered in hot fudge.

3. Ice cream it's what's for dinner.

4. "Could I have a taste of " "You want to try some of " "I want to try um could I try the pistachio?"

5. Bananas, ice cream, peanuts, and fudge these are the ingredients of a banana-split sundae.

6. Making ice cream at home takes a long time and a lot of muscle!

7. An electric ice-cream maker which replaced arm power with a cranking motor makes the job easier but less fun.

8. Nothing tastes better than the first taste of freshly made ice cream nothing except perhaps the next taste.

9. Don't eat too quickly brain-freeze.

10. A danger of ice cream I'll risk it every time.

Correct   Write your own sentence, correctly using dashes for each of the situations indicated below:

1. For emphasis:

   _____

2. To set off a series:

   _____

3. With nonessential elements:

   _____

> **dash**
> long horizontal line that separates words, creating emphasis.

LO5 Real-World Application

Correct The following letter sounds too informal because it contains too many contractions. For any contractions you find, write the line number and full form of the word. Also, if you find any errors with apostrophes, write the line number and show the correct punctuation.

Hanford Building
Supply Company, Inc.

5821 North Fairheights Road
Milsap, CA 94218
Ph: 567-555-1908

June 1, 2011   *1*

Account: 4879003

Mr. Robert Burnside, Controller
Circuit Electronic's Company
4900 Gorham Road   *5*
Mountain View, CA 94040-1093

Dear Mr. Burnside:

This letter's a reminder that your account's past due (presently 60 days).

As of today, we haven't yet received your payment of $1,806.00, originally due March
31. I've enclosed the March 1 invoice. It's for the mitered flange's that you ordered   *10*
January 10 and that we shipped January 28.

You've been a valued customer, Mr. Burnside, and Hanford appreciate's your business.
We've enclosed a postage-paid envelope for your convenience.

If there's a problem, please call (567-555-1908, ext. 227) or email me
(marta@hanford.com). As alway's, we look forward to serving you.   *15*

Sincerely,

Marta Ramones

Marta Ramones'
Billing Department

Enclosures 2

LO6 Real-World Application

Correct Rewrite the following email message, and insert semicolons, colons, hyphens, and dashes where necessary.

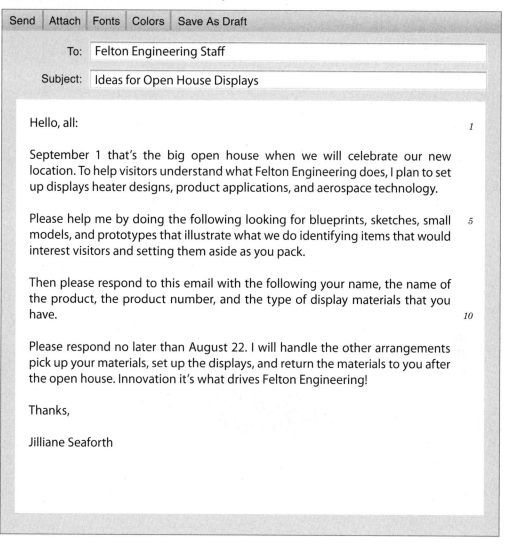

| Send | Attach | Fonts | Colors | Save As Draft |

To: Felton Engineering Staff

Subject: Ideas for Open House Displays

Hello, all: 1

September 1 that's the big open house when we will celebrate our new location. To help visitors understand what Felton Engineering does, I plan to set up displays heater designs, product applications, and aerospace technology.

Please help me by doing the following looking for blueprints, sketches, small   5
models, and prototypes that illustrate what we do identifying items that would interest visitors and setting them aside as you pack.

Then please respond to this email with the following your name, the name of the product, the product number, and the type of display materials that you have.   10

Please respond no later than August 22. I will handle the other arrangements pick up your materials, set up the displays, and return the materials to you after the open house. Innovation it's what drives Felton Engineering!

Thanks,

Jilliane Seaforth

Glossary/Appendix

Understanding the Reading Process

When reading academic texts, be sure to use the **reading process** to gain a full understanding of the material. This graphic shows the reading process in action. The arrows show how you may move back and forth between the steps.

The Reading Process

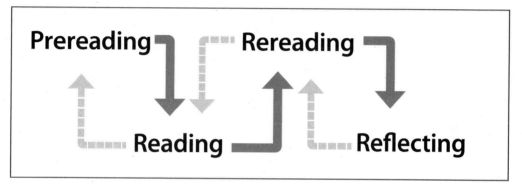

Key Terms to Remember

To use the reading process, you must understand each step in the process.

- **Prereading**—Becoming familiar with the text by reviewing the title, headings, etc.
- **Reading**—Reading the text once for a basic understanding, using a reading strategy such as note taking
- **Rereading**—Completing additional readings as needed until you have a clear understanding of the material
- **Reflecting**—Evaluating your reading experience: *What have you learned? What questions to you still have?*

For additional information, see pages 13–15.

Understanding the Writing Process

When completing a writing assignment, be sure to use the writing process to help you do your best work. This graphic shows the writing process in action. The arrows show how you may move back and forth between the steps.

The Writing Process

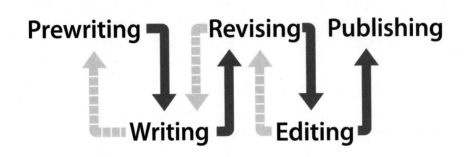

Key Terms to Remember

To use the writing process, you must understand each step in the process.

- **Prewriting**—Starting the process by analyzing the assignment, selecting a topic, gathering details, and finding a focus
- **Writing**—Writing a first draft using your prewriting as a guide
- **Revising**—Improving the content of a first draft
- **Editing**—Checking for style, grammar, mechanics, and spelling
- **Publishing**—Preparing your writing to share or submit

For additional information, see pages 94–99.

Understanding the Structure of Paragraphs and Essays

Paragraphs and essays follow a three-part structure. Knowing the purpose of each part will help you understand reading assignments and develop your own writing.

Three-Part Structure

Paragraph Structure

Topic Sentence
- Names the topic and focus

Body Sentences
- Provide supporting sentences
- Follow a pattern of organization

Closing Sentence
- Wraps up the paragraph

Essay Structure

Opening Part
- Introduces the topic
- Provides background information
- Identifies the main point or thesis

Middle Part
- Supports or develops the main point
- Follows one or more patterns of organization

Closing Part
- Summarizes the key ideas
- Restates the thesis
- Provides final thoughts or analysis

For additional information, see pages 76–77 and 100–105.

Using a Peer Review Sheet

Sharing your writing at various stages is important, but it is especially important when you review and revise a first draft. The feedback that you receive will help you change and improve your essay.

Peer Review Sheet

Essay title: _____

Writer: _____

Reviewer: _____

1. Which part of the essay seems to work best—opening, middle, or closing? Why?

   _____

   _____

2. Which part of the essay needs work—opening, middle, or closing? Why?

   _____

   _____

3. Do the middle paragraphs clearly present each step of the process? Explain.

   _____

   _____

4. Do you understand the process after reading the essay?

   _____

   _____

5. Identify a phrase or two that shows the writer's level of interest.

   _____

   _____

Understanding Word Parts

The next nine pages include common prefixes, suffixes, and roots. Many of our words are made up of combinations of these word parts.

Prefixes

Prefixes are those "word parts" that come *before* the root words (*pre* = before). Depending upon its meaning, a prefix changes the intent, or sense, of the base word. As a skilled reader, you will want to know the meanings of the most common prefixes and then watch for them when you read.

a, an [not, without] amoral (without a sense of moral responsibility), atypical, atom (not cuttable), apathy (without feeling), anesthesia (without sensation)

ab, abs, a [from, away] abnormal, abduct, absent, avert (turn away)

acro [high] acropolis (high city), acrobat, acronym, acrophobia (fear of height)

ambi, amb [both, around] ambidextrous (skilled with both hands), ambiguous, amble

amphi [both] amphibious (living on both land and water), amphitheater

ante [before] antedate, anteroom, antebellum, antecedent (happening before)

anti, ant [against] anticommunist, antidote, anticlimax, antacid

be [on, away] bedeck, belabor, bequest, bestow, beloved

bene, bon [well] benefit, benefactor, benevolent, benediction, bonanza, bonus

bi, bis, bin [both, double, twice] bicycle, biweekly, bilateral, biscuit, binoculars

by [side, close, near] bypass, bystander, by-product, bylaw, byline

cata [down, against] catalog, catapult, catastrophe, cataclysm

cerebro [brain] cerebral, cerebrum, cerebellum

circum, circ [around] circumference, circumnavigate, circumspect, circular

co, con, col, com [together, with] copilot, conspire, collect, compose

coni [dust] coniosis (disease that comes from inhaling dust)

contra, counter [against] controversy, contradict, counterpart

de [from, down] demote, depress, degrade, deject, deprive

deca [ten] decade, decathlon, decapod (10 feet)

di [two, twice] divide, dilemma, dilute, dioxide, dipole, ditto

dia [through, between] diameter, diagonal, diagram, dialogue (speech between people)

dis, dif [apart, away, reverse] dismiss, distort, distinguish, diffuse

dys [badly, ill] dyspepsia (digesting badly), dystrophy, dysentery

em, en [in, into] embrace, enslave

epi [upon] epidermis (upon the skin, outer layer of skin), epitaph, epithet

eu [well] eulogize (speak well of, praise), euphony, euphemism, euphoria

ex, e, ec, ef [out] expel (drive out), ex-mayor, exorcism, eject, eccentric (out of the center position), efflux, effluent

extra, extro [beyond, outside] extraordinary (beyond the ordinary), extrovert, extracurricular

for [away or off] forswear (to renounce an oath)

fore [before in time] forecast, foretell (to tell beforehand), foreshadow

hemi, demi, semi [half] hemisphere, demitasse, semicircle (half of a circle)

hex [six] hexameter, hexagon

homo [man] Homo sapiens, homicide (killing man)

hyper [over, above] hypersensitive (overly sensitive), hyperactive

hypo [under] hypodermic (under the skin), hypothesis

il, ir, in, im [not] illegal, irregular, incorrect, immoral

in, il, im [into] inject, inside, illuminate, illustrate, impose, implant, imprison

infra [beneath] infrared, infrasonic

inter [between] intercollegiate, interfere, intervene, interrupt (break between)

intra [within] intramural, intravenous (within the veins)

intro [into, inward] introduce, introvert (turn inward)

macro [large, excessive] macrodent (having large teeth), macrocosm

mal [badly, poorly] maladjusted, malady, malnutrition, malfunction

meta [beyond, after, with] metaphor, metamorphosis, metaphysical

mis [incorrect, bad] misuse, misprint

miso [hate] misanthrope, misogynist

mono [one] monoplane, monotone, monochrome, monocle

multi [many] multiply, multiform

neo [new] neopaganism, neoclassic, neophyte, neonatal

non [not] nontaxable (not taxed), nontoxic, nonexistent, nonsense

ob, of, op, oc [toward, against] obstruct, offend, oppose, occur

oct [eight] octagon, octameter, octave, octopus

paleo [ancient] paleoanthropology (pertaining to ancient humans), paleontology (study of ancient life-forms)

para [beside, almost] parasite (one who eats beside or at the table of another), paraphrase, paramedic, parallel, paradox

penta [five] pentagon (figure or building having five angles or sides), pentameter, pentathlon

per [throughout, completely] pervert (completely turn wrong, corrupt), perfect, perceive, permanent, persuade

peri [around] perimeter (measurement around an area), periphery, periscope, pericardium, period

poly [many] polygon (figure having many angles or sides), polygamy, polyglot, polychrome

post [after] postpone, postwar, postscript, posterity

pre [before] prewar, preview, precede, prevent, premonition

pro [forward, in favor of] project (throw forward), progress, promote, prohibition

pseudo [false] pseudonym (false or assumed name), pseudopodia

quad [four] quadruple (four times as much), quadriplegic, quadratic, quadrant

quint [five] quintuplet, quintuple, quintet, quintile

re [back, again] reclaim, revive, revoke, rejuvenate, retard, reject, return

retro [backward] retrospective (looking backward), retroactive, retrorocket

se [aside] seduce (lead aside), secede, secrete, segregate

self [by oneself] self-determination, self-employed, self-service, selfish

sesqui [one and a half] sesquicentennial (one and one-half centuries)

sex, sest [six] sexagenarian (sixty years old), sexennial, sextant, sextuplet, sestet

sub [under] submerge (put under), submarine, substitute, subsoil

suf, sug, sup, sus [from under] sufficient, suffer, suggest, support, suspend

super, supr [above, over, more] supervise, superman, supernatural, supreme

syn, sym, sys, syl [with, together] system, synthesis, synchronize (time together), synonym, sympathy, symphony, syllable

trans, tra [across, beyond] transoceanic, transmit (send across), transfusion, tradition

tri [three] tricycle, triangle, tripod, tristate

ultra [beyond, exceedingly] ultramodern, ultraviolet, ultraconservative

un [not, release] unfair, unnatural, unknown

under [beneath] underground, underlying

uni [one] unicycle, uniform, unify, universe, unique (one of a kind)

vice [in place of] vice president, viceroy, vice admiral

Numerical Prefixes

Prefix	Symbol	Multiples and Submultiples	Equivalent	Prefix	Symbol	Multiples and Submultiples	Equivalent
tera	T	10^{12}	trillionfold	centi	c	10^{-2}	hundredth part
giga	G	10^{9}	billionfold	milli	m	10^{-3}	thousandth part
mega	M	10^{6}	millionfold	micro	u	10^{-6}	millionth part
kilo	k	10^{3}	thousandfold	nano	n	10^{-9}	billionth part
hecto	h	10^{2}	hundredfold	pico	p	10^{-12}	trillionth part
deka	da	10	tenfold	femto	f	10^{-15}	quadrillionth part
deci	d	10^{-1}	tenth part	atto	a	10^{-18}	quintillionth part

Suffixes

Suffixes come at the end of a word. Very often a suffix will tell you what kind of word it is part of (noun, adverb, adjective, and so on). For example, words ending in *-ly* are usually adverbs.

able, ible [able, can do] capable, agreeable, edible, visible (can be seen)

ade [result of action] blockade (the result of a blocking action), lemonade

age [act of, state of, collection of] salvage (act of saving), storage, forage

al [relating to] sensual, gradual, manual, natural (relating to nature)

algia [pain] neuralgia (nerve pain)

an, ian [native of, relating to] African, Canadian, Floridian

ance, ancy [action, process, state] assistance, allowance, defiance, truancy

ant [performing, agent] assistant, servant

ary, ery, ory [relating to, quality, place where] dictionary, bravery, dormitory

ate [cause, make] liquidate, segregate (cause a group to be set aside)

cian [having a certain skill or art] musician, beautician, magician, physician

cule, ling [very small] molecule, ridicule, duckling (very small duck), sapling

cy [action, function] hesitancy, prophecy, normalcy (function in a normal way)

dom [quality, realm, office] freedom, kingdom, wisdom (quality of being wise)

ee [one who receives the action] employee, nominee (one who is nominated), refugee

en [made of, make] silken, frozen, oaken (made of oak), wooden, lighten

ence, ency [action, state of, quality] difference, conference, urgency

er, or [one who, that which] baker, miller, teacher, racer, amplifier, doctor

escent [in the process of] adolescent (in the process of becoming an adult), obsolescent, convalescent

ese [a native of, the language of] Japanese, Vietnamese, Portuguese

esis, osis [action, process, condition] genesis, hypnosis, neurosis, osmosis

ess [female] actress, goddess, lioness

et, ette [a small one, group] midget, octet, baronet, majorette

fic [making, causing] scientific, specific

ful [full of] frightful, careful, helpful

fy [make] fortify (make strong), simplify, amplify

hood [order, condition, quality] manhood, womanhood, brotherhood

ic [nature of, like] metallic (of the nature of metal), heroic, poetic, acidic

ice [condition, state, quality] justice, malice

id, ide [a thing connected with or belonging to] fluid, fluoride

ile [relating to, suited for, capable of] missile, juvenile, senile (related to being old)

ine [nature of] feminine, genuine, medicine

ion, sion, tion [act of, state of, result of] contagion, aversion, infection (state of being infected)

ish [origin, nature, resembling] foolish, Irish, clownish (resembling a clown)

ism [system, manner, condition, characteristic] heroism, alcoholism, Communism

ist [one who, that which] artist, dentist

ite [nature of, quality of, mineral product] Israelite, dynamite, graphite, sulfite

ity, ty [state of, quality] captivity, clarity

ive [causing, making] abusive (causing abuse), exhaustive

ize [make] emphasize, publicize, idolize

less [without] baseless, careless (without care), artless, fearless, helpless

ly [like, manner of] carelessly, quickly, forcefully, lovingly

ment [act of, state of, result] contentment, amendment (state of amending)

ness [state of] carelessness, kindness

oid [resembling] asteroid, spheroid, tabloid, anthropoid

ology [study, science, theory] biology, anthropology, geology, neurology

ous [full of, having] gracious, nervous, spacious, vivacious (full of life)

ship [office, state, quality, skill] friendship, authorship, dictatorship

some [like, apt, tending to] lonesome, threesome, gruesome

tude [state of, condition of] gratitude, multitude (condition of being many), aptitude

ure [state of, act, process, rank] culture, literature, rupture (state of being broken)

ward [in the direction of] eastward, forward, backward

y [inclined to, tend to] cheery, crafty, faulty

Roots

A *root* is a base upon which other words are built. Knowing the root of a difficult word can go a long way toward helping you figure out its meaning— even without a dictionary. For that reason, learning the following roots will be very valuable in all your classes.

acer, acid, acri [bitter, sour, sharp] acrid, acerbic, acidity (sourness), acrimony

acu [sharp] acute, acupuncture

ag, agi, ig, act [do, move, go] agent (doer), agenda (things to do), agitate, navigate (move by sea), ambiguous (going both ways), action

ali, allo, alter [other] alias (a person's other name), alibi, alien (from another place), alloy, alter (change to another form)

alt [high, deep] altimeter (a device for measuring heights), altitude

am, amor [love, liking] amiable, amorous, enamored

anni, annu, enni [year] anniversary, annually (yearly), centennial (occurring once in 100 years)

anthrop [man] anthropology (study of mankind), philanthropy (love of mankind), misanthrope (hater of mankind)

anti [old] antique, antiquated, antiquity

arch [chief, first, rule] archangel (chief angel), architect (chief worker), archaic (first, very early), monarchy (rule by one person), matriarchy (rule by the mother)

aster, astr [star] aster (star flower), asterisk, asteroid, astronomy (star law), astronaut (star traveler, space traveler)

aud, aus [hear, listen] audible (can be heard), auditorium, audio, audition, auditory, audience, ausculate

aug, auc [increase] augur, augment (add to; increase), auction

auto, aut [self] autograph (self-writing), automobile (self-moving vehicle), author, automatic (self-acting), autobiography

belli [war] rebellion, belligerent (warlike or hostile)

bibl [book] Bible, bibliography (list of books), bibliomania (craze for books), bibliophile (book lover)

bio [life] biology (study of life), biography, biopsy (cut living tissue for examination)

brev [short] abbreviate, brevity, brief

cad, cas [to fall] cadaver, cadence, caducous (falling off), cascade

calor [heat] calorie (a unit of heat), calorify (to make hot), caloric

cap, cip, cept [take] capable, capacity, capture, reciprocate, accept, except, concept

capit, capt [head] decapitate (to remove the head from), capital, captain, caption

carn [flesh] carnivorous (flesh eating), incarnate, reincarnation

caus, caut [burn, heat] caustic, cauterize (to make hot, to burn)

cause, cuse, cus [cause, motive] because, excuse (to attempt to remove the blame or cause), accusation

ced, ceed, cede, cess [move, yield, go, surrender] procedure, secede (move aside from), proceed (move forward), cede (yield), concede, intercede, precede, recede, success

centri [center] concentric, centrifugal, centripetal, eccentric (out of center)

chrom [color] chrome, chromosome (color body in genetics), chromosphere, monochrome (one color), polychrome

chron [time] chronological (in order of time), chronometer (time measured), chronicle (record of events in time), synchronize (make time with, set time together)

cide, cise [cut down, kill] suicide (killing of self), homicide (human killer), pesticide (pest killer), germicide (germ killer), insecticide, precise (cut exactly right), incision, scissors

cit [to call, start] incite, citation, cite

civ [citizen] civic (relating to a citizen), civil, civilian, civilization

clam, claim [cry out] exclamation, clamor, proclamation, reclamation, acclaim

clud, clus, claus [shut] include (to take in), conclude, claustrophobia (abnormal fear of being shut up, confined), recluse (one who shuts himself away from others)

cognosc, gnosi [know] recognize (to know again), incognito (not known), prognosis (forward knowing), diagnosis

cord, cor, cardi [heart] cordial (hearty, heartfelt), concord, discord, courage, encourage (put heart into), discourage (take heart out of), core, coronary, cardiac

corp [body] corporation (a legal body), corpse, corpulent

cosm [universe, world] cosmic, cosmos (the universe), cosmopolitan (world citizen), cosmonaut, microcosm, macrocosm

crat, cracy [rule, strength] democratic, autocracy

crea [create] creature (anything created), recreation, creation, creator

cred [believe] creed (statement of beliefs), credo (a creed), credence (belief), credit (belief, trust), credulous (believing too readily, easily deceived), incredible

cresc, cret, crease, cru [rise, grow] crescendo (growing in loudness or intensity), concrete (grown together, solidified), increase, decrease, accrue (to grow) crit [separate, choose] critical, criterion (that which is used in choosing), hypocrite

cur, curs [run] concurrent, current (running or flowing), concur (run together, agree), incur (run into), recur, occur, precursor (forerunner), cursive

cura [care] curator, curative, manicure (caring for the hands)

cycl, cyclo [wheel, circular] Cyclops (a mythical giant with one eye in the middle of his forehead), unicycle, bicycle, cyclone (a wind blowing circularly, a tornado)

deca [ten] decade, decalogue, decathlon

dem [people] democracy (people-rule), demography (vital statistics of the people: deaths, births, and so on), epidemic (on or among the people)

dent, dont [tooth] dental (relating to teeth), denture, dentifrice, orthodontist

derm [skin] hypodermic (injected under the skin), dermatology (skin study), epidermis (outer layer of skin), taxidermy (arranging skin; mounting animals)

dict [say, speak] diction (how one speaks, what one says), dictionary, dictate, dictator, dictaphone, dictatorial, edict, predict, verdict, contradict, benediction

doc [teach] indoctrinate, document, doctrine

domin [master] dominate, dominion, predominant, domain

don [give] donate, condone

dorm [sleep] dormant, dormitory

dox [opinion, praise] doxy (belief, creed, or opinion), orthodox (having the correct, commonly accepted opinion), heterodox (differing opinion), paradox (contradictory)

drome [run, step] syndrome (run-together symptoms), hippodrome (a place where horses run)

duc, duct [lead] produce, induce (lead into, persuade), seduce (lead aside), reduce, aqueduct (water leader or channel), viaduct, conduct

dura [hard, lasting] durable, duration, endurance

dynam [power] dynamo (power producer), dynamic, dynamite, hydrodynamics

endo [within] endoral (within the mouth), endocardial (within the heart), endoskeletal

equi [equal] equinox, equilibrium

erg [work] energy, erg (unit of work), allergy, ergophobia (morbid fear of work), ergometer, ergonomic

fac, fact, fic, fect [do, make] factory (place where workers make goods of various kinds), fact (a thing done), manufacture, amplification, confection

fall, fals [deceive] fallacy, falsify

fer [bear, carry] ferry (carry by water), coniferous (bearing cones, as a pine tree), fertile (bearing richly), defer, infer, refer

fid, fide, feder [faith, trust] confidante, Fido, fidelity, confident, infidelity, infidel, federal, confederacy

fila, fili [thread] filament (a single thread or threadlike object), filibuster, filigree

fin [end, ended, finished] final, finite, finish, confine, fine, refine, define, finale

fix [attach] fix, fixation (the state of being attached), fixture, affix, prefix, suffix

flex, flect [bend] flex (bend), reflex (bending back), flexible, flexor (muscle for bending), inflexibility, reflect, deflect

flu, fluc, fluv [flowing] influence (to flow in), fluid, flue, flush, fluently, fluctuate (to wave in an unsteady motion)

form [form, shape] form, uniform, conform, deform, reform, perform, formative, formation, formal, formula

fort, forc [strong] fort, fortress (a strong place), fortify (make strong), forte (one's strong point), fortitude, enforce

fract, frag [break] fracture (a break), infraction, fragile (easy to break), fraction (result of breaking a whole into equal parts), refract (to break or bend)

gam [marriage] bigamy (two marriages), monogamy, polygamy (many spouses or marriages)

gastr(o) [stomach] gastric, gastronomic, gastritis (inflammation of the stomach)

gen [birth, race, produce] genesis (birth, beginning), genetics (study of heredity), eugenics (well born), genealogy (lineage by race, stock), generate, genetic

geo [earth] geometry (earth measurement), geography (earth writing), geocentric (earth centered), geology

germ [vital part] germination (to grow), germ (seed; living substance, as the germ of an idea), germane

gest [carry, bear] congest (bear together, clog), congestive (causing clogging), gestation

gloss, glot [tongue] glossary, polyglot (many tongues), epiglottis

glu, glo [lump, bond, glue] glue, agglutinate (make to hold in a bond), conglomerate (bond together)

grad, gress [step, go] grade (step, degree), gradual (step-by-step), graduate (make all the steps, finish a course), graduated (in steps or degrees), progress

graph, gram [write, written] graph, graphic (written, vivid), autograph (self-writing, signature), graphite (carbon used for writing), photography (light writing), phonograph (sound writing), diagram, bibliography, telegram

grat [pleasing] gratuity (mark of favor, a tip), congratulate (express pleasure over success), grateful, ingrate (not thankful) grav [heavy, weighty] grave, gravity, aggravate, gravitate

greg [herd, group, crowd] gregarian (belonging to a herd), congregation (a group functioning together), segregate (tending to group aside or apart)

helio [sun] heliograph (an instrument for using the sun's rays to send signals), heliotrope (a plant that turns to the sun)

hema, hemo [blood] hemorrhage (an outpouring or flowing of blood), hemoglobin, hemophilia

here, hes [stick] adhere, cohere, cohesion

hetero [different] heterogeneous (different in birth), heterosexual (with interest in the opposite sex)

homo [same] homogeneous (of same birth or kind), homonym (word with same pronunciation as another), homogenize

hum, human [earth, ground, man] humus, exhume (to take out of the ground), humane (compassion for other humans)

hydr, hydra, hydro [water] dehydrate, hydrant, hydraulic, hydraulics, hydrogen, hydrophobia (fear of water)

hypn [sleep] hypnosis, Hypnos (god of sleep), hypnotherapy (treatment of disease by hypnosis)

ignis [fire] ignite, igneous, ignition

ject [throw] deject, inject, project (throw forward), eject, object

join, junct [join] adjoining, enjoin (to lay an order upon, to command), juncture, conjunction, injunction

juven [young] juvenile, rejuvenate (to make young again)

lau, lav, lot, lut [wash] launder, lavatory, lotion, ablution (a washing away), dilute (to make a liquid thinner and weaker)

leg [law] legal (lawful; according to law), legislate (to enact a law), legislature, legitimize (make legal)

levi [light] alleviate (lighten a load), levitate, levity (light conversation; humor)

liber, liver [free] liberty (freedom), liberal, liberalize (to make more free), deliverance

liter [letters] literary (concerned with books and writing), literature, literal, alliteration, obliterate

loc, loco [place] locality, locale, location, allocate (to assign, to place), relocate (to put back into place), locomotion (act of moving from place to place)

log, logo, ogue, ology [word, study, speech] catalog, prologue, dialogue, logogram (a symbol representing a word), zoology (animal study), psychology (mind study)

loqu, locut [talk, speak] eloquent (speaking well and forcefully), soliloquy, locution, loquacious (talkative), colloquial (talking together; conversational or informal)

luc, lum, lus, lun [light] translucent (letting light come through), lumen (a unit of light), luminary (a heavenly body; someone who shines in his or her profession), luster (sparkle, shine), Luna (the moon goddess)

magn [great] magnify (make great, enlarge), magnificent, magnanimous (great of mind or spirit), magnate, magnitude, magnum

man [hand] manual, manage, manufacture, manacle, manicure, manifest, maneuver, emancipate

mand [command] mandatory (commanded), remand (order back), mandate

mania [madness] mania (insanity, craze), monomania (mania on one idea), kleptomania, pyromania (insane tendency to set fires), maniac

mar, mari, mer [sea, pool] marine (a soldier serving on shipboard), marsh (wetland, swamp), maritime (relating to the sea and navigation), mermaid (fabled sea creature, half fish, half woman)

matri [mother] maternal (relating to the mother), matrimony, matriarchate (rulership of women), matron

medi [half, middle, between, halfway] mediate (come between, intervene), medieval (pertaining to the Middle Ages), Mediterranean (lying between lands), mediocre, medium

mega [great, million] megaphone (great sound), megalopolis (great city; an extensive urban area including a number of cities), megacycle (a million cycles), megaton

mem [remember] memo (a reminder), commemoration (the act of remembering by a memorial or ceremony), memento, memoir, memorable

meter [measure] meter (a metric measure), voltameter (instrument to measure volts), barometer, thermometer

micro [small] microscope, microfilm, microcard, microwave, micrometer (device for measuring small distances), omicron, micron (a millionth of a meter), microbe (small living thing)

migra [wander] migrate (to wander), emigrate (one who leaves a country), immigrate (to come into the land)

mit, miss [send] emit (send out, give off), remit (send back, as money due), submit, admit, commit, permit, transmit (send across), omit, intermittent (sending between, at intervals), mission, missile

mob, mot, mov [move] mobile (capable of moving), motionless (without motion), motor, emotional (moved strongly by feelings), motivate, promotion, demote, movement

mon [warn, remind] monument (a reminder or memorial of a person or an event), admonish (warn), monitor, premonition (forewarning) mor, mort [mortal, death] mortal (causing death or destined for death), immortal (not subject to death), mortality (rate of death), mortician (one who prepares the dead for burial), mortuary (place for the dead, a morgue)

morph [form] amorphous (with no form, shapeless), metamorphosis (a change of form, as a caterpillar into a butterfly), morphology

multi [many, much] multifold (folded many times), multilinguist (one who speaks many languages), multiped (an organism with many feet), multiply

nat, nasc [to be born, to spring forth] innate (inborn), natal, native, nativity, renascence (a rebirth, a revival)

neur [nerve] neuritis (inflammation of a nerve), neurology (study of nervous systems), neurologist (one who practices neurology), neural, neurosis, neurotic

nom [law, order] autonomy (self-law, self-government), astronomy, gastronomy (art or science of good eating), economy

nomen, nomin [name] nomenclature, nominate (name someone for an office)

nov [new] novel (new, strange, not formerly known), renovate (to make like new again), novice, nova, innovate

nox, noc [night] nocturnal, equinox (equal nights), noctilucent (shining by night)

numer [number] numeral (a figure expressing a number), numeration (act of counting), enumerate (count out, one by one), innumerable

omni [all, every] omnipotent (all-powerful), omniscient (all-knowing), omnipresent (present everywhere), omnivorous

onym [name] anonymous (without name), synonym, pseudonym (false name), antonym (name of opposite meaning)

oper [work] operate (to labor, function), cooperate (work together)

ortho [straight, correct] orthodox (of the correct or accepted opinion), orthodontist (tooth straightener), orthopedic (originally pertaining to straightening a child), unorthodox

pac [peace] pacifist (one for peace only; opposed to war), pacify (make peace, quiet), Pacific Ocean (peaceful ocean)

pan [all] panacea (cure-all), pandemonium (place of all the demons, wild disorder), pantheon (place of all the gods in mythology)

pater, patr [father] paternity (fatherhood, responsibility), patriarch (head of the tribe, family), patriot, patron (a wealthy person who supports as would a father)

path, pathy [feeling, suffering] pathos (feeling of pity, sorrow), sympathy, antipathy (feeling against), apathy (without feeling), empathy (feeling or identifying with another), telepathy (far feeling; thought transference)

ped, pod [foot] pedal (lever for a foot), impede (get the feet in a trap, hinder), pedestal (foot or base of a statue), pedestrian (foot traveler), centipede, tripod (three-footed support), podiatry (care of the feet), antipodes (opposite feet)

pedo [child] orthopedic, pedagogue (child leader; teacher), pediatrics (medical care of children)

pel, puls [drive, urge] compel, dispel, expel, repel, propel, pulse, impulse, pulsate, compulsory, expulsion, repulsive

pend, pens, pond [hang, weigh] pendant pendulum, suspend, appendage, pensive (weighing thought), ponderous

phil [love] philosophy (love of wisdom), philanthropy, philharmonic, bibliophile, Philadelphia (city of brotherly love)

phobia [fear] claustrophobia (fear of closed spaces), acrophobia (fear of high places), hydrophobia (fear of water)

phon [sound] phonograph, phonetic (pertaining to sound), symphony (sounds with or together)

photo [light] photograph (light-writing), photoelectric, photogenic (artistically suitable for being photographed), photosynthesis (action of light on chlorophyll to make carbohydrates)

plac [please] placid (calm, peaceful), placebo, placate, complacent

plu, plur, plus [more] plural (more than one), pluralist (a person who holds more than one office), plus (indicating that something more is to be added)

pneuma, pneumon [breath] pneumatic (pertaining to air, wind, or other gases), pneumonia (disease of the lungs)

pod (see ped)

poli [city] metropolis (mother city), police, politics, Indianapolis, Acropolis (high city, upper part of Athens), megalopolis

pon, pos, pound [place, put] postpone (put afterward), component, opponent (one put against), proponent, expose, impose, deposit, posture (how one places oneself), position, expound, impound

pop [people] population, populous (full of people), popular

port [carry] porter (one who carries), portable, transport (carry across), report, export, import, support, transportation

portion [part, share] portion (a part; a share, as a portion of pie), proportion (the relation of one share to others)

prehend [seize] comprehend (seize with the mind), apprehend (seize a criminal), comprehensive (seizing much, extensive)

prim, prime [first] primacy (state of being first in rank), prima donna (the first lady of opera), primitive (from the earliest or first time), primary, primal, primeval proto [first] prototype (the first model made), protocol, protagonist, protozoan

psych [mind, soul] psyche (soul, mind), psychiatry (healing of the mind), psychology, psychosis (serious mental disorder), psychotherapy (mind treatment), psychic

punct [point, dot] punctual (being exactly on time), punctuation, puncture, acupuncture

reg, recti [straighten] regiment, regular, regulate, rectify (make straight), correct, direction

ri, ridi, risi [laughter] deride (mock, jeer at), ridicule (laughter at the expense of another, mockery), ridiculous, derision

rog, roga [ask] prerogative (privilege; asking before), interrogation (questioning; the act of questioning), derogatory

rupt [break] rupture (break), interrupt (break into), abrupt (broken off), disrupt (break apart), erupt (break out), incorruptible (unable to be broken down)

sacr, sanc, secr [sacred] sacred, sanction, sacrosanct, consecrate, desecrate

salv, salu [safe, healthy] salvation (act of being saved), salvage, salutation

sat, satis [enough] satient (giving pleasure, satisfying), saturate, satisfy (to give pleasure to; to give as much as is needed)

sci [know] science (knowledge), conscious (knowing, aware), omniscient (knowing everything)

scope [see, watch] telescope, microscope, kaleidoscope (instrument for seeing beautiful forms), periscope, stethoscope

scrib, script [write] scribe (a writer), scribble, manuscript (written by hand), inscribe, describe, subscribe, prescribe

sed, sess, sid [sit] sediment (that which sits or settles out of a liquid), session (a sitting), obsession (an idea that sits stubbornly in the mind), possess, preside (sit before), president, reside, subside

sen [old] senior, senator, senile (old; showing the weakness of old age)

sent, sens [feel] sentiment (feeling), consent, resent, dissent, sentimental (having strong feeling or emotion), sense, sensation, sensitive, sensory, dissension

sequ, secu, sue [follow] sequence (following of one thing after another), sequel, consequence, subsequent, prosecute, consecutive (following in order), second (following "first"), ensue, pursue

serv [save, serve] servant, service, preserve, subservient, servitude, conserve, reservation, deserve, conservation

sign, signi [sign, mark, seal] signal (a gesture or sign to call attention), signature (the mark of a person written in his or her own handwriting), design, insignia (distinguishing marks)

simil, simul [like, resembling] similar (resembling in many respects), assimilate (to make similar to), simile, simulate (pretend; put on an act to make a certain impression)

sist, sta, stit [stand] persist (stand firmly; unyielding; continue), assist (to stand by with help), circumstance, stamina (power to withstand, to endure), status (standing), state, static, stable, stationary, substitute (to stand in for another)

solus [alone] soliloquy, solitaire, solitude, solo

solv, solu [loosen] solvent (a loosener, a dissolver), solve, absolve (loosen from, free from), resolve, soluble, solution, resolution, resolute, dissolute (loosened morally)

somnus [sleep] insomnia (not being able to sleep), somnambulist (a sleepwalker)

soph [wise] sophomore (wise fool), philosophy (love of wisdom), sophisticated

spec, spect, spic [look] specimen (an example to look at, study), specific, aspect, spectator (one who looks), spectacle, speculate, inspect, respect, prospect, retrospective (looking backward), introspective, expect, conspicuous

sphere [ball, sphere] stratosphere (the upper portion of the atmosphere), hemisphere (half of the earth), spheroid

spir [breath] spirit (breath), conspire (breathe together; plot), inspire (breathe into), aspire (breathe toward), expire (breathe out; die), perspire, respiration

string, strict [draw tight] stringent (drawn tight; rigid), strict, restrict, constrict (draw tightly together), boa constrictor (snake that constricts its prey)

stru, struct [build] construe (build in the mind, interpret), structure, construct, instruct, obstruct, destruction, destroy

sume, sump [take, use, waste] consume (to use up), assume (to take; to use), sump pump (a pump that takes up water), presumption (to take or use before knowing all the facts)

tact, tang, tag, tig, ting [touch] contact, tactile, intangible (not able to be touched), intact (untouched, uninjured), tangible, contingency, contagious (able to transmit disease by touching), contiguous

tele [far] telephone (far sound), telegraph (far writing), television (far seeing), telephoto (far photography), telecast

tempo [time] tempo (rate of speed), temporary, extemporaneously, contemporary (those who live at the same time), pro tem (for the time being)

ten, tin, tain [hold] tenacious (holding fast), tenant, tenure, untenable, detention, content, pertinent, continent, obstinate, abstain, pertain, detain

tend, tent, tens [stretch, strain] tendency (a stretching; leaning), extend, intend, contend, pretend, superintend, tender, extent, tension (a stretching, strain), pretense

terra [earth] terrain, terrarium, territory, terrestrial

test [to bear witness] testament (a will; bearing witness to someone's wishes), detest, attest (bear witness to), testimony

the, theo [God, a god] monotheism (belief in one god), polytheism (belief in many gods), atheism, theology

therm [heat] thermometer, therm (heat unit), thermal, thermostat, thermos, hypothermia (subnormal temperature)

thesis, thet [place, put] antithesis (place against), hypothesis (place under), synthesis (put together), epithet

tom [cut] atom (not cuttable; smallest particle of matter), appendectomy (cutting out an appendix), tonsillectomy, dichotomy (cutting in two; a division), anatomy (cutting, dissecting to study structure)

tort, tors [twist] torture (twisting to inflict pain), retort (twist back, reply sharply), extort (twist out), distort (twist out of shape), contort, torsion (act of twisting, as a torsion bar)

tox [poison] toxic (poisonous), intoxicate, antitoxin

tract, tra [draw, pull] tractor, attract, subtract, tractable (can be handled), abstract (to draw away), subtrahend (the number to be drawn away from another)

trib [pay, bestow] tribute (to pay honor to), contribute (to give money to a cause), attribute, retribution, tributary

turbo [disturb] turbulent, disturb, turbid, turmoil

typ [print] type, prototype (first print; model), typical, typography, typewriter, typology (study of types, symbols), typify

ultima [last] ultimate, ultimatum (the final or last offer that can be made)

uni [one] unicorn (a legendary creature with one horn), unify (make into one), university, unanimous, universal

vac [empty] vacate (to make empty), vacuum (a space entirely devoid of matter), evacuate (to remove troops or people), vacation, vacant

vale, vali, valu [strength, worth] valiant, equivalent (of equal worth), validity (truth; legal strength), evaluate (find out the value), value, valor (value; worth)

ven, vent [come] convene (come together, assemble), intervene (come between), venue, convenient, avenue, circumvent (come or go around), invent, prevent

ver, veri [true] very, aver (say to be true, affirm), verdict, verity (truth), verify (show to be true), verisimilitude

vert, vers [turn] avert (turn away), divert (turn aside, amuse), invert (turn over), introvert (turn inward), convertible, reverse (turn back), controversy (a turning against; a dispute), versatile (turning easily from one skill to another)

vic, vicis [change, substitute] vicarious, vicar, vicissitude

vict, vinc [conquer] victor (conqueror, winner), evict (conquer out, expel), convict (prove guilty), convince (conquer mentally, persuade), invincible (not conquerable)

vid, vis [see] video, television, evident, provide, providence, visible, revise, supervise (oversee), vista, visit, vision

viv, vita, vivi [alive, life] revive (make live again), survive (live beyond, outlive), vivid, vivacious (full of life), vitality

voc [call] vocation (a calling), avocation (occupation not one's calling), convocation (a calling together), invocation, vocal

vol [will] malevolent, benevolent (one of goodwill), volunteer, volition

volcan, vulcan [fire] volcano (a mountain erupting fiery lava), volcanize (to undergo volcanic heat), Vulcan (Roman god of fire)

volvo [turn about, roll] revolve, voluminous (winding), voluble (easily turned about or around), convolution (a twisting)

vor [eat greedily] voracious, carnivorous (flesh eating), herbivorous (plant eating), omnivorous (eating everything), devour

zo [animal] zoo (short for zoological garden), zoology (study of animal life), zodiac (circle of animal constellations), zoomorphism (being in the form of an animal), protozoa (one-celled animals)

The Human Body

capit	head	gastro	stomach	osteo	bone
card	heart	glos	tongue	ped	foot
corp	body	hema	blood	pneuma	breathe
dent	tooth	man	hand	psych	mind
derm	skin	neur	nerve	spir	breath

For additional information, see pages 35–36.

Glossary

A

abstract
something that can't be sensed (seen, heard, etc.); a feeling or an idea

abstract nouns
nouns referring to ideas or conditions that cannot be sensed

academic sentences
usually longer sentences with multiple layers of meaning; reveal careful thought on the part of the writer

academic voice
the tone or style used in most textbooks and professional journals; formal and serious

action verb
word functioning as a verb that expresses action

active voice
the voice created when a subject is acting

adjective
a word that modifies a noun or pronoun

adjective phrase or clause
a phrase or a dependent clause functioning as an adjective

adverb
word that modifies a verb, an adjective, an adverb, or a whole sentence

adverb clause
a dependent clause functioning as an adverb

agree in number
when subject and verb are both singular or both plural

ambiguous
unclear or confusing

annotate
to add comments or make notes in a text

antecedent
the noun or pronoun that a pronoun refers to or replaces

APA
American Psychological Association; provides documentation guidelines for the social sciences

appositive
a noun or noun phrase that renames another noun right beside it; usually set off by commas

apostrophe
a punctuation mark (') used to show that a letter or number has been left out or that a word is possessive

argumentation
a discussion or course of reasoning aimed at demonstrating truth or falsehood; relies on logic and sound reasoning

article
common noun markers (*a, an,* or *the*)

audience
the intended reader of a text

auxiliary verbs
helping verbs used with the main verb to indicate tense and other things

B

base word (root)
the word part or base upon which other words are built (*help* is the base for the word *helpful*)

"be" verb
forms of the verb "be" *(is, are, was, were)*; function as linking verbs

C

causal connection
the link between the causes and effects of a topic; usually identified in the thesis statement

causes
the reasons for an action or a condition

chronological
organized by time

citations
sources referred to in research; occur within the text and in a listing at the end of the report

claim
the position or thesis developed in an argument essay

classification
the act of arranging or organizing according to classes or categories

closing
the final part of writing; a closing sentence in a paragraph, a closing paragraph (or two) in an essay

cluster
a strategy to generate ideas graphically; used to select topics and to gather details about a topic

colon
a punctuation mark (:) that introduces an example or list

comma splice
a sentence error that occurs when two sentences are connected with only a comma

common noun
a general noun, not capitalized

comparison-contrast
showing how two or more subjects are similar and different

complete predicate
the predicate with modifiers and objects

complete subject
the subject with modifiers

complex sentence
a sentence with an independent and dependent clause

compound adjective
an adjective made of two more words, hyphenated before the noun but not afterward (*ready-made meals*)

compound-complex sentences
a sentence with two or more independent clauses and one or more dependent clauses

compound noun
noun made up of two or more words (*editor in chief*)

compound predicate
two or more predicates joined by *and* or *or*

compound sentence
two or more simple sentences joined with a coordinating conjunction

compound subject
two or more subjects connected by *and* or *or*

concrete nouns
nouns referring to something that can be sensed

conjunction
word or word group that joins parts of a sentence

content
the ideas and meaning developed in a piece of writing

context
the part of a text that surrounds a particular word; helps determine the word's meaning

contraction
word formed by joining two words, leaving out one or more letters (indicated by an apostrophe)

conventions
the rules governing the standard use of the language

coordinating conjunction
conjunction that joins grammatically equal parts

correlative conjunctions
pair of conjunctions that stress the equality of the parts that are joined

count nouns
nouns that name things that can be counted (*pens, votes, people*)

counterarguments
opposing positions or arguments

cycle chart
a graphic organizer that identifies the steps in a recurring process

D

dangling modifiers
a modifying word, phrase, or clause that appears to modify the wrong word

dash
long horizontal line (—) that separates words or ideas, creating emphasis

declarative sentence
a sentence that express a basic statement

deductive thinking
following a thesis (main idea) with supporting reasons, examples, and facts

definite article
the word *the*

definition
the formal statement or explanation of a meaning of a word

delayed subject
a subject that appears after the verb

demonstrative adjective
a demonstrative pronoun (*this, that, those*) used as an adjective

dependent clause
a group of words with a subject and verb that does not express a complete thought

description
a written creation of an image of a person, place, thing, or idea

dialogue
conversation between two or more people

direct object
a word that follows a transitive verb

documentation guidelines
rules to follow for giving credit for the ideas of others used in a report; MLA and APA provide two common sets of documentation rules

double negative
the nonstandard use of two negatives to express a single negative idea (*I can't hardly sleep*)

double preposition
the nonstandard use of two prepositions together (*off of*)

double subject
error created by following a subject with a pronoun

E

editing
checking revised writing for style, grammar, punctuation, capitalization, and spelling errors

effects
circumstances brought about by a cause or an action

essay
a short piece of writing that uses facts and details to support a claim (thesis)

example
details that demonstrate or show something

exclamation mark
a punctuation mark (!) used at the end of an exclamatory sentence or a word that indicates strong emotion

exclamatory sentence
a sentence that expresses strong emotion

F

feminine
female

first draft
a first attempt to develop writing

focus
a particular part or feeling about a topic that is emphasized in a piece of writing; usually expressed in a thesis statement

formal English
a serious, straightforward style used in most academic writing; objective (sticks to the facts)

fragment
a group of words that does not express a complete thought

freewriting
a prewriting strategy involving rapid, nonstop writing; helps in selecting a topic and gathering details about it

future tense
verb tense indicating that action will happen later

G

gathering grid
a graphic organizer used to identify or gather different types of defining details

gender
masculine, feminine, neuter, or indefinite

gerund
a verb form that ends in *ing* and is used as a noun

graphic organizers
clusters, lists, charts, and other visuals that help writers explore and arrange ideas

H

helping (auxiliary) verb
verbs that work with a main verb to form different tenses and so on

hyphen
a short horizontal line (-) used to form compound words (*in-service*)

I

ideas
the first and main trait of writing; includes the main idea plus supporting details

idiom
a common expression whose meaning is different from its literal meaning (*hit the roof*)

illogical
without logic; senseless, false, or untrue

illustration
the act of clarifying or explaining in writing

implied subject
the word *you* assumed to begin command sentences

indefinite article
the words *a* or *an*

indefinite adjective
an indefinite pronoun (*much, some*) used as an adjective

indefinite pronoun
a pronoun such as *someone* or *everything* that does not refer to a specific person or thing

independent clause
a group of words with a subject and verb that expresses a complete thought

indirect object
a word that comes between a transitive verb and a direct object

inductive thinking
presenting specific details first and concluding with the thesis (main point)

inferences
a logical conclusion that can be made about something that is not actually said or stated in a text

infinitive
a verb form that begins with *to* and can used as a noun (or as an adjective or adverb)

informal English
a relaxed style used in most personal essays; subjective (contains the writer's thoughts and feelings)

interrogative sentence
a sentence that asks a question

italics
a special type style like *this* used to identify titles of books moves, etc.; functions the same as underlining

items in a series
three or more words, phrases, or clauses that are grammatically the same; set off by commas

interjection
a word or phrase that expresses strong emotion

intransitive verb
action verb that does not transfer action to a direct object

irregular verb
a verb in which the principal parts are different words (*give, gave, given*)

K

KWL
a reading strategy identifying what the reader knows, wants to learn, and eventually learns

L

levels of detail
details that contain differing levels of clarifying support

line diagram
a graphic organizer used to identify the main idea and examples in writing

linking verb
verb that connects the subject with a noun or another word; "be" verbs (*is, are, was, were*) are linking verbs

listing
a strategy used to gather ideas for writing

M

main idea (main point)
the idea that is developed in a piece of writing

masculine
male

misplaced modifier
a modifying word, phrase, or clause that has been placed incorrectly in a sentence

MLA
Modern Language Association; provides documentation guidelines for use in the humanities (literature, history, philosophy, etc.)

N

narration
the sharing of a story; a personal narrative shares a true story

neuter
neither male nor female

nominative case
used as a subject or a subject complement

noncount noun
nouns that name things that cannot be counted (*ice, plastic, sunshine*)

noun
a word that names a person, place, thing, or idea

noun clause
a dependent clause that functions as a noun

noun phrase
a noun plus its modifiers

number
singular or plural

O

objective
sticking to the facts; uninfluenced by personal feelings

objective case
used as a direct object, an indirect object, or an object of a preposition

organization
the second important trait; deals with the arrangement of ideas

organized list
an outline-like graphic used to keep track of the information in a report and other forms of writing; customized for personal use

outline
an orderly graphic representation of ideas, following specific rules for arrangement

P

paragraph
a distinct division of writing containing a topic sentence, body sentences, and a closing sentence; usually develops one specific topic

paraphrase
a form of summary writing with explanations and interpretations; may be as long or longer than the source text

participle
a verb form ending in *ing* or *ed* and functioning as an adjective

passive voice
the voice created when a subject is being acted upon

past tense
verb tense indicating that action happened earlier

perfect tense
verb tense that expresses completed action

person
whether the pronoun is speaking, being spoken to, or being spoken about

personal voice
sounds informal and somewhat relaxed; subjective (including the writer's thoughts and feelings)

persuasion
a form of discourse attempting to convince an audience; may appeal to emotion as well as logic

phrase
a group of words that lacks a subject or predicate or both

plagiarism
using the words and thoughts of others without crediting them; intellectual stealing

plot
the different parts of a story that create suspense

plural
referring to more than one thing

points of comparison
the special elements or features used to make a comparison (size, strength, appearance, etc.)

possessive
used to show ownership

predicate
the part of the sentence that tells or asks something about the subject

predicate adjective
adjective that appears after a linking verb

prefix
word parts that come before the base word (*un* is a prefix in *unwind*)

prepositional phrase
a group of words with a preposition, an object, and any modifiers

prereading
becoming familiar with a text by reviewing the title, heading, etc.

present tense
verb tense indicating that action is happening now

prewriting
starting the writing process by analyzing the assignment, selecting a topic, gathering details, and finding a focus

primary sources
information collected directly, such as through firsthand experiences

process
a series of actions, steps, or changes bringing about a result

progressive tense
verb tense that expresses ongoing action

pronoun
word that takes the place of a noun or another pronoun

proper adjective
an adjective based on the name of a specific person, place, thing, or idea; capitalized

proper noun
the specific name of a person, place, thing, or idea; capitalized

publishing
preparing writing to share or submit

purpose
the reason for writing (to inform, to entertain, to persuade, etc.)

Q

question mark
a punctuation mark (?) used an the end of an interrogative sentence (question)

quotation
the specific thoughts or words of other people used in writing

quotation marks
punctuation marks (" ") that set off certain titles, special words, and the exact words spoken by someone

R

rambling sentence
a sentence error that occurs when a long series of separate ideas are connected by one connecting word after another

reading
the second step in the reading process; getting a basic understanding of the text

reading process
a process helping a reader gain a full understanding of a text

rereading
part of the reading process; consists of additional readings and analysis after the first reading

research report
a carefully planned form of informational writing, ranging in length from two or three pages and up

revising
improving the content of a first draft

relative clause
a dependent group of words beginning with a relative pronoun and a verb

relative pronoun
a word—*that, which, who, whom*—that introduces a relative clause

root (base word)
the word part (base) upon which other words are built (*help* is the base in *helpful*)

run-on sentence
a sentence error when two sentences are joined without punctuation or a connecting word

S

satiric voice
the use of humor, fake praise, or sarcasm (ridicule) to make fun of someone or something

secondary sources
information gained through reading what others have learned about a topic

semicolon
a punctuation mark (;) that connects sentences and separates items in some series

sensory details
specific sights, sounds, smells, textures, and tastes

sentences
the thoughts that carry the meaning in discourse; one of the key traits

sequencing
the following of one thing after another

shift in person
when first, second, and/or third person are improperly mixed in a sentence

shift in tense
more than one verb tense improperly used in a sentence

simple predicate
the verb and any helping verbs without modifiers or objects

simple sentence
a complete thought (containing a subject and a verb)

simple subject
the subject without any modifiers

singular
referring to one thing

spatial
organization related to location; often used in descriptions

SQ3R
a reading strategy consisting of survey, question, read, recite, and review

Standard English
English considered appropriate for school, business, and government

story line
the parts of a plot or story; includes exposition, rising action, climax, and resolution

STRAP strategy
a strategy to analyze writing and writing assignments

subject
the part of a sentence that tells who or what the sentence is about

subject complement
as word that follows a linking verb and renames or describes the subject

subjective
including a writer's personal thoughts and feelings

subordinate clause
word group that begins with a subordinating conjunction and has a subject and verb but can't stand alone as a sentence

subordinating conjunction
word or word groups that connect clauses of different importance

summarizing
the process of presenting the core of a text in a condensed form

suffix
a word part coming after a base word (*ful* is a suffix in *healthful*)

T

T-chart
A graphic organizer used to list causes and effects

tense
tells whether the action (verb) happens in the past, present, future, etc.

thesis statement
the statement of the main idea or focus of an essay; usually appears early in the text (often at the end of the first paragraph)

time line
a graphic organizer used to list ideas or events in chronological order

topic sentence
the statement of the main idea in a paragraph

transitions
words and phrases that link ideas in writing

transitive verb
action verb that transfers action to a direct object

traits
the main elements or features in writing; includes ideas, organization, voice, word choice, sentences, and conventions

U

usage error
using the wrong word (*they're* instead of *their*)

V

Venn diagram
a graphic organizer (two intersecting circles) used to identify similarities and differences for comparative writing

verb
A word that expresses action or a state of being

verb phrase
the main verb and any auxiliary verbs

verbal
a construction formed from a verb but functioning as a noun, adjective, or adverb (gerund, participle, or infinitive)

voice
the personality or tone in a piece of writing; one of the traits

W

word choice
the choice of words in a piece of writing; one of the traits

writing (the first draft)
the first attempt to develop a piece of writing; one of the steps in the writing process

writing process
a series of steps to follow to develop a piece of writing; includes prewriting, writing, revising, editing, and publishing